Oxford English Grammar Course

Basic

A grammar practice book for elementary to pre-intermediate students of English

OXFORD
UNIVERSITY PRESS

Great Clarendon Street, Oxford, OX2 6DP, United Kingdom

Oxford University Press is a department of the University of Oxford. It furthers the University's objective of excellence in research, scholarship, and education by publishing worldwide. Oxford is a registered trade mark of Oxford University Press in the UK and in certain other countries

First published in 2011
This updated edition with e-book first published in 2019
2023 2022
10 9 8 7 6 5 4

ISBN: 978 0 19 441482 1 Student's book with answers
ISBN: 978 0 19 441481 4 Student's book and e-book pack with answers

Printed in China

This book is printed on paper from certified and well-managed sources

Michael Swan & Catherine Walter

Oxford English Grammar Course

Basic

A grammar practice book for elementary to pre-intermediate students of English

With answers

OXFORD
UNIVERSITY PRESS

publisher's acknowledgements

The publisher would like to thank the following for permission to reproduce photographs and cartoons:

Alamy pp57 (Isabella Lucy Bird/Visual Arts Library), 109 (Paris/Antony Nettle), 137 (airplane/Antony Nettle), 137 (speedboat/Ron Bedard), 137 (motorbike/Oleksiy Maksymenko), 137 (tractor/Juice Images), 282 (cafe/KIM), 282 (corner/Jim Powell), 282(shopping/STOCK4B GmbH); Ancient Art & Architecture Collection pp45 (ship), 45 (Namibia); Bridgeman Art Library p109 (Sunflowers/National Gallery, London, UK); CartoonStock p86; Corbis UK Ltd. pp137 (yacht/Patrick Ward), 282 (river/Jeff Henry); French Ministry of Culture and Communication p45 (Chauvet); Getty Images pp57 (Ann Carstairs/Mike Powell/TheImage Bank), 282 (diving/PhotoDisk Green/David De Lossy); Greg Evans International pp13, 161 (Taj Mahal), 161 (Edinburgh Castle); Philip Hargraves: p167 (no shirt no shoes); Impact Photos p45 (China); iStockphoto p167 (no hard hat/Linda Steward); Oxford University Press pp45 (Stonehenge/Photodisc), 59 (supermarket), 73; 109 (book/Mark Mason), 117 (spider/Eureka), 117 (cat), 117 (bear), 161 (Tower/Corel);209; 221; 282 (steps/Photodisc), 282 (bike/Photodisc), 282 (skiing/Photodisc), 282 (gate/Photodisc), 282 (fence/Photodisc), 282 (yellow line/Photodisc), 282 (bridge); 205 (Mark Mason); Private Eye p287 (keys/Michael Heath); Punch Cartoon Library pp50; 58; 93, 195 (children, toys/Honeysett), 231, 287 (married/Pete Dredge); Raleigh Cycles p137 (bicycle); Robert Harding Picture Library pp109 (China/Gavin Hellier), 161 (Globe Theatre/Fraser Hall); Robert Thompson pp119; 139 (Marriage Guidance); Royal Geographical Society p109 (North Pole); Sayle Screen Ltd p188; Shutterstock pp117 (dinosaur/Jean-Michel Girard), 117 (penguin/Jan Martin Will), 117 (elephant/Victor Soares), 117 (tiger/pandapaw); Stan Eales p114; The Cartoon Bank pp1; 22; 59; 139 (spell-checker/Marshal Hopkins/Conde Nast Publications), 195 (bed/Peter Steiner/Conde Nast Publications), 218; The Dian Fossey Gorilla Fund International p101; Michael Swan: pp 167 (no cycles/ good food served here, look both ways), 212

Commissioned illustrations by:

Hamesh Alles: p13; Emma Brownjohn/New Division: pp 35, 37, 91, 200; Stefan Chabluk: pp 19, 85, 131, 156, 168(prepositions), 187, 215, 254, 290; Mark Duffin: pp 146, 152, 153, 155, 177, 190, 191, 197, 199, 224, 225(snakes), 230, 241, 256, 261; Paul Daviz/Illustration: pp 183, 203; Richard Coggan: pp 80, 211
Pete Ellis/Meiklejohn Illustrations: pp 33, 154, 223, 228; Maureen and Gordon Gray: pp 169, 211 (people); Joanna Kerr: p178; Pete Lawrence: pp 3, 25, 28, 36, 42, 51, 61, 67, 89, 94. 96, 98, 100, 108, 112, 134, 135, 142, 145, 157, 170, 176, 191, 192, 207, 216, 247, 251, 264, 265, 268, 269, 278, 279, 295; Ed McLachlan: pp 71, 165, 210; Gavin Reece: pp 10, 24, 99, 147, 159, 189, 280, 281

Every effort has been made to trace the owners of copyright material used in this book, but we should be pleased to hear from any copyright holder whom we have been unable to contact.

The authors and publisher are grateful to those who have given permission to reproduce the following extracts and adaptations of copyright material:

p132 *The Sound of Silence* Copyright © 1964 Paul Simon and Bruce Woodley. Used by permission of the Publisher: Paul Simon Music.
p253 Definitions taken from the *Oxford Advanced Learner's Dictionary*, eighth edition, published 2010 © Oxford University Press 2010.

Sources
p73 www.zerocarbonbritain.com
p82 *Lucile* by Owen Meredith
p107 *The Elephant's Child* in *Just So Stories* by Rudyard Kipling
p183 Based on *A contribution to statistics* from *Wislawa Szymborska Poems New and Collected*

contents

authors' acknowledgements

We owe a continuing debt to the many people whose advice and comments helped us with earlier versions of this material. The present book has benefited enormously from the hard work and professionalism of our editorial and design team at Oxford University Press. In particular, we would like to acknowledge the contributions of our remarkable editor, Sarah Parsons, and our equally remarkable designer, Phil Hargraves, who have made it possible for us to write the book that we wanted to, and whose input is evident on every page.

introduction

Who is this book for?

The *Oxford English Grammar Course* (Basic Level) is for all elementary and pre-intermediate learners who want to improve their knowledge of English grammar.

What kind of English does the book teach?

This book teaches the grammar of spoken and written British English. But it can also be used by students of American, Australian or other kinds of English – the grammatical differences are very small and unimportant.

How is the book organised?

There are 22 sections. A section covers one part of English grammar (for example: making questions and negatives; present tense verbs; problems with nouns). Each section contains:

- a presentation page which introduces the point of grammar
- several short units with explanations and exercises
- two 'More Practice' pages: these include 'Grammar in a text' exercises and internet exercises
- a short revision test.

4 Grammar in a text. Put in *a, an, the* or nothing (–).

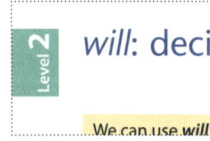

A TRUE STORY

In 1.......... 1969, in 2.......... Portland, 3.......... Oregon, 4.......... man went to rob 5.......... bank. He didn't want 6.......... people in 7.......... bank to know what was happening, so he walked up to one of 8.......... cashiers, wrote on 9.......... piece of 10.......... paper, 'This is 11.......... robbery and I've got 12.......... gun', and showed 13.......... paper to 14.......... cashier. Then he wrote, 'Take all 15.......... money out of your drawer and put it in 16.......... paper bag.' 17.......... cashier read 18.......... message, wrote at 19.......... bottom of 20.......... paper, 'I haven't got 21.......... paper bag' and gave 22.......... paper back to 23.......... robber. 24.......... robber ran out of 25.......... bank.

adapted from a poem by Wisława Szymborska

7 Internet exercise: checking correctness. Use a search engine (e.g. Google). How many hits are there for these expressions? So which are correct?

"too much fast" 40,700	"too fast" 10,900,000: Correct
"everybody is"	"everybody are" ....
"everything are"	"everything is" ....
"most people"	"most of people" ....

Two levels

More basic units are marked 'Level 1'; more advanced units are marked 'Level 2'.

Level 1 present p

Level 2 *will*: deci

One way of using the book: to study particular points

If you want to know more about a particular point (for example present tenses, the difference between *should* and *must*, or the position of adverbs), look in the index (pages 355–362) to find the right unit(s). Read the explanations and do the exercises. Check your answers in the answer key (pages 309–354).

Another way of using the book: for systematic study

If you are working without a teacher, we suggest:

1 DON'T go right through the book from beginning to end – some parts will be unnecessary for you.
2 Choose a Section to study. Section 1, 'be and have', for example? Section 8? Section 19?
3 Read the grammar explanations, do the exercises, and check your answers in the key (pages 309–354).
4 Do some or all of the exercises in the 'More Practice' pages.
5 Go to the revision test at the end of the section, and try some or all of the questions.
6 Check your answers. If you still have problems, look at the explanations again.

Pronunciation

The e-book has a section entitled 'Pronunciation for grammar', which will help you to hear unstressed grammatical words more clearly, and to pronounce structures fluently with good rhythm and stress.

Examinations

This book teaches all of the grammar (and more!) that is needed for Common European Framework Levels A1 and A2, and is suitable for learners studying for Cambridge KET and PET.

If you know everything in the book, will you speak perfect English?

No, sorry!

1 Not many people learn foreign languages perfectly. (And not many people need to.) But this book will help you to speak and write much more correctly.
2 Books like this give short practical explanations. They cannot tell you the whole truth about English grammar, and they cannot give you enough practice to get all the difficult points right. If you follow the rules in this book, you will not make many mistakes. But you will probably need to practise using the structures in different situations. (The website material will help with this.) You will find more complete information about difficult points in the Intermediate Level of the *Oxford English Grammar Course*.
3 Grammar is not the only important thing in a language. You also need a wide vocabulary, and – very important – you need a lot of practice in listening and speaking, reading and writing. Remember: this is a grammar practice book, not a complete English course.

To the teacher: website support

There is a complete lesson-by-lesson **Teacher's Guide** which you can download free from www.oup.com/elt/oegcteachersguides. This supplements the Student's Book exercises with hundreds of additional communicative and out-of-class practice activities, to help students make the move from practising grammar to *using* grammar. It also contains helpful Language Notes showing typical problems students may have with certain structures, often because of cross-language differences.

You can also download **Classroom Tests** for each level to help to show what your students need to study, or how well they have learnt the material you have covered. To access these, take a moment to sign up for free membership of the Oxford Teachers' Club: www.oup.com/elt/teachers/oxfordenglishgrammar.

We hope that you will enjoy using our book.

With our best wishes for your progress in English.

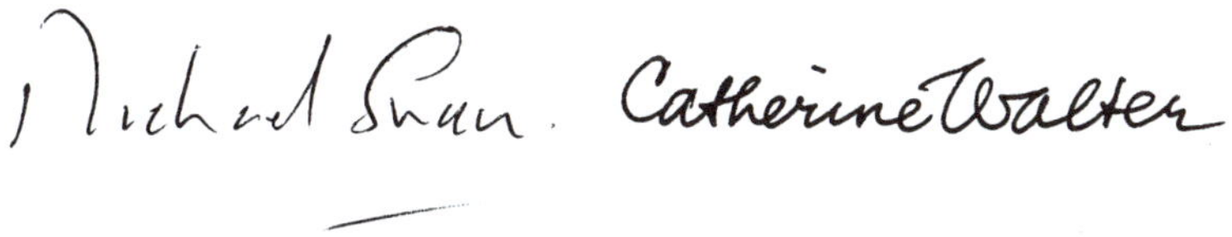

words for talking about grammar

active and **passive:** *I see, she heard* are **active** verbs; *I am seen, she was heard* are **passive** verbs.
adjectives: for example *big, old, yellow, unhappy*.
adverbs: for example *quickly, completely, now, there*.
affirmative sentences or **statements** are not questions or negatives – for example *I arrived*.
articles: *a/an* ('indefinite article'); *the* ('definite article').
auxiliary verbs are used before other verbs to make questions, tenses etc – for example ***do** you think; I **have** finished, she **is** working*. See also **modal auxiliary verbs**.
clause: see **sentence**.
comparatives: for example *older, better, more beautiful, more slowly*.
conditional: a structure using the conjunction ***if***.
conjunctions: for example *and, but, because, while*.
consonants: see **vowels**.
contractions: short forms like *I'm, you're, he'll, don't*.
conversational: see **formal**.
countable nouns: the names of things we can count – for example *one **chair**, three **cars***; **uncountable** (or '**mass**') **nouns**: the names of things we can't count, like *oil, rice*.
determiners: words like *the, some, many, my*, which go before (adjective +) noun.
double letters: *pp, tt, ee* etc.
formal, informal, conversational: We use **formal** language with strangers, in business letters etc: for example 'Good afternoon, Mr Parker. May I help you?' We use **informal** or **conversational** language with family and friends: for example 'Hi, John. Want some help?'
future verbs: for example *I **will go**; Ann **is going to write** to us*.
imperatives: forms like ***Go** home, **Come** and **sit** down, **Don't worry***, which we use when we tell or ask people (not) to do things.
indirect speech: the grammar that we use to say what people say or think: for example *John said **that he was tired***.
infinitives: *(to) go, (to) sleep* etc.
informal: see **formal**.
***-ing* forms:** *going, sleeping* etc.
irregular: see **regular**.
leave out: If we say *Seen John?*, we are **leaving out** *Have you*.
modal verbs or modal auxiliary verbs: *must, can, could, may, might, shall, should, ought to, will* and *would*.
negative sentences are made with *not*: for example *I have **not** seen her*.
nouns: for example *chair, oil, idea, sentence*.
object: see **subject**.
opposite: *hot* is the **opposite** of *cold*; *up* is the **opposite** of *down*.
passive: see **active**.
past perfect tense: see **perfect tenses**.
past progressive tense: see **past tenses**.
past tenses: for example *went, saw, stopped* (**simple past**); *was going, were eating* (**past progressive**).
past participles: for example *gone, seen, stopped*.
perfect tenses: forms with *have/has/had* + past participle: for example *I have forgotten* (**present perfect**); *It has been raining* (**present perfect progressive**); *They had stopped* (**past perfect**).
personal pronouns: for example *I, you, us, them*.
plural: see **singular**.
possessives: for example *my, your; mine, yours; John's, my brothers'*.
prepositions: for example *at, in, on, between*.
present participles: for example *going, sleeping* etc (also called ***-ing* forms**).
present perfect tenses: see **perfect tenses**.

present tenses: for example *He goes* (**simple present**); *She is walking* (**present progressive**).
progressive (or '**continuous**'): for example *I am thinking* (**present progressive**); *They were talking* (**past progressive**).
pronouns: for example *I, you, anybody, themselves*.
question tags: for example *isn't it?, doesn't she?*
reflexive pronouns: *myself, yourself* etc.
regular: plurals like *cats, buses*; past tenses like *started, stopped*; **irregular:** plurals like *teeth, men, children*; past tenses like *broke, went, saw*.
relative clauses: clauses that begin with relative pronouns: for example *the man who bought my car*.
relative pronouns: *who, which* and *that* when they join clauses to nouns: for example *the man* ***who*** *bought my car*.
sentence, clause: A sentence begins with a capital letter (A, B etc) and ends with a full stop (.), like this one. A sentence may have more than one clause, often joined by a conjunction. For example: *I'll come and see you when I'm in London*.
simple past tense: see **past tenses**.
simple present tense: see **present tenses**.
singular: for example *chair, cat, man*; **plural:** for example *chairs, cats, men*.
spelling: writing words correctly: for example, we spell *necessary* with one *c* and double *s*.
subject and **object:** In *She took the money – everybody saw her*, the **subjects** are *she* and *everybody*; the **objects** are *the money* and *her*.
superlatives: for example *oldest, best, most beautiful, most easily*.
tense: *She goes, she is going, she went, she was going, she has gone* are different **tenses**.
third person: words for other people, not *I* or *you*: for example *she, them, himself, John, has, goes*.
uncountable nouns: see **countable nouns**.
verbs: for example *sit, give, hold, think, write*.
vowels: *a, e, i, o, u* and their usual sounds; **consonants:** *b, c, d, f, g* etc and their usual sounds.

other useful words

Here are some other words that are used in this book. Find them in your dictionary and write the translations here.

action ....
choose ....
common ....
complete (*verb*) ....
correct ....
description ....
difference ....
event ....
exclamation ....
explain ....
expression ....
form (*noun*) ....
go on, happen ....
in general ....
introduction ....
join ....
mean (*verb*) ....
meaning ....
necessary ....
news ....
normal ....
normally ....
particular ....
plan ....
polite ....
politely ....
possibility ....
possible ....
practise ....
predict ....
prefer ....
probable ....
pronounce ....
pronunciation ....
repeat ....
report ....
revision ....
rule ....
section ....
similar ....
situation ....
stressed (pronunciation) ....
structure ....
unnecessary ....
unusual ....
use (*noun*) ....
use (*verb*) ....
(word) order ....

list of units

SECTION 1 *be* and *have*

grammar summary

be (*am*/*are*/*is*/*was*/*were*)

- We can use **adjectives**, **nouns** or expressions of **place** after ***be***.
  She ***is late****.* *I****'m hungry****.* ***Are*** *you a* ***doctor****?* ***Is*** *everybody* ***here****?*
- We use a special structure with *be* – ***there is*** – to introduce things: to say that they exist.
  There's *a strange woman at the door.* ***There are*** *some letters for you.*
- *Be* can be an **auxiliary verb** in progressive tenses (see page 23) and passives (see page 94).
  She ***is working****.* *It* ***was made*** *in Hong Kong.*

have (*have*/*has*/*had*)

- We can use ***have*** or ***have got*** to talk about **possession**, **relationships** and some other ideas.
  Do *you* ***have*** *a car?* *I* ***don't have*** *any brothers or sisters.* *Ann* ***has got*** *a headache.*
- And we can use ***have*** to talk about some kinds of **actions**.
  I'm going to ***have a shower****.* *What time* ***do*** *you* ***have breakfast****?*
- ***Have*** can also be an **auxiliary verb** in perfect tenses (see Section 5).
  I ***haven't seen*** *her all day.* *We knew that he* ***had taken*** *the money.*

'And were you good while I was out?'

To be or not to be, that is the question.
(*Shakespeare*: Hamlet)

There's a thin man inside every fat man.
(*George Orwell*)

Is there life before death?
(*Seamus Heaney*)

You can have it all, but you can't do it all.
(*Michelle Pfeiffer*)

If you've got everything,
you've got nothing.
(*Leni MacShaw*)

When I was young there was no respect for the young, and now that I am old there is no respect for the old.
(*J B Priestley*)

be *I am happy today. Are we late?*

	BE: PRESENT				
+	*I am*	*you are*	*he/she/it is*	*we are*	*they are*
?	*am I?*	*are you?*	*is he/she/it?*	*are we?*	*are they?*
-	*I am* ***not***	*you are* ***not***	*he/she/it is* ***not***	*we are* ***not***	*they are* ***not***

I am a doctor. *Are you American?* *We are* ***not*** *ready.*

1 Put in *am*, *are* or *is*.

▶ You ...are... late.
1 We .... very well.
2 My sister .... a doctor.
3 Paul and Ann .... in America.
4 I .... happy today.
5 I think you .... tired.
6 Our house .... very small.
7 I .... nearly ready.

In **conversation** and informal writing, we use **contractions**:
I'm *you're* *he's* *she's* *it's* *John's* *the train's* *we're* *they're*

I'm a doctor. *You're late.* *John's in London.* *The shop's open.* *We're ready.*

2 Write these sentences with contractions.

▶ Claire is ill. ...Claire's ill....
1 We are all tired. ....
2 They are here. ....
3 I am sorry. ....
4 My name is Peter. ....
5 You are early. ....
6 The shop is closed. ....
7 She is at home. ....

To make **questions** (?) with *be*, we put the **verb before the subject**.

STATEMENT +: *I am late.* *The taxi is here.* *We are late.* *Your keys are in the car.*
QUESTION ?: *Am I late?* *Is the taxi here?* *Are we late?* *Are my keys in the car?*

3 Make questions.

▶ Bill / Scottish ...Is Bill Scottish?...
1 Marie / from Paris ....
2 we / very late ....
3 John / in bed ....
4 the boss / here ....
5 your car / fast ....
6 Luke / here ....
7 we all / ready ....
8 I / early ....
9 they / at home ....
10 you / happy ....
11 Joe / married ....
12 this / your house ....
13 that / Jane ....

Do you know all these **question words**? ***who what when where why how***
Contractions with *is*: ***who's what's when's where's why's how's***

Who's *that?* ***What's*** *this?* ***When's*** *the party?* ***Where's*** *the station?* ***Why*** *are we here?* ***How*** *are you?*

4 Put in question words with *are* or *'s*.

▶ '...Who's... that?' 'It's my brother.'
▶ '...Where are... Leo and Amy?' 'In London.'
1 '.................. your name?' 'Maria.'
2 '.................. my glasses?' 'Here.'
3 '.................. your teacher?' 'Mrs Allen.'
4 '.................. the exams?' 'On Tuesday.'
5 '.................. you late?' 'My watch is broken.'
6 '.................. your mother?' 'Not very well.'
7 '.................. Daniel?' 'In hospital.'
8 '.................. those men?' 'I don't know.'
9 '.................. your parents?' 'Very well.'
10 '.................. your birthday?' 'March 17th.'

To make negative (–) sentences with *be*, we put **not** after **am/are/is** or **'m, 're, 's**.

*I **am not** Scottish.* *We **are not** ready.* *I'**m not** tired.* *She'**s not** here.* *They'**re not** my friends.*

We can also make contractions with **n't**: *you **aren't**, she **isn't*** etc (**BUT NOT** ~~*I amn't*~~).

5 Write negative (–) ends for the sentences.

▶ I'm Greek, but (– *from Athens*) I'm not from Athens.
▶ It's winter, but (– *cold*) it's not cold. **OR** it isn't cold.
1 She's tired, but (– *ill*) ....
2 They are in England, but (– *in London*) ....
3 You're tall, but (– *too tall*) ....
4 We are late, but (– *very late*) ....
5 It's summer, but (– *hot*) ....
6 I'm a student, but (– *at university*) ....
7 John's good-looking, but (– *very nice*) ....
8 Anne is at work, but (– *in her office*) ....
9 This is a nice coat, but (– *mine*) ....
10 It's a big car, but (– *very fast*) ....

We often use ***be*** with: ***hungry, thirsty, cold, hot, right, wrong, afraid, interested, what colour?, what size?***
And we use ***be*** with **ages**.

*Have you got anything to eat? I'**m hungry**.* *I'**m cold**.* *It'**s** very **hot** here in summer.*
*'It's late.' 'You'**re right**. Let's go.'* ***Are** you **afraid** of flying?* *I'**m interested** in politics.*
***What colour is** her hair?* ***What size are** your shoes?* *'**How old are** you?' 'I'**m 17**.'*

6 Complete the sentences under the pictures.

▶ She is hungry. 1 He .... 2 She .... 3 .... 4 It ....

7 Put in words from the box.

afraid ✓	cold	colour	hot	hungry	interested	old	right	size	thirsty	wrong	

▶ He is a big man, but he is afraid of her.
1 You think I'm wrong, but I know I'm ....
2 'What .... is that T-shirt?' 'Extra large.'
3 What .... is your car?
4 Sorry, I'm not .... in her problems.
5 'It's the18th today.' 'You're .... – it's the 19th.'
6 'Something to drink?' 'No, thanks. I'm not ....'
7 'It's .... in here.' 'Open a window.'
8 Is it .... here in winter?
9 'How .... is your girlfriend?' 'She's 19.'
10 'I'm .... ' 'Would you like a sandwich?'

In some answers, both contracted forms (for example *I'm, don't*) and full forms (for example *I am, do not*) are possible. Normally both are correct.

Level 1

be: past *Where were you? I was in Glasgow.*

+	*I was*	*you were*	*he/she/it was*	*we were*	*they were*
?	*was I?*	*were you?*	*was he/she/it?*	*were we?*	*were they?*
-	*I was **not***	*you were **not***	*he/she/it was **not***	*we were **not***	*they were **not***
	Contractions: *wasn't, weren't*				

Where were you yesterday? *My mother was a singer.* *I wasn't well last week.*

1 Put in *was* or *were*.

▶ In summer 1990 I ...was... in Brazil.

1 'We .... very happy to see you yesterday.' 'And I .... happy to see you.'
2 Lunch .... OK, but the vegetables .... not very good.
3 I can't find my keys. They .... here this morning.
4 It .... cold and dark, and we .... tired.
5 My grandmother .... a doctor, and her two brothers .... both doctors too.
6 '........... you in London yesterday?' 'No, I .... in Glasgow.'
7 'When .... your exam?' 'It .... yesterday.'
8 'Why .... you late?' 'The train .... late.'

2 Put the words in the correct order to make questions.

▶ Ann at home yesterday was ...Was Ann at home yesterday?...
1 good party was the ....
2 people were the interesting ....
3 teacher father your was a ....
4 everybody was late ....
5 your was driving test when ....
6 Tuesday you where on were ....
7 open windows why the all were ....
8 John's brother school was with at you ....

3 Put in *wasn't* or *weren't* and words from the box. Make sure you understand *actually*. Use a dictionary if necessary.

a teacher	good	in England	in their hotel	interesting ✓	late	warm	well	with Anna

▶ The lesson ...wasn't interesting... Actually, it was very boring.
1 You .... Actually, you arrived 10 minutes early.
2 My father .... Actually, he worked as a bus driver.
3 I .... yesterday. Actually, I was with Susan.
4 The children .... yesterday. The doctor came to see them.
5 We .... last week. We went to Scotland for a few days.
6 The snow .... at Christmas. We couldn't ski.
7 Ann and Peter .... when I phoned.
8 It .... last night. Actually, it was quite cold.

→ For the present perfect of *be* (*I have been* etc), see page 61.

be: future *The bus will be full.*

+	*I/you/he/she/it/we/they* **will be**
?	**will** *I/you/she* etc **be**?
–	*I/you/he* etc **will not be**
	Contractions: *I'll, you'll* etc; *won't* (= *will not*)

It **will be** *cold this evening.* *I'**ll be** at home all day tomorrow.*
Where **will** *we* **be** *ten years from now?* *The exam* **won't be** *difficult.*

1 Look at the table and complete the text.

Tomorrow's temperatures	
Cairo	35°
Rio	30°
Paris	23°
London	3°
Moscow	-18°

0°

Tomorrow ..it will be.. very hot in Cairo.
It .... hot in ....
.... warm in ....
.... cold in ....
.... very cold in ....

2 Change these sentences to affirmative (+) or negative (–).

▶ The bus will not be full. ..The bus will be full.........
▶ She'll be late. ..She won't be late.........
1 I'll be sorry. ....
2 It will not be hot. ....
3 We won't be at home. ....
4 The shops will be closed. ....
5 He'll be in Scotland. ....
6 Lisa will be at school. ....

To make **future questions** with ***be***, we put ***will*** **before the subject**.

STATEMENT +: ***We will*** *be late.* ***Her brother will*** *be here at 10.00.* ***The bus will*** *be full.*
QUESTION ?: ***Will we*** *be late?* *When* ***will her brother*** *be here?* ***Will the bus*** *be full?*

3 Make questions with *will ... be ...?*

▶ you / at home / this evening ..Will you be at home this evening?.........
▶ when / lunch / ready ..When will lunch be ready?.........
1 when / your father / in England ....
2 Ann / at the party / with John ....
3 everybody / here / at 8.00 ....
4 the train / late / again ....
5 when / Joe and Mary / in the office ....
6 the weather / good / tomorrow ....
7 where / you / on Tuesday ....

4 Complete the sentences.

1 (*your age*) This year I am .... In 2000 I ....
Last year I .... Next year I .... In 20..... I ....
2 (*a friend's age*) This year he/she .... In 2000 ....
Last year .... Next year .... In 20..... ....

In some answers, both contracted forms (for example *I'm, don't*) and full forms (for example *I am, do not*) are possible. Normally both are correct.

there is/was *There's a dog in the garden.*

	PRESENT		PAST	
+	*there **is***	*there **are***	*there **was***	*there **were***
?	***is** there?*	***are** there?*	***was** there?*	***were** there?*
–	*there **is not***	*there **are not***	*there **was not***	*there **were not***
	Contractions: *there's; isn't, aren't, wasn't, weren't*			

We use ***there is, there are*** etc to say that something or somebody **exists.**
We often use ***there is, there are*** etc before ***a/an, some*** and ***any***.

***There's a** dog in the garden.* (NOT ~~*A dog is in the garden.*~~)
***Is there any** milk in the fridge?* (NOT ~~*Is any milk …?*~~)
***Were there any** phone calls?* (NOT ~~*Were any phone calls?*~~)
***There are some** letters for you.*
***There isn't** much coffee.*
***There was a** good film last night.*

1 Make some sentences with words from the three boxes, using *there is* etc.

There is/are a lot of There isn't much There aren't many There isn't/aren't any There wasn't/weren't any	water air grass dogs elephants trees cars people computers … (*you think of some more things*)	in Africa in the USA in Antarctica in London on the moon in 1600 … (*you think of some more places or times*)

▶ There are a lot of animals in Africa.
▶ There weren't any cars in 1600.
1 ....
2 ....
3 ....
4 ....
5 ....
6 ....

To make **questions** with *there is* etc, we put *is* etc **before** *there*.

STATEMENT +:	*There **is** a letter for you.*	*There **were** some problems.*	*William says **there are** six eggs.*
QUESTION ?:	***Is there** a letter for me?*	***Were there** any problems?*	*How many eggs **are there**?*

2 Make present or past questions with *there is* etc.

▶ any fruit juice in the fridge (*present*) Is there any fruit juice in the fridge?
▶ any letters for me (*past*) Were there any letters for me?
▶ how many people / in your family (*present*) How many people are there in your family?
1 a doctor here (*present*) ....
2 any trains to London from this station (*present*) ....
3 a special price for students (*past*) ....
4 any mistakes in my letter (*past*) ....
5 much money in your bank account (*present*) ....
6 how many students / in your class (*present*) ....
7 many children at the swimming pool (*past*) ....
8 how many people / at the party (*past*) ....

there is: future *Will there be cars?*

	FUTURE
+	*there **will** be*
?	***will** there be?*
-	*there **will** not be*
	Contraction: *won't* (= *will not*)

***There will be** a public holiday next Tuesday.* ***Will there be** a meeting tomorrow?*
***There will not be** any time for us to see Mary.* ***There won't be** any of my friends at the party.*

1 Complete the sentences with *there will be* and words from the box.

fish	flowers	food	hospital	rain ✓	sun	ten people	trouble	two new students

▶ I think there will be rain .... tomorrow.
1 But I think .... on Tuesday.
2 .... in the class tomorrow.
3 .... in our house at the weekend.
4 One day, perhaps .... enough .... for everybody.
5 .... for supper tonight.
6 .... a new .... in our town next year.
7 'Mum, I've broken a window.' '.................................... when your father comes home.'
8 .... a lot of .... in the garden this summer.

2 Make negative (-) sentences. Use *There will not be* or *There won't be*.

▶ time / see Granny There won't be time to see Granny.
▶ exam / Saturday There will not be an exam on Saturday.
1 meeting / tomorrow ....
2 any trains / Sunday ....
3 any buses / 4 o'clock in the morning ....
4 If you get up late tomorrow, / any breakfast ....
5 anybody / home tomorrow evening ....
6 any children / the party ....
7 a French lesson / Monday evening ....
8 time / have lunch today ....

3 Write questions about life in the year 2100, with *Will there be …?*

▶ (*cars*) Will there be cars?
1 (*trains*) ....
2 (*computers*) ....
3 (*good food*) ....
4 (*different countries*) ....
5 (*governments*) ....
6 (*a lot of problems*) ....
7 (your question) ....

4 Write your answers to the questions in Exercise 3.

▶ There will be cars. OR There won't be cars.
1 ....
2 ....
3 ....
4 ....
5 ....
6 ....
7 ....

In some answers, both contracted forms (for example *I'm*, *don't*) and full forms (for example *I am*, *do not*) are possible. Normally both are correct.

have I have do you have? I don't have

I/you/we/they ***have***
he/she/it ***has***

We can use ***have*** to talk about **possessions**, family (and other) **relationships** and **illnesses**.

I ***have*** *a new car.* *Nina* ***has*** *two sisters.* *Pete* ***has*** *a nice girlfriend.* *We all* ***have*** *colds.*

We also say that people **have** hair, eyes etc; and that things **have** parts.

You ***have*** *beautiful eyes.* *My new car only* ***has*** *two doors.*

1 Circle the correct form.

▶ *John / I* have two brothers. (I circled)
▶ Grace *has / have* a cold. (has circled)
1 *My father / My parents* has two cars.
2 *We all / Sally* have blue eyes.
3 I *have / has* a headache.
4 I see that your brother *have / has* a new girlfriend.
5 *You / Paul* has very long hair.
6 These houses *have / has* big rooms.
7 I can't read this book – it *has / have* 800 pages.
8 *Susie / Susie and Mick* have a really nice flat.

2 Write about three things that you have, and three things that one of your friends or relations has.

1 I have ....
2 I ....
3 ....
4 ....
5 ....
6 ....

We can make **questions** (?) and **negatives** (-) with ***do/does/did*** + **infinitive** (without *to*).
(For questions and negatives without *do*, see page 11.)

STATEMENT +	QUESTION ?	NEGATIVE -
I ***have*** *the keys.*	***Do*** *I* ***have*** *the keys?*	*I* ***do not / don't have*** *the keys.*
Joe ***has*** *a car.*	***Does*** *Joe* ***have*** *a car?* (NOT ~~*Does Joe has*~~ ...)	*Joe* ***does not / doesn't have*** *a car.*

3 Make questions (?) or negatives (-) with *have*.

▶ you / a cat ? Do you have a cat?
▶ Eric / many friends - Eric doesn't have many friends.
1 we / a garden - We don't..........
2 they / any children ? ....
3 Peter / a cold ? ....
4 my aunt / a dog - ....
5 Monica / any brothers or sisters ? ....
6 I / enough money - ....
7 Laura / a boyfriend ? ....
8 Why / you / two cars ? ....

4 Write about three things that you don't have, and three things that one of your friends or relations doesn't have.

1 I don't have ....
2 ....
3 ....
4 ....
5 ....
6 ....

have: past and future

PAST: *I/you/he/she/it/we/they* ***had***

When I was a student I ***had*** *an old Volkswagen.* *Ann* ***had*** *a cold last week.*

We make past **questions** and **negatives** with ***did*** **+ infinitive (without *to*)**.

STATEMENT +	QUESTION ?	NEGATIVE -
Clara ***had*** *a cold.*	***Did*** *Clara* ***have*** *a cold?* (NOT ~~*Did Clara had*~~ …)	*Clara* ***did not / didn't have*** *a cold.*

1 Make sentences about Clara when she was six.

- ▸ a bicycle ? Did she have a bicycle?
- ▸ a dog - She didn't have a dog.
1. a computer - ……………
2. very fair hair + ……………
3. lots of friends - ……………
4. many nice clothes - ……………
5. her own room ? ……………

2 Write sentences about yourself when you were six. Use *I had* and *I didn't have*.

1. I had ……………
2. I didn't have ……………
3. ……………
4. ……………

FUTURE: *I/you/he/she/it/we/they* ***will (not) have***
Contractions: *I'll, you'll* etc; *won't* (= *will not*)

One day, everybody ***will have*** *enough food.* *Julia says that she* ***won't have*** *children.*

To make **future questions** with ***have***, we put ***will*** **before the subject**.

STATEMENT +:	*John will have a car soon.*	*The baby will have blue eyes.*
QUESTION ?:	*Will John have a car soon?*	*Will the baby have blue eyes?*

3 Read the text and complete the sentences about John's future.

This year, John doesn't have money, a job, a house, a girlfriend, a suit or a car. He has a small room, a bicycle, old clothes, a guitar and a cat. But next year:

- ▸ more money + He will have more money.
- ▸ a small room - He won't have a small room.
- ▸ a cat ? Will he have a cat?
1. a job + ……………
2. a bicycle - ……………
3. a car + ……………
4. a house ? ……………
5. a girlfriend ? ……………
6. old clothes - ……………
7. a suit + ……………
8. a guitar ? ……………

In some answers, both contracted forms (for example *I'm*, *don't*) and full forms (for example *I am*, *do not*) are possible. Normally both are correct.

have: actions *He's having a shower.*

We use ***have*** in a lot of common expressions to talk about **actions**.

*I usually **have breakfast** at seven o'clock.* *I'm going to **have a shower**.*
*Would you like to **have something to eat**?* *If Bill comes this weekend we'll **have a party**.*
*Teresa **had a baby** in June.* *Are you **having a good time**?* ***'Have a good flight.'** 'Thanks.'*

1 Look at the pictures and complete the sentences. Use *have*, *has* or *had* with words from the box.

a baby	coffee	dinner	a game	a party ✓	a shower	toast

▶ The people next door ....had a party.................. last night and I couldn't sleep.
1 I .... with John yesterday evening.
2 My boss usually .... at 11 o'clock.
3 Nicole's going to .... in August.
4 I usually .... before breakfast.
5 We always .... for breakfast.
6 Would you like to .... of tennis?

▶ 

1 

2 

3 

4 

5 

6 

We make simple present and past **questions** and **negatives** with ***do/does*** and ***did***.

*We **don't have** parties very often.* ***Does** Kurt **have** eggs for breakfast?*
***Did** you **have** a good journey?* *We **didn't have** a holiday.*

2 Make questions (?) and negatives (–).

▶ (*good time* ?) 'We went to Paris at the weekend.' ....'Did you have a good time?'..............
▶ (*breakfast* –) I got up late this morning, so I ....didn't have breakfast.................
1 (*lunch* ?) What time .... on Sundays?
2 (*good trip* –) Ann was in America last week. ....
3 (*shower* –) The hotel bathroom was very dirty, so I ....
4 (*good flight* ?) Welcome to England, Mr García. ....
5 (*good game* ?) 'Mark and I played tennis this morning.' ....
6 (*coffee* –) .... before I go to bed.

LEARN THESE COMMON EXPRESSIONS WITH *HAVE* (USE A DICTIONARY IF NECESSARY)
have breakfast, lunch, dinner, (a cup of) tea/coffee, a drink, something to eat/drink *have eggs/toast for breakfast, have fish for lunch etc* *have a wash, a shower, a bath* *have a good time, a bad day, a nice evening, a party, a holiday, a game* *have a good flight/trip/journey etc* *have a conversation* *have a baby*

have without *do*: *have got* *Have you got a cat?*

+	I/you/we/they **have got**	he/she/it **has got**
?	**have** I/you etc **got**?	**has** he/she/it **got**?
-	I/you etc **have** not **got**	he/she/it **has** not **got**
	Contractions: *I've, he's* etc; *haven't, hasn't*	

We often use ***got*** with ***have***, especially in spoken English, and especially in the **present**.
This does not change the meaning: we use ***have/has got*** like ***have/has*** to talk about **possession** etc.

- ***I have got*** is the same as ***I have.***
- ***Have you got?*** is the same as ***Do you have?*** (We don't use *do/does* with *have got*.)
- ***She hasn't got*** is the same as ***She doesn't have***.

I've got *a cat.* ***Has*** *she* ***got*** *a dog?* (NOT ~~*Does she have got*~~ …)
I haven't got *a car.* *She's* ***got*** *a sister.* *You'**ve got*** *beautiful eyes.* ***Have*** *you* ***got*** *a cold?*

1 Write about John's possessions etc.

- ▶ a bicycle: ✓ John's got a bicycle.
- ▶ suits: 2 He's got two suits.
- ▶ a horse: ✗ He hasn't got a horse.
- ▶ any children: ✗ He hasn't got any children.

1 brothers: 2 ……………………………………
2 a car: ✗ ……………………………………
3 dogs: 3 ……………………………………
4 a dictionary: ✓ ……………………………………
5 long hair: ✗ ……………………………………
6 any sisters: ✗ ……………………………………

2 Write three sentences about your possessions etc, and three about the possessions of a friend or relation.

1 I've got …………………………… 4 ……………………………
2 …………………………… 5 ……………………………
3 …………………………… 6 ……………………………

To make **questions** (?) with ***have got***, we put ***have/has*** **before the subject**.

STATEMENT +:	*I* ***have*** ***got*** *a cold.*	*Harry's* ***got*** *a fast car.*	*Amy and Juan* ***have*** ***got*** *tickets.*
QUESTION ?:	***Have*** *you* ***got*** *a cold?*	***Has*** *Harry* ***got*** *a fast car?*	***Have*** *Amy and Juan* ***got*** *tickets?*

3 Beth and Tom have got a lot of money. Ask questions with *have got*.

- ▶ they / big house Have they got a big house?

1 they / big garden ……………………………………
2 Beth / good job ……………………………………
3 Tom / big car ……………………………………
4 they / plane ……………………………………
5 they / any horses ……………………………………

Past forms with *got* (***I had got*** etc) are **unusual**. We **don't** use *got* in the **future**.

She ***had*** *a fast car.* (MORE NATURAL THAN *She had got a fast car.*) *I* ***will have***. (NOT ~~*I will have got.*~~)

In some answers, both contracted forms (for example *I'm, don't*) and full forms (for example *I am, do not*) are possible. Normally both are correct.

be and *have*: more practice

1 Contractions. Rewrite these sentences with contractions.

▶ John is tired. *John's tired.*
1 They were not ready. ....
2 We are all here. ....
3 I am not a student. ....
4 Where is your house? ....
5 She will not be late. ....
6 You have got my keys. ....
7 I have not got much time. ....
8 Franz does not live here. ....

2 Contractions. Rewrite these sentences without contractions.

▶ I wasn't ready. *I was not ready.*
1 Tom's late. ....
2 I won't have time. ....
3 Anna's hungry. ....
4 He doesn't have a car. ....
5 She's got two sisters. ....
6 She's right. ....
7 Emma's got beautiful eyes. ....
8 There's a letter for you. ....

3 *Be*. Make questions and negatives. Use negative contractions.

▶ It's summer. (*hot*) *Is it hot? No, it's not hot.* (OR *No, it isn't hot.*)
1 He's Chinese. (*from Beijing*) ....
2 He was ill. (*in bed*) ....
3 We'll be late. (*very late*) ....
4 Her room's cheap. (*very big*) ....
5 They were students. (*at university*) ....
6 She was in the building. (*in her office*) ....
7 They'll have something to drink. (*coffee*) ....
8 They're rich. (*happy*) ....

4 *Have*: questions and negatives. Complete the sentences with *do* or *does*.

▶ I *do* not have much free time.
▶ *Does* Carol have a boyfriend?
1 Dogs .... not have wings.
2 .... England have any high mountains?
3 Ann ....n't have a job just now.
4 .... you have my new address?
5 My brother and I .... not have blue eyes.
6 Maria .... n't speak English.
7 I ....n't have a headache any more.
8 .... your street have any shops?

5 *There is*. Put in expressions from the box.

there's ✓	there are	there was	there weren't	there will be	there won't be
is there	are there	was there	were there	will there be	

▶ *There's* somebody at the door.
1 I think .... an election next year.
2 I'm hungry. .... anything to eat?
3 .... a fascinating programme on TV last night.
4 How many people .... in your family?
5 I wanted to buy shoes, but .... any nice ones in the shops.
6 .... many people at the meeting yesterday?
7 .... two policemen at the door. They want to talk to you.
8 I'm not going to the party. .... any interesting people there.
9 .... a phone call for me while I was out?
10 .... anybody in the office tomorrow?

6 Grammar in a text. Read the text, and then write about yourself.

His name's Noureddin. He's from Rabat, in Morocco. He's a student. He's 21. He isn't married. He's got four brothers and two sisters.
He's interested in music and politics. He isn't interested in sport.

My name's ....
....
....
....
....
....
....

7 Grammar in a text. Put in affirmative (+) or negative (-) forms of *be* or *have*.

Helen ▶ ...is............. fourteen. She 1.................. at a very nice school; she 2.................. interested in the lessons – there 3.................. only two teachers that she doesn't like – and she 4.................. got lots of friends. (Two years ago she 5.................. at a different school; the lessons 6.................. very good, and she 7.................. many friends, so she 8.................. very unhappy.) The school 9.................. a long way from Helen's house, so she gets up early. She 10.................. a quick wash, and then she 11.................. breakfast – cereal and fruit juice if she 12.................. hungry. There 13.................. a school bus, but if it 14.................. very cold her mother takes her by car. In the evenings she 15.................. school work; she 16.................. much difficulty with this, so she usually finishes quickly. Then she 17.................. supper. At ten o'clock she 18.................. very tired, so she 19.................. a bath and goes to bed. On Saturdays and Sundays she gets up at 12.00, 20.................. a quick lunch and goes straight to her computer games.

8 GRAMMAR AND VOCABULARY: relations. Make sure you know the words in the box. Use a dictionary if necessary. Then look at the family tree and write 'true' or 'false' against the sentences.

son	daughter	uncle	aunt	nephew	niece
cousin	grandchild	grandfather	grandmother		

▶ Eric and Sue have four grandchildren. ...True.....
▶ Ruby is Bill's grandmother. ...False.....
1 Toby is Bill's son. ....
2 Bill is Paul's uncle. ....
3 Rosemary is Toby's mother. ....
4 Lily is Bill's niece. ....
5 Ben is Toby's nephew. ....
6 Ruby is Lily's cousin. ....
7 Alice is Bill's aunt. ....
8 Rosemary is Lily's uncle. ....
9 Toby is Ruby's nephew. ....
10 Ruby is Paul's niece. ....

9 Internet exercise. Can you find these on the internet?

1 The name of a song with the words *"there is a house"* ....
2 The name of a song with the words *"once I had"* ....
3 The name of a song with the words *"have a party"* ....

pronunciation for grammar → e-book

be and *have*: revision test

1 Circle the correct form.

▶ (*Is*) / *Are* your brother at home?
1 *Where / Who / How* is the station?
2 *I / We* was in London yesterday.
3 *Are / Have* you thirsty?
4 Alice *is / has* three brothers.
5 My sister *is / has* 25 today.
6 'I *am / have* cold.' 'Put on a sweater.'
7 I *want / won't* be here next week.
8 I *am / are* tired.
9 Emma *is / has* very happy today.
10 There *is / are* a new secretary in the company.
11 Did you *have / had* a good journey?
12 *Do / Does* your father have a car?
13 *Do / Have* you got a cold?
14 *Will be you / Will you be* at the party tonight?
15 *I amn't / I'm not* ready.
16 '*Why / Who / How* are you?' 'Fine, thanks.'
17 Did you *have / has* a good holiday?
18 It's my birthday next week. I *will be / will have* 18.
19 Does John *have / has* a brother?
20 How many people *is / are* there in your family?

2 Correct (✓) or not (✗)?

▶ I don't had breakfast today. ..✗..
1 I'm not ...... I amn't ......
he's not ...... he isn't ......
2 Do you got a bicycle? ......
3 Had you a good journey? ......
4 Jane is having a shower. ......
5 My friends was late. ......
6 Is there any eggs in the fridge? ......
7 I don't have many friends. ......
8 I do have two brothers. ......
9 There won't be a lesson tomorrow. ......
10 I not had breakfast today. ......

3 Change the sentences to questions or negatives.

▶ It's Tuesday. [-] It isn't Tuesday. OR It's not Tuesday.
1 There's a taxi outside. [?] ......
2 Chris has got a headache. [?] ......
3 Joe has a car. [-] ......
4 Ann had a meeting yesterday. [?] ......
5 I had coffee for breakfast. [-] ......
6 There will be an English lesson tomorrow. [?] ......
7 I'm hungry. [-] ......
8 Petra's got a new car. [-] ......
9 She had a nice time at the party. [?] ......
10 The house has got a big garden. [?] ......

4 Make present (PR), past (PA) or future (F) questions.

▶ Peter / Irish (PR) Is Peter Irish?
▶ Jane / have breakfast this morning (PA) Did Jane have breakfast this morning?
1 Rosemary / from London (PR) ......
2 we / early (F) ......
3 Sarah / at home (PA) ......
4 Karim / have a cold (PR) ......
5 your car / fast (PR) ......
6 the manager / in America (F) ......
7 Tim and Anna / students (PA) ......
8 What time / you have lunch today (F) ......
9 you / here tomorrow (F) ......
10 those people / American (PA) ......

In some answers, both contracted forms (for example *I'm*, *don't*) and full forms (for example *I am*, *do not*) are possible. Normally both are correct.

SECTION 2 present tenses

grammar summary

SIMPLE PRESENT: *I work, she works, he doesn't work* etc PRESENT PROGRESSIVE: *I am working, she is working, he isn't working* etc

English has **two 'present' tenses.**

- We use the **simple present** mostly to talk about **things that are always true**, and **things that happen repeatedly.**
  *Dogs **eat** meat.* *My grandmother **lives** in Brighton.* *I **work** every Saturday.*
- We use the **present progressive** (or 'present continuous') to talk about things that are happening just **around the time when we speak.**
  *Look! The dog**'s eating** your shoe.* ***I'm working hard** these days.*
- We can also use the **present progressive** to talk about the **future** (see page 38).
  ***I'm seeing** Lucy tomorrow.*

Some old songs

I like myself

I believe in love

She's leaving home

Am I asking too much?

Is she really going out with him?

Where are you going?

Smoke gets in your eyes

I love Paris in the springtime

She loves me

She loves you

I'm crying

I'm flying

Why do I love you?

Why do fools fall in love?

Why do lovers break each other's hearts?

I don't want to do it

simple present* affirmative *I work; you work; she works*

+	I work	you work	he/she/it work**s**	we work	they work
	I live	you live	he/she/it live**s**	we live	they live
	I stop	you stop	he/she/it stop**s**	we stop	they stop

*I **work** in a bank.* *He **works** in a restaurant.*
*You **live** near my brother.* *She **lives** in Liverpool.*
*We **stop** the lessons at 5.00.* *The train **stops** at York.*

HOW TO MAKE HE/SHE/IT FORMS

- **most verbs:** + -s work ⟶ work**s** know ⟶ know**s** rain ⟶ rain**s**
- **-s, -sh, -ch, -x:** + -es pass ⟶ pass**es** wash ⟶ wash**es** teach ⟶ teach**es** mix ⟶ mix**es**
- **exceptions:** go ⟶ go**es** do ⟶ do**es** have ⟶ ha**s**

1 **Write the *he/she/it* forms.**

catch ✓	come ✓	cook	drink	fetch	fix	live	miss	push
read	run	smoke	stand	start	touch	watch	wish	write

+ -*S*: comes

....

+ -*ES*: catches

....

VERBS ENDING IN -Y

- **vowel + y** -ay, -ey, -oy, -uy: + -s say ⟶ say**s**
- **consonant + y** -dy, -ly, -py, -ry, etc: -y ⟶ -ies fly ⟶ fl**ies**

2 **Write the *he/she/it* forms.**

buy ✓	carry ✓	copy	enjoy	fry	marry	play	stay	study	try

+ -*S*: buys

-*Y* ⟶ -*IES*: carries

3 **Put the words in the correct order.**

▶ eats dog too your much
 Your dog eats too much.

1 live I that house in
...

2 bank Kim in a works
...

3 badly violin plays the very Claire
...

4 Scotland those from children come
...

5 young very look you
...

4 **Circle the correct answers.**

▶ (We) / My friend always wear old clothes.
▶ You / (John) always wears nice clothes.
1 We all / The boss thinks you're wonderful.
2 I / Catherine want a new job.
3 Bread / Books costs a lot.
4 Andy / Andy and Pete sings very well.
5 Sophy / Sophy and Ian like parties.
6 You / She drive too fast.
7 Our cat / Our cats never catches mice.
8 That child / Children makes a lot of noise.
9 That bus / All those buses go to the station.
10 My father / My mother and father teaches English.

* Also called 'present simple'

simple present: use *I work in a bank.*

We use the **simple present** to talk about:

- things that are **always true**.

*The sun **rises** in the east. My parents **live** near Dover.*

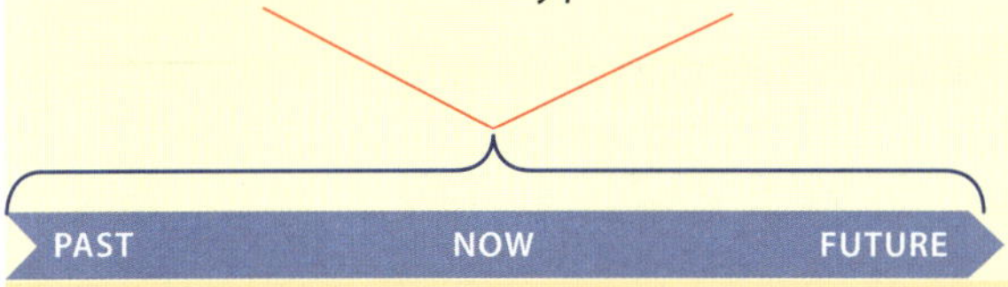

- habits and things that happen **repeatedly**.

*Joe **plays** golf on Saturdays.*

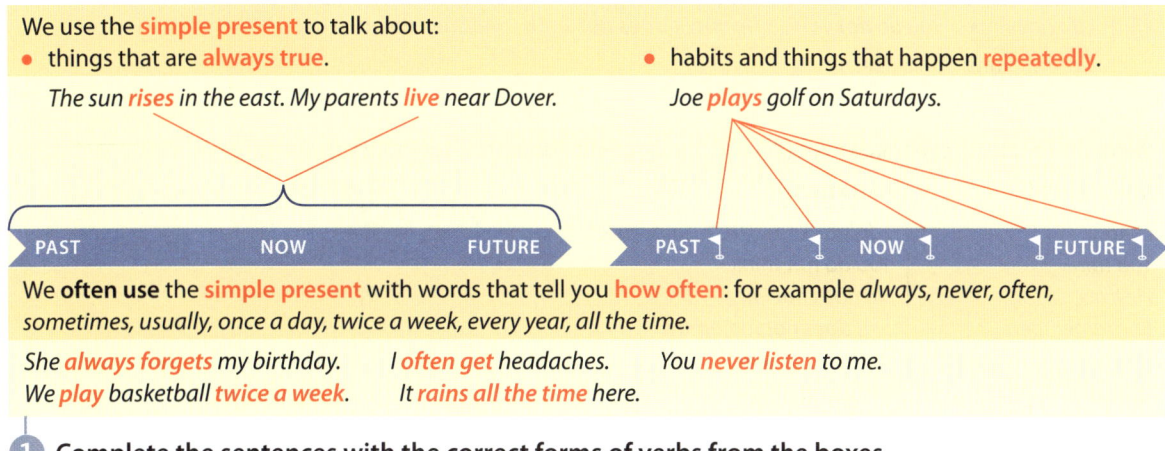

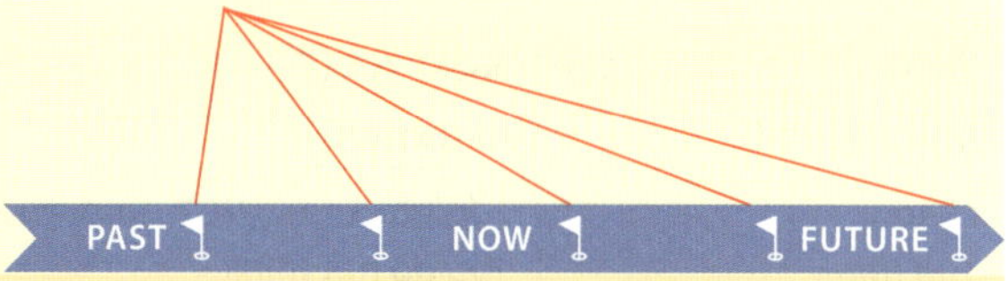

We **often use** the **simple present** with words that tell you **how often**: for example *always, never, often, sometimes, usually, once a day, twice a week, every year, all the time.*

*She **always forgets** my birthday.* *I **often get** headaches.* *You **never listen** to me.*
*We **play** basketball **twice a week**.* *It **rains all the time** here.*

1 Complete the sentences with the correct forms of verbs from the boxes.

ask	get up ✓	go	make	play	speak

▶ Peter always ..gets up.......... late on Sundays.
1 Ann and John sometimes .... tennis at weekends.
2 My mother often .... French at home.
3 Small children .... questions all the time.
4 Sarah .... to Oxford to see her mother twice a week.
5 I .... more mistakes in English when I'm tired.

forget	get	listen	live	watch

6 I often .... people's names.
7 We usually .... to music in the car.
8 My brother .... in Vancouver.
9 I .... a lot of films on TV.
10 My parents .... all their food from supermarkets.

2 Choose suitable verbs in the correct forms to complete the sentences.

▶ The sun ..sets..... in the west. (*live, rise, set*)
1 That woman .... that she .... everything. (*know, think, run, wash*)
2 Our son .... karate. (*read, study, write*)
3 Alice .... to go skiing every year. (*try, play, say*)
4 You always .... very nice clothes. (*look, start, wear*)
5 Andy always .... his car on Saturdays. (*buy, sell, wash*)
6 Most people .... for other people. (*talk, work, teach*)
7 That child never .... 'Thank you'. (*like, say, sing*)
8 He .... in the same chair every evening. (*know, like, sit, stand*)
9 My father .... TV most evenings. (*listen, think, watch*)
10 We always .... what we can't have. (*want, get, forget*)

We do not use a present tense to talk about **how long** something has lasted (see page 65).

*I **have known** her since 1990.* (**NOT** ~~*I know her since 1990.*~~)

In some answers, both contracted forms (for example *I'm, don't*) and full forms (for example *I am, do not*) are possible. Normally both are correct.

simple present negatives *I don't know. She doesn't ski.*

-	*I **do not** work* *you **do not** work* *he/she/it **does not** work* *we/they **do not** work*
	Contractions: *don't, doesn't*

We make simple present **negatives** (-) with ***do/does not*** + **infinitive** (without *to*).

STATEMENT +	NEGATIVE -
I know	*I **do not** know* (NOT ~~*I know not*~~)
You think	*You **do not** think*
He likes	*He **does not** like*
She remembers	*She **does not** remember*
It helps	*It **does not** help*
We want	*We **do not** want*
They understand	*They **do not** understand*

1 Make negative sentences. Use *do not* or *does not*.

▶ I play chess. (*cards*) I do not play cards.
1 You speak very good Arabic. (*Chinese*) ....
2 Bill plays the piano very well. (*guitar*) ....
3 We agree about most things. (*holidays*) ....
4 Alan and John live near me. (*George and Andrew*) ....
5 My father writes novels. (*poetry*) ....
6 Barbara works in London. (*live*) ....
7 Henry likes old books. (*parties*) ....

2 Make negative sentences. Use *don't* or *doesn't*.

1 The train stops at Bristol. (*Cardiff*) It..........
2 I like jazz. (*pop music*) ....
3 Peter remembers names very well. (*faces*) ....
4 We know our Member of Parliament. (*his wife*) ....
5 Alice teaches engineering. (*mathematics*) ....
6 The children play football on Mondays. (*hockey*) ....
7 The shops open on Sunday mornings. (*afternoons*) ....

3 Complete the negative sentences, using words from the box. You can use *do not / does not* or *don't / doesn't*, as you like.

fish	in Britain	much petrol ✓	much tennis
on Sundays	Russian	your phone number	

▶ My car / use My car doesn't use much petrol.
1 Our cat / like ....
2 Melinda / speak ....
3 I / remember ....
4 Oranges / grow ....
5 The postman / come ....
6 We / play ....

4 Choose one verb to make each sentence negative.

▶ It ..doesn't snow.. very often in San Francisco. (*snow, sing, play*)

1 I like football, but I .... cricket at all. (*think, like, remember*)

2 She lives in Japan, but she .... a word of Japanese. (*sing, work, speak*)

3 I'm sorry – I .... your name. (*eat, remember, work*)

4 He works in New York, but I .... what he does. (*know, use, come*)

5 Mary's really tired, but she .... to go to bed. (*help, want, walk*)

6 We .... a big flat – just one bedroom. (*work, play, want*)

7 Phil .... very hard, but he makes a lot of money. (*work, stand, stop*)

8 Gemma's parents .... I'm the right man for their daughter. (*write, read, think*)

5 GRAMMAR AND VOCABULARY: games

Look at the table, and write five or more sentences like this:

Ann plays tennis, but she doesn't play cards.

....

....

....

....

....

....

....

....

....

....

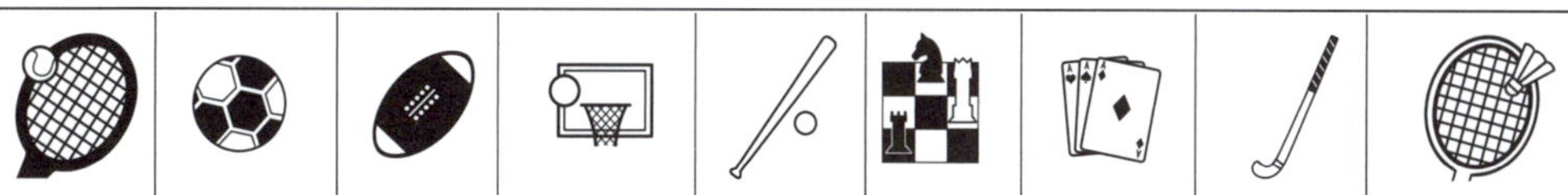

	tennis	football	rugby	basketball	baseball	chess	cards	hockey	badminton
Ann	✓	✗	✗	✓	✗	✗	✗	✗	✓
Pete	✗	✓	✗	✗	✗	✓	✓	✗	✗
Joe	✓	✗	✓	✓	✗	✗	✓	✓	✓
Sarah	✗	✓	✗	✗	✓	✓	✗	✗	✗

6 What games do you play? And what games do you not play?

....

....

NOTE: one negative word is enough (see page 115).

Nobody *understands me.* (**NOT** ~~*Nobody doesn't understand me.*~~)

She ***never*** *phones me.* (**NOT** ~~*She doesn't never phone me.*~~)

In some answers, both contracted forms (for example *I'm, don't*) and full forms (for example *I am, do not*) are possible. Normally both are correct.

simple present questions *Do you remember me?*

?	**do** *I work?* **do** *you work?* **does** *he/she/it work?* **do** *we work?* **do** *they work?*

We make simple present **questions** (?) **with** ***do/does*** **+ subject + infinitive** (without *to*).

STATEMENT +	QUESTION ?
I know	***Do*** *I know?*
You think	***Do*** *you think?* (NOT ~~*Think you?*~~)
He likes	***Does*** *he like?* (NOT ~~*Does he likes?*~~)
She remembers	***Does*** *she remember?*
It helps	***Does*** *it help?*
We want	***Do*** *we want?*
They understand	***Do*** *they understand?*

1 Put in *do* or *does*.

▶ ..Do.......... you know my friend Andy?
▶ ..Does....... this bus go to Cambridge?
1 .... Ann want to come with us?
2 .... your parents live near here?
3 .... you speak Chinese?
4 .... Sarah go to school on Saturdays?
5 .... this shop sell stamps?
6 .... Bill and Harry play golf?

2 Make questions.

▶ They smoke. ..Do they smoke?...
▶ Ashley teaches French. ..Does Ashley teach French?...
1 The Oxford bus stops here. ....
2 The teachers know her. ....
3 You play the piano. ....
4 John works in a restaurant. ....
5 This train stops at York. ....
6 We need more eggs. ....
7 Fatima likes parties. ....
8 Peter speaks Spanish well. ....

Do you know all these **question words**?
what when where who why how how much how many what time

What do *you* ***think?*** (NOT ~~*What think you?*~~) ***Where does*** *Lucy* ***live?*** (NOT ~~*Where lives Lucy?*~~)
How much does *this* ***cost?*** (NOT ~~*How much this costs?*~~)
What time does *the train* ***leave?*** (NOT ~~*What time the train leaves?*~~)

3 Choose the correct subject.

▶ How much does ..the ticket............ cost? (*the ticket / the tickets*)
1 Where do .... live? (*your daughter / your children*)
2 What time does .... start? (*the lesson / the lessons*)
3 What do .... want? (*you / the girl*)
4 When does .... finish? (*the holidays / the holiday*)
5 Why do .... talk so fast? (*that woman / those women*)
6 What do .... think of the new boss? (*you / she*)

→ For questions without *do*, like *Who lives here?*, see pages 108–109.

4 Choose the correct question word and put in *do* or *does*.

how	how many	how much ✓	what	when	where	why

▶ How much does the ticket cost?
1 .... your children live?
2 .... she want?
3 .... the holidays start?
4 .... the teacher talk so fast?
5 .... languages .... he speak?
6 .... you pronounce this word?

5 Make questions.

▶ Where / she live? Where does she live?
1 What / you want? ....
2 What / this word mean? ....
3 What time / the film start? ....
4 How much / those shoes cost? ....
5 Why / she need money? ....
6 How / this camera work? ....
7 Where / you buy your meat? ....
8 Who / you want to see? ....

6 Do you know all these simple present questions? Study them, and then put the correct question into each conversation.

How do you pronounce this word? *How do you spell that?* *What does this word mean?*
How much does it cost / do they cost? *Do you know Anna?* *Where do you live/work?*
What do you do? (= 'What is your job?') *How do you do?* (= 'I'm pleased to meet you.')
What time does the train/bus/plane leave/arrive? *What time does the film/concert/class start?*

1 '..'
'With one c and double s.'
2 '..'
'I'm a taxi driver.'
3 '..'
'I don't know. Look in the dictionary.'
4 '..'
'It gets into the station at 3.00 in the morning.'
5 '..'
'€500.'
6 '..'
'No, but I know her sister.'
7 '..'
'How do you do?'
8 '..'
'I don't know. Look on the cinema programme.'

In some answers, both contracted forms (for example *I'm*, *don't*) and full forms (for example *I am*, *do not*) are possible. Normally both are correct.

simple present: more practice

+	*I/you/we/they* **work**	*he/she/it* **works**
?	**do** *I/you/we/they* **work**?	**does** *he/she/it* **work**?
–	*I/you/we/they* **do not work**	*he/she/it* **does not work**
	Contractions: *don't, doesn't*	

1 Circle the correct answers.

1 Where *do / does* your sister live?
2 *My cat / My cats* don't like fish.
3 This car *don't / doesn't* go very fast.
4 This train *stop / stops* at every station.
5 Why *do English people / English people do* drink so much tea?
6 The post office doesn't *open / opens* on Sundays.
7 When does *your holiday start / start your holiday*?
8 My parents both *play / plays* golf.
9 *That café / Those cafés* stays open all night.
10 Her letters don't *say / to say* very much.

2 Make sentences.

▶ Anu (*live*) in Birmingham + Anu lives in Birmingham.
▶ you (*speak*) Chinese ? Do you speak Chinese?
▶ Sarah (*like*) classical music – Sarah doesn't like classical music.
1 I (*like*) getting up early – ...
2 you (*want*) something to drink ? ...
3 Dan (*play*) football on Saturdays + ...
4 you (*remember*) her phone number ? ...
5 that clock (*work*) – ...
6 she often (*fly*) to Paris on business + ...
7 it (*rain*) much here in summer – ...
8 elephants (*eat*) meat ? ...
9 he (*think*) he can sing ? ...
10 we (*need*) a new car + ...

3 Make sentences like the ones in Exercise 2. Write about yourself.

1 I like ...
2 I don't like ...
3 I want ...
4 I don't want ...
5 I need ...
6 I don't need ...
7 I often ...
8 I never ...
9 I always ...

present progressive*: forms *I'm reading; I'm not working.*

+	*I **am** working*	*you **are** working*	*he/she/it **is** working*	*we/they **are** working*
-	*I **am not** working*	*you **are not** working*	*he/she/it **is not** working* etc	
	Contractions: *I'm, you're, he's* etc (*not*) *...ing; you aren't, he isn't* etc *...ing* *What's he ...ing?, Where's she ...ing?, When's it ...ing?* etc			

We make **present progressive** verbs with ***be*** (*I am, you are* etc – see page 2) + ***...ing***.

*John **is studying** Russian.* *I'**m not working** today.*

We use **contractions** (***I'm**, John**'s**, **isn't*** etc) in **conversation** and **informal writing**.

1 Make present progressive affirmative (+) and negative (-) sentences.

- ▶ The lesson is starting now. (*start* +)
- ▶ Jenny isn't working today. (*work* -)

1 You .... too fast. (*talk* +)
2 The cat .... a bird. (*eat* +)
3 Kevin .... dinner now. (*cook* +)
4 I .... this party. (*enjoy* -)
5 I .... a good book. (*read* +)
6 It .... now. (*rain* -)
7 You .... to me. (*listen* -)
8 I .... very happy today. (*feel* +)
9 Peter .... to school this week. (*go* -)
10 We .... a bit of English. (*learn* +)

HOW TO MAKE *-ING* FORMS

- **most verbs: + *-ing*** — *work* → *working* — *sleep* → *sleeping*
- **verbs ending in *-e*: (~~e~~) + *-ing*** — *make* → *making* — *hope* → *hoping*
- ***-ie* changes to *y* + *-ing*** — *lie* → *lying*

2 Write the *-ing* forms of these verbs.

break breaking clean .... come .... die .... enjoy ....
go .... live .... make .... play .... sing ....
start .... wash .... write ....

DOUBLING (*stopping, running* etc)

- **one vowel + one consonant → double consonant + *-ing*** — *stop* → *stopping* (NOT ~~*stoping*~~) — *run* → *running*
- **two vowels: don't double** — *sleep* → *sleeping* — *wait* → *waiting* (NOT ~~*waitting*~~)
- **two consonants: don't double** — *want* → *wanting* (NOT ~~*wantting*~~) — *help* → *helping*
- **Only double in STRESSED syllables** — *beGIN* → *beginning* BUT *HAPpen* → *happening*

3 Write the *-ing* forms of these verbs.

get .... feel .... put .... hit ....
jump .... rain .... rob .... shop ....
shout .... sit .... slim .... dream ....
stand .... talk .... turn ....
ANswer .... OPen .... VIsit .... forGET ....

* Also called 'present continuous'

In some answers, both contracted forms (for example *I'm, don't*) and full forms (for example *I am, do not*) are possible. Normally both are correct.

present progressive: use *I'm working just now.*

We use the **present progressive** to say that things are happening **now** or **around now**.

I'm working just now. *It's raining again.* *Jane's taking driving lessons.*

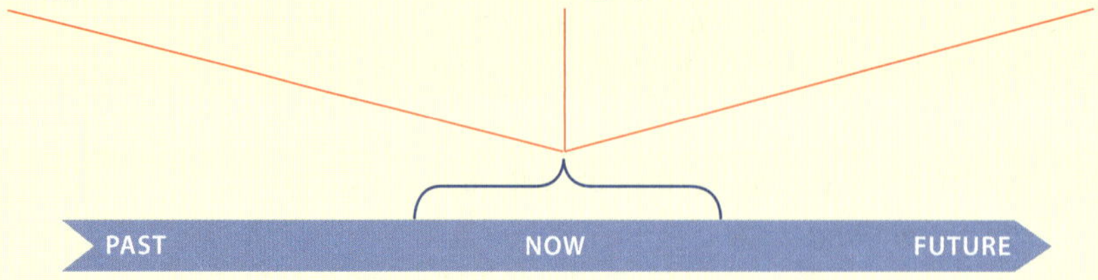

*I'm sorry, I can't come out. I'm **working** just now.* (Compare: *I **work** every day.* – see page 17.)
*Look – it's **raining** again.* (Compare: *It **rains** every day here.*)
*Jane's **taking** driving lessons.* (Compare: *A lot of people **take** lessons with that driving school.*)
*I'm **enjoying** this party.* (Compare: *I usually **enjoy** parties.*)

1 Make present progressive sentences.

▶ Emma / read / the newspaper. Emma's reading the newspaper.
1 The baby / cry / again. ....
2 It / snow / hard. ....
3 You / look / very beautiful today. ....
4 Your coffee / get / cold. ....
5 I / play / a lot of football this year. ....
6 We / wait / for a phone call. ....
7 Chris and Helen / spend / a week in France. ....

2 Look at the pictures and use the verbs in the box to say what Helen is doing.

brush	brush	drink	get up ✓	go	listen	open	read	read	wash

▶ She's getting up.
1 .... her face.
2 .... her teeth.
3 .... to the radio.
4 .... coffee.
5 .... the newspaper.
6 .... her hair.
7 .... letters.
8 .... the door.
9 .... to work.

▶

1

2
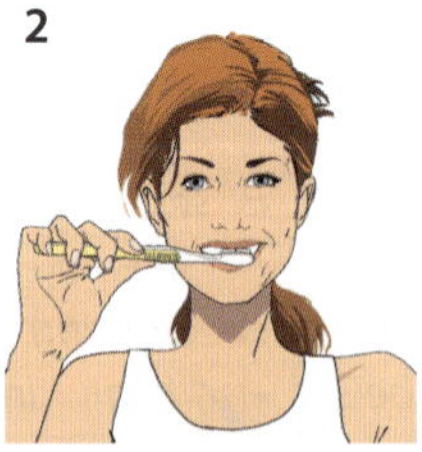
3

4

5

6

7

8

9

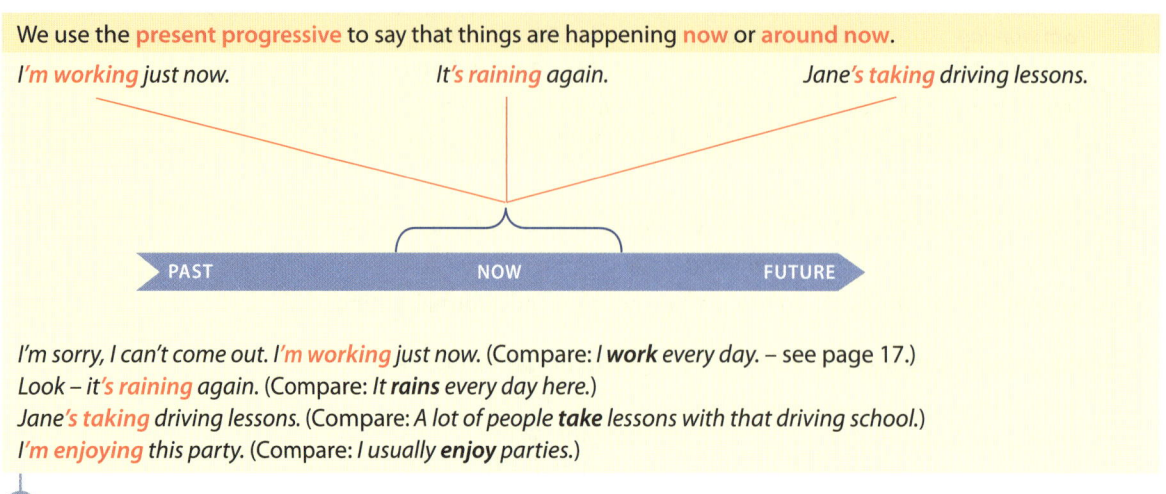

present progressive negatives *He's not listening to me.*

–	*I* **am not** *working* *you* **are not** *working* *he/she/it* **is not** *working* *we/they* **are not** *working*
	Contractions: *I'm not, you're not; he's/she's/it's not, we're not, they're not* Or: *you/we/they aren't, he/she/it isn't*

We make present progressive negatives with ***am/are/is not + …ing***.

I'm not working *this week.*

1 Choose the right verbs and make negative (–) present progressive sentences.

▶ I (*write, play, ask*) you for a lot of money. *I'm not asking you for a lot of money.*

1 He (*listen, stand, start*) to me. ……

2 I (*rain, work, get*) today. ……

3 It (*wear, rain, speak*) now. ……

4 She (*wear, look, wait*) a coat. ……

5 John's students (*wait, like, learn*) very much. ……

6 We (*enjoy, fly, read*) this film. ……

7 You (*live, wait, eat*) much these days. ……

8 I (*sleep, stand, expect*) to pass the exam. ……

9 My computer (*pay, work, write*). ……

10 I (*stop, play, give*) much tennis these days. ……

2 Write negative ends for the sentences.

▶ It's cold, but (– *snow*) *it's not snowing.*

▶ I'm a teacher, but (– *work just now*) *I'm not working just now.*

1 He's a good footballer, but (– *play well today*) ……

2 They are in England now, but (– *live in London*) ……

3 It's a new car, but (– *run well*) ……

4 Everybody says this is a good book, but (*I* – *enjoy it*) ……

5 It's summer, but (*the sun* – *shine*) ……

6 I'm a student, but (– *study at university*) ……

7 She sings when she's happy, but (– *sing just now*) ……

8 I don't have any problems, but (– sleep well these days) ……

9 We're on holiday, but (– *have a good time*) ……

10 I'm crying, but (– *cry because of you*) ……

3 Complete the sentences, using the verbs in the box.

not work	not listen	not rain	not move	not eat

1 The train ……

2 The children ……

3 It ……

4 The cat ……

5 John ……

1

2

3

4

5

NOTE: We **do not** use a present tense to say **how long** something has lasted (see page 65).

I've been waiting since 9.00. (**NOT** ~~*I'm waiting since 9.00.*~~)

In some answers, both contracted forms (for example *I'm, don't*) and full forms (for example *I am, do not*) are possible. Normally both are correct.

present progressive questions *Is it raining?*

?	**am** *I working?* **are** *you working?* **is** *he/she/it working?* **are** *we/they working?*

We make **present progressive questions** with *am/are/is* + **subject** + ***...ing***

STATEMENT +: *It is raining.* *You are working.* *The children are making something.*

QUESTION ?: *Is it raining?* *Are you working?* *What are the children making?*

1 Make questions.

▶ everybody / listen / to me ? Is everybody listening to me?
1 you / wait / for somebody ? ....
2 your boyfriend / enjoy / the concert ? ....
3 those men / take / our car ? ....
4 you / talk / to me ? ....
5 it / snow ? ....
6 we / go / too fast ? ....
7 your computer / work ? ....
8 you read / that newspaper ? ....
9 the bus / come ? ....
10 somebody / cook lunch ? ....

2 Complete the questions.

▶ 'Those people aren't speaking English.' 'What language are they speaking?'
1 'Bill's writing something on the wall.' 'I can't see – what ....'
2 'The train's stopping!' 'Why ....'
3 'They're studying now.' 'What ....'
4 'They're playing a game.' 'What game ....'
5 'I'm going now. Goodbye.' 'Wait! Where ....'
6 'Nadia's telephoning somebody.' 'Who ....'
7 'The baby's eating something.' 'What ....'
8 'Sue's working as a secretary.' 'Where ....'
9 'I'm cooking something good.' 'What ....'
10 'I'm not living with my parents.' 'Where ....'

3 Put in question words and make present progressive questions. (More than one answer may be possible.)

▶ you / do What are you doing?
1 you / go now ....
2 Anne / cry ....
3 he / write ....
4 you / telephone ....
5 they / live ....
6 your brother / study English ....
7 you / cook ....
8 those people / look at me ....
9 the dog / eat ....
10 the children / do ....

present progressive: more practice

+	I **am** working	you **are** working	he/she/it/**is** working	we/they **are** working
?	**am** I working?	**are** you working?	**is**/he/she/it working?	**are** we/they working?
–	I **am not** working	you **are not** working	he/she/it/**is not** working etc	
	Contractions: *I'm, you're, he's* etc *(not) ...ing; you aren't, he isn't* etc *...ing*			

1 Put the words in the correct order. Use contractions (e.g. *it's*) where possible.

▶ me you talking are to ? Are you talking to me?
1 getting are you up ? ....
2 raining is again it . ...
3 not you are listening . ...
4 going where you are ? ....
5 talking fast too I am ? ....
6 I film enjoying not this am . ...
7 laughing those people at are me why ? ....
8 am for you I cooking this not . ...
9 you what drinking are ? ....
10 the baby eating the is newspaper . ...

2 Make present progressive sentences.

▶ I / look for / the station + I'm looking for the station.
▶ you / work / tonight ? Are you working tonight?
▶ it / rain – It's not raining.
1 Peter / try / to save money + ...
2 why / those children / cry ? ....
3 your friends / play football / this afternoon ? ....
4 she / look / very well today – ....
5 I think she / make / a big mistake + ...
6 you / wear / your usual glasses – ....
7 I / start / to learn Spanish + ...
8 the 10.15 train / run / today ? ....
9 David / live with his parents / any more – ....
10 what / you / do / in my room ? ....

3 Complete the text with verbs from the boxes.

1–5: come ✓ look not wear snow walk wear

And Mrs Alexander ▶ is coming down the steps of the plane now. It is very cold and it 1........................ heavily, but she 2........................ very happy. She 3........................ a dark blue dress with a black coat and boots, but she 4........................ a hat. She really is a very beautiful woman. Her husband 5........................ down the steps with her.

6–11: kiss look return say stop try

Now Mrs Alexander and her husband 6........................ at the crowd and smiling. The photographers 7........................ to get nearer, but the police 8........................ them. What a day! At last, after twenty years, this wonderful woman 9........................ to her own country. Now the President 10........................ her hand. What 11........................ he .... to her, do you think?

In some answers, both contracted forms (for example *I'm, don't*) and full forms (for example *I am, do not*) are possible. Normally both are correct.

the two present tenses: the difference

SIMPLE PRESENT: *I work* etc	PRESENT PROGRESSIVE: *I'm working* etc
• things that are **always true** • things that happen **all the time, repeatedly, often, sometimes, never** etc	• things that are happening **now** • things that are happening **around now**
*The sun **rises** in the east.* *She often **wears** red.* *I **play** tennis.*	*The sun **is not shining** today.* *She's **wearing** a blue dress.* *I'm **playing** a lot of tennis these days.*

1 Put the expressions in the correct places.

every day ✓ just now nearly always now ✓ on Fridays these days
this afternoon today very often when I'm tired

SIMPLE PRESENT: *I work* etc

every day ....
....
....

PRESENT PROGRESSIVE: *I'm working* etc

now ....
....
....

2 Use the verbs in the box to complete the sentences.

chase ✓ chase drive eat fly play play rain sell speak work write

Cats ...chase... mice.

▸ 

But ...this cat is not chasing mice....

Cows .... grass.

1 

But this cow ....
....

Planes ....

2 

But this ....
....

It often ....

3 

But ....
.... now.

Luke .... hard.

4 

But ....
.... today.

Ann .... tennis.

5 

But ....
.... now.

John .... English.

6 

But ....
....

Bill .... a bus.

7 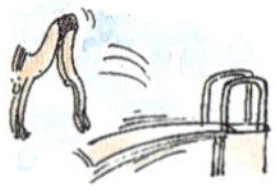

But ....
....

This shop .... books.

8 

But ....
....

Carol .... the piano.

9 

But she ....
....

Simon .... poetry.

10 

But ....
....

Dogs .... cats.

11 

But this ....
....

3 Complete the sentences with the correct verb forms.

▶ 'Do you smoke?' 'No, never.' (*you / smoke*)
▶ 'What are you eating?' 'A cheese sandwich.' (*you / eat*)
1 'Where .... these days?' 'In a garage.' (*she / work*)
2 '... here in summer?' 'Not very often.' (*it / rain*)
3 'Bonjour.' 'Sorry, I .... French.' (*not speak*)
4 'Your English .... better.' 'Oh, thank you.' (*get*)
5 '... golf?' 'Yes, but not very well.' (*you / play*)
6 'Who .... to?' 'My boyfriend.' (*you / write*)
7 'Where's Suzanne?' '... now.' (*she / come*)
8 Well, goodnight... to bed. (*I / go*)
9 Water .... at 100°C. (*boil*)
10 '...?' 'Not yet.' (*that water / boil*)
11 '...?' 'I can't see it.' (*the bus / come*)
12 'That man .... all the time.'
'Yes, and he ....' (*talk; never listen*)
13 'What's Peter's job?' '... film scripts.' (*he / write*)
14 'Summer's coming.' 'Yes, ... warmer.' (*it / get*)
15 'How often ....?' 'Every weekend.' (*you / see your parents*)
16 'Where's your brother?' '... from Scotland today.' (*he / come back*)
17 '... fast?' 'Yes, always. Too fast.' (*John / drive*)
18 'Come and have a drink.' 'Not now. I .... a phone call.' (*wait for*)
19 'What .... at?' 'A very strange bird.' (*you / look*)
20 'What kind of music ....' 'All kinds.' (*you / like*)

4 Make true sentences about yourself.

▶ I often play tennis, but I am not playing tennis now. (*play*)
1 I often ...., but I .... now. (*play*)
2 I sometimes ...., but I .... now. (*wear*)
3 I often ...., but I .... now. (*speak*)
4 I often ...., but I .... now. (*listen*)
5 I sometimes ...., but I .... now. (*read*)
6 I often ...., but I .... now. (*watch*)
7 I sometimes ...., but I .... now. (*buy*)
8 I often ...., but I .... now. (*eat*)
9 I often ...., but I .... now. (*drink*)
10 I never ...., and I .... now. (*?*)

I never vote for anybody. I always vote against. (*W C Fields*)

I never travel without my diary. One should always have something sensational to read in the train.
(*Oscar Wilde*)

I never think of the future. It comes soon enough.
(*Albert Einstein*)

When a dog bites a man, that is not news, because it happens so often. But if a man bites a dog, that is news.
(*John B Bogart, American newspaper editor*)

When a woman isn't beautiful, people always say, 'You have lovely eyes, you have lovely hair'.
(*Anton Chekhov*)

In some answers, both contracted forms (for example *I'm*, *don't*) and full forms (for example *I am*, *do not*) are possible. Normally both are correct.

Level 2

non-progressive verbs *I don't understand.*

Some verbs are most often used in simple tenses, not progressive, even if we mean 'just now'.

*I **like** this weather.* (NOT ~~*I'm liking this weather.*~~) *What **does** he **want**?* (NOT ~~*What is he wanting?*~~)

THE MOST IMPORTANT NON-PROGRESSIVE VERBS

believe, hate, hope, know, like, love, mean, need, prefer, remember, seem, think (= 'have an opinion'), *understand, want*

*I **hate** this music.* *'We're late.' 'I **know**.'* *I **love** that colour.* ***Do** you **understand**?*
*What **does** this **mean**?* *I **need** some help.* *'Tea?' 'I **prefer** juice.'* *Ayesha **seems** unhappy.*

Note also the expressions *It doesn't matter* (= 'It's not important') and *I see* (= 'I understand').

*'I'm sorry I'm late.' '**It doesn't matter.**'* *'There's a problem.' '**I see.**'*

1 Make sentences.

▶ Ayesha / seem / unhappy today [+] ...Ayesha seems unhappy today....
▶ you / need / help [?] ...Do you need help?...
▶ I / know / her name [-] ...I don't know her name....
1 what / this word / mean [?] ....
2 Rob / want / to see the doctor [-] ....
3 she / love / me ! [+] ....
4 Peter / seem / tired [+] ....
5 we / need / a new car [-] ....
6 you / know / that man [?] ....
7 I / hate / this cold weather [+] ....
8 you / like / this music [?] ....
9 I / remember / her address [-] ....
10 you / understand / this letter [?] ....

2 Complete the sentences with verbs from the boxes.

hope	like	need	not matter	not understand	prefer	not remember	want ✓

▶ What ...does... Paul ...want... for his birthday?
1 'Przepraszam!' 'Sorry, I .... '
2 'Would you like some coffee?' 'No, thank you. I .... tea, if that's OK.'
3 'What do you think of this music?' 'I .... it.'
4 I'm going to the shops. .... we .... anything?
5 'I've broken a cup.' 'It .... '
6 I .... it doesn't rain tomorrow.
7 Sorry, I .... your name.

believe	hate	not know	love	mean	see	think

8 .... you .... what she told you?
9 I .... her name or address.
10 .... you .... it's going to rain?
11 'We've got a problem.' 'I .... '
12 'You're crazy!' 'What .... you .... ?'
13 If you .... me, why can't we get married?
14 My father likes most music, but he .... rock.

SOME USEFUL EXPRESSIONS WITH NON-PROGRESSIVE VERBS:

I hope so. *I hope not.* *I think so.* *I don't think so.* *It depends.* *I don't mind.* (= 'It doesn't matter to me.')

*'Will you pass your exam?' **'I hope so.'*** *'Is it going to rain?' **'I hope not.'***
*'Is that Maria over there?' 'Yes, **I think so.**'* *'Are you free on Sunday?' **'I don't think so.'***
*'Can you help me?' **'It depends.** What do you want me to do?'*
*'What would you like to drink?' **'I don't mind.'***

Level 2

3 Choose the best expressions to complete the conversations.

▶ 'Is Ingrid enjoying her holiday?' *'I hope so.'* / *'I don't mind.'*

1 'Agresti, min ruggide flochsch?' *'I don't think so.'* / *'I don't understand.'*
2 'We're not happy with your work.' *'I hope so.'* / *'I see.'*
3 'Is Jeremy coming to dinner?' *'I see.'* / *'I hope not.'*
4 'Do you like this music?' *'I think so.'* / *'I don't remember.'*
5 'Is that Olivia getting into the taxi?' *'I know.'* / *'I don't think so.'*
6 'Who wrote 'War and Peace'?' *'It depends.'* / *'I don't know.'*
7 'It's Tuesday'. *'I think so.'* / *'I know.'*
8 'Can you lend me some money?' *'It depends.'* / *'It doesn't matter.'*
9 'We're too early.' *'I don't know.'* / *'It doesn't matter.'*
10 'What's Phil's address?' *'I don't remember.'* / *'It depends.'*
11 'Sorry, this coffee isn't very good.' *'I don't mind.'* / *'I hope so.'*
12 'Will you pass your exam?' *'I hope so.'* / *'I don't remember.'*
13 'Is Pete in his office?' *'I don't think so.'* / *'I see.'*
14 'Is it going to rain?' *'It depends.'* / *'I hope not.'*
15 'Can you help me?' *'I think so.'* / *'I don't remember.'*

4 Write personal answers.

▶ Will everybody in the world speak English one day? I think so. / I don't think so. / I hope so. / I hope not. / I don't mind. / I don't know.

1 Is your English getting better? ……………………………
2 Will you be rich and famous one day? ……………………………
3 What were you doing at 8.00 in the morning on February 16th last year?
……………………………
4 How many stars are there in the sky? ……………………………
5 Will it rain tomorrow? ……………………………
6 Have you got a good government? ……………………………
7 Will you live to be 100 years old? ……………………………
8 Are there people on other planets? ……………………………
9 Are you a nice person? ……………………………
10 Will you fall in love next week? ……………………………

WHAT YOU SAY	WHAT THEY SAY	WHAT THEY MEAN
'Do you mind if I sit here?'	'No, please do.'	'Go away.'
'I'm sorry I spilt coffee on you.'	'It doesn't matter at all.'	'You clumsy fool.'
'Can you do something for me?'	'It depends. What is it?'	'Certainly not.'
'What shall I sing?'	'I don't mind. Anything.'	'Don't sing.'
'Do you see what I mean?'	'Yes.'	'No.'
'Shall I wear the blue dress or the green one? Which do you prefer?'	'I don't mind. They're both beautiful.'	'A dress is a dress. What's the difference?'
'You don't seem to like the food.'	'Oh, I do. It's delicious.'	'I hate it.'
'I need to be alone.'	'I see.'	'I don't see.'

In some answers, both contracted forms (for example *I'm, don't*) and full forms (for example *I am, do not*) are possible. Normally both are correct.

present tenses: more practice

1 Question words. Choose words from the box to complete the questions.

how	how many	how much	what	what time	when	where	why

1 .... do you want for Christmas?
2 .... does the holiday start?
3 .... does your sister live?
4 .... tickets do you need?
5 .... do you usually get up?
6 .... rice do you want?
7 .... do you need to learn English?
8 .... do you make scrambled eggs?

2 Simple present. Choose the correct verbs to make simple present sentences.

▶ I / hamburgers (+) (*like, drink, play*) I like hamburgers.
▶ Henry / French (?) (*make, speak, work*) Does Henry speak French?
▶ the buses / on Sundays (-) (*speak, play, run*) The buses don't run on Sundays.
1 what language / Brazilians (?) (*run, work, speak*) ....
2 Felix / fast cars (+) (*sing, catch, drive*) ....
3 Annemarie / newspapers (-) (*make, read, clean*) ....
4 my two brothers both / in London (+) (*play, speak, work*) ....
5 dogs / vegetables (-) (*walk, eat, pass*) ....
6 Maria / the piano (-) (*play, make, cool*) ....
7 Peter / at weekends (?) (*work, wear, break*) ....
8 my husband / very well (+) (*want, cook, stop*) ....
9 Roger / to work with animals (+) (*want, play, read*) ....
10 this bus / to Belfast (?) (*work, speak, go*) ....

3 Present progressive. Write true sentences to say what is (not) happening now.

▶ I / work I'm working.
1 I / wear red socks I'm ....
2 it / rain ....
3 I / listen to music ....
4 I / sit on the beach ....
5 I / sing ....
6 I / think about something beautiful ....
7 I / wait for a phone call ....
8 the sun / shine ....
9 the government / make everybody happy ....
10 my English / get better ....

4 Progressive and non-progressive verbs. Correct (✓) or not (✗)?

▶ Are you liking this weather? ✗
▶ I'm working today. ✓
1 You're driving too fast. ......
2 What is this word meaning? ......
3 I'm not wanting a drink just now. ......
4 Where are you living now? ......
5 I'm thinking you're wrong. ......
6 That man is looking like your brother. ......
7 Sorry, I'm not understanding. ......
8 I'm seeing the doctor this morning. ......
9 'I can't pay you today.' 'I see.' ......
10 What are you thinking about? ......

5 Grammar in a text. Complete the text with the correct forms of the verbs in the box.

get up	go	have	like	like	live	look after	not like	not want	work	work ✓

Anna ▶ ..works...... in a circus in the south of England. She 1 .... the animals. Every day she 2 .... at 5.00, she 3 .... breakfast in her tent and then she 4 .... to work with the animals. She 5 .... her life very much, and she 6 .... the other people in the circus, but she 7 .... her boss. She also has problems with her boyfriend, James. He 8 .... 500 miles away, in Scotland, where he 9 .... in a bank. He 10 .... her to stay with the circus.

cry	do	love	not know	not want	not work	read	sit	you think	want

This morning Anna 11 .... She 12 .... in her tent. She 13 .... a letter and she 14 .... In the letter, James says 'I 15 .... you to leave the circus and come to Scotland to be with me. I 16 .... to move to England to be with you, because I'm doing well in my job.' Anna 17 .... what to do. She 18 .... James, but she 19 .... well in her job too. What 20 .... she should do?

6 GRAMMAR AND VOCABULARY: clothes. Use the words in the box to say what the people are (not) wearing. Use a dictionary if necessary.

belt	blouse	boots
cardigan	coat	dress
glasses	hat	jacket
raincoat	shoes	shirt
skirt	socks	suit
sweater	trousers	

John Cathy Sandra David

John is wearing a white shirt, a blue sweater, a blue jacket, grey trousers with a blue belt, blue socks and black shoes. He is not wearing glasses.

Cathy is wearing ....

....

....

Sandra ....

....

....

David ....

....

....

7 Internet exercise. Use the internet to get information about a well-known person. Write some of the information (simple present sentences). Some of these words might be useful.

hate	like	live	work	play	travel	often	always	never

....

....

pronunciation for grammar → e-book

present tenses: revision test

1 Write the simple present *he/she/it* forms.

go ..goes.... catch .... cost .... do .... enjoy .... fly ....
have .... hope .... know .... live .... mix .... pass ....
play .... stand .... teach .... think .... try .... wash ....
wear .... wish .... work ....

2 Write the *-ing* forms.

call ..calling..... begin .... cry .... die .... enjoy .... fly ....
forget .... get .... happen .... hold .... hope .... learn ....
look .... make .... open .... play .... send .... sit ....
sleep .... stop .... take ....

3 Put the words in order to make simple present sentences.

- ▶ Phil / dogs / like (+) Phil likes dogs.
- ▶ know / you / Anna (?) Do you know Anna?
- ▶ open on Sundays / the post office (–) The post office doesn't open on Sundays.

1 work / you / London (?) ....
2 pop music/ like / I (–) ....
3 where / live / James (?) ....
4 coffee / some / want / you (?) ....
5 rain / here / it / a lot (+) ....
6 I / my / every week / wash / car (+) ....
7 Spanish / Luke / speak (–) ....
8 friends / football / play / all your (?) ....
9 a suit / wear / to the office / I (–) ....
10 make / spaghetti carbonara / how / you (?) ....

4 Put the words in order to make present progressive sentences.

1 sister / my / in Spain / travel (+) ....
2 happy / Alice / look / very (–) ....
3 the baby / why / cry (?) ....
4 for the bus / wait / you (?) ....
5 much tennis / I / these days / play (–) ....
6 nice / Tim/ wear / a / very / raincoat (+) ....
7 me / talk / you / about / (?) ....
8 walk / slowly / you / too (+) ....
9 that / what / eat / child (?) ....
10 this / I / enjoy / concert (–) ....

5 Correct (✓) or not (✗)?

1 'Where's Melissa?' 'She's coming now.' ......
2 'Are you smoking?' 'No, never.' ......
3 John cooks dinner just now. ......
4 I work late most Tuesdays. ......
5 Why is she looking at me? ......
6 I'm going skiing every winter. ......
7 You're driving too fast. ......
8 What is this word meaning? ......
9 I'm seeing the doctor this morning. ......
10 'I can't pay you today.' 'I see.' ......
11 Where are you living now? ......
12 What do you think about? ......
13 I think you're wrong. ......
14 That man is looking like your brother. ......
15 'Your English gets better.' 'Oh, thank you.' ......

In some answers, both contracted forms (for example *I'm*, *don't*) and full forms (for example *I am*, *do not*) are possible. Normally both are correct.

SECTION 3 talking about the future

grammar summary

There are **three** common ways to talk about the **future** in English:

- with the ***going to*** structure.
  *I'm really **going to stop** smoking.*
- with the **present progressive**.
  ***I'm seeing** John this evening.*
- with ***will***.
  *Anna **will be** in the office from 10.00 till 2.00.*

We use ***going to*** or the **present progressive** especially when the future has some **present** reality: for example to talk about plans that we have already made.

We can sometimes use the **simple present** to talk about the future.

*Her train **arrives** at 15.37.* *I'll phone you when I **get** home.*
*I'll see you tomorrow if I **have** time.*

Your horoscope for next week

AQUARIUS
(Jan 21 – Feb 18)

Wednesday will bring money, but the money will bring problems.

PISCES
(Feb 19 – March 20)

It will be a difficult week. Don't travel by train.

ARIES
(Mar 21 – Apr 20)

Some very strange things will happen on Tuesday. Try to laugh about them.

TAURUS
(Apr 21 – May 21)

The week will be full of danger. Stay away from children and animals.

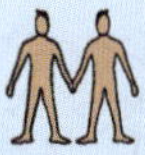

GEMINI
(May 22 – June 21)

Your family will cause problems on Monday. And on Tuesday, Wednesday, Thursday, …

CANCER
(June 22 – July 22)

The week will bring love, excitement and adventure. But not to you.

LEO
(July 23 – Aug 23)

Stay in bed on Thursday. Don't open the door. Don't answer the phone.

VIRGO
(Aug 24 – Sept 23)

You will meet an exciting stranger. Don't believe anything that he says.

LIBRA
(Sept 24 – Oct 23)

You will spend most of the week in hospital. Good luck.

SCORPIO
(Oct 24 – Nov 22)

The week will be bad in many ways. But not as bad as the following week.

SAGITTARIUS
(Nov 23 – Dec 21)

You will make an unexpected journey. It will end badly.

CAPRICORN
(Dec 22 – Jan 20)

Trouble will come from a horse and a washing machine.

going to Look – it's going to rain.

+	*I* ***am going to*** *drive*	*you* ***are going to*** *drive*	*he/she* ***is going to*** *drive* etc
?	***am*** *I* ***going to*** *drive?*	***are*** *you* ***going to*** *drive?*	***is*** *he/she* ***going to*** *drive?* etc
-	*I* ***am not going to*** *drive*	*you* ***are not going to*** *drive* etc	
	For contractions (*I'm, aren't* etc), see pages 2 and 315.		

We often use ***going to*** when we can **see the future in the present** – when a future situation is **starting**, or clearly **on the way**.

Look – it's ***going to rain.***

Rebecca's ***going to have a baby*** *next month.*

1 Look at the pictures. What is going to happen? Use the words in the box.

▶ She is *going to post a letter.*
1 The woman ....
2 He ....
3 She ....
4 The cars ....
5 He ....
6 The ball ....

break the window
crash
drink coffee
have breakfast
play the piano
post a letter ✓
read a letter

▶

1

2

3

4

5

6

We often use ***going to*** to talk about **intentions** – things that people **have decided** (not) to do.

What ***are you going to wear*** *this evening?* *I'm* ***not going to take*** *a holiday this year.*

2 Make questions with *going to*.

▶ you / cook supper *Are you going to cook supper?*
▶ when / your brothers / be here *When are your brothers going to be here?*
1 Jane / change her school ....
2 where / you / put that picture ....
3 what / you / buy for Felix's birthday ....
4 Ethan / play football / tomorrow ....
5 when / you / stop smoking ....
6 Alice / go to university ....
7 you / phone the police ....
8 your mother / come and stay with us ....
9 she / buy that coat ....
10 what / you / tell the boss ....

3 Lindsay is talking about her holiday next week. Look at the pictures and complete the sentences.

do any work	drive to Italy ✓	fly ✓	learn some Italian	read English newspapers
stay in a nice hotel	swim a lot	take photos	visit museums	write postcards

▶ No, I'm not going to fly.
▶ I'm going to drive to Italy.
1 ...
2 ...
3 ...
4 ...
5 ...
6 ...
7 ...
8 ...

4 Make sentences with *going to*.

▶ Andy / start school / next week [+] Andy is going to start school next week.
▶ you / see the dentist [?] Are you going to see the dentist?
▶ I / work this evening [-] I'm not going to work this evening.
1 how / you / get to London [?] ...
2 when / Monica / come and see us [?] ...
3 it / snow [-] ...
4 I / cook fish / for lunch [+] ...
5 when / you / see the doctor [?] ...
6 Angela / marry / her secretary [+] ...
7 John / call / this evening [?] ...
8 I / stop / playing poker [+] ...
9 everybody / watch the football match [+] ...
10 Sally / get the job [-] ...

5 Write some sentences about your intentions. Use *I'm (not) going to ...*

1 I'm ... this evening.
2 ... tomorrow.
3 ... next year.
4 ... when I'm old.
5 ... one day.

NOTE: In informal speech (and songs), we often say ***gonna*** for ***going to***.

In some answers, both contracted forms (for example *I'm*, *don't*) and full forms (for example *I am*, *do not*) are possible. Normally both are correct.

Level 1

present progressive *What are you doing this evening?*

+	*I **am** working*	*you **are** working*	*he/she/it **is** working*	*we/they **are** working*
?	***am** I working?*	***are** you working?*	***is** he/she/it working?*	***are** we/they working?*
–	*I **am not** working*	*you **are not** working*	*he/she/it **is not** working*	
	For contractions (*I'm, aren't* etc), see pages 2 and 315.			

We can use the **present progressive** with a **future meaning**, especially when we talk about **plans for a fixed time and/or place.**

*'What **are** you **doing** this evening?' 'I'**m staying** in.'* *Where **are** you **going** on holiday?*
*Joe'**s coming** to the theatre with us tomorrow.* *I'**m starting** a new job next week.*

1 Make sentences with the present progressive.

▶ when / you / come back ? *When are you coming back?*
▶ I / go / there again – *I'm not going there again.*
1 I / play / baseball tomorrow – ....
2 I / go / to Canada next year – ....
3 we / stay / with Paul and Lucy next week + ...
4 you / work / this evening ? ....
5 what time / your friends / arrive ? ....
6 my company / move / to Scotland next year + ...
7 how / your mother / travel to France ? ....
8 I / see / the dentist on Thursday + ...
9 I / go / to a concert tonight + ...
10 Gary / marry Cathy / after all – ....

2 Look at Harry's diary and correct the sentences.

▶ He's staying in Berlin on Friday night.
No, he's coming back to England on Friday night.
1 He's seeing John Parker on Sunday afternoon.
....
2 He's going to the Birmingham office by car.
....
3 He's having dinner with Stewart on Tuesday.
....
4 He's going to the theatre on Thursday evening.
....
5 His new secretary is starting on Friday.
....
6 Phil and Monica are going to his wedding on Saturday.
....

Sunday
John Parker morning
Monday
to Birmingham (1.15 train)
Tuesday
lunch Stewart 1.00
Wednesday
theatre with Ann and Joe
Thursday
new secretary starting
Friday
to Berlin LH014 8.00;
back LH135 16.40
Saturday
Phil and Monica's wedding

3 A friend of yours is going on holiday soon. Write questions.

▶ when / leave *When are you leaving?*
▶ take / your sister *Are you taking your sister?*
1 where / go ....
2 why / go there ....
3 how long / stay ....
4 stay / in one place ....
5 stay / with friends ....
6 how / travel ....
7 take / the dog ....
8 who / go with you ....
9 when / come back ....

will: predicting *I think it will rain tomorrow.*

+	*I/you/he/she/it/we/they* **will** *work*
?	**will** *I/you/he* etc *work?*
–	*I/you/he* etc **will not** *work*
	Contractions: *I'll, you'll* etc; *won't* (= *will not*)

We use ***will*** + **infinitive** to **predict** – to say things that we **think, guess** or **know** about the **future**.

*I think it **will snow** tomorrow.*
*Bella **won't be** here this evening.*
*Be quick, or you'**ll miss** your train.*
*When **will** you **know** your exam results?*

1 Put the words in the correct order to make affirmative (+) sentences.

▶ here George be will ..George will be here.......... tomorrow.
▶ speak everybody English perhaps will ..Perhaps everybody will speak English.. in the year 2100.
1 begin class will the .... at 9.30.
2 be they'll home .... soon.
3 examination will the difficult be ....
4 walk we'll party the to ....
5 she not speak will me to ....
6 your John answer questions will ....
7 Sunday ten years old will Emily be on ....

2 Make questions with *will*.

1 what time / tomorrow evening's concert / start ? ....
2 when / you and the family / get back / from Paris ? ....
3 you / be / here tomorrow ? ....
4 you and your mother / be / here tomorrow ? ....
5 where / you / be / this evening ? ....
6 the children / have enough money / for the journey ? ....
7 how soon / you know / the answer ? ....

3 Make negatives with *won't* and questions.

▶ 'I ..won't finish.. this work today.' 'When ..will you finish.. it?' (*finish*)
▶ 'John ..won't be.. here tomorrow.' '..Will he be here.. on Tuesday?' (*be*)
1 'Annie .... here at ten.' 'When .... here?' (*be*)
2 'I .... time for lunch.' '.............. time for a sandwich?' (*have*)
3 'You .... a pen in there.' 'Where .... one?' (*find*)
4 'The children .... to school in Ely.' 'Where ....' (*go*)
5 'Dylan .... much money if he sells that car.' 'How much ....' (*get*)
6 'Your car .... ready today.' 'When .... ready?' (*be*)
7 'I .... the exam result today.' 'When .... it?' (*know*)

NOTE: After *I* and *we*, some people say *shall* instead of *will*. The meaning is the same; *will* is more common in modern English.

In some answers, both contracted forms (for example *I'm, don't*) and full forms (for example *I am, do not*) are possible. Normally both are correct.

will: deciding, refusing, promising *I'll answer it.*

We can use ***will*** when we **decide** or **agree** to do things, and when we talk about **refusing** (saying 'no') and **promising**. We **don't** use the **simple present** in these cases.

*OK, I really **will** stop smoking.* *She **won't** speak to me.* *I'**ll** phone you.* (NOT ~~*I phone you.*~~)

Things can 'refuse'.

*The car **won't** start.* *This pen **won't** write.*

We often use ***will*** at the moment when we decide something.

*'There's someone at the door.' 'I'**ll** go.'* (NOT ~~*I go.*~~) *'That's the phone.' 'I'**ll** answer it.'*

1 Put in words from the box with *'ll* or *won't*.

do	go shopping	go to bed ✓	help	open	start	stop	tell ✓	tell	wash

- ▶ I'm tired. I think I'll go to bed.
- ▶ I don't know what he wants. He won't tell us.
1. I .... the cups; can you dry them?
2. 'Can somebody post my letters?' 'I .... it.'
3. 'My motorbike ....' 'No petrol?'
4. I .... Jack that we're going to be late.
5. The baby .... crying. Can you sing to her?
6. 'There's no food in the house.' 'I ....'
7. 'I can't move this table.' 'I .... you.'
8. 'This door ....' 'It's locked.'

2 It's time to change your life. Look at the ideas in the box and write six promises with *will* or *won't* – the most important first.

always think before I speak   be nice to everybody   drive too fast   fall in love every week
go for a walk every day   go to bed early   learn another language / a musical instrument
read more   relax   smile at everybody   smoke   study English every day   talk more slowly
talk to strangers   think about myself too much   work harder   (*your own promise*)

- ▶ I'll talk more slowly.
- ▶ I won't drive too fast.
1. ....
2. ....
3. ....
4. ....
5. ....
6. ....

3 Look at the expressions in the box. Use a dictionary if necessary. Then circle the best answers.

I'll think about it.   I'll see. (= 'I'll think about it.')   (I'll) see you tomorrow/later.
(I'll) see you.   I'll give you a ring/call. (= 'I'll phone you.')   I'll tell you tomorrow/later.

1. 'Mum, can I have an ice cream?' **A** 'I'll see.' **B** 'I'll see you.'
2. 'When do you want to play tennis?' **A** 'I'll see you tomorrow.' **B** 'I'll tell you tomorrow.'
3. 'I've got to go now.' **A** 'I'll see you.' **B** 'I'll think about it.'
4. 'Would you like to come dancing with me?' **A** 'I'll think about it.' **B** 'I'll see you later.'
5. 'Can we talk about it some more?' **A** 'I'll see you.' **B** 'I'll give you a ring.'
6. 'Goodbye now.' **A** 'See you tomorrow.' **B** 'I'll see.'
7. 'What do you want for your birthday?' **A** 'See you.' **B** 'I'll tell you later.'
8. 'Would you like to go to Scotland with me?' **A** 'I'll see you.' **B** 'I'll see.'

simple present for future *Our train leaves at 8.10.*

We can use the **simple present** to talk about **timetables**, cinema/theatre **programmes** and **dates**.

*Our train **leaves** at 8.10.* *What time **does** your flight **arrive**?* *The film **starts** at 7.30.*

1 Put the words in order to make sentences.

▶ leave / the flight / at 9.30 + ...The flight leaves at 9.30.........

▶ the film / what time / start ? ...What time does the film start?.........

▶ at Mill Road / this bus / stop – ...This bus doesn't stop at Mill Road.........

1 start / the next lesson / at 2.00 + ...

2 this term / on March 12th / end + ...

3 when / finish / the concert ? ....

4 we / a lesson / next Thursday / have – ....

5 this bus / at the post office / stop ? ....

6 at 8.00 / start / the play + ...

7 what time / arrive / you / in Rome ? ....

8 the banks / at 3.00 tomorrow / close + ...

9 at every station / stop / the next train + ...

10 when / start / the school holidays ? ? ....

We use the **simple present** with a **future** meaning after ***before, after, while, until, when, as soon as*** and ***if***.

*We'll see you **before** we **go**.* (NOT ... ~~*before we will go.*~~) *We'll have a drink **after** I **finish** work.*
*You can use my bike **while I'm** away.* *He'll phone you **when** he **arrives**.* (NOT ... ~~*when he will arrive.*~~)
*We'll wait **until** Justin **gets** here.* *I'll tell you **if** I **need** money.* *I'll write **as soon as** I **get** home.*

2 Put in the correct verb forms: simple present or *will*-future.

▶ If it ...rains......... , we ...'ll have......... the party inside. (*rain; have*)

1 I .... happy when I .... my exam. (*be; pass*)

2 If you .... now, you .... the train. (*leave; catch*)

3 John says he .... as a taxi-driver if he .... money. (*work; need*)

4 I .... free tomorrow evening, but I .... you on Friday. (*not be; see*)

5 Mary .... Chinese next year after she .... work. (*study; stop*)

6 I .... you to the station as soon as I .... my car keys. (*drive; find*)

7 When he .... her, his life .... a lot. (*marry; change*)

8 .... you .... smoking if the doctor .... you that you must? (*stop; tell*)

9 If we .... to the boss very politely, ... he .... to us? (*talk; listen*)

10 I .... you after I .... back from work. (*phone; get*)

→ For more practice on this point, see pages 236 and 245.

In some answers, both contracted forms (for example *I'm, don't*) and full forms (for example *I am, do not*) are possible. Normally both are correct.

future: more practice

1 ***Going to.* Look at the pictures. What is *going to* happen? Use *going to* with the verbs in the box.**

crash	drink a glass of water	get on a bus	go skiing	go swimming	have dinner
make coffee ✓	play the violin	sing	start running	write a letter	

▶ He's going to make coffee.
1 He's ....
2 She's ....
3 They ....
4 The car ....
5 ....
6 ....
7 ....
8 ....
9 ....
10 ....

2 **Present progressive. A problem. (Use a dictionary if necessary.) Jane is seeing five people next week, one each day: her bank manager, her solicitor, her accountant, her dentist and her doctor. Who is she seeing when? Read the text in the box, fill in the table and complete the sentences.**

> She's seeing her bank manager before her doctor. She's seeing her doctor on Tuesday. She's seeing her dentist two days after her bank manager. She's seeing her accountant two days after her doctor.

1 She's seeing .... on Monday.
2 .... on Tuesday.
3 .... on Wednesday.
4 .... on Thursday.
5 .... on Friday.

Monday	
Tuesday	doctor
Wednesday	
Thursday	
Friday	

3 ***Will.* These are sentences from real conversations. Put in forms of *will* with expressions from the box. (C: the speaker used a contraction: *'ll* or *won't*.)**

change	not snow	start	tell	go to sleep soon

1 You make me so unhappy: I .... crying in a moment. (C)
2 Do you think that all this money .... your life?
3 It .... tonight, will it, John? (C)
4 And they said, 'Benjamin's tired, he ....' (C)
5 She .... you how to do it.

4 **Put the words in order, and make statements (+), questions (?) or negative sentences (-) with *going to* (G), the present progressive (PP), *will* (W) or the simple present (SP).**

- ▶ (G) start work / Robert / tomorrow + ...Robert is going to start work tomorrow.......
- ▶ (PP) again / invite / her / I - ......I'm not inviting her again.......
- ▶ (W) be / in the office tomorrow / Anna ? ......Will Anna be in the office tomorrow?......
- ▶ (SP) leave / our train / at midday + ...Our train leaves at midday.......

1 (G) stop / I / smoking + ...

2 (PP) I / Andrew / tonight / see + ...

3 (G) rain / it - ....

4 (G) marry / Peter / his boss + ...

5 (W) exams / his / pass / Oliver - ....

6 (W) like/ this / you / film + ...

7 (SP) arrive / the bus from London / what time ? ....

8 (PP) I / tomorrow / the car / use - ....

9 (G) steak / I / cook / this evening + ...

10 (G) how / travel / to Ireland / you ? ....

11 (W, SP) I / phone you / when / get home / I + ...

12 (PP) you / on Saturday / work ? ....

13 (W) need / you / for the night / room / a ? ....

14 (G) write / you / to your father ? ....

15 (W) we / enough / for a good holiday / money / have - ....

16 (W) key / find / the / I / where ? ....

17 (W, SP) you / to university / after / leave school / you / go ? ....

....

18 (PP) stay with us / next week / John and Sylvia + ...

19 (G) you / when / have a haircut ? ....

20 (G) get up / soon / you ? ....

5 GRAMMAR AND VOCABULARY: giving directions with *will*. **Complete the letter. Put *'ll* with the verbs and put in the words from the box. Use a dictionary if necessary.**

apple trees	bridge	door	house	key	old house	the road ✓	great time

Dear Pamela and Simon

To find the house: when you get to Llanbrig, drive through the town and take ▶ ...the road..... for Caernarvon. After about 6 km, you (*pass*) ▶ ...'ll pass..... an 1 .... on the left. Immediately after that, you (*come to*) 2 .... a bridge. Turn left after the 3 ...., and very soon you (*come to*) 4 .... a crossroads. Go left again, and you (*see*) 5 .... our 6 .... on the right in about 300m. You (*recognise*) 7 .... it because it's got a green 8 .... and four 9 .... You (*find*) 10 .... the 11 .... under the mat outside the back door. Enjoy your holiday. I'm sure you (*have*) 12 .... a 13 ....

Love

Susan

6 **Internet exercise. Use a search engine (e.g. Google) to find simple sentences that begin:**

1 The government will ....

2 The government will not ....

3 The Prime Minister will ....

4 The Prime Minister will not ....

5 The President will ....

6 The weather will ....

future: revision test

1 Write the contracted forms.

▶ I am going to ..*I'm going to*..........
1 I will ....
2 She will ....
3 It will not ....
4 They are going to ....
5 They will ....
6 They will not ....
7 She is not going to ....
OR ....
8 I am not going to ....

2 Correct (✓) or not (✗)?

▶ You eat with us this evening? ..*✗*..
▶ I'm taking a Spanish exam on Thursday. ..*✓*..
1 'There's somebody at the door.' 'I go.' ......
2 Will Anna and John be here tomorrow? ......
3 I promise I write again soon. ......
4 I'll telling you everything soon. ......
5 The car won't start. ......
6 I'm working in London next week. ......
7 The concert starts at 8.00 this evening. ......
8 Emma's going to have a baby. ......
9 Do you play tennis with Peter this weekend? ......
10 Where will be the party? ......

3 Correct the mistakes.

▶ ~~When you~~ and Karen coming to see us? ..*When are you ...*..........
1 The concert will tonight. ....
2 I will need a visa to go to China? ....
3 Our business will moves out of London next year. ....
4 Alan and Carol not are getting married after all. ....
5 I really going to stop smoking. ....
6 I wo'nt be here tomorrow. ....
7 I phone you after I will get home. ....
8 The secretary will giving you all the information. ....
9 What you're doing at the weekend? ....
10 When will be the meeting? ....

4 Make questions and negative sentences.

▶ Tim will play the trumpet on Tuesday. Fred / flute / Friday ? Serena / saxophone / Saturday –
..*Will Fred play the flute on Friday?*.. *Serena won't play the saxophone on Saturday.*..

1 Susan's seeing Simon on Sunday. Melanie / Martin / Monday ? Tessa / Tom / Tuesday –
....
....

2 Mr Smith is going to study Spanish in Seville. Mr Andrews / Arabic / Algiers ?
Mrs Roberts / Russian / Rome –
....
....

3 Charles will cook chicken for Charlotte. Derek / duck / Dorothy ? Sally / spaghetti / Sam –
....
....

4 William is going to work in West Africa. Harry / take a holiday / Hungary ? Steve / study / Siberia –
....
....

5 Angela is travelling to Amsterdam in August. Oliver / Oslo / October ? Monica / Madagascar / May –
....
....

In some answers, both contracted forms (for example *I'm*, *don't*) and full forms (for example *I am*, *do not*) are possible. Normally both are correct.

SECTION 4 past tenses

grammar summary

SIMPLE PAST: *I worked, she worked, he didn't work* etc
PAST PROGRESSIVE (OR 'PAST CONTINUOUS'): *I was working, she was working, he wasn't working* etc

English has **two 'past' tenses.**

- We use the **simple past** for **complete finished actions**. We often use it in **stories**.
  *I **wrote** ten letters yesterday.* *A man **walked** into a police station and **asked** …*
- We use the **past progressive** to talk about actions which were **unfinished** at a past time.
  *'What **were** you **doing** at 10.00 last night?' 'I **was writing** letters.'*

◀ About 6,000 years ago, somebody painted this picture on a cave wall in Namibia, south-west Africa.

▲ Stonehenge, in southern England, is about 4,800 years old. Who built it? Nobody knows.

◀ About 1,200 years ago, Vikings from Scandinavia made this beautiful ship.

About 2,200 years ago, Shi Huangdi completed the Great Wall of China. ▼

THE CAVE OF CHAUVET-PONT-D'ARC

About 33,000 years ago, in the Stone Age, a man or a woman drew this owl on the wall of a cave in southern France. We don't know anything about the artist, and we never will. We only know that somebody saw an owl, saw that it was beautiful, and recorded its beauty. (When Picasso first saw prehistoric cave art, he said 'We have learnt nothing.') Before the Bronze Age or the Iron Age, before the glaciers covered Europe and went away again, before all of recorded history, an unknown person left a message for us: 'I saw this creature, and I thought it was beautiful'. Thank you, Stone Age artist.

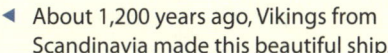

Level 1

simple past: forms *I worked. I went.*

	REGULAR VERBS	IRREGULAR VERBS
+	I/you/he/she/it/we/they **work*ed***	I/you/he/she/it/we/they **went**
?	**did** I/you/he/she/it/we/they **work**?	**did** I/you/he/she/it/we/they **go**?
-	I/you/he/she/it/we/they **did not work**	I/you/he/she/it/we/they **did not go**
	Contraction: *didn't*	

HOW TO MAKE REGULAR SIMPLE PAST FORMS

- **most verbs:** + *-ed* — *work* → *worked* — *help* → *helped* — *rain* → *rained*
- **after -*e*:** + *-d* — *hope* → *hoped* — *like* → *liked*

1 Write the simple past.

walk walked — arrive .... — change .... — cook ....

hate .... — live .... — pass .... — shave .... — watch ....

VERBS ENDING IN -*Y*

- **vowel (*a, e, o*) + *y*** → *-yed* — *play* → *played* — *enjoy* → *enjoyed*
- **consonant (*d, l, r* etc) + *y*** → *-ied* — *try* → *tried* — *reply* → *replied*

2 Write the simple past.

stay .... — study .... — cry .... — annoy .... — carry ....

hurry .... — pray ....

DOUBLING (*stopped, planned* etc)

- **one vowel + one consonant** → ***double consonant* + *-ed*** — ***stop*** → *stopped* (**NOT** ~~*stoped*~~) — ***plan*** → *planned*
- **two vowels: don't double** — ***seem*** → *seemed* — ***wait*** → *waited* (**NOT** ~~*waitted*~~)
- **two consonants: don't double** — *want* → *wanted* (**NOT** ~~*wantted*~~) — ***help*** → *helped*
- **only double in STRESSED syllables** — *preFER* → *preferred* — **BUT** *WONder* → *wondered*

3 Write the simple past.

shop .... — rain .... — start .... — rob .... — slim ....

jump .... — shout .... — slip .... — fit .... — turn ....

VIsit .... — reGRET .... — deVElop .... — GALlop ....

OPen .... — ANswer .... — reFER ....

With **irregular** verbs, you have to learn the simple past forms one by one (see page 299).

go → ***went*** — *see* → ***saw*** — *buy* → ***bought*** — *pay* → ***paid***

4 Write as many of the simple past forms as you can. Check them on page 299, and learn the ones that you don't know.

become .... — begin .... — break .... — bring .... — catch ....

come .... — drink .... — eat .... — fall .... — feel .... — forget ....

get .... — give .... — hear .... — hold .... — keep .... — know ....

learn .... — leave .... — let .... — make .... — pay .... — put ....

read .... — say........... — shut .... — sit .... — speak .... — stand ....

take .... — tell .... — think .... — write ....

simple past: use *I left school in 1990.*

We often use the **simple past** to talk about **when** things happened.

*I **left** school **in 1990**.* *I **didn't see** Ann **yesterday**.* ***What time did** you **arrive**?*

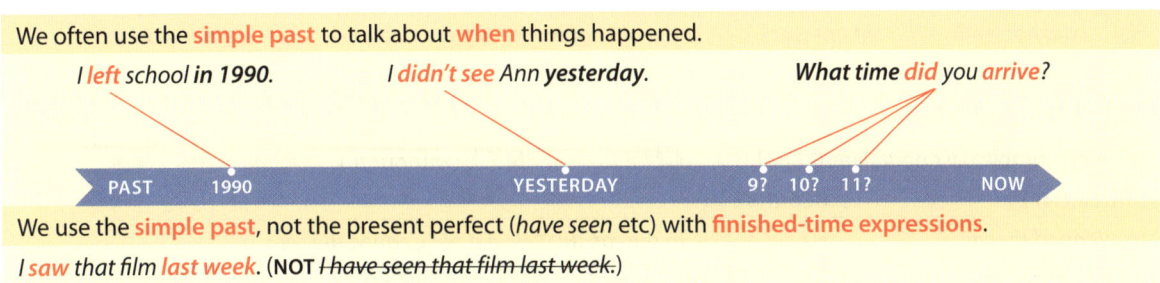

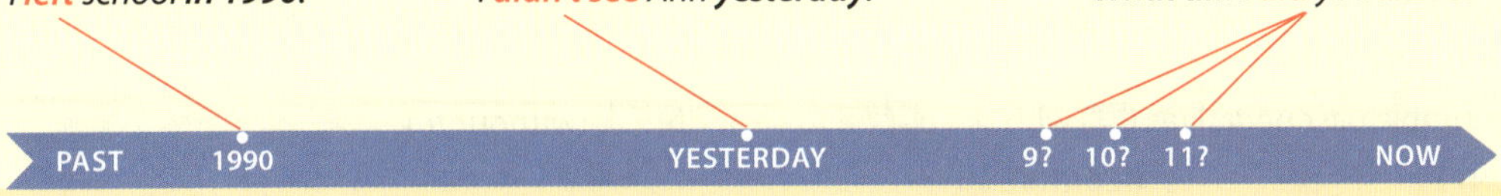

We use the **simple past**, not the present perfect (*have seen* etc) with **finished-time expressions**.

*I **saw** that film **last week**.* (NOT ~~*I have seen that film last week.*~~)
***Did** you **pay** William **on Sunday**?* (NOT ~~*Have you paid William on Sunday?*~~)

1 Put the beginnings and ends together, using the verbs in the box.

die ✓	forget	learn	like	read	speak	stop

0 Shakespeare ..died..........	A birthday on Monday. ......
1 I .... my girlfriend's	B in 1616. ..0..
2 That's a really good book.	C so I .... my lessons last week. ......
3 When we were children	D I .... it last year. ......
4 I didn't .... my piano teacher	E we always .... French at home. ......
5 Where did you	F to speak Spanish so well? ......

Note the **word order** with ***ago***.

*I started this job **three years ago**.* (NOT ... ~~*ago three years.*~~) *It happened **a long time ago**.*

2 How long ago was your last birthday? Ten days ago? Five weeks ago? Eight months ago? Write the answer, and complete the other sentences.

1 My last birthday was ....
2 Last Tuesday was ....
3 Last January ....
4 My third birthday ....

We often use the **simple past** for things that happened **one after another**, for example in **stories**.

*He **parked** his car, **went** into the station and **bought** a ticket. Then he **had** a cup of coffee and ...*

3 Grammar in a text. Put simple past verbs into the story.

1–6:	come	hear	open	say	not see	stand
7–10:	give	hold	not read	take		
11–15:	run	say	not speak	turn	write	

He 1.................. outside her door for a long time. Then he 2.................. her footsteps inside the house. She 3.................. the door and 4.................. out. At first she 5.................. him, but then she 6.................. , 'Oh, hello, Harold.' He 7.................. a paper out of his pocket and 8.................. it to her. She 9.................. it in one hand, but 10.................. it. 'Listen,' he 11.................. . She 12.................. 'I 13.................. you this letter because –' She 14.................. back into the house. He 15.................. and walked slowly down the street.

In some answers, both contracted forms (for example *I'm*, *don't*) and full forms (for example *I am*, *do not*) are possible. Normally both are correct.

simple past: negatives *I did not work. I did not go.*

-	*I* **did not work** *you* **did not work** *he/she/it* **did not work** *we* **did not work** *they* **did not work**
	Contraction: *didn't*

We make simple past negatives (-) with **did not /didn't + infinitive** (without *to*).

STATEMENT +	NEGATIVE -
He ***cleaned*** *the car.*	*He* ***did not clean*** *the car.* (NOT ~~*He did not cleaned the car.*~~)
He ***started*** *early.*	*He* ***did not start*** *early.* (NOT ~~*He did not starts early.*~~)
She ***saw*** *you.*	*She* ***didn't see*** *you.* (NOT ~~*She didn't saw you.*~~)
John ***went*** *to Rome.*	*John* ***didn't go*** *to Rome.*

1 Circle the correct form.

- ▶ I *break* / *broke* a cup yesterday.
- ▶ Ann did not *play* / *played* tennis this morning.
1. Harry *work* / *worked* last Sunday.
2. I didn't *know* / *knew* where I was.
3. I didn't *feel* / *felt* well last night.
4. Alina *come* / *came* to see us at the weekend.
5. I didn't *see* / *saw* Bill at the party.
6. Peter didn't *write* / *wrote* to me for a long time.
7. The train did not *arrive* / *arrives* on time.
8. Julita didn't *like* / *likes* / *liked* her teacher.

2 Make simple past negative sentences.

- ▶ I played hockey last weekend. (*football*) I didn't play football.
1. We spoke Spanish together. (*Arabic*) ....
2. My uncle taught mathematics. (*science*) ....
3. Bill cooked the potatoes. (*the fish*) ....
4. I took my mother to the mountains. (*my father*) ....
5. We told our parents everything. (*the police*) ....
6. I wrote to my sister. (*my brother*) ....
7. I liked the party. (*the music*) ....
8. We knew her address. (*phone number*) ....

3 Complete the sentences with affirmative (+) or negative (-) verbs.

- ▶ I didn't break this window, but (*the other one* +) I broke the other one.
- ▶ I worked last week, but (*the week before* -) I didn't work the week before.
1. He didn't change his trousers, but (*his shirt* +) ....
2. She answered the first question, but (*the others* -) ....
3. He phoned her, but (*go to her house* -) ....
4. I didn't bring any flowers, but (*some chocolates* +) ....
5. She didn't buy a coat, but (*a very nice dress* +) ....
6. I ate the vegetables, but (*the meat* -) ....
7. We kept the photos, but (*the letters* -) ....
8. They didn't speak English, but (*German* +) ....
9. My grandfather shaved on weekdays, but (*at weekends* -) ....

4 Write five things that you didn't do yesterday.

1. I didn't ....
2. ....
3. ....
4. ....
5. ....

simple past questions *Did you pay? What did she say?*

?	***did** I work?* ***did** you work?* ***did** he/she/it work?* ***did** we work?* ***did** they work?*

We make simple past questions (?) with *did* + subject + infinitive (without *to*).

STATEMENT +	QUESTION ?
He cleaned the car.	*Did he clean the car?* (NOT ~~*Did he cleaned the car?*~~)
The class went to Rome.	*Where did the class go?* (NOT ~~*Where did the class went?*~~)

1 Circle the correct form.

- ▶ I *take* / *took* my father to Spain last week.
- ▶ Did you *hear* / *heard* me?
1. Did Theo *bring* / *brought* his wife with him?
2. When did Gemma *start* / *starts* school?
3. I *see* / *saw* Eric in the supermarket yesterday.
4. The lesson *begin* / *began* very late.
5. How did Oliver *break* / *broke* his leg?
6. Why did you *leave* / *left* your job?
7. Did Fred *speak* / *spoke* to you about Andy?
8. Where did that woman *keep* / *kept* all her money?
9. Rolf *learn* / *learnt* English when he was young.
10. Sorry – I *forget* / *forgot* to buy milk.
11. Did you *come* / *came* by train or by bus?
12. What did you *say* / *said*?

2 Make simple past questions.

- ▶ James enjoyed the food, but (*the music* ?) *did he enjoy the music?*
1. She listened to everything, but (*remember it* ?) ....
2. You didn't pay Ryan, but (*the others* ?) ....
3. You liked the book, but (*the film* ?) ....
4. He played football, but (*well* ?) ....
5. You gave them some help, but (*any money* ?) ....
6. She wrote to her sister, but (*her mother* ?) ....
7. He learnt French, but (*English* ?) ....
8. She got up early, but (*early enough* ?) ....
9. You shut the back door, but (*the front door* ?) ....
10. They took the children with them, but (*the dog* ?) ....
11. She felt ill on Sunday, but (*OK yesterday* ?) ....
12. He forgot the name of his hotel, but (*the address as well* ?) ....

3 Make simple past questions with *what, who* and *where.*

- ▶ Pete saw somebody. *Who did he see?*
1. John went somewhere. ....
2. Bill bought something. ....
3. Alice married somebody. ....
4. Mary broke something. ....
5. Mike stayed somewhere. ....
6. Joe studied something. ....
7. Robert studied somewhere. ....
8. Ann wrote something. ....
9. Catherine heard somebody. ....
10. George understood something. ....
11. Helen forgot something. ....
12. Sarah went on holiday somewhere. ....

→ For questions without *did*, like *Who said that?* or *What happened?*, see pages 108–109.

In some answers, both contracted forms (for example *I'm, don't*) and full forms (for example *I am, do not*) are possible. Normally both are correct.

Level 1

simple past: more practice

	REGULAR VERBS	IRREGULAR VERBS
+	*I/you/he/she/it/we/they* **work**ed / **like**d	*I/you/he* etc **went / saw**
?	**did** *I/you/he* etc **work / like?**	**did** *I/you/he* etc **go / see?**
-	*I/you/he/* etc **did not work / like**	*I/you/he* etc **did not go / see**
	Contraction: *didn't*	

1 Complete the sentences with affirmative (+) verbs, questions (?) or negatives (-).

- ▶ She didn't feel well last night, but (*OK this morning* +) ...she felt OK this morning.....
- ▶ 'I bought a new coat yesterday.' ('*shoes too* ?') ...Did you buy shoes too?.....
- ▶ We saw the Eiffel Tower, but (*see Notre Dame* -) ...we didn't see Notre Dame.....
1. I didn't learn much French at school, but (*a lot of Latin* +) ....
2. I remembered to buy the bread, but (*the milk* -) ....
3. I spoke to Alexia's father, but (*her mother* -) ....
4. 'Peter didn't phone yesterday.' ('*this morning* ?') ....
5. I didn't take the bus to London; (*the train* +) ....
6. I know you went to Singapore, but (*Malaysia* ?) ....
7. The train stopped at Edinburgh, but (*Glasgow* -) ....
8. 'Did the children see a film?' ('*two films* +') ....
9. 'I ate your cake.' ('*my chocolates too* ?') ....
10. I studied for the exam, but (*enough* -) ....

2 Make simple past questions.

- ▶ Sarah and her baby came out of hospital. (*When*) ...When did they come out?.....
1. Ann and her brother went on holiday. (*Where*) ....
2. Peter's friends gave him a bicycle. (*Why*) ....
3. The small woman said something. (*What*) ....
4. The children bought something. (*What*) ....
5. I invited somebody to lunch. (*Who*) ....
6. Mary dropped something. (*What*) ....
7. Oliver beat somebody at tennis. (*Who*) ....
8. George wrote to the police. (*Why*) ....
9. Rose asked somebody to marry her. (*Who*) ....
10. Bruno lived in India. (*When*) ....

3 Look at the picture, and complete the sentence correctly.

A did you remember
B did you remembered
C do you remembered
D did you to remember

'That reminds me, dear – .... the sandwiches?'

past progressive* *What were you doing at 8.00?*

+	*I **was** working*	*you **were** working*	*he/she/it **was** working*	*we/they **were** working*
?	***was** I working?*	***were** you working?*	***was** he/she/it working?*	***were** we/they working?*
–	*I **was not** working*	*you **were not** working*	*he/she/it **was not** working* etc	
	Contractions: *wasn't, weren't*			

We make the **past progressive** with ***was/were* + *…ing***. (For spelling rules, see page 23.)

*At 8 o'clock I **was waiting** for a train. What **were** you **doing**?*

We use the **past progressive** to say what was (not) happening **around** (before, at and perhaps after) a **past time**.

*'What **were** you **doing at 8.00**? **Were** you **watching TV**?'* (NOT ~~*What did you do*~~ …)

***'At 8.00?** No, I **wasn't watching** TV. I **was playing** cards.'* (NOT ~~*I played*~~ …)

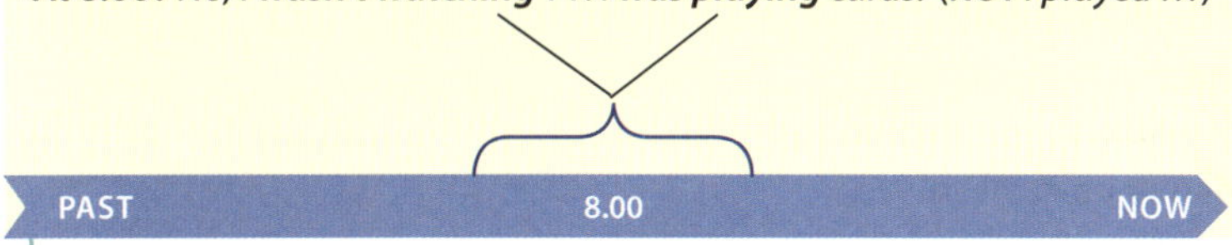

1 What were the people doing yesterday evening? Look at the pictures and complete the sentences with words from the box. Use past progressive verbs.

cook supper	dance	drive home
not watch TV	play cards ✓	

▶ At 9.15 Sarah *was playing cards.*

1 At 10.30 Fred and Alice ……………………

2 At 8.20 Keith ……………………

3 At 7.50 Mary ……………………

4 At 11.00 Oliver ……………………

▶ 

1 

2 

3 

4 

We make past progressive questions with ***was/were* + subject + *…ing***.

STATEMENT + :	*It **was** raining.*	*You **were** working.*	***All the children were** singing.*
QUESTION ? :	***Was it** raining?*	***Were you** working?*	*What **were all the children** singing?*

2 Write questions.

▶ 'At 10.00 I was reading.' (*a newspaper*) *Were you reading a newspaper?*

▶ 'When I saw Peter he was eating.' (*what*) *What was he eating?*

1 'When I went into Alesha's office, she was writing.' (*letters*) ……………………

2 'At lunchtime Richard was shopping.' (*where*) ……………………

3 'At 8.30 Anna was cooking.' (*what*) ……………………

4 'When I arrived, all the children were crying.' (*why*) ……………………

5 'At midnight, Liz and Jack were driving.' (*to Scotland*) ……………………

3 What were you doing at 10 o'clock last night?

……………………………………………………

* Also called 'past continuous'

In some answers, both contracted forms (for example *I'm, don't*) and full forms (for example *I am, do not*) are possible. Normally both are correct.

simple past or past progressive? *I walked / I was walking*

We use the **simple past** to talk about **complete** actions (long or short).
We use the **past progressive** for actions which were **not complete** at a past time.

*Joe **got up** at 7.00 and **worked** from 9.00 to 4.00.*

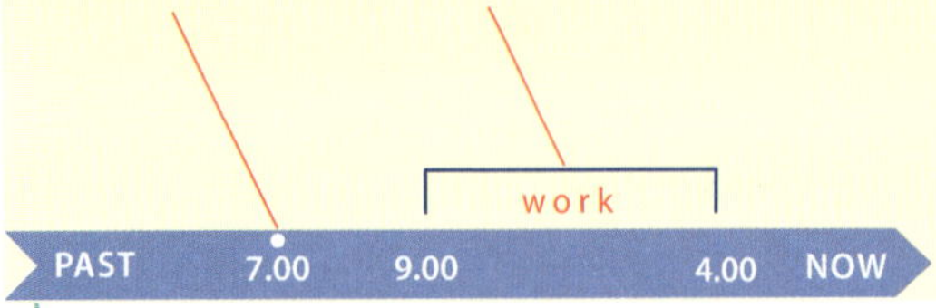

*At 8.00, when Joe came home, I **was reading**.*

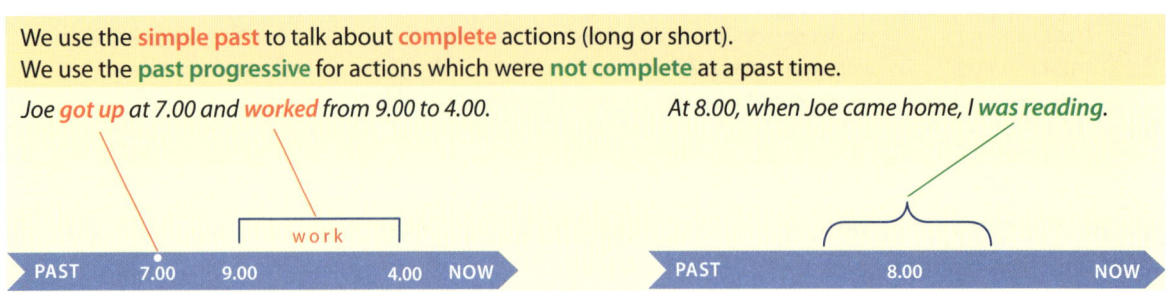

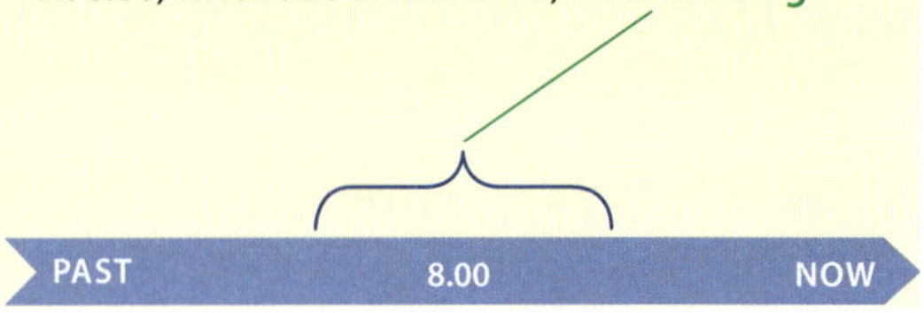

1 Simple past or past progressive?

- ▶ I *lived / was living* in France for eight years. (*lived* circled)
- ▶ Sue *lived / was living* in France when her uncle died. (*was living* circled)

1. At 6.15, when you phoned, I *had / was having* a shower.
2. We *watched / were watching* TV all evening.
3. Matt *watched / was watching* TV when Anita came in.
4. My father *worked / was working* hard all his life.
5. They got married while they *studied / were studying* at London University.
6. Yesterday we *drove / were driving* from Oxford to Edinburgh and back.
7. It was a nice evening, so she *walked / was walking* home from work.
8. I met Sylvie while I *worked / was working* in Japan.
9. At university I *studied / was studying* physics.
10. When I last saw him he *talked / was talking* to a policeman.

2 Complete the sentences with past progressive verbs.

- ▶ When I got home (*the children watch TV* [+]) When I got home the children were watching TV.
- ▶ (*you cycle* [?]) when you broke your leg Were you cycling when you broke your leg?
- ▶ When I saw Joan (*she look* [-]) happy When I saw Joan she wasn't looking happy.

1. At seven o'clock on Friday (*we play cards* [+]) ....
2. When I saw him he was holding the phone but (*talk* [-]) ....
3. When Mary got up (*it snow* [+]) ....
4. When I saw Alice, (*she walk* [-]) very fast ....
5. What (*you do* [?]) at ten o'clock yesterday evening ....
6. When you heard them, (*they talk about me* [?]) ....
7. How fast (*you drive* [?]) when you had the accident ....
8. The doorbell rang when I (*expect* [-]) anybody ....
9. I don't know what I (*do* [+]) at 10.00 on January 13th, 2005 ....
10. I had to drive to London because the trains (*run* [-]) when I left home ....

Note the difference when we use the **past progressive** and the **simple past** together.
Past progressive: longer action or situation.
Simple past: complete shorter action that **happened** while the longer action **was happening**.

*While I **was having** a bath,*

*the phone **rang**.*

*While I **was talking** to my brother,*

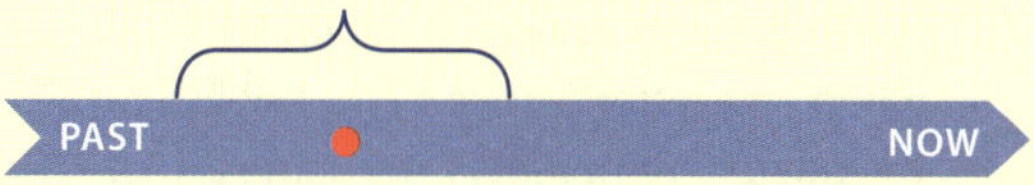

*Bill **came** in.*

3 Put simple past and past progressive verbs in the right places.

▶ While I ..was walking.......... down the road, I ..saw.............................. Bill. (*walk; see*)

1 While I .... the newspaper, the cat .... on to the table. (*read; jump*)
2 Alan .... Helen while he .... in Morocco. (*meet; travel*)
3 Sally .... her leg while she .... (*break; ski*)
4 While I .... , somebody .... my car. (*shop; steal*)
5 Ruth .... me eight times yesterday while I .... (*phone; work*)
6 The police .... me while I .... home. (*stop; drive*)
7 I .... an interesting report on the radio while I .... breakfast. (*hear; have*)
8 Dad .... to sleep again while he .... TV. (*go; watch*)
9 While I .... I .... a glass. (*wash up; break*)
10 I .... my hand while I .... in the kitchen. (*cut; work*)
11 When I .... the house I took my coat because it .... (*leave; snow*)
12 When I .... the door they .... about me. (*open; talk*)
13 The telephone .... while I .... lunch. (*ring; cook*)
14 When I last .... from Harry he .... in Portugal. (*hear; work*)

4 Correct (✓) or not (✗)?

1 This morning I listened to the news before I was going out. ......
2 I walked up to the policeman and asked him the way to the station. ......
3 When Ann arrived I was writing letters. ......
4 The cat was bringing in a mouse while I was having breakfast. ......
5 I didn't go out because when I looked out of the window it rained. ......
6 When I went to sleep the teacher was talking about grammar. ......
7 The teacher was still talking about grammar when I woke up. ......
8 Jenny and Takashi got married while she worked in Tokyo. ......

5 Put in words from the box, in the simple past or past progressive.

drive	open	pass	pull	run	shine ✓	sing	start	turn	turn	wait

It was a beautiful morning. The sun ▶ ..was shining... and birds 1........................ . About five thousand people 2........................ in front of the palace. At 10.00, the guards 3........................ the Palace gates, and the President's car 4........................ out and 5........................ left into Democracy Street. The crowds 6........................ to sing the National Anthem. The President's car 7........................ right into Constitution Square. Then suddenly, just as it 8........................ the Ritz Hotel, a man 9........................ out in front of it and 10........................ a gun from his pocket.

In some answers, both contracted forms (for example *I'm, don't*) and full forms (for example *I am, do not*) are possible. Normally both are correct.

past tenses: more practice

1 Simple past. Make sentences.

▶ the train / stop / at every station [+] The train stopped at every station.
▶ when / my letter / arrive [?] When did my letter arrive?
▶ the doctor / remember / my name [–] The doctor didn't remember my name.
1 what / all those people / want [?] ....
2 all your brothers / send you / birthday cards [?] ....
....
3 the baby / eat / some toothpaste this morning [+] ....
....
4 the teacher / answer / my question [–] ....
5 I / lose / my keys again yesterday [+] ....
6 anybody / phone / while I was out [?] ....
7 The Prime Minister / tell / us that things were getting better [+] ....
....
8 My friends and I / believe / the Prime Minister [–] ....
....
9 Richard / give / me a birthday present [–] ....
10 What time / you / get up / today [?] ....

2 Past progressive. Complete the sentences with past progressive verbs.

▶ When I walked in (*the children fight* [+]) the children were fighting.
▶ What (*you do* [?]) in my office when I came in were you doing
▶ When I had the accident (*I drive* [–]) fast I wasn't driving
1 At 9.00 on Sunday (*we watch TV* [+]) ....
2 When I saw him he was holding a paper, but (*read* [–]) ....
3 When you heard them, (*they speak English* [?]) ....
4 When you got home, what (*the children do* [?]) ....
5 Anna arrived when I (*expect* [–]) her ....
6 I don't know what I (*do* [+]) at 6.00 on February 18th ....
7 When I looked out of the window it (*snow* [+]) again ....
8 I had to drive to work because the trains (*run* [–]) ....
9 How fast (*you drive* [?]) when the police caught you ....
10 When I saw Peter, he (*stand* [+]) and looking up at my window ....
....

3 Simple past and past progressive. Put in the correct verb forms.

▶ They ...told... the police that they ...were playing... cards at 10.00. (*tell; play*)
1 When I .... out of the house I took my umbrella because it .... (*go; rain*)
2 This morning I .... the newspaper before I went out. (*read*)
3 .... you .... the football match last night? (*watch*)
4 When I .... into the room they .... about clothes. (*walk; talk*)
5 At 8 o'clock yesterday morning I .... in the sea. (*swim*)
6 I walked up to the classroom window and .... in. The teacher .... but nobody .... (*look; talk; listen*)
7 The telephone .... as usual, while I .... a bath. (*ring; have*)
8 This time last Friday I .... on the beach. (*lie*)
9 Why .... you .... home early yesterday? (*go*)
10 When I first .... John he .... round the world. (*meet; travel*)

4 Grammar in a text. Complete the text with the correct forms of the verbs in brackets.

Yesterday I ▶ (*get up*) ..got up.................... at 7.00. When I 1 (*look*) .... out of the window it 2 (*rain*) ...., exactly like every other day this week.
I 3 (*wash*) ...., 4 (*get dressed*) ....,
5 (*give*) .... the cat his breakfast, and 6 (*make*) .... coffee.
7 I (*not eat*) .... anything, because I'm never hungry in the morning. Then I
8 (*go*) .... to the bus stop and 9 (*wait*) .... for the bus. It
10 (*not arrive*) ...., as usual, so I 11 (*walk*) .... to the office.
While I 12 (*walk*) ...., I decided once again that it was time to find another job – one with a car. When I 13 (*arrive*) ...., nobody 14 (*work*) .... –
15 everybody (*talk*) .... about the weather. The boss
16 (*come in*) .... and 17 (*tell*) .... everybody to start working, but this 18 (*not make*) .... much difference. I 19 (*sit down*) .... at my desk and 20 (*start*) .... thinking about football.

5 GRAMMAR AND VOCABULARY. Make sure you know all the words in the box. Use a dictionary if necessary. Then try to correct the mistakes. Find the answers on the internet if necessary.

build	climb	compose	discover	make	invent	paint	write

▶ Galileo wrote 'Hamlet'. ..Galileo discovered the moons of Jupiter...................
▶ Shakespeare discovered the moons of Jupiter. ..Shakespeare wrote 'Hamlet'...................
1 Mozart built the Eiffel Tower. ....
2 Leonardo da Vinci directed 'Ivan the Terrible'. ....
....
3 Shah Jehan invented dynamite. ....
4 Alfred Nobel wrote the song 'Help'. ....
....
5 Sergei Eisenstein built the Taj Mahal. ....
6 Gustave Eiffel wrote 'Pride and Prejudice'. ....
7 Edmund Hillary and Tenzing Norgay composed 'The Marriage of Figaro'. ....
....
8 Marie Curie first climbed Mount Everest. ....
9 John Lennon and Paul McCartney discovered radium. ....
....
10 The novelist Jane Austen painted the 'Mona Lisa'. ....
....

6 Internet exercise. What did these people do? Use a search engine (e.g. Google) to find out the answers, if necessary.

1 Alexander Fleming ....
2 Giuseppe Verdi ....
3 Rembrandt van Rijn ....
4 Edmund Whymper ....
5 Mary Shelley ....
6 Stephanie Kwolek ....
7 Christopher Wren ....
8 Akira Kurosawa ....

pronunciation for grammar ➔ e-book

past tenses: revision test

1 Write the simple past forms.

arrive ...arrived... become .... begin .... break .... bring ....
buy .... change .... cry .... develop .... feel ....
go .... hope .... leave .... like .... pay .... start ....
stay .... stop .... watch .... write .... work ....

2 Circle the correct forms.

▶ Why didn't you *phone / phones / phoned*?
1 In the afternoon the rain *stoped / stopped*.
2 You never *visited / visitted* me in hospital.
3 When I arrived she was *makeing / making* coffee.
4 My mother didn't *feel / felt* well yesterday.
5 We usually *speak / spoke* French in my family when I was a child.
6 Henry didn't *told / tell* the police anything.
7 Did you *like / liked* the film?
8 I didn't *saw / seen / see* the accident.
9 John *phoned / was phoning* just when I *went / was going* out.
10 I *played / was playing* football a lot when I was at school.

3 Put in simple past or past progressive verbs.

▶ He ......told...... his wife that he ...was playing... chess at midnight. (*tell*; *play*)
1 I .... as a translator for two years. (*work*)
2 Jenny .... as a translator when she .... Roger. (*work*; *meet*)
3 Liz .... her purse while she .... (*lose*; *shop*)
4 We .... John all evening. (*listen to*)
5 While I .... my car, Ellie .... to talk to me. (*clean*; *stop*)
6 I .... my hand while I .... (*burn*; *cook*)
7 Rick .... when Emma .... home. (*read*; *come*)
8 My mother .... in Dublin all her life. (*live*)
9 While she .... in Chicago she .... ill. (*study*; *get*)
10 The police .... him while he .... out of the bank. (*catch*; *run*)

4 Each sentence has one or two mistakes. Correct them.

▶ I looked out of the window, and I ~~was seeing~~ that it ~~rained~~. ...saw... was raining...
1 Yesterday we were driving from London to Bristol and back. ....
2 At university I was studied engineering. ....
3 Why you were crying when I came in? ....
4 I was begining to get tired, so I was going home. ....
5 We payed the bill and leaved the restaurant. ....
6 While I was shoping, somebody was stealing my bicycle. ....
7 The doorbell ringed while I was cleaning the flat. ....
8 It was a warm day, so we opening all the windows. ....
9 What time you was got up this morning? ....
10 I did lost my keys somewhere when I walked home this evening. ....

In some answers, both contracted forms (for example *I'm*, *don't*) and full forms (for example *I am*, *do not*) are possible. Normally both are correct.

SECTION 5 perfect tenses

grammar summary

(SIMPLE) PRESENT PERFECT: *I have worked, she has worked, he hasn't worked* etc
PRESENT PERFECT PROGRESSIVE: *I have been working, he has been working* etc
PAST PERFECT: *I had worked, she had worked* etc

We use the **present perfect** to talk about **past** actions with some **importance now**.

*I've **written** to John, so he **knows what's happening**.*

We use the **present perfect progressive** mostly to say **how long** things have been going on **up to now**.

*I **have been writing** letters since breakfast time.*

When we are already talking about the past, we use the **past perfect** to talk about an **earlier time**.

*Yesterday I found some old letters that Kate **had written** to me from Germany.*

ANN CARSTAIRS was born in 1976. She is an explorer who has travelled extensively in Asia and Africa. She has also participated in expeditions to the North and South Poles and she has climbed in the Andes and Himalayas.

For the last five years, Ann has been working for the National Institute for Polar Research. She has written four books about her experiences.

ISABELLA LUCY BIRD *(1831–1904)* was a famous explorer. At a time when it was difficult for women to be independent, she travelled in the United States, Persia, China, Japan, Korea and Morocco. She wrote many books about her experiences, illustrated with her own remarkable photographs.

He's not here. He's gone to Paris.

Look what I've found!

Who's taken my coat?

I've made a cake. Would you like some?

Have you ever been to Canada?

I've just had a brilliant idea.

I've already read it.

She's been here since Monday.

The Prime Minister has met workers' representatives. They discussed a number of questions.

I've been studying English for three years.

Nobody was there. They had all gone home.

I knew I'd seen her somewhere before.

present perfect: forms *I have paid. Has she forgotten?*

	REGULAR VERBS			AN IRREGULAR VERB
+	*I **have** worked*	*you **have** worked*	*he/she/it **has** worked* etc	*I **have** seen* etc
?	***have** I worked?*	***have** you worked?*	***has** he/she/it worked?* etc	***have** I seen?* etc
-	*I **have not** worked*	*you **have not** worked* etc		*I **have not** seen* etc
	For contractions (*I've, he's, haven't*), see page 301.			

To make the **present perfect**, put ***have/has*** with the **past participle** (***worked, seen*** etc).
Regular past participles end in ***-ed***, like simple past tenses (for spelling rules, see page 46).

work → ***worked*** *hope* → ***hoped*** *stop* → ***stopped*** *try* → ***tried***

With irregular verbs, the past participle is often different from the simple past tense.
You have to learn the forms one by one (see page 299).

see → ***seen*** *speak* → ***spoken*** *go* → ***gone*** *buy* → ***bought***

1 Write as many of the irregular past participles as you can. Check them on page 299, and learn the ones that you don't know.

become ...become... begin ...begun... break .... bring .... buy ....
come .... drink .... eat .... fall .... forget ....
give .... hear .... hold .... keep .... know ....
learn .... leave .... let .... make .... pay ....
put .... read .... say .... shut .... sit ....
stand .... take .... tell .... think .... write ....

2 Write affirmative (+) or negative (-) present perfect sentences.

▶ I (*speak* +) to the boss ...I have spoken to the boss....
▶ they (*eat* -) anything ...They have not eaten anything....
1 she (*forget* +) my address ....
2 I (*make* +) a mistake ....
3 you (*shut* -)the door ....
4 Alan (*work* +) very hard ....
5 I (*hear* -) from Mary ....
6 John (*learn* -) anything ....
7 I (*break* +) a cup ....
8 we (*buy* +) a new car ....
9 the rain (*stop* +) ....
10 I (*see* -) a newspaper today ....

'Somewhere with no irregular verbs.'

We make present perfect questions with ***have/has*** + **subject** + past participle.

STATEMENT +:	*You have paid.*	*The rain has stopped.*	*The children have gone to Dublin.*
QUESTION ?:	*Have you paid?*	*Has the rain stopped?*	*Where have the children gone?*

3 Make present perfect questions.

▶ John / leave ? Has John left?

▶ why / Fiona / go home ? Why has Fiona gone home?

▶ where / you / put the keys ? Where have you put the keys?

1 we / pay ? ....

2 Tim / phone ? ....

3 you / hear the news ? ....

4 the dogs / come back ? ....

5 what / Barbara tell the police ? ....

6 why / Andy and Sarah / bring the children ? ....

7 what / you / say to Mike ? ....

8 why / everybody / stop talking ? ....

9 you / see / Martin anywhere ? ....

10 who / take / my coat ? ....

11 what / happen ? ....

12 where / my brother / go ? ....

13 why / Peter / close the window ? ....

14 Judith / pass / her exam ? ....

15 the postman / come ? ....

4 Look at the pictures and put the words in the correct order.

lady	you	without	seen	me	have	a

....

seen	I	ball	sorry	your	haven't	no ✓

'No, ...

In some answers, both contracted forms (for example *I'm, don't*) and full forms (for example *I am, do not*) are possible. Normally both are correct.

finished actions: present perfect or simple past?

PRESENT PERFECT: WE THINK ABOUT THE PAST AND THE PRESENT TOGETHER

When we think about the **past and present together,** we normally use the **present perfect**.

I've written to John, so he knows what's happening now.
I've made a cake. Would you like some?
Look – I've bought a new dress.

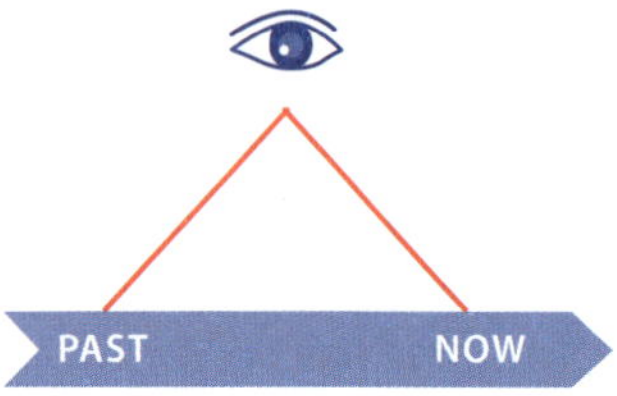

FINISHED ACTION	PRESENT PERFECT	PRESENT
letter (yesterday) →	*I've written to John.* ←	John knows now.
cake (this morning) →	*I've made a cake. Would you like some?* ←	I'm offering you some now.
new dress (last Tuesday) →	*Look – I've bought a new dress.* ←	I'm showing you now.

SIMPLE PAST: WE THINK ONLY ABOUT THE PAST, NOT THE PRESENT

When we think **only about the past**, we most often use the **simple past**.

My grandfather wrote me a lot of letters.
(He's dead now; I'm not thinking about the present.)
I made a cake for the children, but they didn't like it.
(I'm not talking about the present.)
I bought a new dress last Tuesday, for the party.
(I'm thinking only about last Tuesday.)

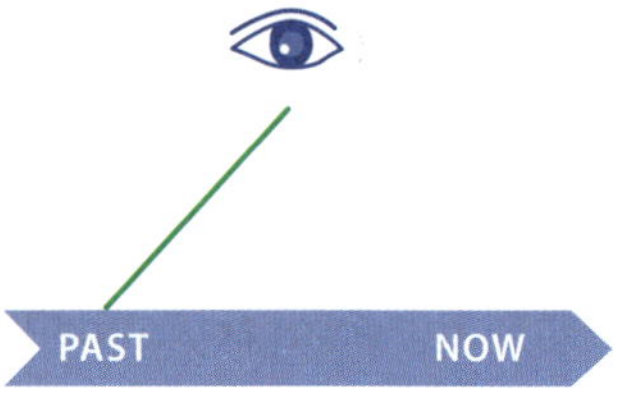

1 Read the sentences and the questions, and circle the correct answers.

- ▸ Ann has bought a new coat. Has she got the coat now? **YES / PERHAPS**
- ▸ Grandma came to stay with us. Is Grandma with us now? **YES / PROBABLY NOT**

1. I made a cup of tea. Is there tea now? **YES / PROBABLY NOT**
2. Eric has made a cake. Is there a cake now? **YES / PROBABLY NOT**
3. Jane went to France. Is she there now? **YES / DON'T KNOW**
4. Marlon has gone to Scotland. Is he there now? **YES / DON'T KNOW**
5. Pat and Al started a business. Is the business still running? **YES / DON'T KNOW**
6. Sue has started guitar lessons. Is she taking lessons now? **YES / DON'T KNOW**
7. The cat has run away. Is the cat at home now? **NO / DON'T KNOW**
8. The doctor sent Bill into hospital. Is he there now? **YES / DON'T KNOW**
9. Pete lost his glasses. Has he got his glasses now? **NO / DON'T KNOW**
10. Joanna has cut all her hair off. Has she got any hair now? **NO / DON'T KNOW**

2 Circle the correct verb forms.

1. Shakespeare *never travelled / has never travelled* in Africa.
2. When I was at school I *studied / have studied* Latin.
3. Rob *lost / has lost* his job, and he can't find another one.
4. We *met / have met* some very interesting people on our last holiday.
5. Look – I *bought / 've bought* some new shoes.
6. My grandmother *left / has left* school at 14.
7. 'Does your father know you're back in England?' 'Yes, I *told / 've told* him.
8. I *made / 've made* mushroom soup. Would you like some?
9. 'What's Rosie's phone number?' 'Sorry, I *forgot / 've forgotten*.'
10. Who *built / has built* Edinburgh Castle?

3 What are the people saying? Look at the pictures and complete the sentences with verbs from the box. Use the present perfect.

break ✓	break	buy	cut	eat	find
give	pass	sell	send	stop	

▶ 'Somebody ..has broken.. the window.'
1 'John .... us a postcard.'
2 'I .... a hat.'
3 'I .... my finger.'
4 'The rain ....'
5 'Look what Peter .... me.'
6 'I .... my car.'
7 'I .... too much.'
8 'I .... an earring.'
9 'I .... my exam!'
10 'I .... my arm.'

4 Put the beginnings and ends together, and put in the present perfect verbs.

break ✓	change	close	find	forget	go	leave	lend	lose	see

0 Joe ..has broken.. his leg,	A 'Sorry. I know him, but I .... his name.' ......
1 Molly can't get into her house	B 'Yes, his girlfriend .... him.' ......
2 'He's looking unhappy.'	C because she .... her keys. ......
3 'Who's that?'	D 'No, I .... it.' ......
4 'That's a good film. Shall we go?'	E so he can't go skiing. ..0..
5 'Where's Louise?'	F 'Yes, she .... her hair-style.' ......
6 'Can I borrow your bicycle?'	G 'We can't. It ....' ......
7 Anton .... a new job.	H 'I think she .... to Ireland.' ......
8 'Shall we have lunch at the Cantina?'	I 'Sorry, I .... it to Maria.' ......
9 'Denise looks different.'	J He's working in a bank now. ......

Note the difference between ***gone (to)*** and ***been (to)*** in present perfect sentences.

'Where's John?' 'He's ***gone to*** *Paris.'* (He's there now.) *Mary's* ***gone*** *swimming. She'll be back at 6.00.*
I've ***been to*** *Italy lots of times* (and come back), *but I've never* ***been to*** *Spain.*

5 Put in *been* or *gone*.

1 'Where's Zoe?' 'She's .... shopping.'
2 Gary's .... shopping. The fridge is full.
3 Have you ever .... to the United States?
4 They're not here. They've all .... out.
5 I haven't .... to the cinema for weeks.
6 Katie's .... to live in Greece.

We don't normally use the **present perfect** with **finished-time expressions**.

I've seen Ann. **OR** *I saw Ann yesterday.* **BUT NOT** *~~I've seen Ann yesterday.~~*

We use the **simple past**, not the present perfect, in stories (see page 47).

A man ***walked*** *into a police station and* ***said*** ... (**NOT** *~~A man has walked~~* ...)

In some answers, both contracted forms (for example *I'm, don't*) and full forms (for example *I am, do not*) are possible. Normally both are correct.

Level 2

time words: present perfect or simple past?

We **don't** normally use the **present perfect** with **finished-time expressions**.

We've found oil in the garden. **BUT NOT** ~~*We've found oil in the garden yesterday.*~~
A plane has crashed at Heathrow Airport. **BUT NOT** ~~*A plane has crashed at 3.15 this afternoon.*~~

1 Circle the words for a finished time.

a few days ago   always   this week   last week   never   now
then   today   yesterday   when   in 1990

2 Correct (✓) or not (✗)?

- ▶ My father has changed his job. ..✓..
- ▶ Andy has gone to Scotland last week. ..✗..
1. Look what Peter has given me yesterday! ......
2. I've seen a great programme last night. ......
3. I think everybody has arrived now. ......
4. When have you talked to Ann? ......
5. We've bought a new car in April. ......
6. I've met my wife when we were students. ......
7. Look what Peter has given me! ......
8. Mary has written to me three weeks ago. ......
9. Sorry – I've forgotten your name. ......
10. I've forgotten Mike's birthday last Tuesday. ......
11. Everybody has gone home at 10 o'clock. ......
12. There's nobody here! What has happened? ......
13. Sally has left school in 2006. ......
14. When have you arrived in London? ......
15. I think Mary has missed the train. ......
16. What have you done then? ......

We can use the **present perfect** to ask if things **have happened up to now**, or to say that they **haven't happened up to now**. This often happens with words for an **unfinished time** (for example ***today***, ***ever***, ***never***).

Has *the boss* ***phoned today****?*   ***Have*** *you* ***ever broken*** *your leg?*
We ***haven't been*** *to Scotland* ***this year****.*   *Mary* ***hasn't written*** *to me* ***this week****.*

Have you ever seen a ghost?

I've never seen one.

3 Make present perfect sentences.

- ▶ Steven / pay / for his lessons ? Has Steven paid for his lessons?
1. you / ever / write / a poem ? ......
2. I / never / climb / a mountain ......
3. Charles / speak / to you / today ? ......
4. Clara / not / tell / me / her new address ......
5. you / ever / lose / your memory ? ......
6. We / not / play / football / this year ......
7. Alex / never / write to me ......
8. you / see Henry / this week ? ......
9. my father / never / drive a car ......
10. the cat / have / anything to eat / today ? ......
11. you / finish / those letters ? ......
12. I / not / pay / for the lessons / this month ......
13. Sally / have a baby ......
14. Lucy / not phone / today ......
15. Corinne / come back / from India ? ......
16. It / stop / raining ......
17. the postman / come / this morning ? ......
18. We / eat / everything in the house ......

We can use the **present perfect** to say **how often** things have happened **up to now**.

*That's a wonderful film. I'**ve seen** it **three times**.* *Sally **has** only **been** to Ireland **once**.*
*We'**ve often wanted** to come and see you.*

4 Make present perfect sentences.

▶ I / break / my arm / three times .... I've broken my arm three times.

1 Joe / change / his job / twice this year

....

2 how often / she / ask / you for money ?

....

3 I / often / try / to stop smoking

....

4 Tom / phone / me / six times this week

....

5 My father / meet / the Prime Minister / twice

....

6 The police / question / Annie / more than once

....

7 I / only / play / rugby / once in my life

....

8 My brother / often / help / me / in my work

....

9 Nobody / ever / understand / her

....

10 I / never / want / to go to the moon

....

5 Present perfect or simple past? Circle the correct answers.

1 *Did you ever go / Have you ever been* to Wales?
2 I *never read / have never read* any of his books.
3 Our team *won / has won* two matches this year.
4 Our team *won / has won* two matches last year.
5 Shakespeare *never went / has never been* to Athens.
6 I haven't bought any clothes *this year / last year*.
7 Julia *stayed / has stayed* with us last week.
8 I worked very hard *today / yesterday*.
9 I *never saw / have never seen* a ghost.
10 When *did John phone. / has John phoned*?

6 Write five things that you didn't do yesterday, and five things that you have never done.

1 I didn't .... yesterday.
2 ....
3 ....
4 ....
5 ....
6 I have never ....
7 ....
8 ....
9 ....
10 ....

→ For the present perfect with *just*, *yet* and *already*, see page 64.

In some answers, both contracted forms (for example *I'm*, *don't*) and full forms (for example *I am*, *do not*) are possible. Normally both are correct.

already, yet and *just*

We often use the present perfect with *already* (= 'earlier than somebody expected'). Note the word order: *already* comes after *have*.

'Newspaper?' 'No, thanks. I've already read it.' *You're late. We've already started.*

1 Complete the sentences with *already* and verbs from the box (present perfect).

cook	finish	get up	go ✓	leave	pay

▶ 'Where's Pete?' 'He's ...already gone... home.'
1 'Shall I pay?' 'No, I ....'
2 'What time's the train?' 'It ....'
3 'Can you wake Helen?' 'She ....'
4 'Let's have fish.' 'I .... chicken.'
5 'When's the film?' 'It ....'

We also often use the present perfect with *yet* (= 'up to now') in questions and negatives. Note the word order: *yet* usually comes at the end of a sentence.

'Have you spoken to John yet?' 'No. He hasn't come in yet.'

2 Make questions (?) and negatives (-) with *yet*.

1 my sister / phone ? ....
2 the postman / come - ....
3 Bill / find a job - ....
4 you / finish that book ? ....
5 I / start work - ....
6 you / have supper ? ....

And we often use the present perfect with *just* (= 'a short time ago'). *Just* comes after *have*.

I've just come back from Spain. *The rain has just stopped.*

3 Do these things, and then write sentences to say what you have just done.

▶ (*touch your ear*) ...I have just touched my ear...
1 (*look at the floor*) ....
2 (*think about your home*) ....
3 (*move your feet*) ....
4 (*put your hand on your head*) ....

4 It is eight o'clock in the morning. Look at the table and say what Angela has (not) done. Use present perfect verbs with *already*, *yet* and *just*.

▶ ...She has just had a cup of coffee...
▶ ...She hasn't got dressed yet...
▶ ...She has already done a lot of work...
1 She .... letters.
2 She .... mother.
3 She .... kitchen.
4 She .... newspaper ....
5 She .... some toast.
6 She .... radio ....

have a cup of coffee	7.55	✓
get dressed	-	✓
do a lot of work	+	✓
write letters	three	
telephone mother	7.57	
clean kitchen	+	
read newspaper	-	
make toast	7.59	
listen to the radio	-	

since and *for* *since Tuesday; for ten years*

TUESDAY ▶ I've been here since Tuesday ▶ NOW

We use the **present perfect**, not the present, to say **how long** something has continued **up to now**.

*I'**ve been** here since Tuesday.* (**NOT** ~~*I am here since Tuesday.*~~)
*I'**ve known** John for ten years.* (**NOT** ~~*I know John for ten years.*~~)

We can say how long with ***since*** or ***for***.
We use ***since*** when we give the **beginning** of the time (for example ***since Tuesday***).
We use ***for*** when we give the **length** of the time (for example ***for three days***).

*I've been here **since Tuesday**.* *I've been here **for three days**.* (**NOT** ... ~~*since three days.*~~)
*I've known Mary **since 2005**.* *I've known Mary **for a very long time**.*
*I've had this car **since April**.* *I've had this car **for six months**.*

1 Put in *since* or *for*.

1 .... six weeks
2 .... Sunday
3 1996
4 .... ten years
5 .... yesterday
6 .... breakfast time
7 .... a long time
8 .... five minutes
9 .... July
10 .... last week
11 .... a day
12 .... this morning

2 How long have you known people? Write sentences.

▶ *I've known my English teacher since September.*
1 I've known .... for ....
2 I've ....
3 ....
4 ....
5 ....

3 How long have you had things? Write sentences.

▶ *I've had these shoes for six months.*
1 I've had my .... since ....
2 ....
3 ....
4 ....
5 ....

4 Make present perfect questions with *How long ...?*

▶ you / be / in this country *How long have you been in this country?*
▶ Rachel / have / her job *How long has Rachel had her job?*
1 you / know / Mike ....
2 you / be / a student ....
3 your brother / be / a doctor ....
4 Andrew / have / that dog ....
5 David and Elizabeth / be / together ....

Be, know and ***have*** are **non-progressive** verbs (see pages 30–31). With most other verbs, we use the **present perfect progressive** (see next page) to say how long things have continued up to now.

*How long **have you been waiting**?*

In some answers, both contracted forms (for example *I'm, don't*) and full forms (for example *I am, do not*) are possible. Normally both are correct.

present perfect progressive* *It's been raining since Sunday.*

+	*I **have been** working*	*you **have been** working*	*he/she/it **has been** working* etc
?	***have** I **been** working?*	***have** you **been** working?*	***has** he/she/it **been** working?* etc
-	*I **have not been** working*	*you **have not been** working* etc	
	For contractions (*I've, he's, haven't* etc), see page 301.		

We make the **present perfect progressive** with ***have/has been* + *…ing***.

*We **have been living** here since April.* *John**'s been working** in the bank for three months.*

We use the **present perfect progressive** (with most verbs) to say **how long** things have been continuing **up to now**. (For *be, have* and *know*, see page 65.)

*I**'ve been learning** English **for four years**.* *It**'s been raining all day**.*
***Have** you **been waiting long**?*

*We**'ve been travelling for six hours.***

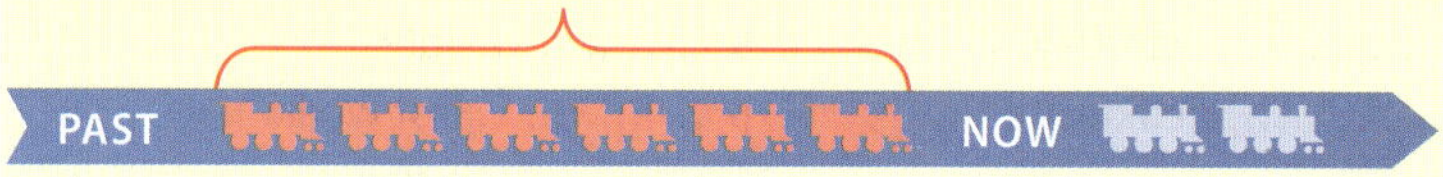

1 Make present perfect progressive sentences. Use *for* or *since* (see page 65).

▶ John started learning Chinese in February. Now it's July. (*for*)
John has been learning Chinese for five months.

▶ It started raining on Sunday. It's still raining. (*since*)
It's been raining since Sunday.

1 Mary started painting the house on Monday. Now it's Friday. (*for*)
……………………………………

2 We started driving at six o'clock. Now it's ten o'clock. (*for*)
……………………………………

3 Anna started working at Smiths in January. (*since*)
……………………………………

4 Joseph started building boats when he was 20. Now he's 40. (*for*)
……………………………………

5 We started waiting for the bus at 8.30. (*since*)
……………………………………

6 Prices started going up last year. (*since*)
……………………………………

7 We started camping on July 20th. (*since*)
……………………………………

8 My father started teaching 40 years ago. (*for*)
……………………………………

9 It started snowing at midnight. Now it's midday. (*for*)
……………………………………

10 The team started training together in June. Now it's September. (*for*)
……………………………………

REMEMBER: we **don't** use **present tenses** to say **how long** things have been going on.

*They**'ve been living** here since 1998.* (NOT ~~*They are living here since 1998.*~~)
*I**'ve been learning** English for three years.* (NOT ~~*I'm learning English for 3 years.*~~)

* Also called 'present perfect continuous'

2 How long have you been learning English?

....

3 Correct (✓) or not (✗)?

- ▶ I'm waiting for her since this morning. ..✗..
- ▶ I've been waiting for her for four hours. ..✓..
- 1 I have been sitting in this office since 9.00. ......
- 2 She's working here since 1998. ......
- 3 We have been driving for about six hours. ......
- 4 How long are Ann and Peter working here? ......
- 5 Sue has been talking on the phone all day. ......
- 6 How long are you learning English? ......
- 7 My brother's living in Glasgow since March. ......
- 8 That man has been standing outside all day. ......
- 9 I'm only playing the piano since Christmas. ......
- 10 Have you been waiting long? ......

4 Look at the pictures and say what the people have been doing. Use the verbs in the box (present perfect progressive).

play	play	swim	teach	travel ✓	write

▶ She has been travelling.

1 .... the piano.

2 .... football.

3 ....

4 .... letters.

5 ....

▶

1

2

3

4

5

In some answers, both contracted forms (for example *I'm*, *don't*) and full forms (for example *I am*, *do not*) are possible. Normally both are correct.

Level 2

past perfect *It had already begun when we arrived.*

+	*I **had** seen*	*you **had** seen*	*he/she/it **had** seen* etc
?	***had** I seen?*	***had** you seen?*	***had** he/she/it seen?* etc
-	*I **had not** seen*	*you **had not** seen*	*he/she/it **had not** seen* etc
	Contractions: *I'd, you'd* etc; *hadn't*		

To make the **past perfect**, put ***had*** with the **past participle** (*worked, seen, lost* etc).

*She didn't phone Alan because she**'d lost** his number.* *It was a film that I **hadn't seen** before.*

1 Make past perfect sentences.

- ▶ I couldn't get in because I ...had forgotten... my keys. (*forget* +)
- ▶ Anna wasn't at home. Where ...had... she ...gone?... (*go* ?)
- ▶ The telephone wasn't working because we ...hadn't paid... the bill. (*pay* -)

1 The woman told me that she .... in China a few years before. (*work* +)
2 Everything in the garden was brown because it .... (*rain* -)
3 The bathroom was full of water. What .... (*happen* ?)
4 I knew I .... that man somewhere before. (*see* +)
5 We were surprised to see Mark, because we .... his letter. (*get* -)
6 After three days the dogs came back home. Where .... (*be* ?)
7 They gave me some money back because I .... too much. (*pay* +)
8 There was nothing in the fridge. I could see that Peter .... the shopping. (*do* -)

We use the past perfect when we are already talking about the past, and want to talk about an earlier past time.

Our train was late, and we ran to the cinema. But the film had already begun.

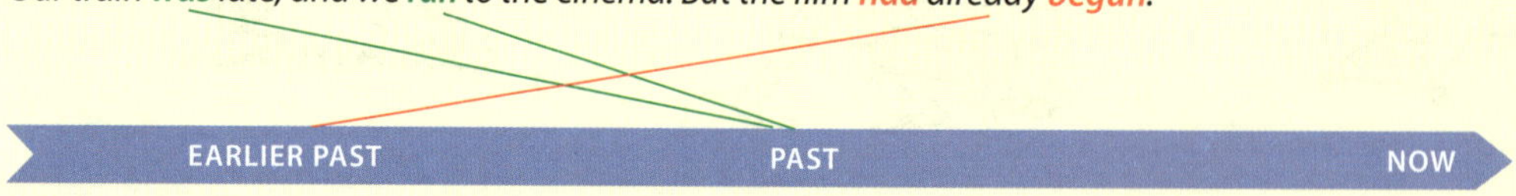

I got out of the car and went into the school. It was empty. Everybody had gone home.
I was glad that I had caught the early bus. *Anna wondered if anyone had told Jim.*
We couldn't understand why Sue hadn't locked the door.

2 Circle the correct answers.

- ▶ I *didn't recognise* / *hadn't recognised* Helen, because she *cut* / *had cut* her hair very short.

1 No one *understood* / *had understood* how the cat *got* / *had got* into the car.
2 Joe *didn't play* / *hadn't played* in the game on Saturday because he *hurt* / *had hurt* his arm.
3 When I *looked* / *had looked* in all my pockets for my keys, I *started* / *had started* to get very worried.
4 Liz *never travelled* / *had never travelled* by train before she *went* / *had gone* to Europe.
5 I *arrived* / *had arrived* at the shop at 5.30, but it *already closed* / *had already closed*.
6 I *didn't have* / *hadn't had* much money after I *paid* / *had paid* all my bills last week.

3 Put in the simple past or the past perfect.

▶ Bill ...didn't tell... anybody how he ...had got... into the house. (*not tell; get*)

▶ Emma ...went... to France last week. Before that, she ...had... never ...been... outside Ireland. (*go; be*)

1 When their mother .... home, the children .... all the sweets. (*get; eat*)

2 Yesterday I .... a man who .... at school with my grandmother. (*meet; be*)

3 It .... to rain, and I .... that I .... my window. (*start; remember; not close*)

4 I .... a letter on my desk that I .... (*find; not open*)

5 I .... Bob I couldn't go to the theatre, but he .... the tickets. (*already tell; buy*)

We use the **past perfect after *when*** to show that something was **completely finished**.

***When** I **had watered** all the flowers, I sat down and had a cool drink.*
***When** Susan **had done** her shopping, she went to visit her sister.*

4 Make sentences using the past perfect after *when*.

▶ Jan finished her dinner. Then she sat down to watch TV.
...When Jan had finished her dinner, she sat down to watch TV....

▶ David phoned his girlfriend. Before that he did his piano practice.
...David phoned his girlfriend when he had done his piano practice....

1 George ate all the chocolate biscuits. Then he started eating the lemon ones.
....

2 I turned off the lights in the office. Then I locked the door and left.
....

3 I borrowed Karen's newspaper. Before that she read it.
....

4 Mark had a long hot shower. Before that he did his exercises.
....

5 Barry phoned his mother with the good news. Then he went to bed.
....

Nothing had changed

When I went back to my old school
nothing had changed.

Well, OK,
the place had closed down.

Doors stood wide,
windows had lost their glass,
ceilings had fallen.

Travellers had camped in the dining-room,
and left their names on the walls.

Wind blew
through the rooms where I had sat for so long
and learnt so little.
Rubbish piled up in the corners.

But nothing important had changed.

→ For the past perfect in indirect speech, see page 265.

In some answers, both contracted forms (for example *I'm, don't*) and full forms (for example *I am, do not*) are possible. Normally both are correct.

perfect tenses: more practice

1 Verb forms. Make questions or negative sentences.

▶ She has finished the book. [–] She hasn't finished the book.

▶ The rain has stopped. [?] Has the rain stopped?

1 All those people have gone home. [?] ....

2 Peter has told us everything. [–] ....

3 The postman has been. [?] ....

4 Pat has spoken to Robert. [?] ....

5 Tim and Angela have bought a house. [–] ....

6 Emma's boyfriend has forgotten her birthday. [?] ....

7 Monica has been working in London all this week. [?] ....

8 I've phoned Joseph. [–] ....

9 Robert and Sally have moved to Ireland. [?] ....

10 We've been working all day. [–] ....

2 Present perfect or simple past? Somebody has just said these sentences. Choose the best answers.

▶ 'Harry has found a new girlfriend.' Has he still got this girlfriend? (YES) / PERHAPS

▶ 'Then a cat came into the house.' Is the cat in the house now? YES / (PROBABLY NOT)

1 'I've made coffee.' Is there coffee now? YES / PROBABLY NOT

2 'So Ross made soup.' Is there soup now? YES / WE DON'T KNOW

3 'And Tom has started Japanese lessons.' Is he taking lessons now? YES / WE DON'T KNOW

4 'Jill and Bob opened a driving school.' Is the school running now? YES / WE DON'T KNOW

5 '… because Pete lost his glasses.' Has he got his glasses now? NO / WE DON'T KNOW

6 'Alan has gone to America.' Is he there now? YES / WE DON'T KNOW

7 'We had a good time in Bulgaria.' Are they there now? YES / NO

8 'July has been a good month for business.' Is it still July? YES / NO

9 'Tony and Maria went to China.' Are they there now? YES / WE DON'T KNOW

10 'Polly has just bought a new coat.' Has she got the coat now? YES / PERHAPS

3 Question formation. Make questions (simple past, present perfect or present perfect progressive).

▶ The letter arrived. (*when*) When did the letter arrive?

▶ Somebody has told her. (*who*) Who has told her?

1 Everybody has already gone home. (*why*) ....

2 Anna's been learning Chinese. (*how long*) ....

3 George closed the door. (*why*) ....

4 Sue and Jeanne have gone on holiday. (*where*) ....

5 The President visited Russia. (*when*) ....

6 Jan's father has been travelling in Wales. (*how long*) ....

7 Something has happened. (*what*) ....

8 Joe has been working in Spain. (*how long*) ....

9 Mary studied medicine. (*where*) ....

10 Somebody has taken my bicycle. (*who*) ....

4 Simple past or past perfect? Complete the sentences.

1 When I .... him, I .... that I .... him before. (*see; know; meet*)
2 He .... enough money for food because he .... so many clothes. (*not have; buy*)
3 The meeting .... when I .... (*already start; arrive*)
4 The car .... down because I .... to put oil in. (*break; forget*)
5 I .... Mary for the first time thirty years ago. (*meet*)
6 After our conversation I .... everything that she .... (*forget; say*)
7 The house was empty. Everybody .... out. (*go*)
8 When he .... work he .... out for a walk. (*finish; go*)
9 When I looked in the fridge, I .... some cheese that I .... six weeks before. (*find; buy*)
10 He .... the door, and then realised that he .... his keys in the house. (*close; leave*)

5 Grammar in a text. Put in the correct forms of the verbs.

not be ✓	happen	have	lose	not pass	spend

Last year ▶ ..was not.................. a good year for Pete and Sonia. Pete 1 .... a car accident and 2 .... a month in hospital, Sonia 3 .... her job, the children 4 .... their school exams, and a lot of other bad things 5 ....

be	buy	change	open	pass

This year 6 .... much better. Pete 7 .... his job, and is making much more money. They 8 .... a new house. Sonia 9 .... a small restaurant, and it's going very well. And the children 10 .... all their exams this time.

6 GRAMMAR AND VOCABULARY: housework. Put simple past verbs into the story. Use a dictionary if necessary.

Once upon a time there was a beautiful girl called Cinderella. Her two sisters made her do all the housework. Every day she (▶ *get*) ..got.............. up early, she (1 *sweep*) .... the floors, she (2 *make*) .... the beds, she (3 *polish*) .... the furniture, she (4 *wash*) .... and (5 *iron*) .... the clothes, she (6 *wash up*) .... all the dishes and (7 *put*) .... them away. She (8 *tidy*) .... all the rooms, and she (9 *do*) .... hundreds of other jobs.

Now put present perfect verbs into the conversation.

SISTERS: Well, Cinderella, have you done everything?
10 .... the floors? 11 .... the beds?
12 .... the furniture? 13 .... the clothes? And 14 .... them? 15...................... the dishes? And 16 .... them away?
17 .... all the rooms?

CINDERELLA: No, I 18 .... anything. I'm going to marry the Prince. Goodbye!

7 Internet exercise. Read the two texts on page 57. Then use the internet to find out information about two other people (one living, one dead), and write a few sentences about their lives. Be careful to use the simple past or the present perfect correctly.

....
....

pronunciation for grammar → e-book

perfect tenses: revision test

1 Put in the past participles.

go ..gone....... break .... bring .... come .... drink .... eat ....
forget .... give .... leave .... make .... stand .... stay ....
stop .... take .... think .... try ....

2 Complete the sentences with simple past verbs or past participles.

▶ I ..wrote...... to my brother yesterday. (*write*)
▶ I haven't ..written.. to my sister for a long time. (*write*)
1 The lessons .... last week. (*begin*)
2 You've .... three cups today. (*break*)
3 Why have you .... home early? (*come*)
4 We .... what they wanted. (*know*)
5 Who has .... my coffee? (*drink*)
6 We .... too much last night. (*eat*)
7 John .... off his bicycle yesterday. (*fall*)
8 I'm sorry, I've .... your name. (*forget*)
9 I've .... my address to the police. (*give*)
10 Somebody has .... my umbrella. (*take*)

3 Circle the correct forms.

▶ Jenny *slept* / *has slept* very badly last night.
1 *We know* / *We've known* / *We've been knowing* John and Andy *for* / *since* years.
2 *I work* / *I'm working* / *I've been working* here since last summer.
3 'Mary *went* / *has gone* to London.' 'When *did she leave?* / *has she left?*'
4 Our football team *already has lost* / *has already lost* ten games this year. It *lost* / *has lost* all its games last year too.
5 *Did you ever drive* / *Have you ever driven* a bus?
6 My brother speaks good English, but he *has never had* / *never had* lessons.
7 *Did you see* / *Have you seen* Paul yet?
8 I *started* / *have started* this job *for eight weeks* / *eight weeks ago* / *ago eight weeks*.
9 *I'm* / *I've been* in this school *for* / *since* five years.
10 How long *do you know* / *have you known* Rebecca?

4 Complete the sentences with the simple past, present perfect or present perfect progressive.

▶ I ..have bought.................... tickets for the match. Do you want to come with me? (*buy*)
▶ My grandfather ..went................ to school in Ireland. (*go*)
▶ How long ..have............... you ..been standing............. there? (*stand*)
1 When .... Mike .... his new watch? (*lose*)
2 That child .... chocolate all day. (*eat*)
3 Andrew isn't here today – he .... an accident. (*just have*)
4 It .... non-stop since Sunday. (*snow*)
5 I .... mathematics from 1996 to 1998. (*study*)
6 'You're looking happy.' 'Yes, I .... my exam.' (*just pass*)
7 How long .... you .... Emma? (*know*)
8 .... you ever .... a poem? (*write*)
9 The company .... a lot of money last year. (*lose*)
10 'Do you like the book I gave you?' 'I .... it yet.' (*not start*)

In some answers, both contracted forms (for example *I'm*, *don't*) and full forms (for example *I am*, *do not*) are possible. Normally both are correct.

SECTION 6 modal verbs

grammar summary

MODAL VERBS: *can, could*	*may, might*	*shall, should*	*will, would*	*must*	*ought to*
PAST AND FUTURE OF MODALS: *be able to*	*have to*				

The **modal verbs** are a special group of **auxiliary verbs.** We use them **before other verbs** to express certain meanings – for example **permission, ability, possibility, certainty.**

Modals have **different grammar** from other verbs. For example, they have **no -*s*** on the third person singular: we say ***he can***, **NOT** ~~*he cans*~~.

Have to, be able to and ***used to*** are similar to modals in some ways, and they are included in this section.

For ***will***, see pages 39–40.

Together we can tackle
CLIMATE CHANGE
Science says 'We must'.
Technology says 'We can'.
Help to get politicians to say 'We will'.

(Adapted from advertisement for Centre for Alternative Technology, Machynlleth, Wales.)

Letters to a magazine

Should I give up smoking?
Should I marry Bob?
Should I move to Woking?
Should I change my job?
Should I dye my hair green?
Should I tell his wife?
Should I ask a magazine
How to live my life?

(Lewis Mancha)

I love mankind, it's people I can't stand.

(Charles M Schulz)

There are three kinds of people:
those who can count, and those who can't.

(George Carlin)

If you can't live without me,
why aren't you dead yet?

(Unknown)

Money can't buy you love.

(Traditional)

modal verbs: introduction *can, must, should etc*

can, could	*may, might*	*shall, should*	*will, would*	*must*	*ought to*

The **modal verbs** are a special group of **auxiliary verbs**.
They are **different** from most other verbs in four ways.

+ INFINITIVES WITHOUT *TO*

After **modals** (except *ought*), we use infinitives without *to*. (After **other** verbs, infinitives have *to*.)

***Can** I use your phone?* (NOT ~~*Can I to use*~~ ...)   *Joe **can't** swim.*   *I **may** be out tonight.*
BUT *I **want** to use her phone.*   *I'd **like** to go home.*   *Joe **seems** to have a cold.*

1 Circle the correct answers.

- ▶ Can you play / to play the guitar? (play)
- ▶ I don't want *play / to play* football today. (to play)

1. Ann seems *be / to be* very tired.
2. Peter hasn't phoned. He must *be / to be* away.
3. Could you *pass / to pass* the orange juice?
4. We hope *get / to get* a bigger flat soon.
5. Chris may *be / to be* here at the weekend.
6. I forgot *speak / to speak* to Janet.

NO -S

Modal verbs have no -*s* on the third person singular (*he/she/it* form). (**Other** verbs have -*s*.)

John can speak Korean. (NOT ~~*John cans*~~ ...)   *Barbara may be late.*   *This must be your coat.*
BUT *Josh **knows** my father.*   *Ann **seems** to be ill.*   *The cat **wants** to go out.*

2 Add -*s* or nothing (-).

▶ Amy play.s... tennis. ▶ Tim can..-... swim. 1 Our cat like..... fish. 2 It may..... rain.
3 She must..... pay now. 4 Harry work..... in London. 5 Kim should..... phone her mother.
6 The train seem..... to be late. 7 Nick might..... come and see us. 8 Tom want..... to go home.

NO *DO*

We make **modal questions** (?) and **negatives** (-) without *do*. (**Other** verbs have *do*.)

Can you help me? (NOT ~~*Do you can help me?*~~)   *You must not tell Philip.* (NOT ~~*You don't must*~~ ...)
BUT *Do you **know** my friend Jeremy?*   *Sally **doesn't cook** very well.*

3 Make questions (?) or negatives (-).
(Negatives in this exercise: *cannot/can't; must not/mustn't; may not*)

- ▶ Claire can't speak Russian. (*Chinese* ?) ...Can she speak Chinese?...
- ▶ Katy must wash her clothes. (*do it now* -) ...She mustn't do it now....

1. Mike can't swim. (*ski* ?) ....
2. John can play football. (*poker* ?) ....
3. Maria must play the piano. (*sing* -) ....
4. Robert may go to Italy. (*go this week* -) ....
5. Emma can visit us on Saturday. (*Sunday* -) ....

NO INFINITIVES OR PARTICIPLES

Modal verbs have no infinitives or participles: ~~*to can, maying, musted.*~~
Instead, we use **other verbs**: *can* → ***be able to*** (see page 81); *must* → ***have to*** (see page 78).

must *You must be home by eleven. Must you go?*

+	*I **must** go*	*you **must** go*	*he/she/it **must** go etc*	(NOT ~~*I must to go*~~, NOT ~~*he/she/it musts go*~~)
?	***must** I go?*	***must** you go?*	***must** he/she/it go? etc*	(NOT ~~*Do I must go?*~~)

In **affirmative** (+) sentences, we use ***must*** when we mean **'This is necessary'**.

*I **must get up** early tomorrow.* *You **must fill in** this form.* (NOT ~~*You must to fill*~~ ...)

*You **must visit** us while we're in Paris.* *Pat and Jan are so nice – we **must see** them again.*

1 Complete the sentences with *must* and verbs from the boxes.

be ✓ go hurry pay speak stop study write

▶ FATHER: You ..must be.. home by eleven.
1 TEACHER: You .... in ink.
2 FRIEND: We .... – we're late.
3 DOCTOR: You .... smoking.
4 TAX OFFICE: You .... the tax now.
5 TEACHER: Your daughter .... harder.
6 BOSS: You .... politely on the phone.
7 MOTHER: That child .... to bed now.

2 Put the beginnings and ends together. Add *must* and verbs from the box.

get up give go go have phone read ✓ see

0 Smith's latest book is her best, I think.	A I .... her tonight. ......
1 I haven't heard from Annie for ages.	B You ..must read.. it. Shall I lend it to you? ..0..
2 I've left my handbag in the restaurant.	C My mother made it; you .... a piece. ......
3 This cake is delicious.	D You .... it. It's a cinema classic. ......
4 'Velocity' is a wonderful film.	E We .... for a walk this weekend. ......
5 I've got a lot of work to do tomorrow.	F You .... me your phone number. ......
6 I'd like to see you again.	G I .... back and get it. ......
7 The woods are full of flowers.	H I .... early. ......

In **questions** (?), we use ***must*** when we mean: **'Is this really necessary?'**
To make **questions** with ***must***, we put *must* before the **subject**.

Must we tell the police when we change addresses? *Must you talk so loud?* *Must you go?*

3 A new student is asking some questions about next week's exam. Complete the questions. Use *Must I ...?* and verbs from the box.

answer bring ✓ come pay sit stay work write

▶ ..Must I bring.. writing paper?
1 .... any money?
2 .... to this room?
3 .... in ink?
4 .... in my usual place?
5 .... every question?
6 .... without a dictionary?
7 .... if I finish early?

Have to (see pages 76–77) means the same as ***must***.
Must has no past (~~*musted*~~) or infinitive (~~*to must*~~). Instead, we use ***had to*** and (***to***) ***have to*** (see page 78).

In some answers, both contracted forms (for example *I'm, don't*) and full forms (for example *I am, do not*) are possible. Normally both are correct.

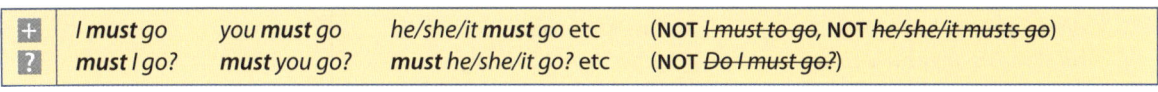

have to Do you have to teach small children?

+	I/you/we/they **have to** go	he/she/it **has to** go
?	**do** I/you/we/they **have to** go?	**does** he/she/it **have to** go?
-	I/you/we/they **do not have to** go	he/she/it **does not have to** go
	Contractions: *don't; doesn't*	

Have to is not a modal verb, but we use it very like *must*.
We use ***have to*** when we want to say **'This is necessary' / 'Is this necessary?'** (like *must*).

*You **have to** drive on the left in Britain.* *I **have to** go to New York for a meeting every month.*
*My sister **has to** work on Saturdays.* *Do your children **have to** take lunches to school?*

1 Complete the sentences with *have to* or *has to* and expressions from the box.

be ✓	be	carry ✓	do	have	have	know	know	like	practise	read	wear

▶ An accountant ..has to be.. good with numbers.
▶ Builders ..have to carry.......... heavy things.
1 A soldier .... a uniform.
2 Students .... a lot of books.
3 A schoolteacher .... children.
4 Cooks .... very clean hands.
5 A politician .... good at speaking.
6 Footballers .... a lot of training.
7 A secretary .... a good memory.
8 A gardener .... about flowers.
9 Doctors .... about drugs.
10 A musician .... a lot.

2 Put the beginnings and ends together. Add *Do/Does ... have to*.

0 'Mary's a swimming teacher.'	A '......................... finish it today?' ......
1 'Here is some work for you and Ian.'	B '......................... speak Spanish?' ......
2 'I want you to go to your aunt's party.'	C '......................... tell you now?' ......
3 'Jo and Alec work for a Mexican firm.'	D '......................... stay until the end?' ......
4 'When would you like your holiday?'	E '..Does she have to.. teach small children?' ..0..
5 'Dad and I are going out tonight.'	F '......................... pay it all now?' ......
6 'That will be 250 Euros.'	G '......................... travel a lot?' ......
7 'Peter works in marketing.'	H 'So .... babysit?' ......

3 Write five things that you have to do every day, or most days.

▶ I have to take the train to work.
1 ....
2 ....
3 ....
4 ....
5 ....

4 Write five things that you never have to do.

▶ I never have to speak Chinese.
1 ....
2 ....
3 ....
4 ....
5 ....

→ For negatives (*do not / don't have to*) see page 77.

mustn't and *don't have to* *We mustn't wake the baby.*

-	*I **must not** go*	*you **must not** go*	*he/she/it **must not** go* etc
-	*I **do not have to** go*	*you **do not have to** go*	*he/she/it **does not have to** go* etc
	Contractions: *mustn't; don't have to*		

Must **has two negatives (-):** we use ***mustn't*** or ***must not*** when we mean **'Don't do this'**.
we use ***don't / do not have to*** when we mean **'This isn't necessary'**.

*You **mustn't** smoke here.* *You **mustn't** take pictures here.* *We **mustn't** wake the baby.*
*You **don't have to** pay now; you can pay when the work is finished.*
*We **don't have to** hurry – we're early.*

1 Complete the sentences with *mustn't* and the verbs in the box.

let	light ✓	make	play	play	smoke	wash

At a campsite:
▶ You mustn't light fires.
1 .... dishes in the showers.
2 .... loud music.
3 .... animals run around.
4 .... in the toilets.
5 .... football.
6 .... noise after 10 pm.

2 Put the beginnings and ends together. Add *don't have to* and verbs from the box.

drive	give	make	make	post	speak	wake ✓

0 You don't have to wake me up;	A I can walk. ......
1 You .... breakfast for me;	B I'll buy *The Times* at the station. ......
2 You .... lunch for me;	C Cathy's going to the post office. ......
3 You .... me to the station;	D I'll just have coffee. ......
4 You .... me your newspaper;	E I've got an alarm clock. ..0..
5 You .... those letters;	F everybody here understands English. ......
6 You .... French;	G I'll have lunch in the canteen. ......

3 *Mustn't* or *don't have to*?

▶ You mustn't pay John – he hasn't done any work
▶ You don't have to pay John – I've already paid him.
1 You .... stay up late tonight – you've got school tomorrow morning.
2 You .... stay up late to wash the dishes – I'll wash them in the morning.
3 We .... leave the door open – the rain will come in.
4 We .... leave the door open – Peter has got a key.
5 You .... write to Deepak about this – I've already written to him.
6 You .... write to Deepak about this – if you do, he'll tell everybody.
7 You .... drive so fast – the police will stop you.
8 You .... drive so fast – we've got a lot of time.
9 I .... look in the cupboard again – I've looked in there twice.
10 I .... look in the cupboard – Holly has put my birthday present in there.
11 You .... phone Maxine now – she's probably asleep.
12 You .... phone Maxine now – tomorrow will be fine.

In some answers, both contracted forms (for example *I'm, don't*) and full forms (for example *I am, do not*) are possible. Normally both are correct.

had to, will have to *I didn't have to pay.*

	PAST: *HAD TO*	FUTURE: *WILL HAVE TO*
+	*I/you/he* etc ***had to*** *go*	*I/you/he* etc ***will have to*** *go*
?	***did*** *I/you/he* etc ***have to*** *go?*	***will*** *I/you/he* etc ***have to*** *go?*
-	*I/you/he* etc ***did not have to*** *go*	*I/you/he* etc ***will not have to*** *go*
	Contractions: *I'll, you'll* etc; *didn't; won't*	

Must has no past or future: ~~*musted*~~; ~~*will must*~~.
We use ***had to*** for the **past** and ***will have to*** for the future of both ***must*** and ***have to***.

My mum ***had to*** *leave school at sixteen.* ***Did*** *you* ***have to*** *tell Jo?* *I* ***didn't have to*** *pay.*
Alice ***will have to*** *start school next September.* *Aled* ***won't have to*** *come.*

1 Write about the things that John had to do (+), and didn't have to do (-), at school.

- (*learn French* +) He had to learn French.
- (*play tennis* -) He didn't have to play tennis.
1. (*learn Russian* -) ....
2. (*learn maths* +) ....
3. (*learn music* -) ....
4. (*play football* +) ....
5. (*write poems* -) ....
6. (*write stories* +) ....

2 Make questions with *Did … have to …?*

- you / learn French at school Did you have to learn French at school?
- Annie / work last Saturday Did Annie have to work last Saturday?
1. Adam / pay for his lessons ....
2. Tina / take an exam last year ....
3. Joe and Sue / wait a long time for a train ....
4. you / show your passport at the airport ....
5. the children / walk home ....
6. Peter / cook supper ....

3 Complete the sentences. Use *'ll have to …, will … have to …?* or *won't have to …* with the verbs in the box.

ask	get	get	go	learn	play	study ✓	tell	work

- Cara wants to be a doctor. She 'll have to study hard.
1. Lucy needs a new passport. She .... a form from the post office.
2. Edward's got a new car, so he .... to work by bus.
3. 'I've got a job with a Swiss company.' '.......... you .... French?'
4. 'Jack wants to be a pianist.' 'He .... for hours every day.'
5. 'Can I go home early?' 'I don't know. You .... the boss.'
6. I'm working next Sunday, but I .... on Saturday.
7. 'Liz wants to go to the US.' '.......... she .... a visa?'
8. I don't know the answer now. I .... you tomorrow.

should *What should I tell John?*

+	*I **should** go*	*you **should** go*	*he/she/it **should** go* etc	(NOT ~~*I should to go*~~)
?	***should** I go?*	***should** you go?*	***should** he/she/it go?* etc	(NOT ~~*do I should go?*~~)
-	*I **should not** go*	*you **should not** go*	*he/she/it **should not** go* etc	
	Contractions: *shouldn't*			

Should is like *must*, but **not so strong**. We use ***should*** for **suggestions, opinions** and **advice.**
Ought to is like *should*, but less common.

*You **should / ought to** be more careful.* *People **shouldn't** drive fast in the rain.* ***Should** I wear a tie?*

1 Choose the best verbs, and complete the sentences with *should* and *shouldn't*.

▶ In a big city, you ...should be... careful with your money. (*be, make, stand*)
1 In an airport, you .... your baggage with you. (*keep, run, stop*)
2 I think everybody .... a foreign language. (*work, learn, teach*)
3 You .... everything in the newspapers. (*write, play, believe*)
4 You .... some fruit or vegetables every day. (*drink, eat, sell*)
5 Doctors say you .... (*work, smoke, get up*)
6 Advertisements .... the truth. (*tell, sell, break*)
7 Small children .... with knives. (*think, play, write*)
8 Parents .... their children's letters. (*read, cook, lie*)
9 People .... fast in towns. (*drive, run, walk*)
10 You .... always .... what you think. (*say, pay, play*)

2 Make questions with *should I*, the question words and verbs from the box.

QUESTION WORDS: What ✓ What What time What time Where Where Who
VERBS: arrive put phone sit tell ✓ wake wear

▶ ...What should I tell... John?' 'Tell him I left early.'
1 .... 'At about 7.00.'
2 '.. first?' 'Mr Andrews.'
3 .... 'Your blue dress.'
4 .... 'At the end of the table.'
5 '.. this box?' 'On the shelf.'
6 '.. you up?' 'Not too early, please.'

We use ***must*** to talk about what's **necessary**, and we use ***should*** to talk about what's **good**.

*I **must** get a new passport: I'm travelling next month.* *I **should** eat more fruit, but I don't like fruit.*

3 Put in *should* or *must*.

▶ 'Do I look OK?' 'You ...should... get a haircut.'
1 I can't go; I .... finish this work.
2 I .... take more exercise.
3 You ....n't smoke near babies.
4 The sign says we ....n't smoke.
5 What .... I do to get a visa?
6 You .... be over 16 to buy cigarettes.
7 'What music .... I play?' 'Mozart.'

In some answers, both contracted forms (for example *I'm, don't*) and full forms (for example *I am, do not*) are possible. Normally both are correct.

can *He can play the piano.*

+	*I **can** go*	*you **can** go*	*he/she/it **can** go* etc	(NOT ~~*I can to go*~~, NOT ~~*he cans go*~~)
?	***can** I go?*	***can** you go?*	***can** he/she/it go?* etc	(NOT ~~*do I can go?*~~)
-	*I **cannot** go*	*you **cannot** go*	*he/she/it **cannot** go* etc	(NOT ~~*I can not go*~~)
	Contraction: *can't*			

*I **can** speak Italian.* *I **can** read Spanish, but I can't speak it.* ***Can** you sing?*

1 Write sentences with *but* about what David can and can't do.

▶ 

1 

2 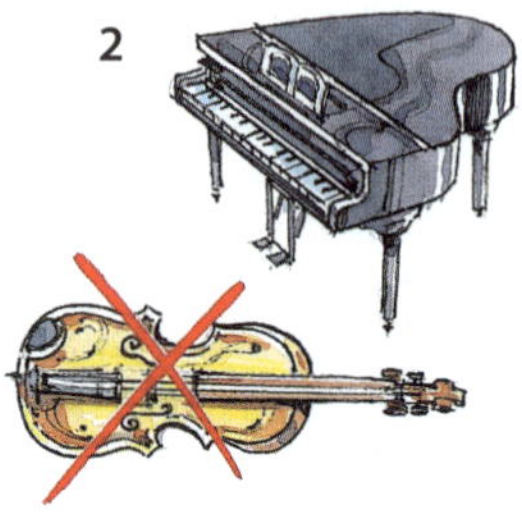

3 

4 

▶ (*speak*) He can speak German, but he can't speak Hindi.
1 (*play*) .... baseball.
2 (*play*) .... the violin.
3 (*remember*) ....
4 (*eat*) .... cherries.

To make questions (?) with *can*, we put **can** before the **subject**.

***Can Bill** swim?* ***Can Alice** speak Chinese?* *When **can I** pay?*

2 Make questions with *can*.

▶ 'Little Lilya is ten months old now.' (*walk*) Can she walk?
▶ 'John is starting the violin.' (*what / play*) What can he play?
1 'My brother wants to work in a restaurant.' (*cook*) ....
2 'My daughter's going to Spain.' (*speak Spanish*) ....
3 'Bill and Lisa want to buy a house.' (*how much / pay*) ....
4 'Can I help in any way?' (*drive a bus*) ....
5 'Some colours look bad on me.' (*wear red*) ....
6 'Jessica and I have got a lovely hotel room.' (*see the sea*) ....
7 'I want to learn the piano.' (*read music*) ....
8 'My brother is looking for a job.' (*what / do*) ....
9 'I can't eat cheese.' (*eat butter*) ....
10 'My sister is one year old today.' (*talk*) ....

3 Write three things that you can do, and three things that you can't do.

1 I can ....
2 I can ....
3 I can ....
4 I can't ....
5 I can't ....
6 I can't ....

could; be able to She couldn't write. I'll be able to drive soon

	PAST			
+	*I **could** go*	*you **could** go*	*he/she/it **could** go* etc	(NOT ~~*I could to go*~~)
?	***could** I go?*	***could** you go?*	***could** he/she/it go?* etc	(NOT ~~*did I could go?*~~)
-	*I **could not** go*	*you **could not** go*	*he/she/it **could not** go* etc	
	Contraction: *couldn't*			

	FUTURE
+	*I/you* etc ***will be able to** go*
?	***will** I/you* etc ***be able to** go?*
-	*I/you* etc ***will not be able to** go*
	Contractions: *I'll, you'll* etc; *won't*

To talk about the **past**, we use ***could***.

*I **could** talk when I was thirteen months old.* *I **could** walk when I was ten months old.*
*I **couldn't** understand the teacher yesterday.* *How **could** you say that to me?*

1 Choose the best verbs, and use them with *could* to complete the story.

My brother's baby was unusual. At three months old she (▶ *say / speak*) ...could say..... 15 words. At a year old she (1 *name / count*) .... all the colours, and she (2 *speak / count*) .... to 100. At three she (3 *read / learn*) .... easy books. She (4 *not think / not write*) .... but she (5 *play / tell*) .... wonderful stories, and she (6 *remember / believe*) .... every story that she heard. She (7 *not walk / not cry*) .... until she was nearly two, though.

2 What could you do at six years old? Look at the words in the box. Use a dictionary if necessary. Then make some sentences with *I could* or *I couldn't*.

climb trees	dance	fight	play chess	play the piano	read	run fast	sing	write

....
....
....

Can does **not** have an **infinitive** (~~*to can*~~). Instead, we use ***(to) be able to***.

*I want **to be able to** speak German.* (NOT ... ~~*to can speak German.*~~) *I'll **be able to** drive soon.*

3 Make sentences with *will be able to*.

▶ I / swim / soon ...I'll be able to swim soon...
1 Little Tim / talk / soon ....
2 I / pay you / next week ....
3 I hope that / go to America / one day ....
4 The doctor / see you / tomorrow ....
5 We / buy a car / next year ....

4 Write about yourself, using *be able to*.

1 I'll .... soon.
2 I'll .... next year.
3 I'll .... one day.
4 I'll always ....
5 I'll never ....

In some answers, both contracted forms (for example *I'm, don't*) and full forms (for example *I am, do not*) are possible. Normally both are correct.

may and *might* *It may snow. I might have a cold.*

+	*I **may** go*	*you **may** go*	*he/she/it **may** go* etc
-	*I **may not** go*	*you **may not** go*	*he/she/it **may not** go* etc
	No contractions: ~~*mayn't*~~		

We use ***may*** to say that things are **possible – perhaps** they are (not) true, or perhaps they will (not) happen.

*'What's that animal?' 'I'm not sure. It **may** be a rabbit.'* *I **may** go to Wales at the weekend.*
*We **may not** be here tomorrow.*

We **do not use** *may* in this way in **questions**.

It may snow. BUT NOT ~~*May it snow?*~~

1 Rewrite the sentences with *may*.

▶ Perhaps Sarah's ill. Sarah may be ill.
▶ Perhaps we won't go out. We may not go out.
1 Perhaps it won't rain. ....
2 Perhaps we'll buy a car. ....
3 Perhaps Joe is not at home. ....
4 Perhaps Anna needs help. ....
5 Perhaps the baby's hungry. ....
6 Perhaps I won't change my job. ....
7 Perhaps she's married. ....
8 Perhaps he doesn't want to talk to you. ....
9 Perhaps you're not right. ....
10 Perhaps I won't be here tomorrow. ....

2 Put the beginnings and ends together; put in *may* with words from the box.

not be decide give go ✓ go not have snow stay

0 'What are your plans for next year?'	A 'I'm not sure. I may go to America.' 0
1 'Are you going to buy that coat?'	B 'Not sure. They .... at home.' ......
2 'Where are your parents going on holiday?'	C 'No. I .... to study physics.' ......
3 'Shall we phone Pete now?'	D 'Yes. I think it ....' ......
4 'It's getting very cold.'	E 'Perhaps; I .... enough money.' ......
5 'What are you doing this evening?'	F 'I don't know. I .... him a sweater.' ......
6 'Are you going to study medicine?'	G 'It's early; he .... out of bed yet.' ......
7 'What are you giving Oliver for his birthday?'	H 'We .... round to Sophie's place.' ......

We may live without poetry, music and art;
We may live without conscience, and live without heart;
We may live without friends, we may live without books;
But civilised man cannot live without cooks.
(Owen Meredith)

Science fiction is the literature of *might be.*
(C J Cherryh)

Note the difference between ***may not*** and ***can't.***

*She **may not be** at home – I'll phone and find out.* (= 'Perhaps she's not at home …')
*She **can't be** at home: she went to Spain this morning.* (= 'She's certainly not at home …')

We can use *can't* to express great surprise or disbelief.

*'Karen's going to marry Des.' 'It **can't be** true. She hates him!'*

3 Put in *may not* or *can't*.

1 We can try that restaurant, but they .... have a table free.
2 There are no lights in the house, and they're not answering the doorbell. They .... be at home.
3 He says he's got lots of money, but it .... be true.
4 'You've won 1 million Euros in the lottery.' 'No, it .... be true!'
5 She says her dog talks to her, but dogs .... talk.
6 I'll ask that policeman, but he .... speak English.
7 'Can you come tomorrow?' 'I'll see. I .... have time.'
8 I .... pass the exam, but I'm hoping for the best.
9 'They've found elephants in Antarctica.' 'That .... be right.'
10 I'm going to see my old primary school teacher tomorrow, but she .... remember me.'

+	*I **might** go*	*you **might** go*	*he/she/it **might** go* etc
?	***might** I go?*	***might** you go?*	***might** he/she/it go?* etc
–	*I **might not** go*	*you **might not** go*	*he/she/it **might not** go* etc
	Contraction: *mightn't*		

We can use ***might*** in the same way as *may* – especially if we are **not so sure** about things.

*'Are you ill?' 'Not sure. I **might** have a cold. Or perhaps not.'* *I **might not** be here tomorrow.*

Might is unusual in questions.

4 John has no money. He is thinking about things that might happen. Put in verbs from the box with *might*.

buy	fall	find	make	send	win ✓

I ▸ ...*might win*... a lot of money in the lottery. Or I 1 .... some money in the street. Or Uncle Max 2 .... me $1,000. Or a rich woman 3 .... in love with me. Or the bank 4 .... a mistake. Or somebody 5 .... my old car.

5 *Might* or *might not*? Circle the correct answers.

▸ Kate had a big lunch, so she *might want* / *(might not want)* to eat this evening.
1 It's getting late. I *might finish* / *might not finish* this work on time.
2 If the traffic gets very bad we *might miss* / *might not miss* the train.
3 If he's had a good day, your dad *might give* / *might not give* you money for the cinema.
4 Andrew's story is so good that his teacher *might believe* / *might not believe* he wrote it.
5 Helen's not feeling well today – I'm afraid she *might pass* / *might not pass* her exam.
6 Alan wasn't at the last meeting. He *might know* / *might not know* the new members.
7 'Where's Tom?' 'He *might be* / *might not be* in the kitchen.'
8 I've got toothache. I *might have to* / *might not have to* go to the dentist tomorrow.
9 I'll do my best, but I *might have* / *might not have* time to help you.
10 I hope we can take the car, but it *might* / *might not* start.

In some answers, both contracted forms (for example *I'm, don't*) and full forms (for example *I am, do not*) are possible. Normally both are correct.

can, could and *may*: permission *Can I use the phone?*

We use ***can I …?*** or ***can we …?*** to **ask** if it is **OK** to do things: to ask permission.

Can *I use the phone, please?* *Mum,* ***can*** *I leave the table now?* ***Can*** *we wait here?*

We often use ***Can I have …?*** and ***Can we have …?*** to ask for things.

Can I have *your address, please?* ***Can we have*** *some water?*

1 Make questions with *Can I …?*

DON'T SAY THIS!	SAY THIS (to your sister, a friend, a waiter, your secretary)
▶ Lend me your pen.	(*borrow*) Can I borrow your pen (, please)?
1 I want a glass of water.	(*have*) ....
2 I'm going to use your pencil.	(*use*) ....
3 I want some more coffee.	(*have*) ....
4 I'll put my coat here.	(*put*) ....
5 Give me some bread.	(*have*) ....
6 Show me those photos.	(*look at*) ....

Could …? is **more formal and polite** than ***can …?***, so we use it, for example, with **strangers, older people, teachers** and **bosses.** ***Could I possibly …?*** is **very** polite.

Could we *leave our luggage here until this afternoon?* ***Could I possibly*** *borrow your paper for a moment?*

2 Make polite questions with *Could I …?*

DON'T SAY THIS!	SAY THIS (to a stranger, a teacher, a boss, an older person)
▶ Lend me your pen.	(*borrow*) Could I borrow your pen, please?
1 I need to use your calculator.	(*use*) ....
2 I'm leaving early today.	(*leave*) ....
3 I want to take your photo.	(*take*) ....
4 Lend me your newspaper.	(*borrow*) ....
5 I'm going to turn on the TV.	(*turn on*) ....
6 I want to open a window.	(*open*) ....

We use ***can/can't***, but not *could/couldn't*, to say that it **is** or **isn't OK** to do things.
(*You can't* is like *you mustn't* – see page 77.)

You ***can*** *leave your books here if you want.* (NOT ~~*You could leave your books*~~ …)
You ***can't*** *use the gym between 1.00 and 2.00.*

3 Put the beginnings and ends together. Add *can* and verbs from the box.

borrow ✓	eat	park	play	turn on	watch

0 If you don't have a torch,	A .... in this car park. ......
1 The children	B they .... the cake in the kitchen. ......
2 Tell the boys that	C you can borrow .... mine. 0
3 If you're cold,	D you .... the heating. ......
4 If you're bored,	E .... in the garden. ......
5 Only teachers	F you .... television. ......

4 **What do the signs tell you? Use *You can't … here* with words and expressions from the box.**

cycle	park ✓	smoke	take photos	use mobile phones

▶ You can't park here.

3 ....

1 ....

4 ....

2 ....

We use ***Can I/we …?*** to **offer help**.

Can I *help you?* ***Can we*** *book the tickets for you?* ***Can I*** *carry those for you?*

5 **Use *Can I …?* to offer help in these situations.**

▶ Your friend has just come home from hospital. Offer to do some shopping for her.
Can I do some shopping for you?

1 You're going to make a cup of tea for yourself. Offer to make one for your sister.
....

2 You work in a shop. A customer walks in. Offer to help her.
....

3 Offer to drive your brother to the station.
....

4 Your friend has got a headache. Offer to get some aspirins for her.
....

In **formal** situations, and when we need to be **very polite**, we often use ***May I …?*** to **ask** if something is **OK**, or ***You may*** (***not***) to **say** that something **is/isn't OK**.

May I *have your name, please, sir?* ***May I*** *use the toilet please, Mrs Roberts?*
You may *open your books now.* ***You may*** *ask questions after the Prince has finished speaking.*
This is a tourist visa: ***you may not*** *take a paid job.* ***You may not*** *leave until the bell rings.*

6 **A teacher is telling her class what to do. Complete the text with *may* and verbs from the box.**

do	leave	not leave	take	talk ✓	not talk	use	use

Please work in groups. You ▶ may talk .... in your group, but please talk quietly. You 1 .... to another group, and you 2 .... the room. You 3 .... your dictionaries. If you want to use other books, you 4 .... them from the shelf; but only one person 5 .... the group at a time. Each group 6 .... the computer for twenty minutes; I will tell you when it is your turn. If you finish before the time is up, you 7 .... other work, but please work quietly.

In some answers, both contracted forms (for example *I'm*, *don't*) and full forms (for example *I am*, *do not*) are possible. Normally both are correct.

can/could you?: requests *Can you lend me a stamp?*

We can **ask people to do things** (make requests) with ***can you …?*** This is **informal**; we often use it when we are talking to **friends**; and also, for example, in **shops** and **restaurants**.

*Joe, **can you** lend me a stamp?* ***Can you** bring me some more butter?*

Could you …? is more **formal** and **polite**; we often use it, for example, when we are talking to strangers, older people, teachers or bosses. ***Could you possibly …?*** is very polite.

*Excuse me, Mr Andrews, **could you** lend me a stamp?*
*I'm sorry to trouble you, but **could you possibly** watch my luggage while I get a coffee?*

1 Complete the sentences with the words from the box.

babysit	clean	drive	give ✓	hold	lend	pass	put	speak	tell ✓	tell	wait

▶ Can you ..give.......... me a receipt?
▶ Could you ..tell.......... me your name?
1 Could you .... me the rice?
2 Can you .... my suit?
3 Can you .... me the time?
4 Could you .... me to the station?
5 Can you .... this bag?
6 Could you possibly .... tonight?
7 Could you possibly .... me a pen?
8 Can you .... these papers away?
9 Could you .... more slowly?
10 Could you .... here for a few minutes?

2 Find better ways of asking people to do these things. (I = informal, P = polite, PP = very polite).

▶ Open the window. (I) ..Can you open the window?..........
▶ Lend me a pen. (P) ..Could you lend me a pen?..........
▶ Help me. (PP) ..Could you possibly help me?..........
1 Open the door. (I) ....
2 Give me an envelope. (P) ....
3 Pass me the sugar. (I) ....
4 Watch my children for a minute. (P) ....
5 Tell me the time. (P) ....
6 Change some dollars for me. (PP) ....
7 Wait outside. (I) ....
8 Translate this letter for me. (PP) ....
9 Come back tomorrow. (I) ....
10 Say it in English. (P) ....

3 Put the words of the caption in the right order.

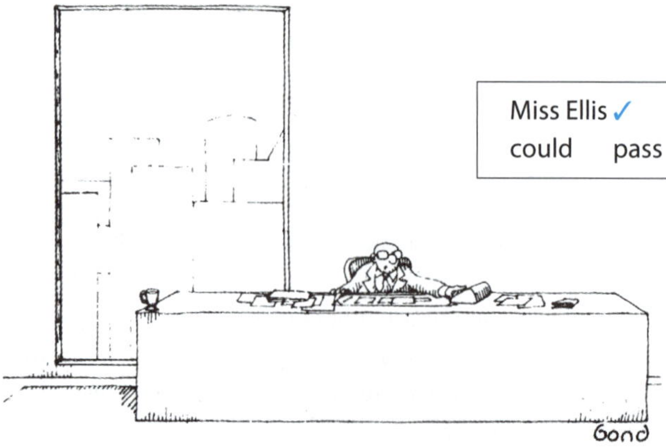

Miss Ellis ✓	here	my	and	come
could	pass	you	coffee	me	in

'Miss Ellis, ...?'

shall in questions *What shall we do?*

Level 2

We often use ***shall I . . . ?*** or ***shall we . . . ?*** when we are asking or suggesting **what to do**.

***Shall I** put the lights on?* *Where **shall we** meet tomorrow?* ***Shall we** go and see Bill?*

1 Make sentences with *shall I . . . ?*

- ▶ put / the meat / in the fridge ? Shall I put the meat in the fridge?
- ▶ what / tell / the police ? What shall I tell the police?

1 what / buy / for Sandra's birthday ? ....

2 when / phone you ? ....

3 pay / now ? ....

4 clean / the bathroom ? ....

5 how many tickets / buy ? ....

6 where / leave the car ? ....

7 what time / come this evening ? ....

8 shut / the windows ? ....

9 when / go shopping ? ....

10 get / your coat ? ....

2 Make sentences with *shall we . . . ?*

- ▶ what time / leave ? What time shall we leave?
- ▶ watch / a film tonight ? Shall we watch a film tonight?

1 go out / this evening ? ....

2 have / a game of cards ? ....

3 how / travel to London ? ....

4 what / do at the weekend ? ....

5 where / go on holiday ? ....

6 look for / a hotel ? ....

7 what time / meet Peter ? ....

8 how much bread / buy ? ....

9 have / a party ? ....

10 when / have the next meeting? ....

We can use ***Shall I . . . ?*** to **offer** politely to **do things for people**.

***Shall I** take your coat?* ***Shall I** make you some coffee?*

3 Make sentences offering to:

- ▶ carry somebody's bag Shall I carry your bag?

1 post somebody's letters ....

2 do somebody's shopping ....

3 make somebody's bed ....

4 read to somebody ....

5 drive somebody to the station ....

6 make somebody a cup of tea ....

7 clean somebody's car ....

8 phone somebody's secretary ....

9 cut somebody's hair ....

10 bring somebody an aspirin ....

In some answers, both contracted forms (for example *I'm*, *don't*) and full forms (for example *I am*, *do not*) are possible. Normally both are correct.

would Would you like a drink? I'd like to be taller.

We often use **would** in the expression ***I'd like*** (= '*I would like*'), to **ask** for things. It is more polite than *I want*.

I'd like *a return ticket, please.* ***I'd like*** *a seat by the window.*

We can **offer** things with ***would you like …?***

Would you like *a drink?* *How many eggs* ***would you like****?*

1 Make sentences with *I'd like …, please* or *Would you like …?*

- ▶ two tickets + I'd like two tickets, please.
- ▶ coffee ? Would you like coffee?
- 1 a black T-shirt + ……………
- 2 an aspirin ? ……………
- 3 the newspaper ? ……………
- 4 an ice cream + ……………
- 5 some more toast ? ……………
- 6 a receipt + ……………

We can use ***would like*** to talk about things that people **want** to do.

I'd like *to learn Chinese.* *What* ***would*** *you* ***like*** *to do on Sunday?*
Would *you* ***like*** *to have lots of brothers and sisters?* *I* ***wouldn't like*** *to be an astronaut.*

2 Which of these things would you like to be or do? Write sentences beginning *I'd like to …* or *I wouldn't like to …*

- ▶ be shorter I'd like to be shorter OR I wouldn't like to be shorter.
- 1 be taller ……………
- 2 be younger ……………
- 3 be older ……………
- 4 go to the moon ……………
- 5 live in a different country ……………
- 6 have a lot of dogs ……………
- 7 write a book ……………
- 8 (*your sentence*) ……………

We often use ***Would you like to …?*** in **invitations.**

Would you like to *come to Scotland with us?*

Don't confuse ***would like*** (= '*want*') and ***like*** (= '*enjoy*'). Compare:

I'd like *some coffee, please.* (NOT ~~*I like some coffee, please.*~~) ***I like*** *coffee but I don't like tea.*
Would you like *to go skating today?* (NOT ~~*Do you like to go …?*~~) ***Do you like*** *skating?*

3 Circle the correct forms.

1 *Do / Would* you like to come to dinner?
2 'Would you like coffee?' *'Yes, I do.' / 'Yes, please.'*
3 I *like / would like* mountains.
4 *Do / Would* you like to go out tonight?
5 I *like / 'd like* to go home now.
6 Do you like dancing? *Yes, I do. / Yes, please.*
7 I *like / would like* to get up late tomorrow.
8 I *don't / wouldn't* like old music.
9 I *don't / wouldn't* like to be an animal.
10 'An apple?' 'Yes, I *like / 'd like* one.'

used to *I used to play the piano.*

+	*I **used to** play*	*you **used to** play*	*he/she/it **used to** play* etc
?	***did** I **use to** play?*	***did** you **use to** play?*	***did** he/she/it **use to** play?* etc
-	*I **did not use to** play*	*you **did not use to** play*	*he/she/it **did not use to** play* etc

*I **used to play** the piano. I **don't play** now.*

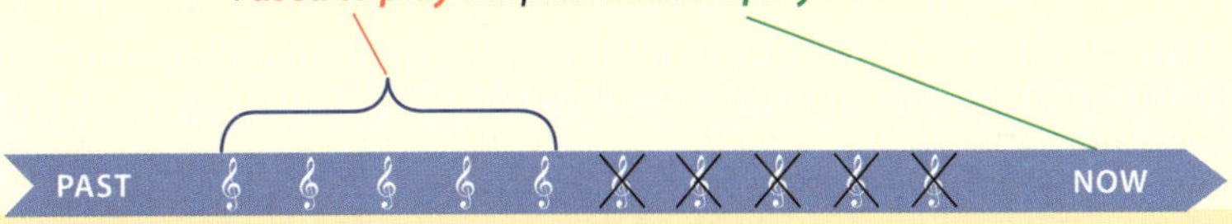

We use ***used to*** + **infinitive** for **finished habits and situations**: things that were true, but are not now. (*Used to* is not really a modal: we make **questions** and **negatives** with ***did***.)

*I **used to play** the piano, but I stopped.* *Pat **used to have** long fair hair.*
*Where **did** you **use to live** before you came here?* *I **didn't use to like** fish, but now I do.*

1 Make sentences about people hundreds of years ago. Begin *(Most) people used to …* or *(Most) people didn't use to …* or *A lot of people used to …*

- ▶ be farmers Most people used to be farmers.
- ▶ have cars People didn't use to have cars.

1 travel on foot or on horses ....
2 go to school ....
3 learn to read ....
4 cook on wood fires ....
5 live very long ....
6 work very long hours ....

To talk about **present** habits and situations, we use the **simple present**, NOT ~~*use to*~~.

*I **play** a lot of tennis.* (NOT ~~*I use to play a lot of tennis.*~~)

2 Make sentences about past and present habits and situations.

- ▶ John / rugby / tennis John used to play rugby. Now he plays tennis.

1 Emily / study German / French ....
2 Paul / live London / Glasgow ....
3 Grace / read a lot / TV ....
4 Dan / driver / hairdresser ....
5 Alice / coffee / tea ....
6 Peter / lots of girlfriends / married ....

3 Make questions about a very old person's past.

- ▶ where / go to school Where did you use to go to school?

1 have dark hair Did ....
2 play football ....
3 where / work ....
4 enjoy your work ....
5 go to a lot of parties ....

4 Write a sentence about your past.

I used to ....

In some answers, both contracted forms (for example *I'm*, *don't*) and full forms (for example *I am*, *do not*) are possible. Normally both are correct.

modal verbs: more practice

1 Forms of modal verbs. Make questions or negatives.

▶ Carol can't speak German. (*Spanish* ?) Can she speak Spanish?

▶ Emma may phone you. (*do it today* -) She may not do it today.

1 Albert can't ski. (*swim* ?) ....

2 Lucy must go to the police. (*go immediately* ?) ....

3 Tom may go to Washington, (*but … go this week* -) ....

....

4 Olivia has to work on Wednesday evening. (*Thursday evening* -) ....

....

5 Paul can play rugby. (*hockey* ?) ....

6 Sarah should see the secretary. (*today* ?) ....

7 Jenny could read when she was five. (*three* -) ....

8 The boss would like some coffee. (*now* ?) ....

9 We may go away next weekend, (*but … might take the children* -) ....

....

10 I must stay awake during the opera. (*go to sleep* -) ....

....

2 Past and future. Change the times of these sentences.

▶ Helen can ski. Helen could ski when she was three years old.

1 I can speak French now. .... on holiday next year.

2 Everybody must fill in a big form. .... last year.

3 Everybody must fill in a big form. .... next year.

4 Can you play the guitar? .... at the next school concert?

5 Must you wear a tie to work? .... in your last job?

6 John can't read very well. .... when he was younger.

7 We can't buy a car. .... before next year.

8 I must see the doctor. .... last week.

9 Everybody can say what they think. .... in the year 3000.

10 You can't sing now. You .... last year.
And you .... next year, either.

3 Advice with *should*. Put the beginnings and ends together.

1 Aunt Mary's thirsty.	A You should give her a saucer of milk. ......
2 I'm getting fat.	B You should buy some new clothes. ......
3 My girlfriend's angry with me.	C You should buy a new one. ......
4 The cat needs a drink.	D You should make her a cup of tea. ......
5 My hair's falling out.	E You shouldn't buy so many electronic gadgets. ......
6 I'm tired.	F You should take more exercise. ......
7 I don't like Anna's new hairstyle.	G You should practise your service. ......
8 I never have any money.	H You should study grammar. ......
9 I don't play tennis very well.	I You shouldn't go to bed so late. ......
10 The car won't go.	J You shouldn't tell her. ......
11 My clothes are all out of fashion.	K You should change your shampoo. ......
12 My English teacher says I make too many mistakes.	L You should tell her you love her. ......

4 **Permission and requests. Make these sentences more polite. (Different answers are possible.)**

▶ Give me some water. *Can/Could/May I have some water?*
1 I want a cup of coffee. ....
2 Can I take a photograph of you? ....
3 Close the door, John. ....
4 I need you to help me. ....
5 Give me that newspaper. ....
6 Will you clean my bicycle, please? ....
7 Can I borrow some money from you? ....
8 Let me use your phone. ....
9 Hold this. ....
10 Wash all my clothes before tomorrow. ....

5 **GRAMMAR AND VOCABULARY: eight useful things. Complete the sentences with *you can* and expressions from the box. Use a dictionary if necessary.**

cook food ✓	keep food cool	keep food very cold	make copies
make phone calls	take photos	wash clothes	wash plates, cups etc

▶ With a cooker *you can cook food.*
1 With a scanner ....
2 With a freezer ....
3 With a washing machine ....
4 With a fridge ....
5 With a mobile phone ....
6 With a dishwasher ....
7 With a camera ....

a cooker

a scanner

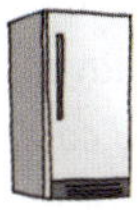
a freezer

a washing machine

a fridge

a mobile phone

a dishwasher

a camera

6 **GRAMMAR AND VOCABULARY: jobs. Complete the sentences with *might be* and words from the box. Use a dictionary if necessary.**

a businessman	a chef	a farmer ✓	a gardener	a lawyer
an opera singer	a pilot	a politician	a vet ✓	

▶ Little Henry likes animals. When he grows up *he might be a farmer or a vet.*
1 Little Angela loves aeroplanes. She might ....
2 Little George is interested in money. ....
3 Little Amrita likes singing and she has a very loud voice. ....
4 Little Peter likes talking. ....
5 Little Alice likes arguing. ....
6 Little John likes cooking. ....
7 Little Ruby likes flowers. ....

7 **Internet exercise. Use a search engine (e.g. Google) to find three short simple sentences with "*will be able to*" and three with "*will have to*".**

1 .... 4 ....
2 .... 5 ....
3 .... 6 ....

pronunciation for grammar → e-book

modal verbs: revision test

1 Correct (✓) or not (✗)?

- ▶ John cans swim. ..✗...
- ▶ I must go now. ..✓...

1 I don't must see Andrew today. ......
2 Anna can't to speak English. ......
3 Last year I must sell my car. ...
4 Would you like to have some coffee? ......
5 It may rain tomorrow. ......
6 Can you singing? ......
7 Must you go? ......
8 I may not be here this evening. ......
9 Do you use to smoke? ......
10 Alex musts work harder. ......

2 Circle the correct verbs.

▶ (*Can*) / *Might* / *Mustn't* I help you?

1 If you travel to Morania you *can* / *should* / *must* have a visa.
2 You *shouldn't* / *don't have to* / *couldn't* laugh at old people.
3 Passengers *must* / *must not* / *should not* smoke in the toilets.
4 I think you *should* / *must* / *may* eat less and take more exercise.
5 You *mustn't* / *may not* / *don't have to* tell me if you don't want to.
6 You *may* / *have to* drive on the left in Britain.
7 We *don't have to* / *mustn't* pay now, but we can if we want to.
8 I *may not* / *could not* be here this evening.
9 She isn't answering the phone. She *shouldn't* /*can't* be at home just now.
10 People *should* / *have to* smile more often.

3 Choose the correct verbs to rewrite the sentences with the same meaning.

▶ I know how to swim. (*can/may*) ...I can swim....................

1 It is necessary for you to phone Martin. (*must/might*) ....
2 It is possible that Ann will be here this evening. (*can/might*) ....
3 It is not necessary for you to wait. (*mustn't/don't have to*) ....
4 It's not good for people to watch TV all the time. (*mustn't/shouldn't*) ....
....
5 Do you want me to open a window? (*shall/will*) ....
6 It is important for people to cooperate. (*may/should*) ....
7 John smoked when he was younger. (*used to/would*) ....
8 It is possible that it will rain. (*can/may*) ....
9 Alan knows how to speak Spanish. (*can/could*) ....
10 I would like you to help me. (*Can/Should*) ....

4 Grammar in a text. Choose the best modal verbs to complete the quotations.

1 Those who *can* / *can't* / *shall*, do. Those who *can* / *can't* / *shall*, teach. (*Traditional*)
2 We *may* / *can* / *must* love one another or die. (*W H Auden*)
3 It is not enough to succeed. Others *can* / *may* / *must* fail. (*Gore Vidal*)
4 You *shall* / *could* / *may* fool all the people some of the time; you *must* / *can* / *shall* even fool some of the people all the time; but you *can't* / *couldn't* / *wouldn't* fool all of the people all the time. (*Abraham Lincoln*)

In some answers, both contracted forms (for example *I'm*, *don't*) and full forms (for example *I am*, *do not*) are possible. Normally both are correct.

SECTION 7 passives

grammar summary

When **A** does something to **B**, there are often two ways to talk about it: '**active**' and '**passive**'.

- We use **active** verbs if we want **A** to be the **subject**.
  Mrs Harris ***cooks*** *our meals.* *Andrew* ***broke*** *the window.*
- We use **passive** verbs if we want **B** to be the **subject**.
  Our meals ***are cooked*** *by Mrs Harris.* *The window* ***was broken*** *by Andrew.*

We make **passive verbs** with ***be*** (*am, are, is* etc) + **past participle** (*cooked, broken* etc).
Passive verbs have the **same tenses** (simple present, present progressive, present perfect etc) as **active** verbs.
For a list of active and passive tenses, see page 300.

'I'm afraid, Mr Klesmerod, that your blood type has been discontinued.'

Do you know? (Answers at the bottom of the page)

1 Which of these is used to boil water?
A a fridge B a sink C a kettle D a hot water bottle

2 Which US President was killed in a theatre?
A Lincoln B Kennedy C Eisenhower D Nixon

3 Which game is played with a racket?
A golf B cricket C football D tennis

4 If you are being served, where are you?
A in a shop B in a church C in the sea D in hospital

5 The Olympic Games have never been held in:
A Melbourne B Tokyo C London D Chicago

6 Which of these metals was discovered by Marie Curie?
A uranium B radium C gold D platinum

7 Which of these was not written by Shakespeare?
A Hamlet B The Sound of Music C Othello D Julius Caesar

8 Which country was governed by the Pharaohs?
A Sweden B China C Egypt D Japan

Answers: 1C, 2A, 3D, 4A, 5D, 6B, 7B, 8C

passives: introduction *English is spoken in Australia.*

When **A** does something to **B**, there are often two ways to talk about it: '**active**' and '**passive**'.
We use **active** verbs if we want **A** to be the **subject**.
We use **passive** verbs if we want **B** to be the **subject**.
We make **passive** verbs with ***be*** (*am, are, is* etc) + **past participle** (*cooked, seen* etc).

A → **B**

ACTIVE				PASSIVE			
A		**B**		**B**		**(by A)**	
Mrs Harris	***cooks***	*our meals.*		*Our meals*	***are cooked***	*by Mrs Harris.*	
Andrew	***broke***	*the window.*		*The window*	***was broken***	*by Andrew.*	
Somebody	***saw***	*her*	*in Belfast.*	*She*	***was seen***		*in Belfast.*
The government	***will close***	*the hospital*	*next year.*	*The hospital*	***will be closed***		*next year.*

Passive verbs have the **same tenses** (simple present, present progressive, present perfect etc) as **active** verbs.
For a list of active and passive tenses, see page 300.
Note the use of ***by*** in passives, to say **who** or **what** does the action.

Our meals are cooked ***by Mrs Harris****.* (NOT …~~*from Mrs Harris.*~~)

1 Which picture goes with which sentence?

▶ The policeman helped the old lady. ......
1 The policeman was helped by the old lady. ......
2 The car hit a tree. ......
3 The car was hit by a tree. ......
4 Annie loves all dogs. ......
5 Annie is loved by all dogs. ......
6 The Queen photographed the tourists. ......
7 The Queen was photographed by the tourists. ......

A

B

C

D

E

F

G

H

2 Circle the correct answer.

1 English *speaks / spoken / is spoken* in Australia.
2 I *studied / was studied* French for three years at school.
3 We *spent / was spent* too much money on holiday.
4 This window *broke / was broken* by your little boy.
5 Her clothes *made / are made* in Paris.
6 This book *written / was written* by my brother.
7 The new university *will open / will opened / will be opened* by the Prime Minister.
8 Ann *was driving / was driven* much too fast, and she *stopped / was stopped* by the police.
9 This house *built / was built* in 1800.
10 Everybody *had / was had / was have* a good time at the party.

simple present passive *We are woken by the birds.*

+	*I **am** woken*	*you **are** woken*	*he/she/it **is** woken* etc
?	***am** I woken?*	***are** you woken?*	***is** he/she/it woken?* etc
-	*I **am not** woken*	*you **are not** woken*	*he/she/it **is not** woken* etc
	For contractions (*I'm, isn't* etc), see pages 2, 301.		

We use the **simple present passive** like the simple present active, for things that are **always true**, and things that happen **all the time, repeatedly, often, sometimes, never** etc (see page 17).

*I **am paid** every two weeks.* *Is Jeremy **liked** by the other children?* *Stamps **aren't sold** here.*

→ For spelling rules for adding *-ed* to verbs, see page 46; for irregular past participles, see page 299.

1 Complete the sentences with *am/are/is*.

▶ A lot of paper ...is...... made from wood.
1 What .... this called in English?
2 Jane .... paid on the first of every month.
3 I .... often sent to the Singapore office.
4 .... any classes taught on Wednesdays?
5 More chocolate .... eaten in the US than in any other country.
6 Not very much .... known about Shakespeare's childhood.
7 We .... woken by the birds every morning.
8 .... you seen by the same doctor every week?

2 Put simple present passive verbs into these sentences.

▶ A lot of olive oil ...is used........................ in Greek cooking. (*use*)
1 Arabic .... from right to left. (*write*)
2 Those programmes .... by millions of people every week. (*watch*)
3 Stamps .... in most newsagents in Britain. (*sell*)
4 The police say that nothing .... about the child's family. (*know*)
5 In English, 'ough' .... in a lot of different ways. (*pronounce*)
6 Spanish .... in Peru. (*speak*)
7 Cricket .... by two teams of eleven players. (*play*)
8 Our windows .... once a month. (*clean*)

3 Make simple present negatives and questions.

▶ 'Those computers ...are not made.. in America.' (*not make*)
'Where ...are they made?......................................' 'In China.'
1 'My name .... with a Y.' (*not spell*)
'How ....' 'L, E, S, L, I, E.'
2 'That kind of bird .... around here, usually.' (*not see*)
'Where ....' 'In warmer countries.'
3 '*Where* .... like *were*.' (*not pronounce*)
'How ....' 'Like *wear*.'
4 'Diamonds .... in Scotland.' (*not find*)
'Where ....' 'In South Africa, for example.'
5 'My sister .... very well.' (*pay*)
'How much ....' 'I don't remember.'

In some answers, both contracted forms (for example *I'm, don't*) and full forms (for example *I am, do not*) are possible. Normally both are correct.

future passive *Tomorrow your bicycle will be stolen.*

+	*I* ***will be*** *woken*	*you* ***will be*** *woken*	*he/she/it* ***will be*** *woken* etc
?	***will*** *I* ***be*** *woken?*	***will*** *you* ***be*** *woken?*	***will*** *he/she/it* ***be*** *woken?* etc
-	*I* ***will not be*** *woken*	*you* ***will not be*** *woken*	*he/she/it* ***will not be*** *woken* etc
	For contractions (*I'll, won't* etc), see page 301.		

We use the **future passive** like the future active (see page 39), to say things that we **think, guess** or **know** about the future, or to ask questions about the future.

One day all the work ***will be done*** *by machines.* *Where* ***will*** *the match* ***be played****?*

1 Make future passive sentences with the verbs from the box.

clean	close ✓	finish	open	send	speak

▸ The motorway ......will be closed...... for three days.
1 The museum .... by the Queen.
2 One day English .... everywhere.
3 This job .... in a few days.
4 Your room .... while you're out.
5 Your tickets .... to you next week.

2 Make future passive negatives and questions.

▸ 'The football match ......won't be played...... on Saturday.' (*play*)
'When ......will it be played?......' 'On Sunday.'
1 'The visitors .... to the hotel by bus.' (*take*)
'How .... there?' 'By taxi.'
2 'The new library .... in the Central Square.' (*build*)
'Where ....' 'Behind the Police Station.'
3 'English .... at the conference.' (*speak*)
'What language ....' 'Chinese.'

3 Make five future passive sentences from the table.

Next year Tomorrow Next week Tonight One day In 20 years	your bed / bicycle / breakfast / food / clothes / dinner / glasses / house / room / work	clean / cook / do / eat / make / send to Canada / steal / wash / take away	by	a small man in a raincoat / a black cat / two old ladies / a beautiful woman / people from another world / the President / a big dog / your old friend Peter / a machine

Tomorrow your bicycle will be stolen by your old friend Peter.
....
....
....
....
....

simple past passive *I was stopped by a policeman.*

+	*I **was** woken*	*you **were** woken*	*he/she/it **was** woken* etc
?	***was** I woken?*	***were** you woken?*	***was** he/she/it woken?* etc
–	*I **was not** woken*	*you **were not** woken*	*he/she/it **was not** woken* etc
	For contractions (*wasn't* etc), see page 301.		

We use the **simple past passive** like the simple past active, for **complete finished actions and events** (see page 47).

*This table **was made** by my grandfather.* *Was the letter **signed**?* *We **weren't met** at the door.*

1 Complete the sentences with *was/were*.

1 The fire.................. seen in Renton, a kilometre away.
2 Most of the matches.................. won by Indian teams.
3 These keys.................. found in the changing room yesterday – are they yours?
4 We couldn't find the station, but we.................. helped by a very kind woman.
5 I.................. stopped by a policeman in Green Road this morning.
6 Yesterday a man.................. caught trying to burn down the Town Hall.

2 Put simple past passive verbs into these sentences.

1 Our passports .... by a tall woman in a uniform. (*take*)
2 These books .... in the classroom on Monday. (*leave*)
3 I don't think this room .... yesterday. (*clean*)
4 We .... at the airport by a driver from the university. (*meet*)
5 Nobody .... what was happening. (*tell*)
6 He .... away to school when he was twelve. (*send*)

3 Make simple past passive negatives and questions.

► 'We ...weren't paid... when we finished the work.' (*not pay*)
'When ...were you paid?...' 'Two months later.'
1 'My father .... in England.' (*not educate*)
'Where ....' 'In Germany.'
2 'The letters .... on Tuesday.' (*not post*)
'When ....' 'On Thursday.'
3 'This .... in butter.' (*not cook*)
'How ....' 'In margarine.'
4 'My suit .... in England.' (*not make*)
'Where ....' 'In Hong Kong.'
5 'The restaurant bill .... in cash.' (*not pay*)
'How ....' 'With a credit card.'

We use a past passive structure – ***to be born*** – to give somebody's date or place of birth.

*I **was born** in 1964.* (NOT ~~*I born in 1964.*~~ NOT ~~*I am born in 1964.*~~) *My sisters **were born** in Egypt.*

4 Write a sentence about your date and place of birth.

I ....

In some answers, both contracted forms (for example *I'm, don't*) and full forms (for example *I am, do not*) are possible. Normally both are correct.

present progressive passive *It's being cleaned.*

+	*I* ***am being*** *watched*	*you* ***are being*** *watched*	*he/she/it* ***is being*** *watched* etc
?	***am*** *I* ***being*** *watched?*	***are*** *you* ***being*** *watched?*	***is*** *he/she/it* ***being*** *watched?* etc
-	*I* ***am not being*** *watched*	*you* ***are not being*** *watched*	*he/she/it* ***is not being*** *watched* etc
	For contractions (*I'm, isn't* etc), see pages 2 and 301.		

We use the **present progressive passive** like the present progressive active, for things that are happening **now** (see page 24), or for things that are **planned for the future** (see page 38).

'Where's the carpet?' 'It's ***being cleaned****.'* *When* ***are*** *you* ***being seen*** *by the doctor?*

1 Questions and answers. Use the words in the box to complete answers to the questions. Use the present progressive passive.

the grass / cut ✓	he / watch	I / send	it / clean	it / paint	it / rebuild	my hair / cut
she / interview	the engine / repair	my watch / repair	we / follow			

▶ 'Can we play on the football pitch?' 'No, *the grass is being cut.*'
1 'Can't you wear your blue suit tonight?' 'No, ...'
2 'Did Alice get that new job?' 'Not yet – .... today.'
3 'What time is it?' 'Sorry, I don't know: ....'
4 'Why the big smile?' .... to Hawaii for a week.'
5 I usually read a magazine while ....
6 I think .... by a police car.
7 'Where's your car?' 'At the garage. ....'
8 The school is closed this year. ....
9 George doesn't know that .... by the police.
10 I can't use my office this week because ....

2 Imagine you are in a busy hotel at midday. Make sentences to say what is being done.

▶ *(beds / make)* *Beds are being made.*
1 *(bills / pay)* ....
2 *(coffee / make)* ....
3 *(drinks / serve)* ....
4 *(food / prepare)* ....
5 *(baggage / bring down)* ....
6 *(money / change)* ....
7 *(new guests / welcome)* ....
8 *(reservations / take)* ....
9 *(phones / answer)* ....
10 *(rooms / clean)* ....

present perfect passive *The house has been sold.*

+	*I* **have been** *seen*	*you* **have been** *seen*	*he/she/it* **has been** *seen* etc
?	**have** *I* **been** *seen?*	**have** *you* **been** *seen?*	**has** *he/she/it* **been** *seen?* etc
–	*I* **have not been** *seen*	*you* **have not been** *seen*	*he/she/it* **has not been** *seen* etc
	For contractions (*I've* etc), see page 301.		

We use the **present perfect passive** like the present perfect active (see pages 60-65), to talk about past actions and events which are **important now** – for example, when we give people news.

The house on the corner **has been sold.** *We* **haven't been invited** *to Anna's party.*

1 News: put the verbs into the present perfect passive.

▶ A new university ...has been opened... in Kew today by the Prince of Wales. (*open*)
1 Lord Retlaw .... for drunk driving. (*arrest*)
2 An old painting from a school in Wales .... for $250,000 by an American museum. (*buy*)
3 An 18-year-old soldier .... in an accident in Devon. (*kill*)
4 The two lost children .... alive and well in a London park. (*find*)
5 An unknown actor .... to star in the new film of 'Macbeth'. (*choose*)
6 The old hospital in the town centre .... (*close*)
7 'What's the problem?' 'My bicycle ....' (*steal*)
8 I .... to write something for the local newspaper. (*ask*)
9 All the papers for next week's meeting .... (*lose*)
10 Everybody in the class .... to Stacey's party. (*invite*)

2 'It's never been done.' Make a sentence for each picture.

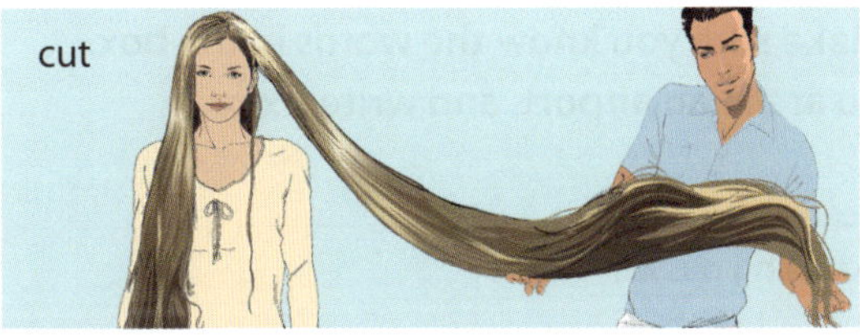

▶ ...It's never been cut....

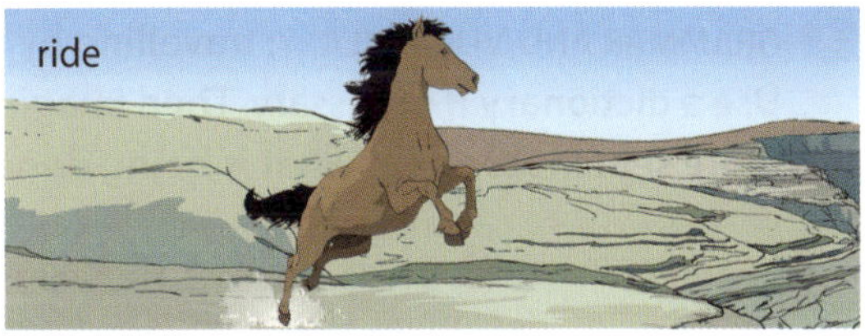

1 ....

2 ....

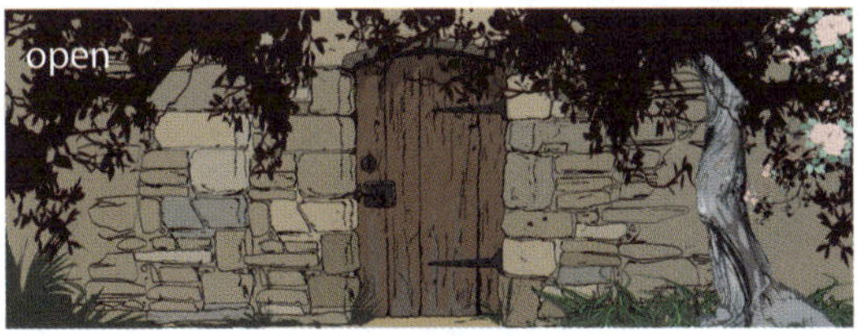

3 ....

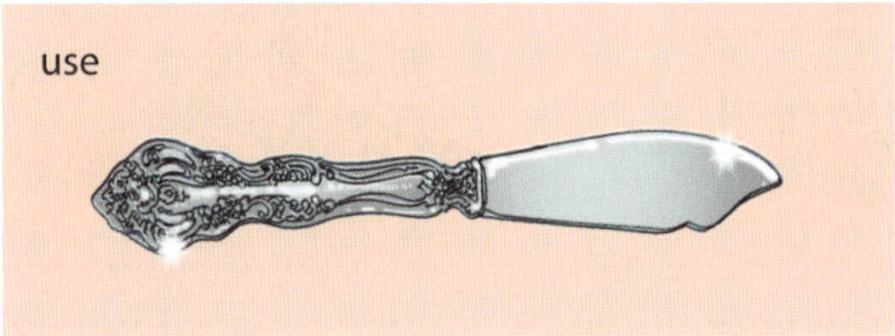

4 ....

5 ....

In some answers, both contracted forms (for example *I'm*, *don't*) and full forms (for example *I am*, *do not*) are possible. Normally both are correct.

passives: more practice

1 Tenses. Put in simple present, simple past or future passive verbs.

- ▶ 'Frankenstein' ..was written.. by Mary Shelley. (*write*)
- ▶ The repairs ..will be finished.. before next Tuesday. (*finish*)

1 Butter .... from milk. (*make*)
2 Last night two men .... in a fight in a nightclub. (*kill*)
3 One day all our work .... by machines. (*do*)
4 English .... as a second language by millions of people. (*speak*)
5 This computer .... in Japan. (*make*)
6 All the footballers .... by a doctor before the match last Sunday. (*examine*)
7 This room .... every day. (*clean*)
8 You .... of the test results as soon as possible. (*inform*)
9 The new road .... in July next year. (*open*)
10 Diamonds .... in several countries in Africa. (*find*)

2 Present progressive passive. Imagine that you are in a busy hotel at one o'clock. All the hotel staff are on strike (they have stopped work) because they want more money. Write sentences about six things that are not being done. Some useful words:

baggage	bills	coffee	drinks	food	money
new guests	reservations	rooms	telephones		

Beds are not being made.

....

3 GRAMMAR AND VOCABULARY: travelling by air. Make sure you know the words in the box. Use a dictionary if necessary. Then imagine you are in an airport, and write six or more sentences about what is being done.

SUBJECTS:	arriving passengers, baggage ✓, boarding passes, cars, departures, passports, reservations, tickets
VERBS:	announce, check, make, meet, park, print, sell, x-ray ✓

Baggage is being x-rayed.

....

4 Tenses. Put in present perfect passive or present progressive passive verbs.

▶ 'Is the Army Museum still in Green Street?' 'No, it has been closed.' (*close*)
1 Don't look now, but I think we .... (*follow*)
2 Hello, police? I'd like to report a theft. My handbag .... (*steal*)
3 'Why did you take the bus?' 'My car ....' (*repair*)
4 I think someone's been in my room – some books .... (*move*)
5 'There's nobody here.' 'No, all the students .... home.' (*send*)
6 'When .... you ....' 'Tomorrow morning.' (*interview*)
7 A group of suspected terrorists .... by the police. (*arrest*)
8 Another group of suspected terrorists ...., but they .... (*not arrest, watch*)
9 The hospital will be closed for two years, while it .... (*rebuild*)
10 James .... to join the local football team. (*ask*)

5 Grammar in a text. Put in simple present active or passive verbs.

© The Diana Fossey Gorilla Fund International 2001

Gorillas (▶ *find*) are found in several countries in Central Africa. They are about 1.6 metres tall, and they (1 *cover*) .... with black or brown hair. Gorillas' lives (2 *spend*) .... in groups. Each group has five to ten gorillas in it. The gorillas in a group (3 *walk*) .... about 0.5 to 1.0 km per day, looking for food. They (4 *not eat*) .... all the leaves in one part of the forest before moving on; some leaves (5 *leave*) .... on the trees and plants.
At night gorillas (6 *sleep*) .... in nests; these nests (7 *make*) .... of branches and leaves. The number of gorillas living in Africa today (8 *not know*) .... but it is certain that this number is getting smaller. Why? Because in the countries where the gorillas (9 *live*) .... more and more trees (10 *cut down*) .... every year.

6 Internet exercise. Use a search engine (e.g. Google) to find short simple sentences with the following verbs. Write the sentences.

"are made" ....
"is spoken" ....
"will be spent" ....
"are being built" ....
"have been seen" ....
"were given" ....
"were sent" ....
"was arrested" ....

pronunciation for grammar → e-book

passives: revision test

1 Circle the correct passive or active verb form.

▶ This book *written* / *was written* by my uncle.
1 Derek *posted* / *was posted* his letter to the university today.
2 We did a lot of work for the school, but we *didn't pay* / *weren't paid*.
3 My friend Douglas *speaks* / *is spoken* seven languages.
4 The letter H *doesn't pronounce* / *isn't pronounced* in French.
5 A new hospital *will build* / *will be built* in the town centre.
6 You can't come in here – the room *is cleaning* / *is being cleaned*.
7 We *have invited* / *have been invited* to John's party tonight.
8 This sauce *makes* / *is made* with oil and vinegar.
9 French *speaks* / *is spoken* in Belgium.
10 John *broke* / *is broken* his leg last week.

2 Correct (✓) or not (✗)?

▶ English is spoken in New Zealand. ..✓...
▶ I am born in Manchester. ..✗...
1 I was studied German for three years. ......
2 Emma invited to a party by her boss. ......
3 How is written your name? ......
4 'Where's your coat?' 'It's being cleaned.' ......
5 Our car has been stolen. ......
6 When is that window broken? ......
7 This book was written from my father. ......
8 I was taken to the opera by a friend of mine. ......
9 The new road will finished in July. ......
10 Our house was built in 1850. ......

3 Put in the correct passive tenses.

▶ 'The Birds' ..was directed.. by Alfred Hitchcock. (*direct*)
▶ You ..will be paid.. next week. (*pay*)
1 'Is the library still downstairs?' 'No, it ....' (*move*)
2 A new hospital .... here next April. (*open*)
3 Somebody has been in my handbag. Some money .... (*take*)
4 'Where's your black sweater?' 'It ....' (*wash*)
5 You .... your examination results before the weekend. (*tell*)
6 'My car ....' 'Well, tell the police.' (*steal*)
7 This phone .... in China. (*make*)
8 Spanish .... in most of South America. (*speak*)
9 The windows .... nearly every week. (*clean*)
10 I .... to help you. What can I do? (*ask*)
11 There was a fight at the football match on Saturday, and one man .... (*kill*)
12 Do you think all translation .... by computers one day? (*do*)
13 'When .... the match ....?' 'Tomorrow.' (*play*)
14 Three computers .... from the school since Christmas. (*steal*)
15 The factory closed suddenly last week, and all the workers .... away. (*send*)
16 This kind of cheese .... from goats' milk. (*make*)
17 Alice .... by a car the other day, and her leg .... (*hit*; *break*)
18 Your letter .... now – it will be ready in five minutes. (*translate*)
19 It says in today's paper that gold .... in Scotland. (*find*)
20 'Have you done those letters?' 'Not yet. They .... by five o'clock.' (*finish*)

In some answers, both contracted forms (for example *I'm*, *don't*) and full forms (for example *I am*, *do not*) are possible. Normally both are correct.

SECTION 8 questions and negatives

grammar summary

To make **questions**, we normally put an **auxiliary verb** (*be, have, can* etc) **before the subject.**

John has gone. → ***Has John** gone?* *She's leaving.* → *When **is she** leaving?*

To make **negatives**, we put ***not*** or ***n't*** **after an auxiliary verb.**

*John **is** working.* → *John **is not** working.* *I **could** swim* → *I **couldn't** swim.*

If there is **no other auxiliary** verb, we use ***do***.

*I **live** in Manchester.* → *Where **do** you live?* *He said 'Hello'.* → *What **did** he say?*

She likes cold weather. → *She **doesn't** like cold weather.*

We do **not** use ***do*** when a **question word** is the **subject**.

***What** happened?* (NOT ~~*What did happen?*~~)

Who are you?

Who were you talking to
when I came in just now
and you put down the phone?
Who were you thinking about
when I asked you
and asked you again
and you answered 'Why, no one'?
Who were you with last night
when you came home late
and said you'd been walking alone?

What was I hoping for
that first day
when I knocked on your door?
What was I thinking about
when I first asked you out?
Who was I looking at
when I first sat looking at you?

Who are you?

I didn't do the housework

I didn't feed the goldfish,
I didn't make the bed,
I didn't study algebra.
I watched a film instead.

I didn't practise on the flute,
I didn't write to Jean,
I didn't visit Aunty May.
I read a magazine.

I didn't do the housework.
I started. Then I quit,
and wrote a poem just to say
I love you. This is it.

yes/no questions *Is the taxi here? Do I need a visa?*

AM I? HAVE YOU? CAN SHE? DO YOU? DOES HE?

All ***yes/no* questions** begin with a **verb**.
To make questions: put an auxiliary verb before the subject.
(Auxiliary verbs are *be* (*am, are* etc), *have/has/had, will, would, can, could, shall, should, may, might* and *must*.)

STATEMENT +:	*The taxi is coming.*	*Ann has arrived.*	*The train will be late.*	*You can pay.*
QUESTION ?:	*Is the taxi coming?*	*Has Ann arrived?*	*Will the train be late?*	*Can you pay?*

1 Put the words in the right order to make questions.

- ▶ you ready are .... Are you ready?
- ▶ telephoned she has Mary .... Has she telephoned Mary?
- ▶ swim your brother can .... Can your brother swim?

1 tired are you ....
2 he at is home ....
3 go must now you ....
4 Spanish they speak can ....
5 tomorrow Derek be here will ....
6 Aunt Ruth will arrive by train ....
7 forgotten her keys she has ....
8 your sister is playing tennis ....
9 coffee some like you would ....
10 your home secretary gone has ....

If there is **no auxiliary verb:** put *do/does/did* before the subject and use the **infinitive** (without *to*).

STATEMENT +: *I need a visa.*
QUESTION ?: *Do I need a visa?* (**NOT** ~~*Need I a visa?*~~, **NOT** ~~*Do I to need a visa?*~~)

STATEMENT +: *John wants to go home.*
QUESTION ?: *Does John want to go home?* (**NOT** ~~*Does John wants to go home?*~~)

STATEMENT +: *She knew Naomi.*
QUESTION ?: *Did she know Naomi?* (**NOT** ~~*Did she knew Naomi?*~~)

2 Make questions with *you*.

You want to know if somebody:

- ▶ understands .... Do you understand?
- ▶ called you .... Did you call me?

1 drinks coffee at bedtime ....
2 likes classical music ....
3 knows your friend Andrew ....
4 went skiing last winter ....
5 works in London ....
6 lives in a flat or a house ....
7 watches a lot of TV ....
8 remembered to buy bread ....
9 saw Barbara last weekend ....
10 plays tennis ....

3 Make questions with *she*.

You want to know if somebody:

▶ plays football .... Does she play football?
1 speaks Arabic ....
2 knows Mr Peters ....
3 works at home ....
4 lived in Birmingham ....
5 went home last week ....
6 plays the piano ....
7 rides horses ....
8 likes working with children ....
9 travelled a lot last year ....
10 drives to work ....

We **don't** put ***do*** with **other auxiliary verbs.**

***Can you** swim?* (NOT ~~*Do you can swim?*~~)

4 Choose the correct question.

▶ (**A**) Will you be ready soon? **B** Do you will be ready soon?
▶ **A** Live you in London? (**B**) Do you live in London? **C** Are you live in London?
1 **A** Do you are tired? **B** Do you tired? **C** Are you tired?
2 **A** Do you must go now? **B** Must you go now?
3 **A** Do you speak Japanese? **B** Speak you Japanese? **C** Are you speak Japanese?
4 **A** Do you have been to New York? **B** Have you been to New York?
5 **A** Were you go to work by car? **B** Did you go to work by car? **C** Went you to work by car?
6 **A** Can she sing? **B** Does she can sing?
7 **A** Is Judy looking for a job? **B** Does Judy looking for a job? **C** Is Judy look for a job?
8 **A** You said something? **B** Did you said something? **C** Did you say something?

Only put **one verb** before the **subject**.

***Is her father** working today?* (NOT ~~*Is working her father today?*~~)
***Has your brother** got children?* (NOT ~~*Has got your brother children?*~~)
***Did those people** telephone again?* (NOT ~~*Did telephone those people again?*~~)

5 Put the verbs in the right place to make questions.

▶ Are / your parents / to dinner (*coming*) .... Are your parents coming to dinner?
1 Did / the police / the drug dealers (*catch*) ....
2 Have / Lucy and Felicia / from their holiday (*come back*) ....
3 When do / English children / school (*start*) ....
4 What is / that man / in the garden (*doing*) ....
5 Are / the buses / next week (*running*) ....
6 Has / the film (*started*) ....
7 Has / John's letter / yet (*arrived*) ....
8 Is /Alicia / today (*working*) ....
9 Does / Paul / your girlfriend (*know*) ....
10 Why is / Kate (*cry*) ....

→ For more practice with present questions, past questions etc, see Sections 2–5.

→ For question tags like *It's late, isn't it?*, see pages 288–289.

In some answers, both contracted forms (for example *I'm, don't*) and full forms (for example *I am, do not*) are possible. Normally both are correct.

question words *When will you see her?*

WHERE IS ...? WHEN CAN ...? WHY DOES ...?

Questions with ***where, when, why*** etc normally have the same word order as ***yes/no* questions** (pages 104–105).
We put ***am/are/is/was/were*** or another **auxiliary verb** (*have, will, can* etc) before the **subject**.

STATEMENT +:	*Anna is in Russia.*	*I will see her on Tuesday.*
QUESTION ?:	*Where is Anna?*	*When will you see her?* (NOT ~~*When you will see her?*~~)

If there is **no other auxiliary verb**, we use ***do/does/did*** + **infinitive** (without *to*).

STATEMENT +:	*He likes his job.*	*I came here to learn English.*
QUESTION ?:	*How does he like his job?*	*Why did you come here?* (NOT ~~*Why you came here?*~~)

1 Make questions with the words in the boxes.

how	when ✓	when	where ✓	where	why

▶ (*you staying?*) 'Where are you staying?' .... 'At the Park Hotel.'
▶ (*you arrive?*) 'When did you arrive?' .... 'Last night.'
1 (*you here?*) .... 'To see Scotland.'
2 (*you been today?*) .... 'To Edinburgh.'
3 (*you going to Glasgow?*) .... 'Next weekend.'
4 (*you like Scotland?*) .... 'It's great!'

how	when	when	where	why

5 (*you come here?*) .... 'By car.'
6 (*you come by car?*) .... 'I like driving.'
7 (*you live?*) .... 'In Germany.'
8 (*you leaving?*) .... 'Next Tuesday.'
9 (*we see you again?*) .... 'I'll be back next summer.'

We often ask questions with ***how*** + **adjective/adverb.**

How old *is your sister?* ***How tall*** *are you?* ***How fast*** *can you run?*

2 Here are some common expressions with *how*. Use them to complete the questions.

How old ...? ✓	How far ...?	How long ...?	How tall ...?
How big ...?	How fast ...?	How often ...?	How well ...?

▶ How old are .... you?' '37 next birthday.'
1 '........ your house from here?' 'About 5 km.'
2 '........ John?' 'Very tall – nearly two metres.'
3 '........ she driving?' 'The police say she was doing 160 km/h.'
4 '........ you see your parents?' 'Every week.'
5 '........ Petra's flat?' 'Very small – just one room and a bathroom.'
6 '........ you stay in China?' 'I was there for six months.'
7 '........ you speak Spanish?' 'Not very well.'

Some questions begin with ***what*** **+ noun.**

What time *is the film?* ***What time*** *does the train leave?* (NOT USUALLY ~~*At what time ...?*~~)
What colour *are her eyes?* (NOT ~~*What colour have ...?*~~) ***What colour*** *is your car?*
What size *are you?* (buying clothes) ***What size*** *would you like?*
What sort of *books do you read?* ***What sort of*** *films do you like?* (OR ***What kind of*** *...?*)

3 Put the beginnings and ends together, and put in an expression with *What ...*

0 ...What time... does her plane arrive?'	A 'Eight o'clock, if it's not late.' ...0..
1 '................ is the baby's hair?'	B '................ , small or large?' ......
2 '................ music do you play?'	C 'She hasn't got any.' ......
3 'I'd like a packet of rice, please.'	D 'Pop, mostly.' ......
4 'Can I borrow one of your sweaters?'	E 'I don't remember – it was very late.' ......
5 '................ holidays do you prefer?'	F 'Sure. .... would you like? Blue? Green?' ......
6 '................ did you get home?'	G 'Extra large.' ......
7 'I need a sweater.' '................ are you?'	H 'We usually go to the mountains.' ......

To ask for **descriptions**, we often use ***What is/are/was/were ... like?***

*'Where have you been?' 'In Ireland.' '**What was** the weather **like**?' 'OK.'*
*'**What's** your new boyfriend **like**?' 'He's very nice.'*
*'My brother writes detective stories.' 'Yes? **What are** they **like**?' 'Not very good, really.'*

4 Make questions with *What ... like?*, using expressions from the box.

your new girlfriend	your new house	your new car	your new job
your new boss ✓	your new school	your new neighbours	

▶ ...What's your new boss like?... 'He's not very good at his job.'
1 .... 'She's a lot of fun.'
2 .... 'Very noisy. They have parties all night.'
3 .... 'OK – it's a bit slow.'
4 .... 'Great – we've got much more room.'
5 .... 'It's interesting. I travel a lot.'
6 .... 'The teachers aren't much good.'

GRAMMAR AND VOCABULARY: **some more useful questions**

Where are you from? *Where do you come from?* (NOT ~~*From where ...?*~~ – see page 111)
How long have you been here? *How long are you here for?* (= 'Until when ...?')
How long does it take to get to London? *How long does it take to learn English?*
How do you spell that word? *How do you pronounce this word?*

→ For questions with *who*, *what* and *which*, see page 108.

I keep six honest serving-men
(They taught me all I knew):
Their names are What and Why and When
And How and Where and Who.

(Rudyard Kipling)

question-word subjects *Who phoned? What happened?*

When ***who*** and ***what*** are **subjects**, we make questions **without *do/does/did***. Compare:

'Who^{SUBJ} *phoned?' 'Mike*^{SUBJ} *phoned.'* (NOT ~~*'Who did phone?'*~~)
'Who^{OBJ} ***did*** *you see?' 'I saw Mike*^{OBJ}*.'*
'What^{SUBJ} *happened?' 'Something*^{SUBJ} *terrible happened.'* (NOT ~~*'What did happen?'*~~)
'What^{OBJ} ***did*** *he say?' 'He said something*^{OBJ} *terrible.'*

The same thing happens when subjects begin with ***which***, ***what***, or ***how much/many***.

Which team won? (NOT ~~*Which team did win?*~~) *What country won the World Cup in 1966?*
How many people work here? (COMPARE *How many people*^{OBJ} ***did*** *you*^{SUBJ} *see?*)

1 Circle the correct form.

▶ Who *lives* / *does live* in that house? (lives)
▶ What *happened* / *did happen* to Joe? (happened)
1 Who *plays* / *does play* the piano?
2 What *made* / *did make* that noise?
3 Who *married she?* / *did she marry?*
4 What *means this word?* / *does this word mean?*
5 What *said you?* / *did you say?*
6 Who *told* / *did tell you?*

2 Make present (PR) or past (PA) questions.

▶ car / belong / to Mary (*which* – PR) Which car belongs to Mary?
▶ you / buy / glasses (*how many* – PA) How many glasses did you buy?
1 people / come / to her party (*how many* – PA) ....
2 Peter / catch / train (*which* – PA) ....
3 bus / go / to the station (*which* – PR) ....
4 Douglas / speak / languages (*how many* – PR) ....
5 Alice / like / music (*what sort* – PR) ....
6 music / keep / the baby quiet (*what sort* – PR) ....

3 Look at the picture and complete the sentences.

▶ Who loves Fred? Alice and Mary.
1 Who does Fred love? ....
2 .... Ann? ....
3 .... love? Joe.
4 .... Alice? ....
5 .... love? Mary.
6 .... love? Ann.
7 .... Nobody.

4 Can you write four more questions and answers about the picture?

1 ....
2 ....
3 ....
4 ....

5 Make questions. Ask about the words in italics.

► (a) John broke *the window*. (b) *John* broke the window.
(a) What did John break? (b) Who broke the window?

1 (a) Melissa bought *a coat*. (b) *Melissa* bought a coat.
....

2 (a) The bus hit *that tree*. (b) *The bus* hit that tree.
....

3 (a) *Rose* lost the office keys. (b) Rose lost *the office keys*.
....

4 (a) Paul teaches *Arabic*. (b) *Paul* teaches Arabic.
....

5 (a) *Mike* hates computers. (b) Mike hates *computers*.
....

6 Write questions about the pictures, using the words in the box. Do you know the answers? (They are at the bottom of the page.)

build ✓	build	paint	first reach	write

► Who built the Eiffel Tower?
1 ....
2 ....
3 ....
4 ....

► The Eiffel Tower

1 The North Pole

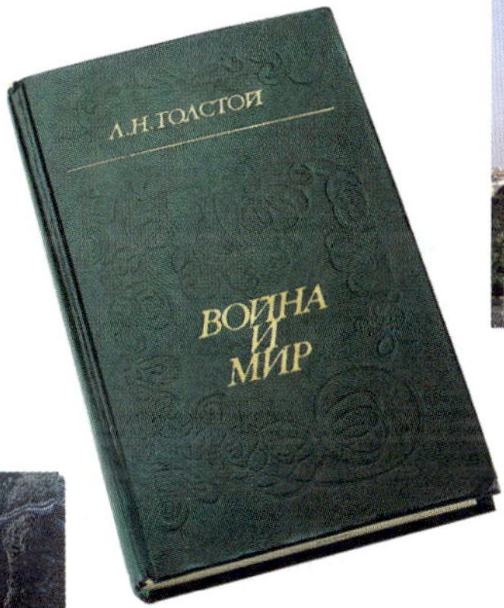

2 *War and Peace*

3 The Great Wall of China

4 *Sunflowers*

7 Write questions about books, plays or songs. Ask some people.

Who wrote ....
....

→ For the difference between *which* and *what*, see page 322. For *whom*, see page 322.

► Gustave Eiffel. 1 Robert Peary in 1909 2 Leo Tolstoy 3 The emperor Shi Huangdi (and a lot of other people) 4 Van Gogh

In some answers, both contracted forms (for example *I'm, don't*) and full forms (for example *I am, do not*) are possible. Normally both are correct.

questions with long subjects *Are Ann and her mother and father coming?*

Be careful when questions have **long subjects**. The word order does not change.

Is	*Ann*	*coming tomorrow?*
Are	*Ann and her mother*	*coming tomorrow?*
Are	*Ann and her mother and father and Uncle George*	*coming tomorrow?* (NOT ~~*Are coming tomorrow Ann ...?*~~)

What time will the bus for the dinner and dance leave? (NOT ~~*What time the bus ... will leave?*~~)
Have Bill and Jenny and their children arrived? (NOT ~~*Have arrived Bill and Jenny ...?*~~)
Where did the President and his wife stay? (NOT ~~*Where stayed...?*~~ OR ~~*Where did stay ...?*~~)
Is the food for the children's party ready? (NOT ~~*Is ready ...?*~~)

1 Make *yes/no* questions.

▶ The boss's secretary travels a lot.
Does the boss's secretary travel a lot?

1 Your sister Caroline is talking to the police.
....

2 All the people here understand Spanish.
....

3 Most of the football team played well.
....

4 The man at the table in the corner is asleep.
....

2 Make questions with question words.

▶ The President and her husband live in Madrid.
Where do the President and her husband live?

1 A ticket for Saturday's concert costs €15.
How much ....

2 The film about skiing in New Zealand starts at 8.00.
What time ....

3 The second word in the first sentence means 'kind'.
What ....

4 The man in the flat downstairs wants to change his job.
Why ....

3 Put the words in the correct order.

1 laughing / why / all those people / are / ?
....

2 is / eating / that big black dog / what / ?
....

3 going / everybody in your family / to Scotland / for Christmas / is / ?
....

4 what game / those children / playing / are / ?
....

5 Lola and her friends / studying / are / where / ?
....

6 those people over there / French / are / speaking / ?
....

prepositions in questions *Who did you go with?*

We often put a **preposition** (*with, at, for* etc) at the end of a question with ***Who*** …? or ***What*** …?, especially in spoken English.

*Who did you go **with**?* (More natural than *With whom did you go?*) *Who is that letter **for**?*
*What are you looking **at**?* *What's she talking **about**?*

We also ask questions with ***Where*** … ***from****?* and ***Where*** … ***to****?*

*'Where do you come **from**?'* (OR *'Where are you **from**?'*) *'Malaysia.'* *Where shall I send the letter **to**?*

1 Put in prepositions from the box.

about	about	for ✓	for	from	from	in	on	to	to	to	with	with

▶ What are you looking ..for.........?
1 Who did Ann send the money ....?
2 Where is your wife ....?
3 What's your book ....?
4 What are you thinking ....?
5 What subjects are you interested ....?
6 Where does Franz come ....?
7 Who are you in love .... now?
8 What are you all waiting ....?
9 Who are you writing ....?
10 Who are you going on holiday ....?
11 Who shall I send the money ....?
12 Which flight are you travelling ....?

2 Write questions beginning *Who/What* and ending with prepositions.

▶ ..Who did you buy your car from?.......... 'I bought my car from Henry.'
1 .... 'I'm thinking about life.'
2 .... 'Alice works for my aunt.'
3 .... 'We were talking about you.'
4 .... 'I'm interested in most things.'
5 .... 'We're looking at that aeroplane.'
6 .... 'I stayed with Eric.'
7 .... 'I work with Sylvia.'
8 .... 'I spent the money on travel.'
9 .... 'The film was about Russia.'
10 .... 'You can get tickets from my office.'

In conversation, we often ask short questions with ***Who/What/Where*** + **preposition**.

'I'm going camping.' ***'Who with?'*** *'William wants to talk to you.'* ***'What about?'***

3 Complete the questions with one word.

1 'I'm thinking.' '............... about?'
2 'I've got a letter.' '............... from?'
3 'She hit him.' '............... with?'
4 'She's getting married.' '............... to?'
5 'I'm going to America.' '............... with?'
6 'Jamie's writing a book.' '............... about?'
7 'I'm writing postcards.' 'Who ....?'
8 'I've bought a present.' 'Who ....?'
9 'Jane has arrived.' '............... from?'
10 'I've got a question.' '............... about?'
11 'Send this box.' 'Where ....?'
12 'I'm making a cake.' 'Who ....?'

In some answers, both contracted forms (for example *I'm, don't*) and full forms (for example *I am, do not*) are possible. Normally both are correct.

negatives *Dogs can't fly. I don't know why.*

AM NOT HAVE NOT WILL NOT CANNOT DO NOT

To make negative sentences: put ***not*** after an **auxiliary verb**.
(Auxiliary verbs are: *be* (*am* etc), *have/has/had, will, would, can, could, shall, should, may, might, must.*)

*It **is not** raining.* *I **have not** seen Bill.* *She **cannot** understand me.*

In **conversation** we usually use **contractions** (see page 301):
aren't isn't wasn't weren't haven't hasn't hadn't won't (= 'will not') *wouldn't*
can't couldn't shan't shouldn't mightn't mustn't
We say *I'm not*, NOT ~~*I amn't*~~. We can also say *you're not* (= 'you aren't'), *he's not, she's not* etc.

*It **isn't** / It**'s not** raining.* *We **weren't** at home.* *I **haven't** seen Ben.*
*She **can't** understand me.* *You **mustn't** tell anybody.* *I**'m not** ready.*

1 Make negative sentences. Use contractions.

▸ Dogs can swim. (*fly*) Dogs can't fly.
1 Milk is white. (*red*) ....
2 The children are at school. (*at home*) ....
3 Max has been to Japan. (*Egypt*) ....
4 You must give this letter to Erica. (*her mother*) ....
5 I'll be here tomorrow. (*in the office*) ....
6 I could talk when I was two years old. (*swim*) ....
7 We were in London yesterday. (*Birmingham*) ....
8 I'm Scottish. (*English*) ....

2 Write five things that you can't do. Here are some suggestions.

dance	draw	drive	play chess/bridge etc	play the piano/guitar etc
remember faces	remember names	ride a horse	sing	
speak French/Chinese etc	understand maths			

▸ I can't speak German.
1 ....
2 ....
3 ....
4 ....
5 ....

'There are three things that I can't remember: names, faces, and I've forgotten the other.'

3 Write five things that you probably won't do next week. Here are some suggestions.

go to New York	get married	get rich	play football	become President
write a poem	buy a car	make a cake	read Shakespeare	climb Mount Everest

▸ I probably won't go to Paris next week.
1 ....
2 ....
3 ....
4 ....
5 ....

If there is no auxiliary verb, we use **do/does/did** + **not/n't** + infinitive (without *to*).

I like → *I* ***don't*** *like* *She knows* → *She* ***doesn't*** *know* (NOT ~~*She doesn't knows*~~)
He arrived → *He* ***did not*** *arrive* (NOT ~~*He did not arrived*~~) *It rained* → *It* ***didn't*** *rain*

4 Make negative sentences.

▶ Cats eat meat. (*potatoes*) Cats don't eat potatoes.
▶ Cervantes wrote 'Don Quixote'. (*Mozart*) Mozart didn't write 'Don Quixote'.
1 Shakespeare lived in London. (*New York*) ....
2 Dictionaries tell you about words. (*phone books*) ....
3 The earth goes round the sun. (*round the moon*) ....
4 Most Algerians speak Arabic. (*Russian*) ....
5 Fridges keep food cold. (*cookers*) ....
6 The Second World War ended in 1945. (*1955*) ....
7 John knows my parents. (*my sister*) ....

5 Use expressions from the two boxes, and write eight things that you don't do.

buy socks dance go to sleep play football play the violin ride a bicycle speak English sing study mathematics write poetry

after breakfast at Christmas at school in London in the bath in the middle of the night in the middle of the road in the sea on the bus on the telephone on Tuesdays

▶ I don't buy books in London.
1 ....
2 ....
3 ....
4 ....
5 ....
6 ....
7 ....
8 ....

6 Complete these negative sentences. Use *aren't, haven't, doesn't* etc.

1 'What's the time?' 'I .... know.'
2 'What was the film like? 'It .... very good.'
3 'Would Stella like some coffee?' 'No, she .... drink coffee.'
4 I .... seen William for weeks. Is he OK?
5 Pat and Jim .... very happy with their new car.
6 'Can I see you tomorrow?' 'I .... be here. How about Tuesday?'
7 'Was the lesson any good?' 'I .... understand a word.'
8 She .... buy the coat; it was too expensive.
9 The baby .... got much hair.
10 'Can we go?' 'In a minute. I .... ready.'

→ For more practice with present negatives, past negatives etc, see Sections 2–5.

NOTE: one negative word is enough (see page 115).

Nobody understands me. (NOT ~~*Nobody doesn't understand me.*~~)
She never phones me. (NOT ~~*She doesn't never phone me.*~~)

In some answers, both contracted forms (for example *I'm, don't*) and full forms (for example *I am, do not*) are possible. Normally both are correct.

Level 2

not and *no*

We use ***not*** to make a **word, expression** or **clause negative.**

__Not surprisingly__, we missed the train. (NOT ~~*No surprisingly*~~ *…*)
The students went on strike, but __not__ the teachers. (NOT *…* ~~*no the teachers.*~~)
I can see you tomorrow, but __not__ on Thursday.
I have __not__ received his answer.

We use ***no*** with a **noun** or ***-ing* form** to mean **'not any'** or **'not a/an'** (see page 115).

__No teachers__ went on strike. (= *There __weren't any__ teachers on strike.*)
I've got __no Thursdays__ free this term. (= … ***not any*** *Thursdays* …)
I telephoned, but there was __no answer__. (= … ***not an*** *answer.*)
NO SMOKING

1 Put in *not* or *no*.

1 I work hard, but .... at weekends.
2 She was .... able to understand him.
3 They had .... butter left in the shop.
4 They repaired my watch, but .... properly.
5 We've got .... time to talk now.
6 I can come round, but .... tonight.
7 They did .... want to help.
8 'Do you smoke?' '.............. usually.'
9 She's a woman with .... sense of humour.
10 'Shall I put some music on?' 'OK, but .... too loud.'

2 Change *not any/a* to *no*.

▶ I haven't got any money. *I've got no money.*
1 There aren't any newspapers. ....
2 There isn't any time. ....
3 There weren't any letters. ....
4 I didn't see a light. ....
5 He didn't give an answer. ....

We **don't usually put *not*** with the **subject**. Instead, we use a structure with ***it***.

It wasn't Bill *who phoned, it was Pete.* (NOT ~~*Not Bill phoned*~~ *…*)

Level 2

negatives with *nobody, never* etc *Nobody loves me.*

We can make negative sentences with ***nobody, nothing, nowhere, never, no, hardly*** (= 'almost not') and similar words. With these words, we **do not** use ***not*** or ***do/does/did***.

__Nobody__ loves me. (NOT ~~*Nobody doesn't love me.*~~)
He said __nothing__. (NOT ~~*He didn't say nothing.*~~)
She __never__ writes to me. (NOT ~~*She doesn't never write to me.*~~)
I've got __no__ money. (NOT ~~*I haven't got no money.*~~)
I can __hardly__ understand him. (NOT ~~*I can't hardly understand him.*~~)

1 Put the words in order to make sentences.

▶ up father early my gets never ...My father never gets up early....
1 lives house nobody that in ....
2 my understand I'll dog never ....
3 children me the nothing told ....
4 money I no have ....
5 the could road I see hardly ....

2 Change the sentences.

▶ She didn't say anything. (*nothing*) ...She said nothing....
1 I didn't see anybody. (*nobody*) ....
2 We didn't have any trouble. (*no*) ....
3 My parents don't go out. (*never*) ....
4 I looked for the dog, but it wasn't anywhere in the house. (*nowhere*) ....
....
5 I didn't eat anything yesterday. (*nothing*) ....
6 It didn't rain for three months. (*hardly*) ....
7 John didn't speak, Mary didn't speak, Bill didn't speak. (*nobody*) ....

3 Make the sentences negative.

▶ I drink coffee. (*not*) ...I don't drink coffee....
▶ I drink coffee. (*never*) ...I never drink coffee....
▶ Somebody telephoned. (*nobody*) ...Nobody telephoned....
1 My grandmother drives fast. (*never*) ....
2 Andrew plays the guitar. (*not*) ....
3 When she talked, I understood. (*nothing*) ....
4 I like Ann's new shoes. (*not*) ....
5 Something happened this morning. (*nothing*) ....
6 There's somewhere to sit down in the station. (*nowhere*) ....
....
7 I watch TV. (*hardly*) ....
8 Somebody wants to play tennis. (*nobody*) ....

I never hated a man enough to give him diamonds back.
(*Zsa Zsa Gabor*)

I have nothing to say, and I am saying it, and that is poetry.
(*John Cage*)

Sometime they'll give a war and nobody will come.
(*Carl Sandburg*)

In some answers, both contracted forms (for example *I'm, don't*) and full forms (for example *I am, do not*) are possible. Normally both are correct.

questions and negatives: more practice

1 Questions with and without *do/did*. Ask about the words in *italics*.

▶ *She* said something. Who said something?
▶ She said *something*. What did she say?
1 *Julia* cooked dinner. ....
2 Julia cooked *eggs*. ....
3 *The ball* hit Joe. ....
4 The ball hit *Joe*. ....
5 Sarah plays *the guitar*. ....
6 *Sarah* plays the guitar. ....
7 Beth speaks *eight languages*. ....
8 *Beth* speaks eight languages. ....
9 *Dad* ate Mum's breakfast. ....
10 Dad ate *Mum's breakfast*. ....

2 Prepositions in questions. Write questions for these answers.

▶ I was thinking about you. Who were you thinking about?
1 I went with Henry. ....
2 I'm writing to Margaret. ....
3 I bought it for my mother. ....
4 The letter's from my uncle. ....
5 We were talking about life. ....
6 I carried it in a paper bag. ....
7 I sold my car for €1000. ....
8 She hit him with her umbrella. ....
9 I sent the flowers to Caroline. ....
10 She comes from Denmark. ....

3 Long subjects. Put in auxiliary verbs to make questions.

▶ why / Jake and his wife / go / to Moscow last year Why did Jake and his wife go to Moscow last year?
▶ the 7.15 train / run on Saturdays Does the 7.15 train run on Saturdays?
1 why / all those people / looking at me ....
2 Anna and Oscar / have lunch together / yesterday ....
3 that man in the dark coat / work / for the government ....
4 the football team / playing / in Scotland / next Saturday ....
5 what / those children / doing / in the garden ....
6 what / the first word in this sentence / mean ....
7 Tom and his sister / staying / at your house / this week ....
8 when / Emma's teacher and her class / going / to Paris ....
9 what / that strange woman / say to you ....
10 when / Mary and Phil / get married ....

4 ***Not, nobody, never* etc. Make negative sentences.**

- ▶ I read newspapers. (*not*) I don't read newspapers.
- ▶ I read newspapers. (*never*) I never read newspapers.
- ▶ Somebody spoke. (*nobody*) Nobody spoke.

1 My father eats meat. (*never*) ……………………

2 Peter likes jazz. (*not*) ……………………

3 There's something to do in this town. (*nothing*) ……………………

4 I understood everything. (*nothing*) ……………………

5 Sally plays the piano. (*not*) ……………………

6 I go to the cinema. (*hardly*) ……………………

7 Something happened. (*nothing*) ……………………

8 Somebody wants to talk to you. (*nobody*) ……………………

9 I've got some money. (*no*) ……………………

10 I've got enough money. (*not*) ……………………

5 **Grammar in a text. Read the poem, and then write one yourself.**

Just you wait and see

I'm getting older.
There isn't time to do everything.
I can't speak German
or climb mountains.
I can see
I'm not going to be a ballet dancer
or an opera singer.
I'll never discover a new planet
or run a two-hour marathon
or write the novel of the century.
But I'll do something good.
Just you wait and see.

Your poem

I'm getting older.
There isn't time to do everything.
I can't ……………………
or ……………………
I can see
I'm not going to ……………………
or ……………………
I'll never ……………………
or ……………………
or ……………………
But I'll ……………………
Just you wait and see.

6 **GRAMMAR AND VOCABULARY. Make sure you know the words in the box, Use a dictionary if necessary. Then read statements 1–6 and correct the five that are wrong.**

cat	dinosaur	elephant	grizzly
bear	hunt	insect	penguin
spider	tiger		

- ▶ Penguins can fly. Penguins can't fly.

1 Adult grizzly bears can climb trees. ……………………

2 Elephants live for 50–70 years. ……………………

3 Tigers live in Africa. ……………………

4 The first people hunted dinosaurs. ……………………

5 Spiders are insects. ……………………

6 Cats can see when there is no light. ……………………

7 **Internet exercise. Get information from the internet (in English) about some of the animals in Exercise 6, or about some other animals. Then write some negative information about the animals, using *can't, don't, aren't* etc.**

……………………

……………………

pronunciation for grammar → e-book

questions and negatives: revision test

1 Correct the mistakes or write 'Correct'.

▶ ~~Speak you~~ English? Do you speak
▶ Did you understand? Correct
1 Does your brother living with you? ....
2 Are coming to the party all your friends? ....
3 Did you see Tom yesterday? ....
4 Play you football? ....
5 Why you are tired? ....
6 What time does the lesson start? ....
7 What is your boss like? ....
8 Where I can pay? ....
9 Who did tell you that? ....
10 Did Sarah phoned yesterday? ....
11 Not speak English. ....
12 I couldn't find my glasses nowhere. ....
13 I'm no ready yet. ....
14 I had no money. ....
15 At what are you looking? ....
16 I never work at weekends. ....
17 She didn't say nothing. ....
18 This sentence is no right. ....
19 Nobody didn't help me. ....
20 She works in China, but no in Beijing. ....

2 Complete the questions.

▶ 'What time is the film?' 'Eight o'clock.'
1 '...................... is that?' 'My brother.'
2 '...................... did you go home?' 'I was tired.'
3 '...................... were you born?' 'In Scotland.'
4 '...................... is Roger?' '27 next birthday.'
5 '...................... is her hair?' 'Black.'
6 '...................... are you?' '1 metre 84.'
7 '...................... music do you like?' 'Pop.'
8 '...................... can you sprint?' 'I can do 100m in 12.4 seconds.'
9 '...................... are your shoes?' '42.'
10 '........... is John's new girlfriend .... ?' 'She's very nice.'

3 Make negative sentences.

▶ I can speak French. (*Spanish*) I can't speak Spanish.
1 Kelly is at home. (*at work*) ....
2 I've forgotten your name. (*your face*) ....
3 Peter drives buses. (*taxis*) ....
4 We went to Spain. (*Portugal*) ....
5 You must use this phone. (*that one*) ....
6 Henry eats fish. (*meat*) ....
7 These people play rugby. (*soccer*) ....
8 Luke broke his arm. (*his leg*) ....
9 I'll be at home in the morning. (*the afternoon*) ....
10 Elisabeth reads magazines. (*books*) ....

4 Make questions with *she and her sisters*.

▶ live in England? Do she and her sisters live in England?
1 been to America? ....
2 like dancing? ....
3 can swim? ....
4 be here tomorrow? ....
5 go to the party yesterday? ....
6 ever studied history? ....
7 can drive? ....
8 phone last night? ....
9 talking to Philip when you saw them? ....
10 get married soon? ....

In some answers, both contracted forms (for example *I'm, don't*) and full forms (for example *I am, do not*) are possible. Normally both are correct.

SECTION 9 infinitives and *-ing* forms

grammar summary

> INFINITIVES: *(to) go, (to) break, (to) see* etc
> -ING FORMS (ALSO CALLED 'GERUNDS'): *going, breaking, seeing* etc

We can use both *-ing* forms and infinitives as subjects (but *-ing* forms are more common).
__Smoking__ is bad for you. (More natural than ***To smoke** is bad for you.*)

We can use **infinitives** to say **why** we do things.
*I got up early **to catch** the 7.15 train.*

After some verbs we use **infinitives**; after **others** we use ***-ing* forms**.
*I **expect to pass** my exams.* (NOT ~~*I expect passing*~~ …) *I'll **finish studying** in June.* (NOT ~~*I'll finish to study*~~ …)

We can use **infinitives after some adjectives** and **nouns**.
*She's **ready to leave**. I'm **glad to see** you. I've got **work to do**.*

After **prepositions** we use ***-ing* forms**, not infinitives.
*You can't live **without eating**.* (NOT … ~~*without to eat.*~~)
*I usually watch TV **before going** to bed.* (NOT … ~~*before to go to bed.*~~)

Infinitives often have ***to*** before them; but not always.
*I want **to go** home, but I can't **go** now.*

How I stopped smoking

I started smoking when I was 16. I didn't really want to smoke, but at that age it's important to imitate your friends. Once I had started, of course, it was hard to stop. And smoking gave me something to do with my hands. Whenever I met strangers, I couldn't help reaching for a cigarette to give me confidence, to make me look (I thought) cool and sophisticated.

Soon I couldn't get through a day without smoking twenty or thirty cigarettes. But smoking made me feel ill and smell bad, and I was tired of feeling ill and smelling bad. And I realised that it was stupid to spend so much money on a ridiculous habit. So I tried to stop. Hundreds of times. I kept on giving up. I became an expert on giving up smoking. Nothing worked: I always started again.

At last I had a piece of luck. I got terrible bronchitis – so bad that I simply couldn't smoke. It lasted for months. And when I finally recovered, I realised that I had broken the habit. I didn't have to start smoking again.

And I never did.

THAT CAT WANTS TO GO OUT
ROBERT THOMPSON

infinitives: using *to* *I want to go. Must you go?*

We usually put *to* with infinitives.

*I want **to go** home.* (NOT ~~*I want go home.*~~) *It's important **to get** enough sleep.*
*I telephoned my sister **to say** sorry.*

But we use infinitives without *to* after *do/does/did* in questions and negatives (see pages 104 and 113).

***Does** John **speak** Russian?* (NOT ~~*Does John to speak ...?*~~) *I **didn't understand**.*

We also use infinitives without *to* after **modal verbs** (*can, could, may, might, will, would, shall, should, must* – see Section 6).

*I **can't swim**.* (NOT ~~*I can't to swim.*~~) ***Must** you **go** now?* *We **should find** a hotel.*

1 Put in *to* or nothing (–).

- ▶ I don't want ..to...... stay at school.
- ▶ What time does the train ..–........ leave?
1. Do you .... play golf?
2. It's nice .... be at home again.
3. Sorry – I can't .... help you.
4. It may .... snow this weekend.
5. I must .... remember .... phone Andy.
6. Do we .... have .... buy petrol?
7. Jane seems .... be tired today.
8. I hope .... see you again soon.

2 Put in words from the box, with or without *to*.

ask ✓	buy	go	hear	help	learn	lend ✓	see	send	stop

- ▶ I'm writing ..to ask.................. for your help.
- ▶ Can you ..lend...................... me some money?
1. Maria went to America .... English.
2. Can you .... me with the cooking?
3. I'd like .... you for a moment.
4. Where did you .... those boots?
5. I expect .... from my family soon.
6. I don't want .... by bus.
7. I must .... Tom some money.
8. You really should .... smoking.

We make **negative infinitives** with ***not (to)*** + **verb**.

*Try **not to forget** your keys.* (NOT ... ~~*to not forget*~~ ...) *Be careful **not to wake** Paul up.*
*I told you **not to telephone** me here.* *I'm sorry **not to stay** longer.*
*The company did **not make** any money last year.* *You must **not park** in front of the school.*

3 Put in *not to* with infinitives from the box.

break	go to sleep	have	have	laugh ✓	make	play	see	talk	tell	wake

- ▶ Please try ..not to laugh.......................... when David sings.
1. It's nice .... a headache any more.
2. Be careful .... those glasses.
3. Please try .... in the lessons.
4. Tell the children .... so much noise.
5. I'd like .... so much work.
6. Hannah must learn .... about herself all the time.
7. Remember .... me up tomorrow morning.
8. It's important .... Sheila about Peter and Sandra.
9. We'll be sorry .... you tomorrow.
10. Please tell Amir .... the trumpet after midnight.

infinitive of purpose *She went to Paris to study music.*

We use an **infinitive with *to*** to say **why** we do something.

*I turned on the TV **to watch** the news.* *Joanna went to Paris **to study** music.*

1 Complete the sentences with the infinitives of the verbs in the box.

ask for	buy	catch	drive	finish	hear	learn	meet	relax	turn on ✓	wait for

▶ Use this button ...to turn on... the computer.
1 Oliver got up early .... Mark to the station.
2 I was late, so I ran .... my bus.
3 Ann wrote to me .... Joe's address.
4 I sat in the waiting room .... the doctor.
5 Bob's gone to the airport .... his uncle.
6 I went to town on Saturday .... a present for my cousin's birthday.
7 I stayed up late last night .... my English homework.
8 Alice went to Beijing .... Chinese.
9 I turned on the radio .... the latest news.
10 I listen to music ....

2 Complete the sentences with the infinitives of the verbs in the box.

buy	clean	earn	get	get up	go ✓	go	make	open	tell	wish

▶ Mum gave us some money ...to go... to the cinema.
1 I stood on a chair .... the top of the fridge,
2 Roger's gone to town .... a book.
3 We moved closer to the fire .... warm.
4 Use this key .... the front door.
5 I left a note .... George about the meeting.
6 Jane got a part-time job .... some pocket money.
7 I bought some good boots .... walking in the mountains.
8 Alice phoned Sue .... her a happy birthday.
9 I put the kettle on .... a cup of tea.
10 I set the alarm clock .... early.

3 Put the beginnings and ends together, using verbs from the box with *to*.

buy	cut	dry	open	see	wash ✓

0 You use soap	A ...to wash... yourself. ..0..
1 You use a knife	B .... things in shops. ......
2 You use a torch	C .... and close doors. ......
3 You use money	D .... yourself. ......
4 You use a key	E .... things into pieces. ......
5 You use a towel	F .... in the dark. ......

In some answers, both contracted forms (for example *I'm*, *don't*) and full forms (for example *I am*, *do not*) are possible. Normally both are correct.

verb + infinitive *I hope to be an airline pilot.*

After **some verbs** we use **infinitives**, usually with ***to***.

*I **hope to go** to Ireland later this year.* *Did Jeremy **agree to help** you with your work?*

1 Read the texts, and write down the verbs that are followed by an infinitive with *to*.

I'm eighteen, and I hope to be an airline pilot. My parents have agreed to pay for lessons if I do well in my exams. My brother says girls shouldn't be pilots, but I refuse to listen to him.

- ▶ hope to
- ▶ agreed to
- 1 ....

When I started to work here, my boss promised to give me interesting work, travelling to Europe and Asia. I expected to enjoy my job. But all my work is boring, and I don't do any travelling. I've tried to talk to my boss, but she doesn't listen. Now I've decided to look for another job.

- 2 ....
- 3 ....
- 4 ....
- 5 ....
- 6 ....

I've always been afraid of water. Then one day last year I thought, 'I don't want to live like this'. So I found some special lessons for people like me. I'm learning to swim, and next summer I plan to take water-skiing lessons.

- 7 ....
- 8 ....
- 9 ....

I needed to be at work early this morning. But I forgot to set my alarm clock, and I woke up at 7.30 instead of 6.30. Then everything seemed to go wrong. I had no clean shirts, the bus was late, …

- 10 ....
- 11 ....
- 12 ....

I began to learn karate four years ago, and I've continued to go to lessons twice a week since then. I love it. I've visited some other karate clubs, but I prefer to learn at my own club, because the teaching is so good.

- 13 ....
- 14 ....
- 15 ....

After ***begin, start, continue*** and ***prefer*** we can also use ***-ing*** forms with the same meaning.

*When did you **begin to learn / begin learning** karate?*
*I **started to have / started having** these headaches about a month ago.*
*The President **continued to speak / continued speaking** for an hour and a half.*
*I **prefer to live / prefer living** in the country – the city is too noisy.*

→ For *-ing* forms after *try* and *forget*, see page 308.

Love . . . Everyone feels it,
has felt it, or expects to feel it.
(*Anthony Trollope, 1883*)

War will stop when men refuse to fight.
(*Pacifist slogan, 1936*)

We must learn to live together as brothers . . .
(*Martin Luther King, 1964*)

Gentlemen always seem
to remember blondes.
(*Anita Loos, 1925*)

He preferred to be good
rather than to seem good.
(*Sallust, of Cato, 54 B.C.*)

Stop the world, I want to get off!
(*Anthony Newley, 1961*)

2 Complete the sentences with verbs from the boxes and *to*.

1–4: agree decide expect ✓ need plan ✓ try

▶ **ALICE**: 'The exam seemed easy. I was surprised when I got a low mark.'
Alice ...expected to... pass the exam; she was surprised when she got a low mark.

▶ David and Cathy have got plane tickets and hotel reservations for Corsica.
David and Cathy are ...planning to... go to Corsica.

1 Annie is going to Singapore. A visa is necessary, and she hasn't got one.
Annie .... get a visa.

2 **JANE**: 'Could you possibly lend me £5?'
ANDY: 'Sure.'
Andy has .... lend £5 to Jane.

3 **JOE**: 'Shall I go to the cinema or stay at home? Cinema, perhaps? No, I'll stay at home.'
Joe has .... stay at home.

4 Lizzie was expecting a call from Sarah. Sarah rang the number, but it was engaged.
Sarah .... phone Lizzie, but the number was engaged.

5–10: forget learn promise refuse start want

5 Oliver lives in the US, but he took all his driving lessons in France.
Oliver .... drive in France.

6 **PATRICK**: 'I will write to you every day, Barbara.'
Patrick has .... write to Barbara every day.

7 **BOB**: 'I was going to post a birthday card to my mother, but I didn't remember.'
Bob .... post his mother's birthday card.

8 **PHILIP**: 'Please, please lend me your car.'
AGNES: 'No, no, no and no.'
Agnes has .... lend her car to Philip.

9 Helen's parents are sending her to England for two weeks. Helen is not happy.
Helen doesn't .... go to England.

10 Susan said her first word when she was seven months old.
Susan .... talk when she was seven months old.

11–15: begin continue hope prefer seem

11 Mark plays the piano and the trumpet. The trumpet is his favourite.
Mark can play the piano, but he .... play the trumpet.

12 Ling usually stops work at 5.00, but yesterday she didn't stop until 7.00.
Ling .... work until 7.00 yesterday.

13 John swims every day; he's going to try for the national team next year.
John .... be in the national swimming team next year.

14 'I'm not sure, but I think Rebecca was worried yesterday evening.'
Rebecca .... be worried yesterday evening.

15 Irene sat down to write a letter to her brother yesterday, but she didn't finish it.
Irene .... write a letter to her brother yesterday.

→ For infinitives in indirect speech (after *tell*, *ask* etc), see pages 125 and 269.

→ For sentences like *I don't want to*, see page 293.

In some answers, both contracted forms (for example *I'm*, *don't*) and full forms (for example *I am*, *do not*) are possible. Normally both are correct.

Level 2

verb + object + infinitive *He wants me to cook.*

We often say that we **want somebody to do** something.

*My boyfriend **wants me to do** all the cooking.* (**NOT** … ~~*wants that I do all the cooking.*~~)

We can use ***would like*** in the same way.

***I'd like you to listen** to this song.* (**NOT** ~~*I'd like that you listen*~~ …)

1 Make sentences with *want* or *would like*.

▶ **MRS LEWIS:** Ann, can you post my letters, please? (*want*)
Mrs Lewis wants Ann to post her letters.

1 **SARAH:** John, could you cook tonight? (*would like*)
....

2 **POLICEMAN:** Please move your car, sir. (*want*)
.... the man ....

3 **MOTHER:** Helen, please wash your face. (*want*)
Helen's mother .... her..........

4 **BILL:** Andy, can you help me? (*would like*)
..........him.

5 **ROGER:** Karen, could you lend me some money? (*would like*)
.... lend him ....

6 **JESSIE:** Be quiet for a minute, Peter. (*want*)
....

7 **DAVID:** Alice, can you have dinner with me? (*would like*)
....

8 **MIKE:** The government should put more money into schools. (*would like*)
....

9 **LUCY:** Bill, stop playing that terrible music. (*want*)
....

10 **MARY:** Gordon, could you make the bed for once? (*would like*)
....

2 Different people want Alice to do different things. Complete the sentences.

buy a better guitar	buy him	do something ✓	go to America with him	go to Russia with her
lend her	spend every weekend	stop	study	take him for	work

▶ Everybody wants her to do something...............
1 Her boss .... harder.
2 Her little brother .... a bicycle.
3 Her dog .... a walk.
4 Her boyfriend ....
5 Her friend Martha .... a blue dress.
6 Her guitar teacher ....
7 Her mother .... at home.
8 Her sister ....
9 The people downstairs .... playing loud music at night.
10 Her father .... economics.

We can use some other verbs like this. For example: ***ask***, ***expect***, ***help***, ***need***, ***tell***.

*I **asked Peter to go** to America with me.* *The doctor **told me to take** a holiday.*
*We don't **expect you to work** at weekends.* *I **need you to translate** this letter.*

Level 2

3 Change the sentences.

▶ They thought that we would be late. (*expect*) They expected us to be late.
1 I didn't say to Alan 'Go home.' (*tell*) ....
2 I said to Fred 'Please be quiet.' (*ask*) ....
3 Do you think she'll phone? (*expect*) ....
4 I carried the books with Joe. (*help*) I helped ....
5 The policewoman said to me 'Show me your driving licence.' (*tell*) .... me .... her ....
6 Ann finished the work with me. (*help*) Ann ....
7 I said to the shop assistant 'Can you help me?' (*ask*) ....
8 You must stay with me. (*need*) I need ....
9 I think she'll pass her exam. (*expect*) ....
10 Some people must help with the party. (*need*) I need ....

4 Dan's family wanted different things from him. Write sentences.

▶ His mother: 'Be happy'. His mother wanted him to be happy.
▶ His grandfather: 'Don't be a politician'. His grandfather didn't want him to be a politician.
1 His father: 'Get rich'
....
2 His sister Isabel: 'Be good at sport'.
....
3 His brother Andy: 'Go to university'.
....
4 His sister Nicole: 'Don't got to university'.
....
5 His brother Henry: 'Be a racing driver'.
....
6 His grandmother: 'Be a doctor'.
....
7 His friend Anthony: 'Have an easy life'.
....
8 His maths teacher: 'Study maths'.
....
9 His literature teacher: 'Study literature.'
....
10 His music teacher: 'Don't study music. Please.'
....

5 What do/did people want you to do/be in life?

▶ My parents want me to be a doctor.
▶ My teacher wanted me to study engineering.
....
....
....
....

In some answers, both contracted forms (for example *I'm*, *don't*) and full forms (for example *I am*, *do not*) are possible. Normally both are correct.

it with infinitive subjects *It's nice to be here with you.*

We don't often begin sentences with infinitive subjects (like *To be here with you is nice*).
More often, we begin with *it* and put the infinitive later.
The structure *It is/was* etc + adjective + infinitive (with *to*) is very common.

It's nice to be here with you. *It was good to see you again.* *It's important to remember people's names.*

1 Change these sentences to make them more natural.

▶ To take your passport is necessary. It's necessary to take your passport.

1 To phone John was not necessary.
....

2 To understand that woman is impossible.
....

3 To stay in bed late on Sundays is nice.
....

4 To say 'No' is sometimes difficult.
....

5 To make our children happy was easy.
....

6 To tell the truth is sometimes dangerous.
....

7 To eat out in restaurants is expensive.
....

8 To learn a foreign language perfectly is almost impossible.
....

9 To travel is nice.
....

10 To visit my parents was good.
....

2 Complete these sentences about a summer holiday. Use *It was* and words from the box.

a bit hard to understand	dangerous to swim	expensive to eat	impossible to be
interesting to see	nice to have	really good to get away ✓	very easy to make

▶ It was really good to get away from home and work.
1 .... sunshine every day.
2 .... how other people live.
3 Sometimes .... the language if people talked fast.
4 .... friends.
5 .... in restaurants, but the food was wonderful.
6 The sea was beautiful, but ....
7 There were so many things to do that .... bored.

3 **What do you think? Make sentences beginning *It's*, using words from the box. Use a dictionary if necessary.**

always	often	sometimes	never	right	wrong	good
bad	necessary	stupid	dangerous			

- ▶ take exercise *It's always good to take exercise.*
- 1 tell the truth ....
- 2 relax ....
- 3 save money ....
- 4 give money to beggars ....
- 5 drive fast ....
- 6 fight ....
- 7 be polite to older people ....
- 8 dress well ....
- 9 smoke ....
- 10 work very hard ....

4 GRAMMAR AND VOCABULARY: **learning and using a language: what is important?**

Make sure you know the words in the box. Use a dictionary if necessary.
Then make sentences with *It's important to …*, *It's not necessary to …* or *It's important not to ….*
Different answers are possible: for ours, see the answer key.

bilingual	comprehension	correctness	immediate	mistake	practise	pronunciation
regularly	results	rules	translate	vocabulary		

LEARNING

- ▶ study regularly *It's important to study regularly.*
- ▶ study six hours a day *It's not necessary to study six hours a day.*
- ▶ expect immediate results. *It's important not to expect immediate results.*
- 1 practise grammar ....
- 2 translate everything ....
- 3 read a lot ....
- 4 read things that interest you ....

PRONUNCIATION

- 5 have perfect pronunciation ....
- 6 have good enough pronunciation ....

GRAMMATICAL CORRECTNESS

- 7 make too many mistakes ....
- 8 speak without mistakes ....

COMPREHENSION

- 9 practise listening to English ....

VOCABULARY

- 10 know 3,000–5,000 words ....
- 11 know 50,000 words ....
- 12 have a good English-English dictionary ....
- 13 have a good bilingual dictionary ....

In some answers, both contracted forms (for example *I'm*, *don't*) and full forms (for example *I am*, *do not*) are possible. Normally both are correct.

adjective + infinitive *glad to find you at home*

We can use **infinitives** (with *to*) after **adjectives** to say **why we feel** *afraid, glad, happy, pleased, sad, surprised, unhappy* etc.

*Mum will be **glad to find** you at home.* *I'm **pleased to meet** you.*

1 Put in suitable adjectives or infinitives.

▶ John was ..happy.... to get home after a long day at work. (*sorry, afraid, happy*)
1 Hello. I'm very glad .... you. (*meet, tell, like*)
2 I was sorry not .... Barbara at the party. (*forget, talk, see*)
3 I'm .... to say that I've got bad news for you. (*glad, sorry, surprised*)
4 I'm .... to wake her up – she always shouts at me when I do. (*excited, pleased, afraid*)
5 We were pleased .... a free weekend at last. (*work, have, know*)
6 When I got home, I was surprised .... a policeman in the kitchen. (*get, leave, find*)
7 I was not .... to hear that I had failed my exam. (*surprised, sorry, sad*)
8 Anna was not .... to find that the cat had brought a mouse in. (*sad, pleased, unhappy*)
9 I was sorry .... home and go to America. I knew I would miss my family. (*get, stay, leave*)
10 We're always .... to go on holiday. (*surprised, sad, happy*)

We can use **infinitives** (with *to*) after **adjectives** to say **what we think** of things that people do. We do this with adjectives like *clever, crazy, right, silly, stupid* and *wrong*.

*You're **crazy to think** you can get there in an hour.* *You were **clever to bring** an umbrella.*

2 Write sentences with infinitives.

▶ Angela carries all her money in one bag. She's wrong.
Angela's wrong to carry all her money in one bag.

▶ Annie got to the airport early. She was clever.
Annie was clever to get to the airport early.

1 Eleanor listens to Mark. She's silly.
....

2 Elizabeth took the train without a ticket. She was wrong.
....

3 I sat on my glasses. I was stupid.
....

4 I washed a white shirt with a red one. I was wrong.
....

5 You believe Luke. You're silly.
....

6 You eat a good breakfast. You're right.
....

7 You lent money to Chris. You were crazy.
....

8 I thought the new Prime Minister was a good man. I was stupid.
....

9 Rebecca told Peter she loved him. She was wrong.
....

10 I stayed in bed until lunchtime. I was right.
....

adjectives with *enough*/*too* + infinitive *too tired to sing*

After **adjective + *enough***, we can use an **infinitive** (with *to*). Note the word order – see page 176.

*Julie's **old enough** to drive now.* (NOT ~~*Julie's enough old*~~ …)   *John isn't **strong enough** to carry that.*

1 Make sentences with *is/isn't old enough to* … .

Alice is 13.	Mark is 16.	Cathy is 17.
John is 18.	Liz is 21.	

- ▶ John *is old enough to drive* a car.
- ▶ Alice *isn't old enough to drive* a car.
1. Alice .... part-time.
2. Alice .... home.
3. Mark .... school.
4. Cathy .... home.
5. Cathy .... vote.
6. John .... his name.
7. Liz .... a bus.

IN BRITAIN – AT WHAT AGE CAN YOU …?

When you are	you can
13	work part-time
16	leave home
17	leave school
18	drive a car
18	vote
18	change your name
21	drive a bus

2 Rewrite these sentences using … *enough to* … .

1. Laurie is not very tall, so he can't play basketball. He's ....
2. Annie's only 14, so she can't vote. ....
3. I'm not very strong. I can't open this bottle. ....
4. My French is good. I can read a newspaper. ....
5. Peter isn't very old. He can't go out by himself. ....
6. Rob is intelligent. He will do well at university. ....

After ***too* + *adjective***, we can use an infinitive (with *to*).

*I'm **too tired** to sing.*   *Alice was very afraid – **too afraid** to speak.*

3 Change two sentences into one. Use *too* … *to* … .

- ▶ I'm very sleepy. I can't drive. *I'm too sleepy to drive.*
1. Helen is very ill. She can't work. ....
2. My grandfather is very old. He can't travel. ....
3. I'm very bored. I can't listen any longer. ....
4. Cara's very hot. She can't play tennis. ....
5. I'm very hungry. I can't work. ....
6. I'm very tired. I can't drive. ....
7. I was very afraid. I couldn't move. ....
8. Molly was very ill last week. She couldn't go to school. ....
9. Our dog's very fat. It can't run. ....
10. My mother's very deaf. She doesn't understand what people say. ....

....

Middle age: the age when you are too old to play tennis and too young to play golf.
(Ansel Adams)

In some answers, both contracted forms (for example *I'm*, *don't*) and full forms (for example *I am*, *do not*) are possible. Normally both are correct.

Level 2

noun/pronoun + infinitive *some letters to write*

We can often use **infinitives with *to*** after **nouns**.

*I've got **some letters to write**.* *Sorry – I haven't got **any money to lend** you.*

1 Complete the sentences with the expressions from the box.

dress to wear	film to watch	friend to see	homework to do
letters to post	shopping to do	stories to tell ✓	

▶ My uncle always has very interesting ..stories to tell.......... about his year in Nepal.
1 Please can I go out tonight, Dad? I've got no ....
2 I'm going to the post office – have you got any ....
3 I think I'll stay at home tonight. I'm a bit tired, and there's a good .... on TV.
4 Have you got a .... to the party, or will you have to buy one?
5 If you've got any .... , we can go to the supermarket later.
6 I'll be home a bit late tonight – I've got a .... after work.

We can use **infinitives with *to*** after words like ***somebody***, ***anything*** and ***nowhere*** (see page 172).

*Would you like **something to drink**?* *I haven't got **anything to read**; can I borrow this book?*
*There's **nothing to eat** in the fridge.* *Those poor people have **nowhere to live**.*

2 Complete the sentences with *somebody* etc and the verbs *in italics*.

▶ POLICEMAN: Move on, please. There's (*see*) ..nothing to see...........................
1 I can't go to the party: I don't have (*wear*) ....
2 Could I possibly use this table? I need (*work*) ....
3 When I arrived, there was (*do*) .... – all the work was finished.
4 Everyone in our class was ill today, so our teacher had (*teach*) ....
5 I'll be with you in a few minutes – I have (*finish*) ....
6 All my friends are out of town tonight, and I've got (*go*) ....
7 Everybody needs (*love*) ....
8 My brother couldn't find (*stay*) .... in Bristol.
9 I'm looking for (*help*) .... me with the disco on Saturday.
10 Your arms are full – give me (*carry*) ....

NOTHING TO EAT

She had nothing to eat.
They made a film about her
because she had nothing to eat.

Her husband
was killed in the war.
They wrote a book about
how he was killed in the war.

Her mother and brother
were executed by the revolutionaries.
There was an opera about it.

Both her children died
(there was no hospital).
You can see the photographs
at an exhibition in London.

Then somebody wrote a poem.

Still
she had nothing to eat.

-ing forms as subjects *Smoking is bad for you.*

We often use ***-ing* forms** (also called 'gerunds') as **subjects** – more often than infinitives.

***Smoking** is bad for you.* (More natural than *To smoke is bad for you.*)
***Swimming** is good exercise.* ***Driving** makes me tired.* ***Travelling** takes a lot of my time.*

1 Complete the sentences.

▶ ...swimming... is slower than ...running... (*running; swimming*)
1 .... is more dangerous than .... (*reading; skiing*)
2 .... is faster than .... (*flying; going by train*)
3 .... costs more than .... (*washing; eating*)
4 .... is easier than .... (*speaking; writing*)
5 .... is harder than .... (*listening; understanding*)
6 .... is more interesting than .... (*shaving; shopping*)
7 .... is more tiring than .... (*resting; working*)
8 .... is more dangerous .... (*smoking; driving*)

2 Make three more sentences like the ones in Exercise 1. Use some of the words in the box.

cycling	learning	running	shopping	sleeping	teaching	thinking	writing

1 ....
2 ....
3 ....

We can put **objects** after ***-ing* forms**.

***Learning languages** is difficult and takes time.* (NOT … ~~*are difficult*~~ … – *learning* is singular.)
***Eating chocolate** does not make you slim.*

3 Complete this list of activities with verbs from the box (use *-ing* forms). Then number them in order of interest: 1 = most interesting (for you); 8 = least interesting.

buy	cook	learn	listen to	look after	meet	play	read

.... cards .... poetry .... music ......
.... meals .... languages .... friends ......
.... children .... clothes ......

In notices, you often see ***NO*** before ***-ing* forms**.

NO SMOKING ***NO WAITING***

4 GRAMMAR AND VOCABULARY: public notices
Which words go with which notice? Use a dictionary if necessary.

NO PARKING ..1.. NO SMOKING ......
NO FISHING ...... NO CYCLING ......
NO CAMPING ......

In some answers, both contracted forms (for example *I'm*, *don't*) and full forms (for example *I am*, *do not*) are possible. Normally both are correct.

preposition + ...ing *Thank you for coming.*

After **prepositions**, we use **-*ing* forms** of verbs.

*The children are tired **of going** to the same place every summer.* (NOT ... ~~are tired of to go to~~ ...)
*She spoke for an hour **without using** notes.* (NOT ... ~~without to use~~ ...)
*Thank you **for coming**.* *I worry **about spending** too much money.*
*We're thinking **of going** to Jamaica for Christmas.*

→ For spelling of *-ing* forms, see page 23.

1 Put the beginnings and ends together.

0 Every morning, my dad worries about	A being late for his train. ..0..
1 Please don't leave without	B watering my garden while I'm on holiday. ......
2 I don't like the idea of	C telling me that you're going. ......
3 Are you interested in	D going to Vienna with us next weekend? ......
4 I'll pay you for	E working all my life. ......
5 I never get tired of	F being able to fly. ......
6 Thank you very much for	G selling his house. ......
7 My brother's thinking of	H drinking lots of coffee. ......
8 I can't work without	I reading. ......
9 Sometimes I dream of	J babysitting. ......

2 Add *-ing* forms of the verbs in the box.

ask	be ✓	close	get	go	hear	ski	smoke	wash	watch	work

▶ Alice dreams of ...being... an opera singer, but she can't sing very well.
1 I'm tired of .... the same old stories; doesn't John realise he's boring us?
2 Which British Prime Minister was famous for .... big cigars?
3 I'm thinking of .... to Greece next summer – have you ever been there?
4 Eric's interested in .... football on television, but not in playing it.
5 Don't worry about .... the dishes – I'll wash them in the morning.
6 She ran out without .... the door.
7 They didn't pay me much for .... in their garden.
8 Jessica and Rob are talking about .... married.
9 I'm not very good at ...., but I like it.
10 She took my bike without ....

People talking without speaking,
People hearing without listening, . . .
'Fools,' said I, 'You do not know
Silence like a cancer grows.'

(from *'Sound of Silence',* song by Paul Simon)

3 Make sentences with *very / quite / not very good at ...ing* or *bad at ...ing*.

	RUN	SWIM	CYCLE	DRAW	SING
JANE	★	●	☆	❍	☆
BOB	☆	●	❍	★	☆
SUE	★	★	☆	❍	☆
MARK	★	☆	★	☆	❍

KEY
★ VERY GOOD
☆ QUITE GOOD
❍ NOT VERY GOOD
● BAD

▶ *(Jane / run, swim)* Jane is very good at running, but bad at swimming.

▶ *(Sue / run, cycle)* Sue is very good at running, and quite good at cycling.

1 *(Bob / run, cycle)* ....

2 *(Sue / draw, run)* ....

3 *(Mark / swim, run)* ....

4 *(Bob / swim, sing)* ....

5 *(Jane / run, cycle)* ....

6 *(Mark / sing, draw)* ....

7 *(Jane / draw, sing)* ....

8 *(Sue / sing, swim)* ....

4 What are you good or bad at? Write some sentences about yourself.

....

....

We use ***by ...ing*** and ***without ...ing*** to say **how** people do something.

I earn my pocket money ***by working*** *in a petrol station.* *She passed her exams* ***without studying****.*

5 Make sentences with *by ...ing* or *without ...ing*.

▶ When I left the house this morning, I didn't close the windows.
I left the house this morning without closing the windows.

▶ Ali got a wonderful job. He was in the right place at the right time.
Ali got a wonderful job by being in the right place at the right time.

1 Ellie stayed awake. She drank lots of coffee.

....

2 Paul drank three glasses of water. He didn't stop.

....

3 Charles woke us up. He turned the TV on.

....

4 You can find out the meaning of a word. Use a dictionary.

....

5 Mike paid for his new house. He didn't borrow any money.

....

6 Helen lost her driving licence. She drove too fast, too often.

....

7 Carl did all his homework. He didn't ask for any help.

....

8 Teresa cooks all her food. She doesn't use any salt.

....

Sometimes *to* is a preposition (for example *I look forward* ***to*** *your answer*).
In this case we must use *-ing* forms of verbs after *to*.

I look forward ***to hearing*** *from you.* (NOT ~~*I look forward to hear from you.*~~)

In some answers, both contracted forms (for example *I'm, don't*) and full forms (for example *I am, do not*) are possible. Normally both are correct.

verb + …*ing* *I can't help feeling unhappy.*

After some verbs we use ***-ing*** forms.
Some of these verbs are: ***keep*** (***on***) (='continue', 'not stop'), ***finish***, ***stop***, ***give up*** (='stop', for habits), ***go***, ***can't help*** (='can't stop myself'), ***spend*** (time), ***mind***, ***suggest***, ***practise***, ***enjoy***.

*I **can't help feeling** unhappy.*　*Do you **mind sharing** a room?*　*Alex has **gone swimming**.*

1 Complete the sentences with *-ing* forms. (For spelling rules, see page 23.)

▶ We enjoy ....playing.... tennis in the morning. (*play*)
1 Has Julia finished .... her photos? (*take*)
2 Robert's given up .... sweets. (*eat*)
3 'Where's Helen?' 'She's gone ....' (*shop*)
4 I have to practise .... so I can pass my test. (*drive*)
5 Alec suggested .... at the supermarket. (*stop*)
6 On Sunday I spent three hours .... in the garden. (*work*)

2 Write sentences using the expressions in the box with *-ing* forms.

He can't help	She enjoys ✓	They've just finished	He's given up	They're going
All that week, it kept	She's practising	She's suggesting ✓	It's just stopped	

▶ She enjoys skiing.

▶ She's suggesting going to Rome.

1 ....

2 ....

3 ....

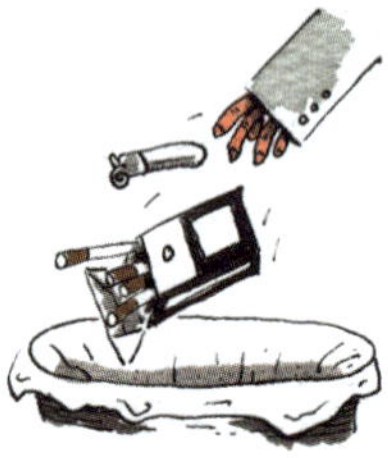

4 ....

5 ....

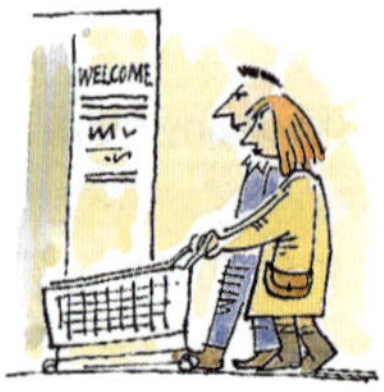

6 ....

7 ....

We use ***–ing* forms after *love*, *like*, *(not) mind*** (= '(not) dislike'), ***dislike*, *hate***.

3 Put in *-ing* forms of the verbs in the box.

cook	eat	get up ✓	play	shop	study	wash	watch	watch	wear	work

▸ I hate ...getting up... in the winter before the sun is up.
1 George dislikes .... dishes, so he often eats out.
2 I don't like playing baseball, but I like .... it.
3 I don't mind .... late if my boss asks me.
4 Joe's two-year-old sister loves .... with her toys in the bath.
5 Jenny and her sister like .... each other's clothes.
6 When I was at school, I hated .... history.
7 I like .... nature programmes on TV.
8 I hate .... in supermarkets.
9 My father likes ...., and we all like ...., so we go well together.

4 Write about ten things you love/hate etc doing. Use expressions from the box or write about other things.

cooking dinner for friends	dancing until 1 a.m.	eating out with friends	getting up early
listening to loud music	lying on a sunny beach	reading novels	swimming in the ocean
travelling to new places	walking in the mountains	walking in the rain	watching old films

▸ ...I love walking in the mountains....
1 ....
2 ....
3 ....
4 ....
5 ....
6 ....
7 ....
8 ....
9 ....
10 ....

After ***love*, *like*** and ***hate*** we can also use **infinitives with *to*** with the same meaning.

*I **love to sing**. = I **love singing**.* *Rachel **likes to go out / going out** with friends.*
*Mum **hates to cook / cooking** on an electric cooker.*
(**BUT NOT** ~~*I dislike to listen to opera.*~~ **AND NOT** ~~*Do you mind to wait for a few minutes?*~~)

In some answers, both contracted forms (for example *I'm*, *don't*) and full forms (for example *I am*, *do not*) are possible. Normally both are correct.

infinitives and *-ing* forms: more practice

1 Adjective or noun + infinitive. Complete the sentences with infinitives.

▶ (I saw Daniel.) I was happy *to see Daniel.*
▶ (I need to do some shopping.) I've got *some shopping to do.*
1 (I found a cat in my bed.) I was surprised ....
2 (She left her job.) She was wrong ....
3 (I can't buy a car.) I've got no money ....
4 (I gave Peter money.) I was crazy ....
5 (We said goodbye to Aunt Emma.) We were glad ....
6 (I didn't have time to phone you.) I was sorry ....
7 (I couldn't work because I was tired.) I was too ....
8 (Somebody must post these letters.) Here are some ....
9 (Somebody must wash the dishes.) I've got no time ....
10 (I need a drink.) I need something ....

2 Infinitive of purpose. Put the beginnings and ends together, and put in infinitives (with *to*) from the box.

catch	cut	impress	keep	learn	look for	make ✓	make	pay	stop	watch

0 Toby gave Lucy some flowers	A *to make* her feel better. *0*
1 Alicia went to America	B .... coffee. ......
2 I switched the TV on	C .... my head warm. ......
3 I took two aspirins	D .... English. ......
4 Carolyn went to the kitchen	E .... the news. ......
5 I'm wearing a hat	F .... my headache. ......
6 I have to work in the evenings	G .... food. ......
7 I used a small knife	H .... for my new car. ......
8 Jack bought some new clothes	I .... the potatoes into pieces. ......
9 We all ran as fast as we could	J .... his girlfriend. ......
10 The cat got up on the table	K .... the train. ......

3 *-ing* form subjects. Put these activities in order of interest (for you) and make sentences with *more interesting*.

driving	listening to music	playing chess	reading	studying English	studying history
talking to friends	watching birds	watching TV	cycling		

▶ *Driving is more interesting than watching birds. Watching birds is more interesting than listening to music.*

....

....

....

....

....

....

....

....

4 Grammar in a text. Complete the text with expressions from the boxes.

1–4: glad to leave ✓	happy not to have	pleased to find	sorry to say	unhappy to think

Five years ago, I went to Australia to start a new job. I was ▶ ..glad to leave.................. London, but I was very 1.................................. goodbye to my friends and family, and my mother was 2.................................. that I would be so far away. I was a bit afraid of my new life, so I was 3.................................. any problems when I arrived. Sydney was beautiful, and I was 4.................................. friendly people in the office, an interesting job and a lovely apartment.

5–7: happy to be	pleased to see	surprised to find

Everything went well in Australia, but I never felt really at home there, and in the end I decided to come back. Today I arrived in London, for the first time in five years. I was 5.................................. so many changes, but I am really 6.................................. here again. On the way from the airport I started to cry – I was so 7.................................. a big red London bus.

5 GRAMMAR AND VOCABULARY: vehicles. Make sure you know the words in the box. Use a dictionary if necessary. Then look at the advertisements and say what the advertisers want you to buy.

bike	motorbike	motorboat	plane	tractor ✓	yacht

▶ ..They want me to buy a tractor.............

1 ....

2 ....

3 ....

4 ....

5 ....

products, contact Trakta for the address of your nearest dealer.
Trakta Tractors
Quality & Performance
Trakta Tractors (UK) Ltd.,
Belmarsh Court, Belmarsh Park, Cheltenham,

1

Heathield H300 Hybrid
• 4130 Molloy frame • 24-speed Hitalo gears

2

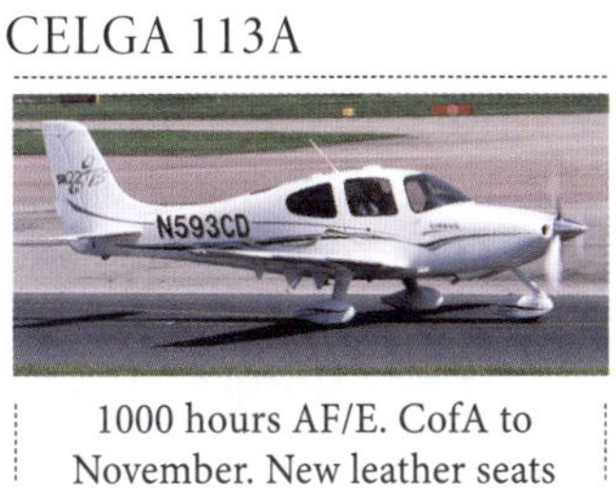

CELGA 113A
N593CD
1000 hours AF/E. CofA to November. New leather seats

3

M marissini yachts
... OUT IN FRONT
Marissini yachts offers a select

4

SORENSEN
Sorensen... Setting a new standard in design and performance.

5

BARRIES
new spec machines arriving
NOW
CALL US FOR THE BEST DEALS
machines to clear DVR300..........£5590
ALPHA............£5450

6 Internet exercise. Find three advertisements on the internet. Write some words from each advertisement, and say what the advertisers want you to do or buy.

....

....

....

infinitives and *-ing* forms: revision test

1 Put in the correct form of the verb.

- ▶ I promise ...to phone... you every day. (*phone*)
- ▶ She suggested ...seeing... a doctor. (*see*)
1. We agreed .... together. (*work*)
2. I didn't expect .... John there. (*see*)
3. I'm really going to stop .... (*smoke*)
4. I can't keep .... – I'm too tired. (*drive*)
5. Iris has decided .... a car. (*buy*)
6. The boss refused .... to me. (*talk*)
7. I thought of .... you a birthday card, but I forgot. (*send*)
8. They still haven't finished .... (*talk*)
9. Bill doesn't want .... with us. (*come*)
10. Your English is good, but you must practise .... (*speak*)

2 Correct the mistakes or write 'Correct'.

- ▶ I want ~~seeing~~ you. ...to see...
- ▶ Can I help you? ...Correct....
1. It's necessary to get a visa. ....
2. I hope to not have problems at university. ....
3. I went to Mexico for learning Spanish. ....
4. His parents wanted him to be a doctor. ....
5. You can get there faster by take the train. ....
6. I stopped to smoke last year. ....
7. She keeps telephoning me. ....
8. We decided going by bus. ....
9. I'm glad to see you. ....
10. Learning languages is difficult. ....
11. I don't want that you pay for me. ....
12. It's dangerous to smoke. ....
13. We need getting tickets. ....
14. You can't live without to eat. ....
15. I often think about change my job. ....
16. I was wrong to say that to her. ....
17. I would like see you again. ....
18. Is it necessary to buy a ticket now? ....
19. Try to not forget your keys. ....
20. You must pay now. ....

3 Write sentences with *want*.

- ▶ **ROBERT** → **PAUL**: tell / everything ...Robert wants Paul to tell him everything....
1. **ANNA** → **BETH**: look after / children ....
2. **JOE** → **JACK**: lend / money ....
3. **PETER'S MOTHER** → **PETER**: clean / room ....
4. **SAM** → **JOE**: go shopping ....

Write sentences with *would like*.

- ▶ **ALICE** → **OLIVIA**: make / coffee ...Alice would like Olivia to make coffee....
5. **TOM** → **SARAH**: pass / newspaper ....
6. **MIKE'S PARENTS** → **MIKE**: study / medicine ....
7. **THE BOSS** → **EMMA**: answer / phone ....

Write sentences with *not want*.

- ▶ **CAROL** → **ROBERT**: drive fast ...Carol doesn't want Robert to drive fast....
8. **MARY** → **JACK**: look / her / like that ....
9. **HARRY** → **JIM**: say / anything / police ....
10. **MARIA'S MOTHER** → **MARIA**: fall in love / pop singer ....

In some answers, both contracted forms (for example *I'm*, *don't*) and full forms (for example *I am*, *do not*) are possible. Normally both are correct.

SECTION 10 special structures with verbs

grammar summary

Several different structures are practised in this section:

- **structures with *get***
  *It's **getting** late.* *I **got** a letter.* ***Get** out!*
- **verbs followed by prepositions**
  ***Look at** this.*
- **phrasal verbs**
  ***Hurry up** – we're late.*
- **verbs with two objects**
  *Can you lend **me some money**?*
- ***have something done***
  *I **have my hair cut** every week.*
- ***let's***
  ***Let's go** and see a film tonight.*
- **imperatives**
  ***Come** in and have some coffee.*

'Don't embarrass me again, spell-checker.'

Level 1

structures with *get* *get up; get your coat; it's getting cold*

Get has **different meanings** in **different structures**.
Get **+ direct object**: 'receive, fetch, obtain, buy …'

Get your coat – it's time to go. *She* ***got a letter*** *from her mother.*

Get **+ adjective**: 'become'

It's ***getting cold****.* *The problem is* ***getting worse****.*

Get **+ adverb particle / preposition**: 'move, change position'

What time do you usually ***get up****?* *It takes me an hour to* ***get to*** *work.*
I couldn't ***get on*** *the bus because it was full.*

1 Complete the sentences using expressions with *get*.

▶ My English is ...getting better...................
1 I need to .... some .... out of the bank.
2 Antonia .... her car and drove away.
3 I .... a long .... from Arthur this morning.
4 What are you doing in my room? ....!
5 If you go out in the rain without a coat, you'll ....
6 If you don't put on a sweater, you'll ....
7 We have to .... the bus at the next stop.
8 If I don't have breakfast, I .... really .... about eleven o'clock.
9 I'm .... ing .... , I think I'll go to bed.
10 It .... early in winter.

Get is often used with a **past participle**. Common expressions:
get burnt *get dressed* *get undressed* *get changed* *get hurt* *get lost*
get married *get divorced* *get broken*
This structure can be similar to a passive verb.

Joe ***got arrested*** *for drunk driving last week.* (= … 'was arrested' …)
We never ***get invited*** *anywhere.*

2 Complete the sentences with *get* and verbs from the box (use past participles).

break	burn	change	divorce	dress	invite	lose	marry	send ✓	steal	undress

▶ When he was 12 he ..got sent.................................. away to boarding school.
1 I forgot to take the chicken out of the oven and it ....
2 Anna and Brian have only been married for a year, but they're ....
3 His glasses .... when he fell off his bike.
4 I'm going to .... and go to bed.
5 Every time he goes walking in the country he ....
6 If you leave your bag there, it'll ....
7 That child takes hours to .... in the morning.
8 'Shall we go swimming?' 'OK. I'll just go and .... '
9 Do you think we'll .... to Roger's party?
10 Sarah and Oliver .... in a beautiful little church in the country.

verbs with prepositions *Wait for me.*

With some verbs, we put a **preposition** (*for, to, at* etc) **before an object.**

***Wait for** me!* (NOT ~~*Wait me!*~~) *I **listen to** a lot of music.* (NOT ~~*I listen a lot of music.*~~)

1 Put the beginnings and ends together, and put in verbs from the box.

0–4:	ask	believe ✓	belong	laugh	wait
5–9:	happened	listen	look	talks	think

0 Do you ...believe........	A at my pronunciation. ......
1 I know my English is bad, but please don't	B for it and I'll give it to you. ......
2 If you're late, I'll	C for you. ......
3 If you want anything, just	D in life after death? ..0...
4 Does this coat	E to you? ......
5 I've got something important to say: please	F about himself. ......
6 Their garden is wonderful.	G about the future. ......
7 Megan lives from day to day. She doesn't	H at those roses! ......
8 He's very boring: he always	I to her? ......
9 Paula's an hour late. What's	J to me. ......

2 Look again at Exercise 1, and write the preposition after each verb.

ask ..for...... believe .... belong .... happen .... laugh ....
listen .... look .... talk .... think .... wait ....

You ***arrive at*** a place, or ***in*** a very big place (NOT ~~to~~).

*The train **arrives at** Oxford Station at 17.15.* *When did you **arrive in** Britain?*

You get ***into/out of*** a car; you ***get on/off*** a bus, train, plane or ship.

*I **got out of** the taxi at Piccadilly Circus.* *We **got off** the bus at Trafalgar Square.*

Look after = 'watch and take care of'; ***look for*** = 'try to find'.

*Could you **look after** the children this evening?* *I'm **looking for** my glasses.*

You ***pay*** a person or a bill; you ***pay for*** something that you buy.

*'Have you **paid Joe**?' 'Yes, I **paid his bill** last week.'* *Can you **pay for** the drinks?*

3 Put in the correct preposition or – (= no preposition).

1 Don't wait .... me if I'm late.
2 What time did you arrive .... the airport?
3 Don't listen .... him – he's being stupid.
4 I'm looking .... John's house while he's away.
5 We're looking .... a bigger house.
6 Did you ask .... coffee?
7 We need to talk .... money.
8 'Whose is that car?' 'It belongs .... Carola.'
9 I forgot to pay .... the tickets.
10 I don't want to think .... the future.
11 She got .... her car and drove away.
12 I couldn't get .... the bus because it was full.
13 'What's happened .... your hand?' 'I cut it on some glass.'
14 The children still believe .... Father Christmas.
15 When I got .... the train I realised I'd forgotten my ticket.
16 Can you pay .... the taxi driver?
17 When did you arrive .... Ireland?
18 She got .... the car and went into her house.
19 Why are you looking .... me?
20 We had to get .... the plane because there was a bomb.

→ For more about prepositions, see pages 273–286.

In some answers, both contracted forms (for example *I'm, don't*) and full forms (for example *I am, do not*) are possible. Normally both are correct.

phrasal verbs *Come in, take off your coat and sit down.*

Some verbs have **two parts.** The second part is a small **adverb** (*back, away, out* etc).
These verbs are called 'phrasal verbs'.
The small adverbs are not the same as prepositions (but some of them look the same).

SOME COMMON PHRASAL VERBS
be in/out/away/back *get out* *get up* *go away* *go/come back* *go on* (= 'continue') *go in/out* *hurry up* *lie down* *look out* *look round* *sit down* *stand up* *turn round* *wake up*

'Can I speak to Ann?' 'She's not ***in****.'* ***Come back*** *soon.* *This headache won't* ***go away****.*
Look out! ***Come in*** *and* ***sit down****.* *It's time to* ***get up****.*

1 Complete the sentences.

▶ The door opened and I went ...in....
▶ ...Come... back and see us soon.

1 I usually .... up at seven o'clock in the morning.
2 Shall we .... out this evening?
3 I heard a noise behind me and turned ....
4 I can't go .... Can we stop for a minute?
5 I'm going home for a bit. I'll be .... after lunch.
6 Hurry .... We're late.
7 I'm not feeling well. I'm going to .... down for an hour.
8 'I love you.' '............... away!'

2 Look at the pictures and complete the captions.

1 Wake ....!

2 Please sit ....

3 Come ....!

Some **phrasal verbs** can have **objects**.

SOME COMMON PHRASAL VERBS THAT CAN HAVE OBJECTS
bring back *fill in* (*a form*) *fill up* *give back* *give up* (= 'stop doing') *let in* *look up* (*something in a dictionary* etc) *pick up* *put down* *put on* (*clothes*) *switch/turn on/off* (*lights, electrical appliances*) *take away* *take off* (*clothes*) *throw away* *turn up/down* (*radio, TV, heater*) *wash up* (*cups, plates* etc)

Please ***fill in this form*** *and post it.* *I'm trying to* ***give up smoking****.*
I ***put on my best clothes*** *for the interview.* *Shall I* ***switch on the lights****?*
Could you ***turn down the radio****?* *Don't* ***throw away the newspaper****.*

In phrasal verbs, ***up*** often means '**completely**'.

I'll ***cut up*** *the wood.* *Let's* ***clean up*** *the house.* ***Fill up*** *your glass.* *I* ***tore up*** *her letter.*

3 Here are some sentences from books and conversations. Complete the phrasal verbs with words from the boxes.

back	down	down	off	on	on	up

1 It was a good feeling to put .... dry clothes and eat a large cooked breakfast.
2 Switch .... the kettle and sit on that chair while I make tea.
3 Put .... your paper and listen to me.
4 Switch .... the lights when you are not using them.
5 It's hot in here. Do you mind if I turn .... the heater a bit?
6 If you find a café, could you bring .... a couple of sandwiches?
7 I think I'll wash .... the plates and cups now.

break	fill	give	let	look	pick	take

8 If you want to know what grammar is, ... up the word in the dictionary.
9 You can't .... up a newspaper these days without reading about terrible things.
10 She got ill and had to .... up her job.
11 He .... in six goals in four games.
12 Why did you have to .... in the form?
13 I .... off my shoes whenever I can.
14 .... up the firewood into little pieces, can you?

The **small adverb** can usually go before or after the **object**.

*Switch **on the kettle**.* OR *Switch **the kettle on**.* *He let **in six goals**.* OR *He let **six goals in**.*

When the **object** is a pronoun (*him, her, it* etc), the **small adverb** must go after it.

*Switch **it on**.* (NOT ~~*Switch on it.*~~) *He let **them in**.* *Take **it away**.*

4 Change the sentences twice.

▶ She put on her coat. *She put her coat on.* *She put it on.*
▶ I washed up the plates. *I washed the plates up.* *I washed them up.*
1 Could you turn down the TV? ....
2 You can throw away the potatoes. ....
3 Why don't you take off your glasses? ....
4 Please put down that knife. ....
5 Shall I fill up your glass? ....
6 I'll switch on the heating. ....

In some answers, both contracted forms (for example *I'm, don't*) and full forms (for example *I am, do not*) are possible. Normally both are correct.

verbs with two objects *Take the boss these letters.*

SOME VERBS THAT CAN HAVE TWO OBJECTS

bring	*buy*	*cook*	*fetch*	*find*	*get*	*give*	*lend*	*make*	*offer*	*pass*
pay	*promise*	*read*	*send*	*show*	*teach*	*take*	*tell*	*write*		

Some **verbs** can have **two objects**. Two different structures are possible:

1 VERB + PERSON + THING	2 VERB + THING + *TO/FOR* + PERSON
*I **gave** Peter lunch yesterday.*	*I **gave** lunch to Peter yesterday.*
*Could you **take** the boss these letters?*	*Could you **take** these letters to the boss?*
*I've **made** everybody tea.*	*I've **made** tea for everybody.*

Most often, we use **verb** + person + thing, especially with personal pronouns (*me, you* etc).

*Can I **show** you my photos?* *I **wrote** her a long letter, but she never answered.*
*I'm going to put John to bed and **tell** him a story.* *I've **bought** you a present.*

1 Change the structure.

▶ Send Alison the bill. Send the bill to Alison.
▶ I'll make some tea for you. I'll make you some tea.
1 I lent Joe my bicycle yesterday. ....
2 I often read stories to Lucy. ....
3 Carol teaches small children maths. ....
4 Ruth showed the photo to the others. ....
5 Amanda often gives her mother flowers. ....
6 Could you buy a newspaper for me? ....
7 I found a hotel room for my parents. ....
8 Pass this paper to Mr Andrews. ....
9 Luke has written a letter to Joy. ....
10 I want to get a good watch for Peter. ....

2 Who gave who what? Write sentences. Put the person before the thing.

JOE: chocolates → **SALLY**: a book → **FRED**: flowers → **ANNIE**: a picture → **LUKE**: a sweater → **MARY**: a camera → **JOE**

▶ Joe gave Sally chocolates.
1 Sally ....
2 ....
3 ....
4 ....
5 ....

3 Can you complete these quotations with words from the box?

buy	find	give	give	lend ✓

▶ Friends, Romans, countrymen, lend me your ears. (*Shakespeare: 'Julius Caesar'*)
1 A four-year-old child could understand this. Run out and .... me a four-year-old child. (*Groucho Marx: 'Duck Soup'*)
2 .... me liberty or .... me death. (*Patrick Henry*)
3 Money can't .... you love. (*Traditional*)

We don't use *describe, explain, say, suggest* or *borrow* in the verb + person + thing structure.
(NOT ~~*Explain me this.*~~ NOT ~~*She said me 'hello'.*~~ NOT ~~*Can I borrow you a stamp?*~~)

have something done I have my hair cut every week.

If you ***have something done***, you **don't do it yourself**; somebody does it for you.

*I **have my hair cut** every week.*   *I **have my car serviced** at the garage every 10,000 km.*

Fred cuts his hair himself.

Eric has his hair cut at Franco's.

1 **Ann is very practical: she likes doing things herself. Bill is not so practical: he has things done by other people. Complete the sentences.**

▶ Ann checks her oil herself. Bill has his oil checked .... at the garage.
1 Ann checks her tyres herself. Bill .... at the garage.
2 Ann changes her oil herself. Bill .... at the garage.
3 Ann repairs her car herself. Bill .... at the garage.
4 Ann cleans her shoes herself. Bill .... on the way to work.
5 Ann does the gardening herself. Bill .... for him.
6 Ann types her letters herself. Bill .... by his secretary.

2 **Make sentences with *should have* …**

▶ John's car is running badly. (*check*) He should have it checked. ....
1 Mary's watch isn't going. (*repair*) ....
2 Mike's trousers are dirty. (*clean*) ....
3 Steve and Helen's kitchen window is broken. (*repair*) ....
4 Pete's hair is getting very long. (*cut*) ....
5 Tom and Janet's new car has done 10,000 km. (*service*) ....
6 Emma's eyes are giving her trouble. (*check*) ....
7 Jasper's roof lets water in. (*repair*) ....
8 Daniel's phone makes funny noises. (*check*) ....

In some answers, both contracted forms (for example *I'm*, *don't*) and full forms (for example *I am*, *do not*) are possible. Normally both are correct.

imperatives *Come in. Don't worry.*

Imperatives are like **infinitives without *to***. We use them, for example, to **tell people what to do**, to give them **advice**, or to give them **friendly invitations**.

***Turn** left at the next crossroads.* *Always **hold** the tennis racket like this.* (NOT ~~*Hold always*~~ …)
***Pay** here.* ***Try** again.* ***Come** and **have** dinner with us.* ***Have** some more meat.*

Negative imperatives begin ***do not***, ***don't*** or ***never***.

*Please **do not park** here.* ***Don't listen** to him.* ***Never tell** her that she's wrong.* (NOT ~~*Tell her never*~~ …)

1 Which words go with which picture?

▶ DRIVE SLOWLY ..A..
1 TURN LEFT ......
2 DON'T TOUCH ......
3 DO NOT PICK FLOWERS ......

2 How do you get from the station to Church Street? Complete the directions.

go ✓	go	take	turn	turn	turn

▶ ...Go........ out of the station, 1 .... right, and 2 .... down Station Road. 3 .... left into Platt Street, then 4 .... the first road on the right. After the car park, 5 .... left, and Church Street is the second on the right.

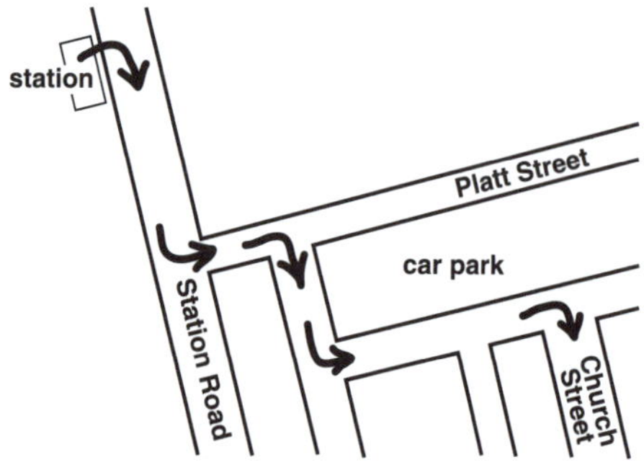

3 GRAMMAR AND VOCABULARY: some common imperative expressions

Make sure you know the expressions in the box. Use a dictionary if necessary. Then complete the sentences.

1–5: Be careful! Have a good journey/holiday Help! Hurry up! Look out! ✓ Sleep well
6–11: Come in Don't forget … Don't worry Follow me Have some (more) …
Make yourself at home Sit down Wait for me!

▶ ...Look out!.. There's a child crossing the road in front of you!
1 .... We're going to be late.
2 .... There's ice on the steps.
3 .... I can't swim!
4 '..' 'Thanks. I'll send you a postcard.'
5 'I'm going to bed.' 'Goodnight. ....'
6 'I'll be home late tonight.' 'OK. .... your keys.'
7 .... I can't walk as fast as you!
8 .... coffee.' 'No thanks. If I drink any more I won't be able to sleep.'
9 'I'd like to speak to the manager, please.' 'Of course, sir. ...., please.'
10 'Jill's gone into hospital.' '.. She'll be all right.'
11 Hello. .... in and ....
Please..

We don't use imperatives, even with *please*, to ask for things politely (see page 86).

Could you tell me the time? (NOT ~~*Tell me the time, please.*~~)

let's (suggestions) *Let's go.*

We can make **suggestions** with ***let's*** (or *let us* – very formal) + **infinitive without *to***.

I'm tired. ***Let's go*** *home.* ***Let's eat*** *out this evening.* ***Let's see*** *what's on TV.*

The negative is ***Let's not*** … or ***Don't let's*** … (informal).

Let's not go *camping this summer.* ***Let's not tell*** *John about Mary and Pete.*
Don't let's invite *that fool Raymond.*

1 **Look at the pictures and complete the suggestions, using *Let's (not)* …**

▶ Let's go for a walk.
1 Let's not ……………………………………
2 …………… play …………………………
3 …………………………………… cards.
4 …………… go …………………… ing.
5 ……………………………………………
6 ……………………………………………
7 …………… watch ………………………
8 …………… go …………………………

▶ 

1 

2 

3 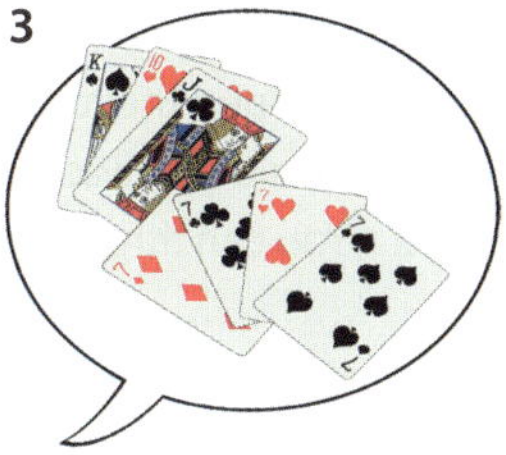

4 

5 

6 

7 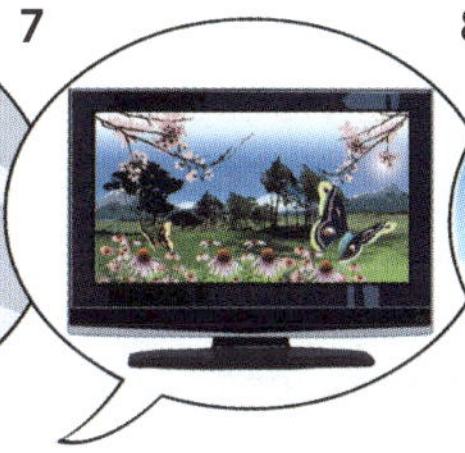

8 

2 **GRAMMAR AND VOCABULARY: cities and countries**

Do you know the English names for cities and countries round the world? Complete the conversations using names in the box. Use a dictionary if necessary.

Athens	Bangkok	Beijing	Copenhagen	Istanbul	Lisbon ✓	Marrakesh
Mexico City	Moscow	Prague	Rio	Vienna	Warsaw	

▶ 'I'd like to visit Portugal.' 'Let's go to Lisbon.'
1 'I'd like to visit Greece.' 'Let's go to ……………………………………'
2 'It would be nice to see Denmark.' 'Let's go ……………………………………'
3 'I want to see Austria.' 'Let's ……………………………………'
4 'I've always wanted to see the Czech Republic.' ……………………………………
5 'I'm interested in seeing Poland.' ……………………………………
6 'What about a holiday in Russia?' ……………………………………
7 'Morocco sounds interesting.' ……………………………………
8 'I've never been to Turkey.' ……………………………………
9 'What about Thailand this year?' ……………………………………
10 'I'd love to see China.' ……………………………………
11 'It's time to see Mexico.' ……………………………………
12 'Brazil this summer, OK?' ……………………………………

In some answers, both contracted forms (for example *I'm*, *don't*) and full forms (for example *I am*, *do not*) are possible. Normally both are correct.

special structures with verbs: more practice

1 Phrasal verbs. Put in the missing words.

▶ I'm really tired. I'm going to *lie* down for half an hour.
1 Hurry ....! We're late.
2 Don't turn ...., but somebody is following us.
3 Can you .... in this form?
4 The radio's too loud. Can you .... it down?
5 It's dark. I'll switch .... the lights.
6 It's cold. .... on your coat.
7 Shall I wash .... these plates?
8 She borrowed my shoes and never brought them ....
9 'I must talk to you.' 'No! .... away!'
10 It's 6.30. Time to .... up.

2 Phrasal verbs with objects. Change the sentences twice.

▶ He put on his glasses. *He put his glasses on. He put them on.*
▶ I turned the radio down. *I turned down the radio. I turned it down.*
1 Could you wash up the cups? ....
2 You can throw away those papers. ....
3 Why don't you take your coat off? ....
4 You need to fill in this form. ....
5 Please bring my bicycle back. ....
6 Let me fill up your glass. ....
7 Please put down that gun. ....
8 I'll switch the TV on. ....
9 Can you cut up the onions? ....
10 Pick your coat up. ....

3 Verbs with two objects. Change the structure.

▶ Send John this letter. *Send this letter to John.*
▶ Can you make some coffee for me? *Can you make me some coffee?*
1 Alice sent her sister €500. ....
2 Sarah bought ice creams for the children. ....
3 Let's send Granny a postcard. ....
4 Ruth showed the photo to the others. ....
5 I gave some flowers to the secretary. ....
6 Can you find John's address for me? ....
7 I found a hotel for Aunt Patsy. ....
8 Take these papers to Mrs Lewis. ....
9 I've given George all the information. ....
10 I want to buy a nice present for my sister. ....

4 Imperatives. Complete the sentences.

▶ Be ..careful.. with those glasses – they break easily.

1 .... in and close the door.
2 Don't .... Everything will be all right.
3 Goodbye! .... a good journey.
4 Look ....! There's a car coming.
5 .... yourself at home.
6 ....! I can't turn the water off!
7 Goodnight. .... well.
8 'Where's the Director's office?' 'I'll show you. .... me.'
9 '............... a good holiday.' 'Thanks. I'm sure we will.'
10 Don't .... to phone us when you arrive.

5 Grammar in a text. Read the text and put in imperatives from the box. Use a dictionary if necessary.

1–5:	fetch	hold	let	pick	put	
6–10:	continue	get	get	open	throw	
11–16:	blow	drink	find	kneel	remove	telephone

Instructions for giving a cat a pill

1 .... up the cat. 2 .... it in your left arm like a baby. 3 .... your right forefinger and thumb at the sides of the cat's mouth and push the mouth open, holding the pill in your left hand. Put the pill into the cat's mouth. 4 .... the cat close its mouth and swallow the pill.

Pick up the pill from the floor and 5 .... the cat from behind the sofa. Pick up the cat. Hold it in your left arm like a baby and 6 .... as before.

Fetch the cat from the bedroom and 7 .... the pill away. 8 .... another pill out of the packet. Hold the cat in your left arm, holding its back legs tightly with your left hand. 9 .... the cat's mouth and push the pill to the back of the mouth with your right forefinger. Hold the mouth shut while you count to ten.

10 .... the pill out of the goldfish bowl. Get the cat down from the top of the wardrobe. Wrap the cat in a towel. 11 .... on the floor, holding the cat firmly between your knees. Put the pill in the end of a drinking straw. Force the cat's mouth open with a pencil and 12 .... down the drinking straw.

Check the label to make sure the pill is not harmful to humans. 13 .... a glass of water to take the taste away. Put a bandage on your arm and 14 .... the blood from the carpet with cold water and soap. 15 .... the fire brigade to get the cat down from the tree across the road.

16 .... a new home for the cat. Get a dog.

6 Internet exercise. Use a search engine (e.g. Google) to find simple sentences with the following phrasal verbs: *pick up, bring back, switch on, throw away, fill up*. Write them here.

....
....
....
....
....

pronunciation for grammar → e-book

special structures with verbs: revision test

1 Which is/are correct? Circle the letter(s) of the correct sentence(s). One, two or more answers may be correct for each question.

1 A He picked up the plate.
B He picked the plate up.
C He picked up it.
D He picked it up.

2 I don't repair my car myself. I …
A repair it in the garage.
B let it repair in the garage.
C let repair it in the garage.
D have repaired it in the garage.
E have it repaired in the garage.
F have it repair in the garage.

3 A I sent some flowers to my mother.
B I sent some flowers my mother.
C I sent to my mother some flowers.
D I sent my mother some flowers.

4 A DO NOT OPEN THIS WINDOW
B NOT OPEN THIS WINDOW
C DON'T OPEN THIS WINDOW
D OPEN NOT THIS WINDOW

5 A Let's to play cards.
B Let's playing cards.
C Let's play cards.

6 A Let's not go home.
B Let's don't go home.
C Not let's go home.
D Let's go not home.

7 A I got out the bus at the station.
B I got off the bus at the station.
C I got on the bus at the station.
D I got down from the bus at the station.

8 A Don't listen to!
B Don't listen him!
C Don't listen!
D Don't listen to him!

9 A They're looking at a hotel.
B They're looking a hotel.
C They're looking for a hotel.
D They're looking to a hotel.

10 A I'm getting cold.
B Can you get some bread?
C Get out of here.
D Let's get married.

2 Put in the correct preposition or – (= no preposition).

1 What's happened .... Tom? He's an hour late.
2 I usually arrive .... the station at 8.30.
3 'Have you lost something?' 'I'm looking .... my keys.'
4 'You look happy.' 'Yes, I'm thinking .... my holiday.'
5 I had to wait .... the bus for half an hour this morning.
6 Have you paid .... the tickets?
7 Could you look .... the children for half an hour?
8 Who's paying .... the bill for lunch?
9 My parents don't like me to ask .... money.
10 I got .... the bus and sat down.
11 Listen .... this – it's really interesting.
12 Anna still believes .... Father Christmas.
13 Do you belong .... a political party?
14 I'll sing, but please don't laugh .... me.
15 I need to talk .... the secretary.
16 Look ....! There's your brother.
17 I send money .... my parents every week.
18 You can pay .... the driver when you get .... the bus.
19 They talked .... sport all evening – it was very boring.
20 My girlfriend comes .... Ireland.

In some answers, both contracted forms (for example *I'm*, *don't*) and full forms (for example *I am*, *do not*) are possible. Normally both are correct.

SECTION 11 articles: *a/an* and *the*

grammar summary

A/An shows that we are talking about **one person or thing.** We often use *a/an*:

- in **descriptions**

  *She's **an** interesting person.* *He's got **a** loud voice.*

- when we say **what something is**, or what somebody's **job** is.

  *This is **a** return ticket.* *I'm **an** engineer.*

The usually means 'You know which one(s) I'm talking about'.

*Can I use **the** phone?* (The hearer knows that this means 'your phone'.)

Nouns used **without articles** often have a special meaning.

*I dislike **cats**.* (This means 'all cats'.)

Most Western European languages have articles. So if you speak (for example) French, German, Spanish or Greek, you will not have too many problems with *a/an* and *the*: they are used mostly in the same way as your articles. There are a few differences: see pages 156–161. If you speak a non-Western-European language (for example Russian, Polish, Arabic, Chinese, Japanese), you may find articles more difficult. Study all of this Section, especially pages 154–155.

There is a mountain far away.
And on the mountain stands a tree.
And on the tree there is a branch.
And on the branch there is a nest.
And in the nest there is an egg.
And in the egg there is a bird.
One day the bird will fly.
One day we will be free.

(old folk song)

An Englishman, an Irishman, a Scotsman and a Welshman went into a pub. The Englishman . . .

Shut the door and turn off the lights when you go, will you?

We've got offices in Australia, Canada and the United States.

He's a doctor and she's an engineer.

There's some bacon in the fridge if you're hungry.

My wife's from California.

I'll meet you at the Palace Hotel in Clark Street at 8.00.

He's got a very nice smile.

You have beautiful eyes.

We went to the Czech Republic on holiday last year.

I'm afraid Ann's in hospital again.

We both studied at Birmingham University.

People are strange.

a/an; pronunciation of *the*

We use *a* before a consonant sound (for example, the normal sound of *b, c, d, f, g, h*).

a book *a coat* *a house* *a letter* *a new idea*

We use *an* before a vowel sound (for example, the normal sound of *a, e, i, o, u*).

an address *an egg* *an idea* *an old house*

1 Put in *a* or *an*.

▶ ..a.. ticket ▶ ..an.. afternoon 1 ...... bicycle 2 ...... airport 3 ...... shop
4 ...... holiday 5 ...... exercise 6 ...... day 7 ...... American 8 ...... student

We choose *a* or *an* because of **pronunciation**, not spelling.

- *a house, a hand, a head* BUT *an hour* /aʊə/ (the *h* is silent, so *hour* is like *our*)
- *an uncle, an umbrella,* BUT *a university* (pronounced *'you-niversity'*), *a European* (pronounced *'you-ropean'*), *a uniform* (pronounced *'you-niform'*), *a useful book*
- *an orange, an opera, an office* BUT *a one-pound stamp* (pronounced *'wun …'*)

2 Put in adjectives.

▶ a car (*expensive*) ..an expensive car..
▶ an address (*new*) ..a new address..
1 a friend (*old*) ....
2 an apple (*big*) ....
3 a child (*unhappy*) ....
4 a train (*early*) ....
5 an uncle (*rich*) ....
6 a job (*easy*) ....
7 an exercise (*hard*) ....
8 a language (*European*) ....
9 a book (*small*) ....

Before a consonant sound we pronounce *the* as /ðə/ (like the end of *mother*).
Before a vowel sound we say /ði/ (it rhymes with *see*).

3 Pronounce:

the beginning the woman the child the time the place the house the horse
the end the old man the office the address the American
the hour the one the university the European the uniform

4 GRAMMAR AND VOCABULARY: seven useful things

Complete the sentences with words from the box. Use *a* or *an*.

alarm clock

calculator

torch

envelope

hammer

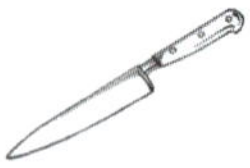
knife

tin-opener ✓

▶ You use ..a tin-opener.. to open tins.
1 You can use .... when you send a letter.
2 .... is useful for mathematics.
3 You can see at night with ....
4 You can put nails into wood with ....
5 .... is useful for cutting things.
6 .... wakes you up in the morning.

countable and uncountable *a car, cars; petrol*

Countable nouns are words like *car, book, chair*. They are the names of things that you can count: you can say '*one car*', '*two books*', '*three chairs*'. They can be **singular** (*a cat, one book*) or **plural** (*two chairs, lots of books*).

Uncountable nouns are words like *smoke, rice, water, petrol*. These are things that you can't count: you can say 'smoke', but not '~~one smoke~~' or '~~two rices~~' or '~~three waters~~'. Uncountable nouns are only **singular**. (For more information, see page 198.)

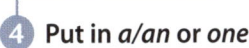

1 Singular countable, plural countable or uncountable? Write 'SC' (singular countable), 'PC' (plural countable) or 'U' (uncountable) against the words.

bird SC	bottles PC	blood U	children	flower	love ......
meat	mountains	music	nose	oil	photos ......
piano	river	snow	songs	table	windows ......

We use ***a/an*** only before **singular countable** nouns.
(*A/An* is a bit like ***one***: you can't say ~~*one houses*~~ or ~~*one air*~~.)

SINGULAR COUNTABLE	PLURAL COUNTABLE	UNCOUNTABLE
a house	*houses* (NOT ~~*a houses*~~)	*air* (NOT ~~*an air*~~)
a car	*cars*	*petrol*

2 Put in *a/an* or nothing (–).

▶ Jake's father makes ....–.... films.
▶ I need ....a.... new bicycle.
1 I never drink .... milk.
2 Jane is .... old friend.
3 Most .... cars use .... petrol.
4 I often listen to .... music.
5 The police are looking for him with .... dogs.
6 My room has got .... really big window.
7 That child wants .... new shoes.
8 She was wearing .... orange skirt.
9 They live in .... very nice house.
10 I never have .... sugar in .... coffee.

We often use an **uncountable noun** (**without *a/an***) to say what something is **made of**.

*The walls in the house were all **made of glass**.* *This sweater is **made of silk**.*

3 GRAMMAR AND VOCABULARY: materials. Put in words from the box. Use a dictionary if necessary.

brick	cotton	glass	leather	metal	plastic	silk	stone	wood	wool

▶ Shoes are made of leather or plastic.
1 Socks are made of ....
2 Cars are made of ....
3 Houses are made of ....
4 Shirts are made of ....
5 Tables are made of ....

We use ***one*** instead of *a/an* when the **exact number** is important. Compare:

*Can I have **a** cheese sandwich?* (NOT ~~*Can I have one cheese sandwich?*~~)
*No, I asked for **one** sandwich, not two!* *I only want **one** sandwich.*

4 Put in *a/an* or *one*.

▶ She's got ....a.... nice coat.
▶ She's only got ....one.... coat.
1 Can I have .... boiled egg?
2 No, I said .... egg, not two.
3 I've got .... problem. Can you help?
4 She's only got .... child.
5 John's got .... beautiful sister.
6 .... girlfriend is enough.

In some answers, both contracted forms (for example *I'm, don't*) and full forms (for example *I am, do not*) are possible. Normally both are correct.

the and *a/an* *Let's see a film. I didn't like the film.*

We use ***the***, not ***a/an***, to talk about somebody or something, when the speaker and hearer **both know about** this person or thing; when they both know **which one(s)**. **In other cases** we use ***a/an***.

Can I borrow the car?

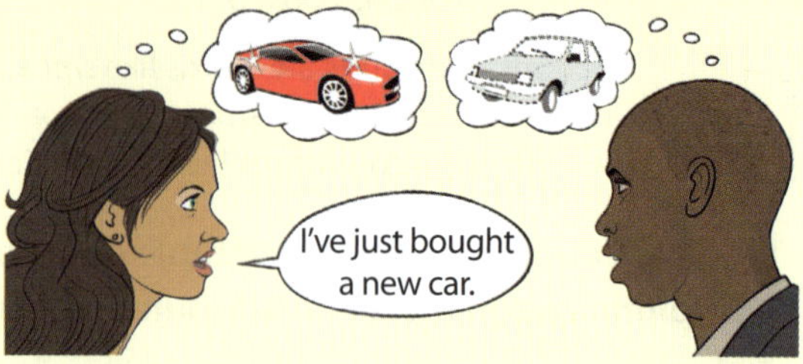
I've just bought a new car.

THE	*A/AN*
*Could you close **the door**?* (You know which door.)	*Could you open **a window**?* (I don't mind which window.)
*I'm going to **the post office**.* (You know which one – the one near here.)	*Is there **a post office** near here?*
*Can I use **the phone**?* (= 'your phone')	*Have you got **a phone**?*
*I didn't like **the film**.* (= 'the one that we saw')	*Let's go and see **a film**.*
*He looked at **the moon**.* (There's only one.)	*He looked at **a tree**.*
*She's in **the front room**.* (You know which room – I'm telling you.)	*I need **a room** for tonight.*
*She came on **the 8.15 train**.* (You know which train – I'm telling you.)	*She arrived in **an old taxi**.*
*How much is **the red coat**?* (You know which coat – I'm telling you.)	*I've just bought **a new coat**.*

1 Put in *a/an* or *the*.

▶ I walked up to her house, rang ..the...... bell and opened ..the...... door.
▶ He lives in ..a........ small village.
1 Look – that's John walking across .... street.
2 Can I use .... bathroom?
3 I need .... English-French dictionary – have you got one?
4 I know .... good restaurant – shall I reserve .... table for tonight?
5 Where's .... teacher? She's very late.
6 I want .... long holiday in .... sun.
7 Who's .... man in your office?
8 I'm leaving on .... 4.30 bus.
9 'Which is your coat?' '.......... green one.'
10 Claire's looking for .... new job.
11 Why are you looking at .... sky?
12 I'll meet you at 4.30 at .... bus stop outside .... police station.

We use ***the*** before ***only***; ***first***, ***second*** etc; and **superlatives** like ***oldest***, ***most*** (see page 223).

*She's **the only** woman for me.* *I live on **the second** floor.*
*It's **the oldest** restaurant in Glasgow.* *He bought **the most expensive** one.*

2 Put the beginnings and ends together, and put in *a/an* or *the*.

0 Sarah's ..the......	A cup of coffee? ......
1 I've got	B first train tomorrow morning? ......
2 John's	C hottest day of the year. ......
3 What time is	D most intelligent person in our family. ..0..
4 Yesterday was	E only boy in the class. ......
5 Would you like	F present for you. ......

We often use *a/an* to talk about **a** person or thing **for the first time**; and *the* when we talk about **the** person or thing **again**.

A man walked up to a policeman. The man took out a map and asked the policeman …

3 Put in *a/an* or *the*.

A BAG IN A BAG

This is ▶ ..a...... true story. Once I went into 1 .... big sports shop because I wanted 2 .... sports bag. 3 .... assistant came up to me, and I told him what I wanted. 4 .... assistant brought me three different bags. I chose 5 .... smallest one and paid for it. 6 .... assistant put 7 .... bag in 8 .... large plastic bag. I told him one bag was enough, and asked him to take 9 .... bag out of 10 .... other bag. He did so, but he looked very unhappy as I walked out of 11 .... shop.

REMEMBER: we **don't** use ***a/an*** with **plurals**. We can use ***the*** with **plurals**.

*She's wearing **black shoes**.* (NOT … ~~*a black shoes.*~~) *She bought **the shoes** last week.*

4 GRAMMAR AND VOCABULARY: animals, birds and other creatures

Make sure you know the words in the box. Use a dictionary if necessary. Then look at the groups of pictures and complete the sentences. Put in *a/an* or *the*.

ant	camel ✓	eagle	frog	monkey	mouse (*plural* mice)	parrot	pigeon	snake	spider

GROUP A

▶ This is a ..camel.. It's ..the.. biggest animal in ..the.. group.
1 This is .... It's .... smallest animal in .... group.
2 This is .... It's .... most intelligent ....

GROUP B

3 This is .... It's .... fastest bird in .... group.
4 This is .... It's .... only blue and yellow .... in ....
5 This is .... It's .... smallest ....

GROUP C

6 This is .... It's .... only creature with eight legs in ....
7 This is .... It's .... creature with six legs in ....
8 This is .... It's .... with no legs ....
9 This is .... It's .... green creature ....

In some answers, both contracted forms (for example *I'm, don't*) and full forms (for example *I am, do not*) are possible. Normally both are correct.

a/an *She's a doctor.*

We use ***a/an*** when we say **what** something is, or **what job** somebody does.

*A pony is **a** small horse.* *Canada is **a** big country.* *My sister is **an** electrician.*

REMEMBER: we **don't** use ***a/an*** with **plurals**.

*Ponies are small **horses**.* (NOT … ~~a small horses.~~)

1 Say what these people's jobs are. Use the words in the box.

builder	cook	dentist	doctor ✓	driver	hairdresser
musician	photographer	shop assistant	teacher		

▶ She's a doctor.
1 He's a ……………………………
2 He's ……………………………
3 She's ……………………………
4 He……………………………
5 She……………………………
6 She……………………………
7 He……………………………
8 She……………………………
9 He……………………………

2 Complete the sentences with your own ideas.

1 …………………………… is a good film.
2 …………………………… is a bad film.
3 …………………………… is a terrible singer.
4 …………………………… is an interesting book.
5 …………………………… is a great man/woman.
6 …………………………… are beautiful animals.
7 …………………………… is a/an ……………………………

3 GRAMMAR AND VOCABULARY: kinds of things

Look up these words in a dictionary if necessary:
building, (musical) instrument, vehicle, tool, container.
Now change these to true singular sentences.

▶ Cars are buildings. A car is a vehicle.
▶ Houses are instruments. A house is a building.
1 Bags are vehicles. ……………………………
2 Hammers are containers. ……………………………
3 Pianos are buildings. ……………………………
4 Buses are tools. ……………………………
5 Screwdrivers are containers. ……………………………
6 Guitars are tools. ……………………………
7 Boxes are instruments. ……………………………
8 Hotels are vehicles. ……………………………

a/an: describing people *She's got a nice smile.*

We often use ***a/an*** in **descriptions.**

*She's got **a** quiet voice.* (NOT … ~~*the quiet voice.*~~) *He's got **a** friendly face.*

REMEMBER: we **don't** use ***a/an*** with **plurals** or **uncountable nouns.**

*She's got **blue eyes.*** (NOT … ~~*a blue eyes.*~~) *He's got **long hair.*** (NOT … ~~*a long hair.*~~)

1 Look at the pictures and complete the sentences. Use the words in the box, and add *a/an* if necessary.

big beard	big ears	big nose ✓	dark hair	long neck	loud voice	nice smile ✓

▶ She's got ..a nice smile..........

▶ He's got ..a big nose..........

1 She's got ....

2 He's got ....

3 She's got ....

4 He's got ....

5 She's got ....

▶

▶

1
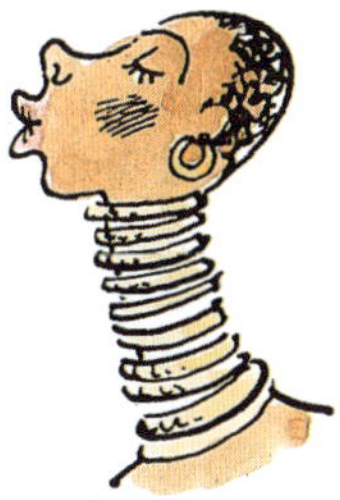

2

3

4

5

2 Here are two descriptions of the same person. Put in *a* or nothing (–).

A 'My name's Sandra. I'm tall and slim. I've got ▶ ....–.... blue eyes, ▶ ....a.... small nose, 1 .... big mouth and 2 .... dark hair. I think I've got 3 .... nice smile. I wear 4 .... glasses.'

B 'Sandra's got 1 .... very friendly face with 2 .... lovely smile. She's got 3 .... long dark hair and 4 .... blue eyes. She's got 5 .... long legs, and she's very pretty. She's wearing 6 .... blue dress today. She's got 7 .... nice voice.'

3 Write a short description (two or three sentences) of a friend of yours. Use some words from Exercises 1 and 2.

....

....

....

DESCRIPTIONS WRITTEN BY ENGLISH 7-YEAR-OLDS

my Dad

He's got green eyes like me. He has got light brown hair in some places.

My Friend

My friend is Annie Lydford. Annie's got short hair and loves horses. Annie has blue eyes and a round head with a short haircut down to her forehead. Annies always happy and she makes a really good friend.

In some answers, both contracted forms (for example *I'm, don't*) and full forms (for example *I am, do not*) are possible. Normally both are correct.

talking in general without *the* *People are funny.*

We do not normally use ***the*** to talk about people or things **in general**. ***The*** does not mean 'all'. We use ***the*** to talk about **particular** people or things (see page 154).

GENERAL	PARTICULAR
People *are funny.*	***The people*** *in that house are funny.*
I like ***music****.*	***The music****'s too loud – can you turn it down?*
Sugar *is fattening.*	*Could you pass* ***the sugar****?*
She's interested in ***dogs*** *and* ***horses****.*	*'Why are* ***the dogs*** *barking?' 'There's somebody outside.'*

1 Make some sentences from the words in the boxes.

Artists Builders Cats Dogs Horses Photographers Pianists Shop assistants Students Teachers	build don't eat don't like eat learn like paint play sell take teach	cats dogs grass houses meat music photos pictures things

- ▶ Dogs don't like cats.
- ▶ Teachers teach things.

1 ....
2 ....
3 ....
4 ....
5 ....
6 ....
7 ....
8 ....

2 Circle the correct forms.

- ▶ *The old people* / *Old people* often forget *the things* / *things.*
- ▶ I like talking to *the old ladies* / *old ladies* who live in that house.

1 *The books* / *Books* are expensive in my country.
2 'Where shall I put *the books* / *books*?' 'On the floor.'
3 Japanese is a difficult language for *the English people* / *English people*.
4 *The flowers* / *Flowers* are beautiful. Thank you very much!
5 *The life* / *Life* is sometimes hard.
6 I don't understand *the words* / *words* of that song.
7 *The food* / *Food* in this restaurant is very expensive.
8 *The water* / *Water* turns into *the ice* / *ice* at 0°C.
9 Why are *the windows* / *windows* open in this room?

3 Here are some common sayings about men and women (not all true!). Complete the sentences with words from the box, and give your opinion.

drivers	lost ✓	money	things	things	think	think	understand	understand

- ▶ Men never ask the way when they're lost .... **TRUE / NOT TRUE**

1 Men are better .... than women. **TRUE / NOT TRUE**
2 Women are more careful with .... than men. **TRUE / NOT TRUE**
3 Women .... men. Men don't .... women. **TRUE / NOT TRUE**
4 Women .... that men will change, but they don't. **TRUE / NOT TRUE**
5 Men don't .... that women will change, but they do. **TRUE / NOT TRUE**
6 Men pay too much for .... that they want. Women buy .... that they don't want because they're cheap. **TRUE / NOT TRUE**

4 **Read the two texts and then write one yourself.**

I love snow.
I like poetry, art and walking.
I don't like football, big dictionaries or hot weather.
I hate telephones, banks, vegetable soup, pop music and small dogs.

I hate writing letters.
I don't like swimming or opera.
I like children, apples, sport, television and cheese.
I love computers, history, dancing, cats, nice clothes and shopping.

....
....
....
....

5 GRAMMAR AND VOCABULARY: interests

Choose some words from the box to complete the sentences. Use a dictionary if necessary. Don't use *the*!

art	chess	dancing	football	history	music	opera	photography
poetry	politics (*singular*)	skating	swimming	tennis	travel		

1 I like ....
2 I don't like ....
3 I like .... better than ....
4 I love ...., but I hate ....
5 I enjoy ....
6 I think .... is interesting, but .... is boring.
7 .... is difficult.
8 I'm good at ...., but I'm not so good at ....
9 I prefer .... to ....
10 I'm not interested in ....
11 Most people are interested in ....
12 Not many people are interested in ....

In some answers, both contracted forms (for example *I'm*, *don't*) and full forms (for example *I am*, *do not*) are possible. Normally both are correct.

names *Mary, Africa, the USA*

NAMES WITHOUT *THE*: PEOPLE, LANGUAGES, MOST PLACES

- **people: ~~*the*~~**

Mary *works for* ***Dr Andrews****.* (NOT ~~*The Mary … the Dr Andrews.*~~)
General Parker *Prince Charles* *Aunt Elizabeth*

- **languages: ~~*the*~~**

Sorry, I don't speak ***Russian****.* (NOT ~~*… the Russian.*~~)

- **most place-names (for example continents, countries, states, lakes, mountains, towns, streets): ~~*the*~~**

Barry's from ***Texas****.* (NOT ~~*… the Texas.*~~)
Africa *Cuba* *Queensland* *Dublin* *Lake Geneva* *Mount Everest*
Wall Street *Piccadilly Circus* *Hyde Park* *Times Square*

1 Complete the sentences with words from the boxes.

Lake Superior	London	Oxford Street	Peru	Queensland ✓	Spanish	Uncle Eric

▶ Queensland .... is in Australia.
1 They speak .... in ....
2 Here's a postcard from .... He's been swimming in ....
3 .... is in the centre of ....

Africa	France	Kilimanjaro	Napoleon	Switzerland

4 .... was a very small man.
5 .... is the highest mountain in ....
6 .... is next to ....

NAMES WITH *THE*: SOME PLACES

- **deserts, rivers, seas and oceans** (but not lakes!): ***the***

the *Sahara Desert* ***the*** *Thames* ***the*** *Rhine* ***the*** *Mediterranean* ***the*** *Atlantic*

- **plural names: *the***

the *Netherlands* ***the*** *United States /* ***the*** *USA* ***the*** *Alps*

- **expressions with *Republic/Kingdom/etc*: *the***

the *Czech Republic* ***the*** *United Kingdom*

- **large areas of the world: *the***

the *West* ***the*** *Middle East* ***the*** *Far East*

2 Circle the correct answers.

▶ I once went on a boat on the *Rhine* / *Lake Victoria.*
▶ We're going to drive right across *Europe* / *Sahara Desert.*
1 Ann's just come back from the *Himalayas / Mount Everest.*
2 My sister works in *Netherlands / Denmark.*
3 I'd like to learn *Japanese / the Japanese.*
4 My parents are on holiday in the *South Africa / People's Republic of China.*
5 Here's a photo of Max in *USA / Trafalgar Square.*
6 Alan's living in a small town near the *Barcelona / Mediterranean.*
7 We have friends in *Ireland / Republic of Ireland.*
8 Wales is the smallest country in the *Great Britain / United Kingdom.*
9 There are a lot of Spanish-speaking people in the *USA / America.*

BUILDINGS WITH *THE*

- **most names of buildings: *the***

the *Hilton Hotel* — ***the*** *Old Mill Restaurant*
the *Globe Theatre* — ***the*** *British Museum*
the *Eiffel Tower* — ***the*** *Taj Mahal*
the *Great Pyramid*

Edinburgh Castle

EXCEPTIONS

- **place-name + *Airport, Station, Cathedral, University, Palace, Castle, School*: ~~*the*~~**

Oxford Airport — *Glasgow Central Station*
Exeter Cathedral — *Cambridge University*
Buckingham Palace — *Didcot Junior School*

- **name + possessive *'s*: ~~*the*~~**

St Paul's Cathedral — *McDonald's*

the Tower of London

the Globe Theatre

the Taj Mahal

3 Put *the* before five of these buildings, and nothing (–) before three.

▶ ..the.. Taj Mahal ▶ ..–.. Halloran's Restaurant 1 .... Old Steak House
2 .... National Gallery of Modern Art 3 .... Central Museum
4 .... Birmingham Airport 5 .... Sheraton Hotel 6 .... New Theatre
7 .... Jenner's Hotel 8 .... Canterbury Cathedral

4 Put in *the* or nothing (–).

1 .... American English 2 .... Asia 3 .... Blue Train Restaurant
4 .... Dominican Republic 5 .... Florida 6 .... Gobi Desert
7 .... Lake Michigan 8 .... Metropolitan Museum 9 .... Mississippi (River)
10 .... Mount Kenya 11 .... New York 12 .... North Sea 13 .... Paris
14 .... Regent Street 15 .... Rocky Mountains 16 .... Trafalgar Square
17 .... Egypt 18 .... White House 19 .... Whitehall Theatre 20 .... Far East

In some answers, both contracted forms (for example *I'm, don't*) and full forms (for example *I am, do not*) are possible. Normally both are correct.

special cases *in bed; after lunch; a hundred; …*

NO ARTICLE (~~THE~~): COMMON EXPRESSIONS WITHOUT *THE* (1)

- **meals: ~~the~~**

to have breakfast/lunch/dinner; before/at/after/for breakfast etc

- **days, dates, public holidays, months and years: ~~the~~**

on Tuesday(s); on September 17th; at Christmas; in July; in 2006

- ***this/next/last* + a day or longer period of time: ~~the~~**

this Monday; next Friday; last week; next month; this summer; last year

1 Complete the sentences with words from the boxes.

breakfast ✓	Easter	lunch	next	Saturdays	Tuesday	winter

▶ I usually just have toast and coffee for ...breakfast....

1 Let's have .... together on ....
2 We usually go to Scotland at ....
3 I'm working at home .... week.
4 It got very cold last ....
5 I play tennis with Rob on ....

August 23rd	Christmas	last	September	1616	this

6 My holiday is in .... year.
7 Lindsay's birthday is on ....
8 Shakespeare died in ....
9 The whole family always comes together at ....
10 We went to California .... summer.

NO ARTICLE (~~THE~~): COMMON EXPRESSIONS WITHOUT *THE* (2)

- **places and activities: ~~the~~**

to/at/from school/university/college; to/in/out of church/prison/hospital/bed; at home; to/at/from work; on holiday

- **transport: expressions with *by*: ~~the~~**

by car/bus/bicycle/plane/train/underground/boat and *on foot*

2 Complete the sentences with words from the box.

bed	car	church	foot	home	holiday	hospital	prison	school	university	work

1 I usually stay in .... late at the weekend.
2 Jake's going to .... to study business.
3 Most of the people in our village go to .... on Sundays.
4 I was in .... for a week when I broke my leg.
5 If I go to .... by .... it takes half an hour.
6 Uncle George comes out of .... in June.
7 I'm not going there on .... – it's raining.
8 'Is Kirsten at ....?' 'No, sorry, she's out.'
9 'Are you working in August?' 'No, I'm on ....'
10 We had to learn Latin at ....

A/AN (BEFORE SINGULAR COUNTABLE NOUNS)

- **after *with*, *without* and *as***

*I did the translation **with a** dictionary.* (**NOT** ... ~~*with dictionary.*~~)
*You can't get in **without a** ticket.* (**NOT** ... ~~*without ticket.*~~)
*She's working **as a** bus-driver.*

- **after *haven't/hasn't got***

*We **haven't got a** fax.* (**NOT** ~~*We haven't got fax.*~~)

- **in exclamations with *What ...!***

***What a** crazy idea!*

- **before *hundred/thousand/million***

***a hundred** days* ***a thousand** people* ***a million** dollars*

3 Put the beginnings and ends together, and put in *a/an*.

0 What	A .... American passport. ......
1 I didn't listen to the programme; I haven't got	B ....a.... terrible day! ..0..
2 I want a house with	C .... garden. ......
3 I went to sleep on the sofa and used my coat as	D .... hundred times. ......
4 I've told you	E .... million people in our city. ......
5 There are about	F .... blanket. ......
6 You can't work there without	G .... radio. ......
7 Phil's working as	H .... stupid idea! ......
8 What	I .... job. ......
9 It's hard to live without	J .... tourist guide. ......

THE: COMMON EXPRESSIONS WITH *THE*

the same; the country/sea/mountains; on the right/left; at the top/bottom/side/front/back; in the middle; at/to the cinema/theatre; on the radio (**BUT** *on TV*)

*Her hair is **the same** colour as her mother's.* (**NOT** ~~*Her hair is same colour*~~ ...) *We live in **the country.***
*I prefer **the mountains;** she prefers **the sea.*** *Our house is the second **on the right.***
*Write your name **at the top** of the page.* *I don't often go **to the cinema.***

4 Make sentences.

▶ Anne's house / the first / left ....Anne's house is the first on the left....
1 Patrick and I work / same office ....
2 We / going / theatre / tonight ....
3 My room / top / house ....
4 Would you like / live / country? ....
5 We usually go / mountains / Christmas ....
6 Joe always sits / back / class ....
7 Suzie's office / right ....
8 I would like / live near / sea ....
9 Why are you driving / middle / road? ....
10 Please sign your name / bottom / this paper ....

POSSESSIVES

We **don't** use ***a/an*** or ***the*** with ***my, your*** etc (see page 188).

***your** address* (**NOT** ~~*the your address*~~) ***my** friend / a friend of mine* (**NOT** ~~*a my friend*~~)

In some answers, both contracted forms (for example *I'm, don't*) and full forms (for example *I am, do not*) are possible. Normally both are correct.

articles: more practice

1 Mixed article uses. Put in *a, an, the* or nothing (–).

1 My sister lives in .... big flat.
2 'Where's .... phone?' 'In .... kitchen.'
3 Andy's brother is .... architect.
4 I'm taking .... 10.15 train.
5 Most people like .... animals.
6 Do you play .... tennis?
7 .... music's too loud – please turn it down.
8 All our furniture is made of .... wood.
9 Carola has got .... beautiful brown eyes.
10 I don't want to be .... student for the next five years.
11 I'm not interested in .... politics.
12 Can I switch on .... lights?
13 .... vegetarians don't eat .... meat.
14 .... petrol is very expensive these days.
15 We haven't seen .... sun for a week.
16 Where did you put .... butter?
17 I often listen to .... music when I'm driving.
18 .... life is sometimes hard.
19 I don't like .... fish.
20 Perhaps .... people are more interesting than .... grammar.

2 Names and special article uses. Correct (✓) or not (✗)?

1 The Canada is a big country. ......
2 Have you ever seen Eiffel Tower? ......
3 Andy works at Apollo Theatre. ......
4 The River Rhone runs into the Mediterranean Sea. ......
5 Hello. I'm at the Oxford Station. ......
6 Would you like to work as teacher? ......
7 He was in bed at 10.00. ......
8 We live in a small town in south. ......
9 Please write your address at the top of the page. ......
10 I don't eat much for the lunch. ......

3 Countable or uncountable? How many countable and uncountable nouns can you find in these advertisements?

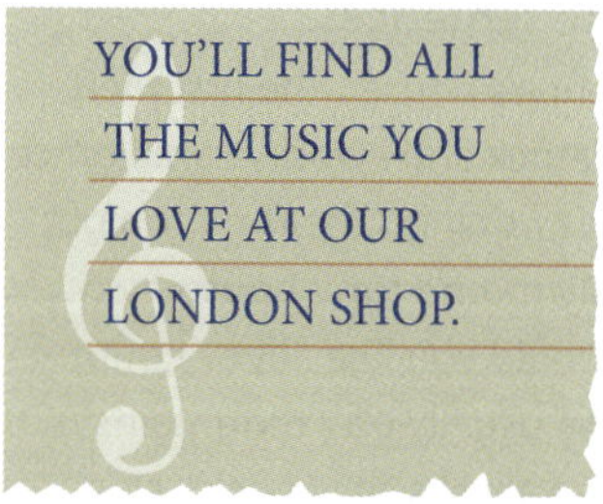

COUNTABLE: ....
....

UNCOUNTABLE: ....
....

4 Grammar in a text. Put in *a, an, the* or nothing (–).

A TRUE STORY

In 1 .... 1969, in 2 .... Portland, 3 .... Oregon, 4 .... man went to rob 5 .... bank. He didn't want 6 .... people in 7 .... bank to know what was happening, so he walked up to one of 8 .... cashiers, wrote on 9 .... piece of 10 .... paper, 'This is 11 .... robbery and I've got 12 .... gun', and showed 13 .... paper to 14 .... cashier. Then he wrote, 'Take all 15 .... money out of your drawer and put it in 16 .... paper bag.' 17 .... cashier read 18 .... message, wrote at 19 .... bottom of 20 .... paper, 'I haven't got 21 .... paper bag' and gave 22 .... paper back to 23 .... robber. 24 .... robber ran out of 25 .... bank.

5 GRAMMAR AND VOCABULARY: materials

Learn some or all of the words in the box. Use a dictionary. Then write some sentences to say what your clothes and other possessions are made of.

brick	cotton	china	diamond	glass	gold	leather	metal	paper
plastic	rubber	silk	silver	stone	synthetic fibre	wood	wool	

▸ *My shoes are made of leather and rubber.* (NOT *~~... the leather ...~~*) ....

....

....

....

....

....

....

....

....

....

6 Internet exercise. Use a search engine (e.g. Google) to find the names of the following in Britain, Australia, Canada or the USA. Write them using articles correctly.

1 a river ....
2 a lake ....
3 a mountain ....
4 a part of the country ....
5 a hotel ....
6 a station ....
7 an airport ....
8 a tourist attraction ....
9 a cathedral ....
10 a museum ....

pronunciation for grammar → e-book

articles: revision test

1 Put in *a* or *an*.

1 .... address
2 .... student
3 .... English student
4 .... university student
5 .... bus
6 .... old woman
7 .... house
8 .... hour's lesson
9 .... one-pound coin
10 .... uncle

2 Countable or uncountable? Put in *a* or nothing (–).

1 I don't like .... beer.
2 Peter is .... very good friend.
3 Does your car use .... petrol or .... diesel?
4 Do you listen to .... music while you're studying?
5 I prefer .... dogs to .... cats.
6 My flat has got .... very small kitchen.
7 I need .... new jeans.
8 Nadia was wearing .... blue dress.
9 They live in .... small town.
10 I never have .... milk in .... tea.

3 Put in *a, an, the* or nothing (–).

1 Rob has got .... very long hair.
2 .... books are very expensive.
3 .... life can be difficult.
4 Ayesha's leaving on .... 10.30 plane.
5 Do you drink .... beer?
6 'Where's .... toilet?' 'At the top of .... stairs.'
7 I like watching .... sport on TV.
8 My second brother is .... engineer.
9 It's hot in here. Can I open .... windows?
10 She stood at her door for a long time looking at .... moon.
11 Most people like .... children.
12 John's very interested in .... science.
13 I liked everything in the film except .... music.
14 Why did you put .... shoe in .... fridge?
15 These socks are made of .... silk.
16 I watch .... football, but I don't play it.
17 I'd like to be .... student again.
18 My mother thinks .... animals are nicer than .... people.
19 .... children don't usually like .... vegetables.
20 Andy lives in .... houseboat.

4 Correct the mistakes or write 'Correct'.

▶ I live in ~~the France~~. France
▶ I was born in London. Correct.
1 Can I speak to the Professor Anderson? ....
2 Greek is a difficult language. ....
3 We've just been to Czech Republic. ....
4 The Soviet Union was founded in 1922. ....
5 She's from Texas. ....
6 Carol has just spent two months in hospital. ....
7 I'll see you the next Tuesday. ....
8 You can't go there without passport. ....
9 Joe's studying to be doctor. ....
10 In Britain people drive on the left. ....

In some answers, both contracted forms (for example *I'm, don't*) and full forms (for example *I am, do not*) are possible. Normally both are correct.

SECTION 12 determiners

grammar summary

this, that, these, those	*some, any, no*	*enough*	*all, each, every, both, either, neither*
much, many, a little, a few	*more, most*	*a lot, lots*	*(a/an, the)* *(my, your* etc*)*

Determiners are words that come at the beginning of noun phrases, before adjectives. Determiners help to show **which** or **how many** people/things we are talking about.

***this** old coat* ***some** strange ideas* ***all** English words* ***enough** people*

Most determiners are explained and practised in this section. ***A/An*** and ***the*** have a separate section on pages 151–166. ***My***, ***your*** etc are explained together with pronouns on pages 188–189.

Somebody, anything, nowhere etc are included here. These are not determiners, but it is more convenient to deal with them in this section.

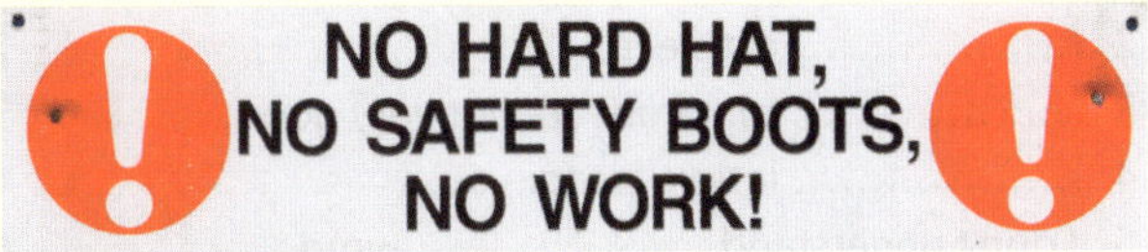

this, that, these and *those*

We can use *this* and *these* to talk about things that are here, near to us.
We can use *that* and *those* to talk about things that are there, not near.

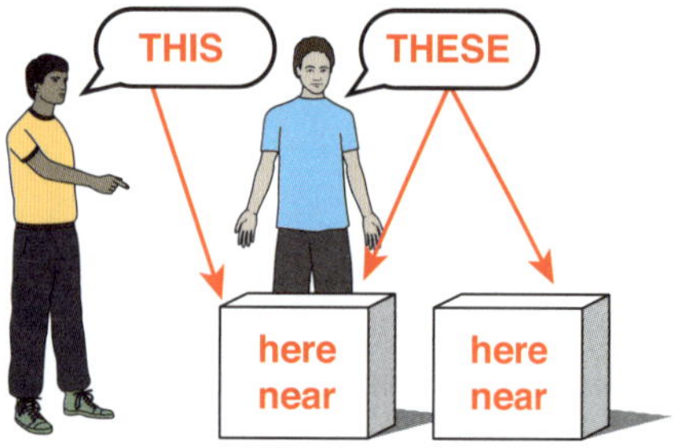

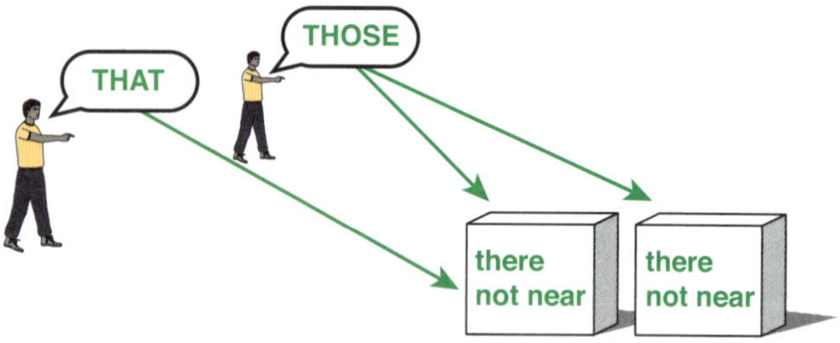

1 Put in *this* or *these*.

▶ Do you like ...this... dress?
1 Do you like .... shoes?
2 .... cat sleeps all day.
3 .... tomatoes are not very good.
4 .... letters are for you.
5 I don't understand .... word.

2 Put in *that* or *those*.

▶ Ann lives in ...that... house over there.
1 Who are .... people?
2 Could you pass me .... papers?
3 I don't think .... train is ours.
4 .... glasses look very nice.
5 Why is she running after .... man?

3 GRAMMAR AND VOCABULARY: cutlery and crockery
Use the words in the box to make ten or more sentences about the colours of the things in the picture. Use a dictionary if necessary.

cup	plate	saucer	knife ✓	fork	spoon	glass	napkin	jug	bowl

This knife is black. Those knives are silver.
....
....
....
....

We can use ***this*** and ***these*** to talk about things that are **happening now** or **starting now**.
We can use ***that*** and ***those*** to talk about things that are **finished**.

*I like **this** music.* *Listen to **these** sentences.*
***That** lesson was boring.* *Did you answer **those** letters yesterday?*

4 Circle the correct answer.

▶ *Do / Did* you like that film?
1 *I'm enjoying / I enjoyed* these lessons.
2 This game *was / will be* hard.
3 *These / Those* potatoes weren't very nice.
4 That holiday *is / was* great!
5 Do you remember *this / that* funny hotel in France?
6 May I have *this / that* dance with you?
7 I'm going to enjoy *this / that* meal.
8 That political speech *is / was* really stupid.
9 Did you understand *this / that* explanation?
10 Listen to *this / that* letter from Karen.

We can use *this, that, these* and *those* **without nouns**.

*I don't like **this**.* *Look at **these**.* *Who said **that**?* ***Those** are pretty.*

We can use ***this*** to **introduce people**, and to introduce ourselves on the telephone.

***This** is my friend Carla.* ***This** is Alex. Can I speak to Fred?*

5 Put in *this, that, these* or *those*.

▶ I don't like living in ...this... country.
1 Could you bring .... box to me, please?
2 Why did you say ....?
3 .... is Peter – is Mary at home?
4 Who are .... people over there?
5 Listen – you'll like .... story.
6 Wait – I can't walk fast in .... shoes.
7 '........................ is my sister Helen.' 'How do you do?'
8 .... was a wonderful meal – thanks.
9 I'm not enjoying .... conversation.
10 Do you remember .... people that we met in Greece?
11 Let's leave .... party.
12 The meal was nice, but I didn't like .... wine much.
13 Could you take .... letters to the post office?
14 I thought Geoff looked silly in .... shorts.
15 Is .... your mother coming out of the police station?
16 Where are you? I can't see very well with .... glasses.
17 We're going to win .... match. You wait and see.
18 What are .... birds on the roof?
19 I can't eat .... apple – it's too hard.
20 I'll never forget .... ten days with Barbara.

In some answers, both contracted forms (for example *I'm, don't*) and full forms (for example *I am, do not*) are possible. Normally both are correct.

some and any *I need some sugar. Have you got any?*

He's got some problems.

She hasn't got any problems.

We use **some** and **any**, not *a/an*, with uncountable and plural nouns.
They mean 'a limited number or quantity'.
We use **some** in **affirmative** (+) sentences.
We use **any** in **negative** (-) sentences, and in most questions.

*I'd like **some** water.* *Here are **some** flowers for you.*
*I haven't got **any** money.* *There aren't **any** trains today.*
*Have you got **any** sugar?* *Do you speak **any** other languages?*

1 Circle the correct answers.

▶ I'd like *some / any* help.
1 There aren't *some / any* letters for you.
2 Have you got *some / any* brothers or sisters?
3 We need *some / any* more milk.
4 She's got *some / any* interesting friends.
5 Are there *some / any* restaurants near here?
6 I'm having *some / any* problems with my car.
7 I didn't have *some / any* breakfast today.
8 He hasn't done *some / any* work for ten years.
9 Do you know *some / any* Americans?

2 Complete the sentences with *any* and words from the box.

English newspapers	games	foreign languages	help ✓	more to drink	sleep

▶ Harriet likes to do things by herself: she doesn't want any help.
1 No, I'm not thirsty – I don't want ....
2 Joe doesn't speak ....
3 Our team hasn't won .... this year.
4 I didn't get .... last night.
5 I couldn't find .... at the shop.

We use **some** in questions which expect the answer 'Yes' – for example **offers** or **requests**.

*Would you like **some** more coffee?* *Could I have **some** bread?*

3 Write sentences with *some*.

1 (*Ask for coffee*) Could I have ....
2 (*Offer bread*) Would you like ....
3 (*Offer rice*) ....
4 (*Ask for tomatoes*) ....
5 (*Offer more potatoes*) ....
6 (*Ask for more milk*) ....

We use ***any*** with words like ***never, without*** or ***hardly*** (= 'almost not'), which have **negative** meanings.

*They **never** give me **any** help.* *I got there **without any** difficulty.* *You made **hardly any** mistakes.*

4 **Put the beginnings and ends together.**

0 I finished the work without	A any rain. ......
1 I was tired, so I went to bed without	B some rain, at last. ......
2 I'm going to do	C any work in the garden. ......
3 Yesterday we had	D some work in the house. ......
4 In July we hardly had	E any supper. ......
5 She never does	F some supper. ......
6 You're hungry. I'll make you	G any help. ..0..

We can use *some* and *any* **without nouns** if the meaning is clear.

*'Can you lend me some money?' 'Sorry, I haven't got **any**.'* *'I need some more envelopes.' 'I'll bring you **some**.'*

5 **Complete the answers with words from the box and put in *some* or *any*.**

buy	good	got ✓	more ✓	put	tomorrow	want	you

▶ 'How many children has he got?' 'He hasn't ..got any..........'
▶ 'This is wonderful soup.' 'Have ..some more..................'
1 'How much did the flowers cost?' 'I didn't .... '
2 'We need light bulbs.' 'I'll get ....'
3 'Where's the sugar?' 'There's .... in front of .... '
4 'Why didn't you buy any cheese?' 'Because I didn't ....'
5 'Shall we go to the cinema?' 'There aren't .... films.'
6 'The car needs oil.' 'But I've just .... in.'

NOTE: ***Any*** is used in negative sentences, but is **not negative**. ***Not … any*** (or ***no*** – see page 114) is negative.

*Sorry, I **haven't** got **any** time / I've got no time.* (NOT ~~*Sorry, I've got any time.*~~)

6 **Complete the sentences with negative past-tense verbs. Use words from the box.**

ask	be	do	find	get ✓	have

▶ I didn't ..get................... any letters today.
1 There .... any fruit in the shops.
2 John .... any work at university.
3 The hotel .... any free rooms.
4 The policeman .... me any questions.
5 We .... any open petrol stations.

7 **GRAMMAR AND VOCABULARY: possessions**

Have you got any of the things in the box? Use a dictionary if necessary. Write some sentences with *some* or *any*.

aspirins	ballpoint pens	dollars	jewellery	keys	love letters
make-up	red shoes	stamps	string	ties	white socks

I've got some ballpoint pens. I haven't got any red shoes.
....
....
....

In some answers, both contracted forms (for example *I'm, don't*) and full forms (for example *I am, do not*) are possible. Normally both are correct.

somebody, anything, nowhere, ...

somebody	*someone*	*something*	*somewhere*	*anybody*	*anyone*	*anything*	*anywhere*
nobody	*no one*	*nothing*	*nowhere*	*everybody*	*everyone*	*everything*	*everywhere*

Somebody and ***someone*** mean the same; so do ***anybody*** and ***anyone*** etc.
The difference between ***somebody*** etc and ***anybody*** etc is the same as the difference between ***some*** and ***any*** (see pages 170–171). For *every*, see page 179.

__Somebody__ telephoned for you. *Has __anybody__ seen my keys?* *She didn't speak to __anyone__.*
I've got __something__ for you. *Do you want __anything__ from the shops?* *He lives __somewhere__ in London.*
She never goes __anywhere__. *__Nothing__ happened.* *__Everyone__ knew that.*

1 Complete the words.

▸ Is ...any...body at home?
1 'What did you say?' 'No..............'
2 I haven't seen Amy ....where.
3 There's ....one at the door.
4 Can I do any.............. to help?
5 You can find Coca-Cola every..............
6 No.............. understands me.
7 'Where did you go at the weekend?' ....where – we stayed at home.'
8 I want to tell you some...............
9 Every.............. in my family has blue eyes.
10 I don't know ....body who plays rugby.
11 Every.............. in this shop is expensive.
12 I want to live ....where warm.

2 These are sentences from real conversations. Can you complete them with *somebody, anything* etc?

1 Does .... want to speak about that?
2 The poor woman has .... to go.
3 It doesn't cost ....
4 .... said 'thank you': not one man.
5 Ten people in one room with no bath, no water, ...
6 What can you buy for a woman who has ....?

After ***nobody/no one, everybody/everyone, everything*** and ***nothing*** we use **singular** verbs.

Everybody __knows__. (NOT ~~*Everybody know.*~~) *Everything __is__ OK.* *Nothing __happens__ here.*

3 Put in verbs from the box. Use singular forms.

agree	be	be	happen	have	know

1 Nobody .... where she lives.
2 Everything .... to me.
3 Everything .... interesting to somebody.
4 .... everybody here?
5 .... everybody got a drink?
6 No one .... with me.

One negative word (like ***nothing, never, not***) is normally enough (see page 115).

She __never__ says anything. (NOT ~~*She never says nothing.*~~ OR ~~*She doesn't never*~~ ...)

4 Correct (✓) or not (✗)?

1 We couldn't find a hotel nowhere. ......
2 Does anybody know Penny's phone number? ......
3 Can I ask you something? ......
4 Nobody want to go home. ......
5 I don't want something, thank you. ......
6 Don't say nothing to Alan about Olivia. ......
7 Everybody needs help sometimes. ......
8 Do anybody want another drink? ......
9 Anybody doesn't understand me. ......
10 I don't never want to take nothing from nobody. ......

Note the difference between ***no one*** and ***none***. ***No one*** means '*nobody*'; ***none*** means '*not any*'.

__No one__ can help me. *I wanted some plums, but there were __none__ in the shop.*

much and *many* How much milk? How many languages?

We use ***much*** with **singular** (uncountable) nouns, and ***many*** with **plurals**.

*Do you listen to **much music**?* *Do you go to **many concerts**?*

1 Put in *much* or *many*.

▶ She doesn't speak ..much.. English.
▶ She doesn't buy ..many.. clothes.
1 I haven't got .... time.
2 Do you play .... football?
3 There aren't .... people here.
4 Are there .... Americans in your company?
5 We don't have .... rain in summer.
6 I don't eat .... meat.
7 Have you travelled to .... countries?
8 We don't watch .... films.
9 Was there .... traffic on the road?
10 Not .... tourists visit our town.
11 Do you know .... songs?
12 She doesn't have .... trouble with English.
13 There aren't .... birds in the garden.
14 She doesn't get .... money in her new job.
15 There hasn't been .... rain this year.

So many worlds,
so much to do,
so little done.

(*Alfred Lord Tennyson*)

We use ***how much*** with **singular** (uncountable) nouns, and ***how many*** with **plurals**.

***How much milk** do you want?* ***How many languages** are there in the world?*

2 Write the questions. Do you know the answers? (See the bottom of the page.)

▶ plays / Shakespeare / write ..How many plays did Shakespeare write?..
1 symphonies / Beethoven / write ....
2 cents / in a dollar .... are there ....
3 kilometres / in a mile ....
4 states / in the USA ....
5 blood / in a person's body .... is there ....
6 air / we breathe / every minute .... do we ....
7 points / you get / for a try in rugby union ....
8 food / an elephant / eat every day ....

We can use ***much*** and ***many*** **without nouns** if the meaning is clear.

*'Have you got any money?' 'Not **much**.'* *'How many people were there?' 'Not **many**.'*

Much and ***many*** are used mostly in **questions** and **negatives**. They are unusual in spoken affirmative (+) sentences. In an informal style, we prefer expressions like ***a lot of*** (see page 174).

*'Do you get **much** snow in winter?' 'Not **much**, but we get **a lot of** rain.'* (NOT … ~~*we get much rain.*~~)
*'Have you got **many** English friends?' 'No, I haven't got **many** English friends. But I've got **a lot of** American friends.'* (NOT USUALLY … ~~*I've got many American friends.*~~)

Answers to Ex 2: ▶ thirty-seven 1 nine 2 a hundred 3 1.6 4 fifty 5 5–6 litres 6 6–7 litres 7 five 8 up to a hundred kilos

In some answers, both contracted forms (for example *I'm, don't*) and full forms (for example *I am, do not*) are possible. Normally both are correct.

a lot of and *lots of*

A lot of and ***lots of*** are common in an informal style. They mean the same.

*I haven't got **a lot of** time just now.* *He's got **lots of** money and **lots of** friends.*

We can use both expressions before singular (uncountable) or plural nouns.

- ***a lot of / lots of*** + singular subject: singular verb

  ***A lot of** his work is good.* ***Lots of** his work is good.* (NOT ~~*Lots of his work are good.*~~)

- ***a lot of / lots of*** + plural subject: plural verb

  ***A lot of** his ideas are good.* (NOT ~~*A lot of his ideas is good.*~~) ***Lots of** his ideas are good.*

If we use *a lot* or *lots* **without** a **noun**, we **don't** use *of*.

*'Have you got **a lot of** work?' 'Yes, **a lot**.'* (NOT ~~*Yes, a lot of.*~~)

1 Circle the correct answer.

1 Lots of people *have / has* computers now.
2 There *is / are* lots of cinemas near here.
3 Lots of snow *has / have* fallen today.
4 'Problems?' 'Yes, *a lot / a lot of*.'
5 A lot of my friends *work / works* in London.
6 'Any letters for me?' '*A lot / A lot of*.'
7 A lot of things *need / needs* to change.
8 There *is / are* lots of food in the fridge.

In affirmative (+) sentences in conversation, ***a lot of*** and ***lots of*** are more natural than *much/many* (see page 173).

We eat a lot of vegetables.
(NOT ~~*We eat many vegetables.*~~)
This car uses lots of petrol.
(NOT ~~*This car uses much petrol.*~~)

not much hair *not many teeth*

a lot of / lots of hair *a lot of / lots of teeth*

Plenty of can be used in the same way as ***a lot of / lots of***.

2 Put in *plenty of* with words from the box.

eggs	food	ideas	paint ✓	patience	time	warm clothes	water

What do you need:

▶ if you're painting a big house? *plenty of paint*
1 if you're very hungry? ....
2 if you've got a lot of work? ....
3 if you work with small children? ....
4 if you're in the Arctic? ....
5 if you're making a big omelette? ....
6 if you're crossing the desert? ....
7 if you're writing a novel? ....

3 GRAMMAR AND VOCABULARY: towns

Make sure you know the words in the box. Use a dictionary if necessary. Then write four sentences about a town, using *a lot of / lots of / plenty / not much / not many*.

bookshops	cinemas	hotels	industry	libraries	markets	nightlife
parks	restaurants	theatres	traffic			

▶ *In Oxford there are a lot of museums; there is not much industry.*
1 In ....
2 ....
3 ....
4 ....

a little and *a few* *a little English; a few words*

We use ***a little*** with **singular** (uncountable) nouns, and ***a few*** with **plurals.**

*If you're hungry, we've got **a little soup** and **a few tomatoes**.*

1 Put in *a little* or *a few*.

1 I know .... English.
2 I speak .... words of Spanish.
3 I'll be on holiday in .... days.
4 Can you give me .... help?
5 Grace will be ready in .... minutes.
6 Could I have .... more coffee?
7 I'd like to ask you .... questions.
8 I'm having .... trouble with the police.
9 The soup needs .... more salt.
10 I'm going away for .... weeks.

Little and ***few*** (without *a*) have a rather **negative** (−) meaning (like ***not much/many***).
A little and ***a few*** have a more **positive** (+) meaning (like ***some***).

*We've got **a little** food in the house if you're hungry.* (= 'some, better than nothing')
*There was **little** food in the house, so we went to a restaurant.* (= 'not much, not enough')
*His lesson was very difficult, but **a few** students understood it.* (= 'more than I expected')
*His lesson was so difficult that **few** students understood it.* (= 'not many, hardly any')

2 Circle the correct answer.

▶ I have *little* / *a little* time to read newspapers and no time at all to read books.
1 Come about 8 o'clock; I'll have *little / a little* time then.
2 There was *little / a little* water on the mountain, and we all got very thirsty.
3 Foreign languages are difficult, and *few / a few* people learn them perfectly.
4 I'm going to Scotland with *few / a few* friends next week.
5 I've brought you *few / a few* flowers.
6 Life is very hard in the Arctic, so *few / a few* people live there.
7 She was a difficult woman, and she had *few / a few* friends.
8 'Would you like something to drink?' '*Little / A little* water, please.'

Little and ***few*** are rather **formal**; in **conversation** we use ***not much/many*** or ***only a little/few***.

*There **wasn't much** food in the house.* OR *There was **only a little** food in the house.*
*The lesson was so difficult that **not many / only a few** students understood it.*

3 Make these sentences more conversational.

▶ I speak little English. *I only speak a little English* OR *I don't speak much English.*
1 There was little room on the bus. ....
2 Few people learn foreign languages perfectly. ....
3 She has few friends. ....
4 We get little rain here in summer. ....
5 This car uses little petrol. ....
6 There are few flowers in the garden. ....
7 Our town gets few tourists. ....
8 We have little time to catch the train. ....

We can use (*a*) ***little*** and (*a*) ***few*** **without nouns** if the meaning is clear.

'Have you got any money?' ***'A little.'*** *'Did you buy any clothes?'* ***'A few.'***

In some answers, both contracted forms (for example *I'm, don't*) and full forms (for example *I am, do not*) are possible. Normally both are correct.

enough money; fast enough

We put *enough* **before nouns.**

Have you got enough money for the bus? *There aren't enough plates for everybody.*

1 Look at the pictures and complete the descriptions.

1 not .... food 2 .... strings 3 .... seats 4 ....

2 Use *enough* with words from the box to complete the sentences.

buses ✓	chairs	girls	money	salt	time	work

▸ You need a car in our village, because there aren't ...enough buses....
1 Have you got .... to finish the work?
2 There were plenty of boys at the party, but not ....
3 We couldn't sit down because there weren't ....
4 I won't pass the exam because I haven't done ....
5 I've got just .... for a ticket to America.
6 This soup isn't very nice. There's not .... in it.

We put *enough* **after adjectives and adverbs.**

This room isn't big enough. (NOT ... ~~*enough big*~~) *You're not walking fast enough.*

3 GRAMMAR AND VOCABULARY: common adjectives

Check the words in the box with a dictionary if necessary. Then complete the list with *not ... enough*.

bright	clear	comfortable	deep	easy	fresh	interesting ✓	loud

	POSSIBLE PROBLEMS		POSSIBLE PROBLEMS
▸ a book	not interesting enough	4 an exercise	....
1 an alarm clock	....	5 an explanation	....
2 a chair	....	6 eggs	....
3 a lamp	....	7 a swimming pool	....

4 Put *enough* with each word.

▸ old ...old enough...	3 beds	7 milk ....
▸ people ...enough people...	4 often	8 help ....
1 warm	5 quiet	9 sweet ....
2 early	6 children	10 young ....

We can use *enough* **without a noun** if the meaning is clear.

'More coffee?' 'No, thanks. I've got ***enough****.'*

too, too much/many and *not enough*

We use ***too*** with **adjectives** and **adverbs**. We use ***too much/many*** with **nouns**.
These give the opposite meaning to 'not enough'.

*This coffee's **too cold**.* (**NOT** … ~~*too much cold*~~ …) *He drives **too fast**.*
*I've got **too much work** and not enough time.* *You ask **too many questions**.*

not hot enough *too hot*

1 Put in *too, too much* or *too many*.

1 .... old
2 .... trouble
3 .... problems
4 .... money
5 ill
6 .... work
7 .... hot
8 .... students
9 .... cars
10 .... difficult

2 GRAMMAR AND VOCABULARY: common adjectives
Make sure you know the words in the box. Use a dictionary if necessary. Then change the expressions.

cheap	dry	expensive	fast ✓	hard	heavy	high	light	low
narrow	short	slow ✓	soft	tall	thick	thin	wet	wide

▸ not fast enough = too slow
▸ too slow = not fast enough
1 not high enough = ...
2 not tall enough = ...
3 not heavy enough = ...
4 not hard enough = ...
5 too narrow = ...
6 too expensive = ...
7 too dry = ...
8 too thick = ...

3 A man is going walking in the mountains for three days. Look at the things that he is taking and give your opinion, using (*not*) *enough* or *too much/many*. Use a dictionary if necessary.

HE IS TAKING		YOUR OPINION
1 packet of soup	▸	not enough soup
1 camera	▸	enough cameras
8 maps	▸	too many maps
5 pairs of socks	1	....
1 pair of boots	2	....
3 pocket torches	3	....
1 tube of sun-cream	4	....
2 waterproof jackets	5	....
2 pairs of sunglasses	6	....
10 kg of bread	7	....
2 kg of cheese	8	....
100 cl of water	9	....
1 orange	10	....
1 bar of chocolate	11	....
1 small bar of soap	12	....
3 toothbrushes	13	....

In some answers, both contracted forms (for example *I'm, don't*) and full forms (for example *I am, do not*) are possible. Normally both are correct.

all all my friends are here; my friends are all here

All can go **with a noun** or **with a verb**.

All the trains *stop at Cardiff.* *The trains* ***all stop*** *at Cardiff.*
All the courses *begin on Monday.* *The courses* ***all begin*** *on Monday.*
All birds *lay eggs.* *Birds* ***all lay*** *eggs.* ***All my clothes*** *need cleaning.* *My clothes* ***all need*** *cleaning.*

1 Change the sentences.

- ▶ All my family like travelling. My family all like travelling.
- ▶ The buses all run on Sundays . All the buses run on Sundays.
1. All the films start at 7 o'clock. ……
2. Our secretaries all speak Arabic. ……
3. The children all went home. ……
4. All these coats cost the same. ……
5. All languages have grammar. ……
6. The people all voted for the Radical Conservatives. ……
7. All my friends live in London. ……
8. These houses all need repairs. ……
9. All those shops belong to the same family. ……
10. Children all need love. ……

Note the **word order** when ***all*** goes **with a verb**. *All* goes:
1 **before** one-word verbs

The guides ***all speak*** *German.* *The visitors* ***all arrived*** *this morning.* *We* ***all got*** *up late.*

2 **after auxiliary verbs** (*will, have, can* etc) and after *are* and *were*.

The guides ***can all*** *understand Spanish.* (NOT *… ~~all can understand Spanish.~~*)
The visitors ***have all*** *arrived.* (NOT *… ~~all have arrived.~~*) *We* ***were all*** *tired.* (NOT *~~We all were tired.~~*)

2 Put *all* with the verb.

- ▶ Cars break down sometimes. Cars all break down sometimes.
- ▶ Mark's friends have gone home. Mark's friends have all gone home.
1. The offices close at weekends. ……
2. The lessons will start on Tuesday. ……
3. These children can swim. ……
4. Our windows are dirty. ……
5. Sorry, the tickets have gone. ……
6. We went to New York for Christmas. ……
7. The shops will be open tomorrow. ……
8. We stopped for lunch at 12.30. ……
9. These watches are too expensive. ……
10. The lights have gone out. ……

We **don't** normally use ***all*** without a noun to mean '**everybody**' or '**everything**'.

Everybody *knows that.* (NOT *~~All know that.~~*) *I've forgotten* ***everything.*** (NOT *~~I've forgotten all.~~*)

All human beings are born free and equal in dignity and rights.
(*Universal Declaration of Human Rights*)

Justice is open to all people in the same way as the Ritz Hotel.
(*Judge Sturgess*)

all and *every; each*

Level 2

We use ***every*** with **singular** nouns and verbs. Compare:

All people are *interesting.*	***Every person is*** *interesting.* (NOT ~~*Every person are*~~ ...)
All teachers make *mistakes.*	***Every teacher makes*** *mistakes.*

We can use other determiners (*the, my, this* etc) after ***all***, but not after ***every***. Compare:

All the *shops were closed.*	***Every*** *shop was closed.* (NOT ~~*Every the shop*~~ ...)

1 Rewrite the sentences with *every*.

▶ All the buses were late. Every bus was late.

1 All animals breathe air. ....

2 She's read all the books in the library. ....

3 I paid all the bills. ....

4 All the computers are working today. ....

5 All languages have verbs. ....

6 All London trains stop at Reading. ....

7 I've written to all the customers. ....

8 All the glasses are dirty. ....

9 All children can be difficult. ....

10 All the roads were closed. ....

Each and ***every*** are similar. We use ***each*** for **two or more**, but we use ***every*** for **three or more**.

*She had a bag in **each** hand.* (NOT ... ~~*in every hand.*~~) *She had a ring on **each/every** finger.*

2 Can you change *each* to *every* in these sentences?

▶ He's got six earrings in each ear. No.

▶ I work each day except Sunday. Yes. ... every day except Sunday.

1 There's a pub on each side of the road. ....

2 She wrote a careful answer to each letter. ....

3 He works in London and Paris, and he's got a girlfriend in each city. ....

....

4 She wears a watch on each wrist. ....

5 My parents are strange, but each one is strange in a different way. ....

....

6 Each house in this street looks the same. ....

Note the difference between *every day* (= 'on Mondays, Tuesdays, Wednesdays etc') and *all day* (= 'from morning to night').

The restaurant is open ***all day***, ***every day*** except Sunday.

'Behind every successful man is a good woman.' (*Traditional*)

'Behind every successful man stands a surprised mother-in-law.' (*Hubert Humphrey*)

'Behind every successful woman stands a good man, looking rather confused.' (*E Stabetsi*)

'Behind every successful man is a woman, behind her is his wife.' (*Groucho Marx*)

In some answers, both contracted forms (for example *I'm, don't*) and full forms (for example *I am, do not*) are possible. Normally both are correct.

both, either and *neither*

We use *both*, *either* and *neither* to talk about **two** people or things.
Both (●● = 'one and the other') has a plural noun.
Either (●● = 'one or the other') has a singular noun.
Neither (●● = 'not either, not one and not the other') has a singular noun.

*'Are you free on Monday or Wednesday?' 'I'm free on **both days**.'*
*'Which day is better for you?' '**Either day** is OK.'*
*'About four o'clock?' 'No, sorry, I'm not free on **either afternoon**.'*
*'What about Thursday or Saturday, then?' 'No, **neither day** is any good.'*

1 Put in *both*, *either* or *neither*.

1 .... children are very tall.
2 I'm busy on .... afternoons.
3 'Which room can I have?' 'You can have .... room. .... rooms have a view of the sea.'
4 .... students tried the exam, but .... student passed.
5 I'm lucky – I can write with .... hand.
6 It's very heavy: use .... hands to carry it.
7 .... coat will look good on you. Why don't you buy one of them?
8 I don't like .... coat. And .... coats are very expensive.
9 'Do you want your holiday in July or August?' '.............. month will be fine.'
10 .... my brothers studied medicine, but .... brother works as a doctor.
11 I paid for .... tickets – Ann's and mine.
12 'What do *precipitate* and *recursion* mean?' 'I don't know .... word.'

2 GRAMMAR AND VOCABULARY: things that come in twos
Make sure you know all these words. Use a dictionary if necessary. Then complete the sentences, using *both*.

ankle ✓	direction	earring	end	eye	knee	parent	sex	side	sock	team

▶ I hurt both ankles playing football.
1 Cars are parked on .... of the road.
2 .... her .... are doctors.
3 Traffic on the road was very slow in ....
4 .... are playing really badly.
5 She hurt .... skiing.
6 I've lost .... my .... – have you seen them anywhere?
7 Police were stopping cars at .... of the bridge.
8 That child has got holes in .... of his ....
9 I need new glasses. Both .... are getting worse.
10 His shop sells clothes for ....

determiners and *of* *most people; most of us*

We use **determiners** (*some, any, much, many, more, most, few, enough* etc) with ***of*** before **other determiners** (*the, this, my* etc) and before personal pronouns (*it, us* etc).

DETERMINER + *OF*	DETERMINER WITHOUT *OF*
• before *the*: ***some of** the people here*	***some** people* (NOT ~~*some of people*~~)
• before *this* etc: ***too many of** those books*	***too many** books* *I've got **too many**.*
• before *my* etc: ***a few of** our friends*	***a few** friends* *She has **a few**.*
• before *it, us* etc: ***enough of** it* ***most of** them*	***enough** milk* ***most** students*

1 Change the expressions.

▶ some houses (*those*) some of those houses
1 not much milk (*the*) ....
2 any friends (*my*) ....
3 enough meat (*that*) ....
4 some big plates (*the*) ....
5 a few ideas (*her*) ....
6 most mistakes (*these*) ....
7 too many students (*the*) ....
8 more potatoes (*those*) ....
9 not much money (*my*) ....
10 not enough work (*his*) ....

2 Put in *of* or nothing (–).

▶ Some – people don't like her.
▶ Some of the people in the class don't like her.
1 Can you lend me some more .... money?
2 I've lost some .... the addresses.
3 I don't like many .... his books.
4 She knows a few .... those people.
5 'Do you like jazz singers?' 'Some ....'
6 There wasn't enough .... food for everybody.
7 I didn't have much .... time to talk to her.
8 A few .... us want to change things.
9 I spend a lot .... my time in Scotland.
10 We haven't got any more .... eggs.
11 I've got some .... bread, but not much ....
12 She didn't understand much .... it.

Note the difference between ***most people/things*** (**in general**) and ***most of the people/things*** (**particular ones**).

***Most people** like dancing.*
*You can pay by credit card in **most shops**.*
***Most of the people at the party** were dancing.*
***Most of the shops here** are open on Sundays.*

3 Put in *most* or *most of the*.

1 .... people talk to themselves.
2 I know .... people in our village.
3 .... people on the bus had no tickets.
4 .... people like music.
5 .... cars are expensive.
6 There are students in .... houses in this street.
7 .... cats eat fish.
8 Our cat eats .... things: fish, meat, biscuits, cheese, ...
9 I understand .... words in this book.
10 She's very friendly: she gets on well with .... people.

NOTE: we often drop *of* after *all* and *both*. After *a lot / lots / plenty* we always use *of* with a noun or pronoun (see page 174).

***All (of)** my friends.* ***Both (of)** her parents.* ***a lot of** problems,* (NOT ~~*a lot problems*~~)

determiners: more practice

1 Demonstratives; *some* and *any*. Put in the correct forms.

▶ Have you got ...any........... shampoo? (*some / any*)
1 Listen to .... You'll love it! (*this / that*)
2 I didn't like .... film yesterday. (*this / that*)
3 Who are .... people in John's car? (*these / those*)
4 '.................. is my friend Beth.' 'How do you do?' (*this / that*)
5 'Look at .... earrings.' 'Where?' 'On my ears, of course!' (*these / those*)
6 You never tell me .... about your work. (*something / anything*)
7 I didn't have .... breakfast this morning. (*some / any*)
8 'This is good ice cream.' 'Would you like .... more?' (*some / any*)
9 'What are you thinking about?' '..................' (*Anything / Nothing*)
10 We got to London .... any difficulty. (*with / without*)

2 Mixed determiners. Put in *all*, *each*, *every*, *everybody*, *everything*, *both*, *either* or *neither*.

1 Has .... student arrived?
2 Hold the string at .... end.
3 Tell me ....
4 She stayed in bed .... day yesterday.
5 We're open .... day except Tuesday.
6 'Tea or coffee?' 'No, ... , thanks.'
7 I can write with .... hand.
8 I can write with .... hands.
9 Do you know .... here?
10 Not .... animals can swim.

3 Mixed determiners. Circle the correct forms.

1 Can I give you my answer tomorrow? I need *little / a little* time to think.
2 His ideas are so difficult that *few / a few* people understand them.
3 There were only *a little / a few* people at the meeting.
4 I'd like to ask you *few / a few* questions, if I may.
5 Too much work, too *little / few* time.
6 James always has *much / lots of* money.
7 Were there *much / many* girls at the party?
8 A lot of my friends *think / thinks* I'm wrong.
9 Am I driving *too / too much* fast?
10 Are those shoes *big enough / enough big*?

4 *Of* with determiners. Put in the correct forms.

1 .... the children enjoyed the show. (*Most / Most of*)
2 .... people like animals. (*Most / Most of the*)
3 .... us are meeting at Joe's tomorrow evening. (*A few / A few of*)
4 Have you seen .... good films recently? (*any / any of*)
5 I've invited .... my friends to come round this evening. (*some / some of*)
6 She finished .... the work, but not .... it. (*most / most of / all / all of*)
7 Have you got .... milk? (*enough / enough of*)
8 You ask .... questions. (*too many / too many of*)
9 'How many books have you got to read?' '..................................' (*A lot / A lot of*)
10 I don't like .... these books. (*many / many of*)

5 GRAMMAR AND VOCABULARY: common adjectives with *somebody* etc. **Check that you know all the adjectives in the box. Use a dictionary if necessary.**

big	boring	fast	high	hot	intelligent	interesting	nice	old	red	rich
round	small	sour ✓	sweet	tall	thin	useful	useless	young	warm	

Now find these in the picture. Write the letters.

- ▶ something high ..k...
- 1 something big ......
- 2 something small ......
- 3 something red ......
- 4 something round ......
- 5 something fast ......
- 6 somebody old ......
- 7 somebody young ......
- 8 somebody tall ......
- 9 somebody thin ......
- 10 somebody rich ......

Now write your own examples for:

- ▶ something sour .....a lemon.....
- 1 somewhere very hot ....
- 2 somewhere warm ....
- 3 something sweet ....
- 4 something useful ....
- 5 somebody intelligent ....
- 6 something interesting ....
- 7 something useless ....
- 8 something boring ....
- 9 somebody nice ....

6 Grammar in a text. Circle the correct forms.

SOME STATISTICS

Those who always know better: perhaps *half us* / *half of us* (circled).
Those who are not sure: *most the rest* / *most of the rest*.
Those who don't know how to be bad: very *few* / *few of*.
Those who think they are important: *a lot* / *a lot of*.
Those who are always afraid of someone or something: *most us* / *most of us*.
Those who are glad to help, if it doesn't take too long: nearly *half* / *half of*.
Those who can be happy: *some us* / *some of us*, not very many.
Those who are kind alone but cruel in crowds: half or more.
Those who will kill you if they think they have to: it's best not to know *how many* / *how many of*.
Those who only take from life and give nothing: maybe 30% (I wish I were wrong).
Those who are lost and ill in the dark: nearly everybody, sooner or later.
Those who are good: *a lot* /*a lot of*.
Those who are good and understanding: hardly anybody.
Those that we should feel sorry for: almost everybody.
Those who are dead at the end: *all us* / *all of us*.

adapted from a poem by Wisława Szymborska

7 Internet exercise: checking correctness. Use a search engine (e.g. Google).
How many hits are there for these expressions? So which are correct?

"too much fast" ....40,700....	"too fast" ....10,900,000: Correct....
"everybody is"	"everybody are" ....
"everything are"	"everything is" ....
"most people"	"most of people" ....

pronunciation for grammar → e-book

determiners: revision test

1 Correct the mistakes and rewrite the sentences.

▶ Would you like little more coffee? *Would you like a little more coffee?*
1 He spoke fast, but I understood all. ....
2 I'm hungry, but there isn't nothing to eat. ....
3 She has much money. ....
4 A lot of us was at the party last night. ....
5 Most of people think I'm right. ....
6 He was carrying a heavy bag in every hand. ....
7 Everything are very difficult. ....
8 I like every kinds of music. ....
9 I think you're driving too much fast. ....
10 If everybody are ready, we can go. ....

2 Circle the correct forms.

1 I'm enjoying *this / that* game.
2 *This / That* lesson was really hard.
3 I've had a postcard from *these / those* people we met in America.
4 What's *this / that* thing in the tree over there?
5 Hello. *This / That* is Mike. Can I speak to Anna?
6 There's *somebody / anybody* on the phone for you.
7 *I need / I don't need* some help.
8 Could I have *some / any* more coffee?
9 Anna hardly said *anything / nothing* all evening.
10 We never go *somewhere / anywhere* interesting.

3 Put in the correct forms.

1 Let me tell you .... my problems. (*all / every / each*)
2 .... everybody ready to leave? (*Is /Are*)
3 .... her parents are doctors. (*Either / Each / Both*)
4 I pronounced .... word separately, very slowly. (*all / each / both*)
5 Not .... bird can fly. (*all / every / either*)
6 'Is there anything to drink?' 'There's .... orange juice.' (*a little / a few / any*)
7 There was .... to do in the town, so we stayed at home most evenings. (*a little / little / anything*)
8 It's nice to spend .... time alone, sometimes. (*a little / little / a little of / little of*)
9 I've been to Scotland .... times. (*a little / a few / a little of / a few of*)
10 'Do you speak Russian?' '..................' (*A little / A little of / A few / A few of*)
11 Children ask .... questions. (*lots / lots of / much / many*)
12 I don't go to .... parties. (*a lot / many / many of*)
13 I've got .... problems. (*too / too much / too many / too many of*)
14 She didn't eat .... breakfast. (*much / many / many of*)
15 There .... lots of time before the shop closes. (*is / are*)
16 There's a pub at .... end of our street. (*each / every / all / both*)
17 She thinks she knows .... (*all / all of / everything*)
18 I practise karate .... day except Tuesday. (*all / either / every*)
19 'Which car can I have?' 'Sorry – .... car is free.' (*neither / either / any / both*)
20 I'd like .... sweet. (*something / something of*)

In some answers, both contracted forms (for example *I'm, don't*) and full forms (for example *I am, do not*) are possible. Normally both are correct.

SECTION 13 personal pronouns; possessives

grammar summary

I, you, he, she, it, we, you, they	*me, you, him, her, it, us, you, them*
my, your, his, her, its, our, your, their	*mine, yours, his, hers, ours, yours, theirs*
myself, yourself, himself, herself, itself, ourselves, yourselves, themselves	*each other*

We use **pronouns** when it is not necessary, or not possible, to use a more exact noun phrase.

Mrs Parker phoned. ***She*** *said …* (The speaker uses the personal pronoun *she* because it is not necessary to repeat *Mrs Parker*.)

Ann talks to ***herself*** *all the time.* (It is unnecessary to repeat *Ann*.)

In this section we explain **personal pronouns** (*I, me, you* etc); **possessives** (*my, your* etc and *mine, yours* etc); **reflexive pronouns** (*myself, yourself* etc); and ***each other***.
Indefinite pronouns (*somebody, anything* etc) are explained in Section 12, together with *some* and *any*.
Relative pronouns (*who, which* etc) are explained in Section 19.

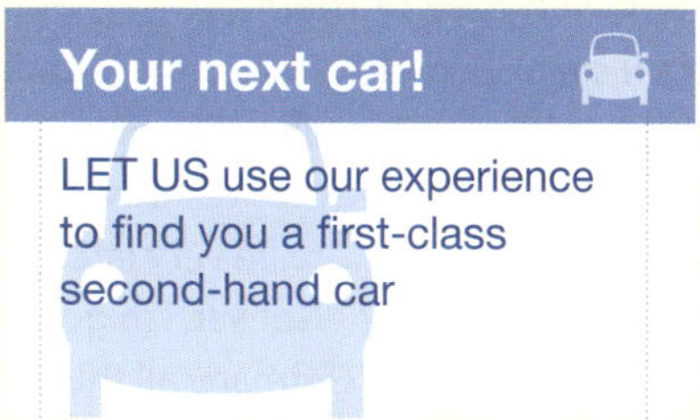

6-piece stainless steel
chef's knife set
worth £150
yours completely FREE
when you buy your furniture from us!

Your next car!
LET US use our experience to find you a first-class second-hand car

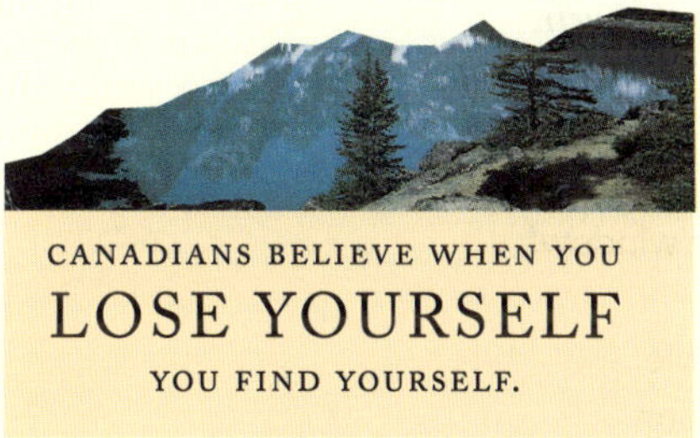

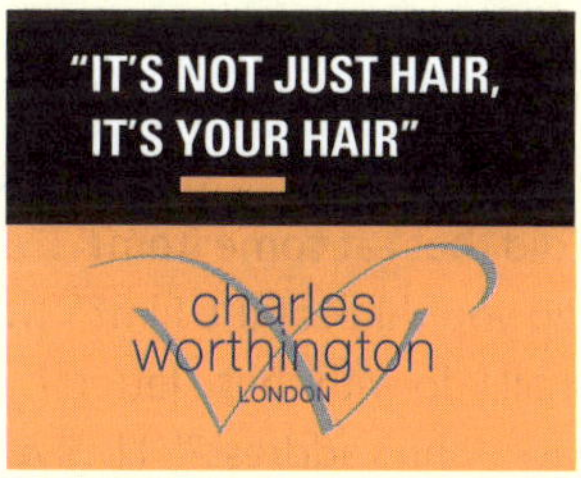

CANADIANS BELIEVE WHEN YOU
LOSE YOURSELF
YOU FIND YOURSELF.

Presents for him, her, you and them!

"IT'S NOT JUST HAIR, IT'S YOUR HAIR"
charles worthington
LONDON

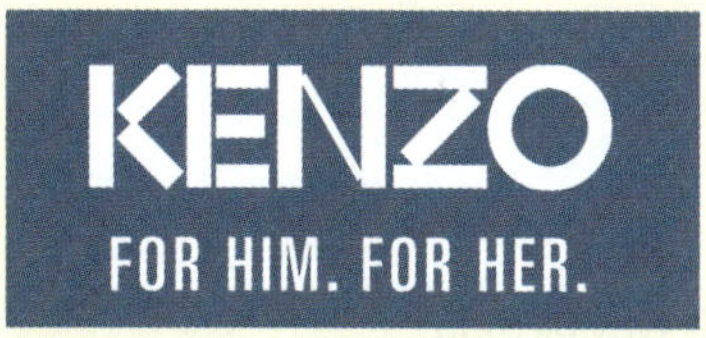

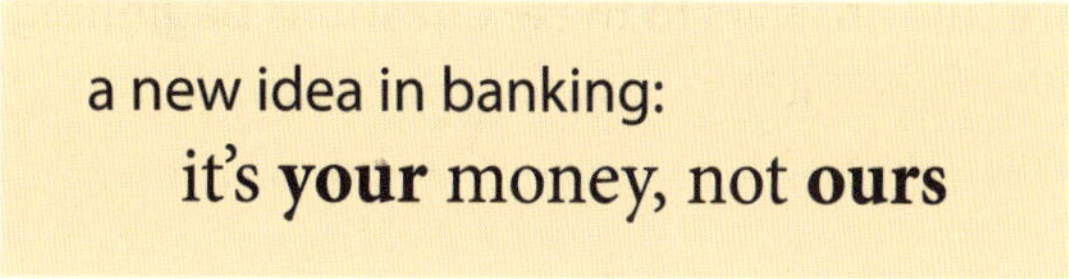

FOR HIM. FOR HER.

FIND YOURSELF IN ONE BITE
luxury Belgian chocolates

yours for just £20:

a new idea in banking:
it's your money, not ours

personal pronouns: *I* and *me* etc

SUBJECTS	*I*	*you*	*he*	*she*	*it*	*we*	*you*	*they*
OTHER USES	*me*	*you*	*him*	*her*	*it*	*us*	*you*	*them*

SUBJECTS: *I, HE* ETC — *I like Mary. He needs help. They want your address.*

OBJECTS: *ME, HIM* ETC — *Mary doesn't like **me**. Help **him**. Don't tell **them** anything.*

AFTER PREPOSITIONS: *ME, HIM* ETC — *Look **at me**. Why is Jane **with him**? Is that **for us**?*

AFTER *BE*: *ME, HIM* ETC — *'Who's there?' 'It's **me**.'* (NOT ~~*'I am.'*~~ OR ~~*'It is I.'*~~) *'Is that Joe?' 'Yes, that's **him**.'*

INFORMAL ANSWERS: *ME, HIM* ETC — *'Who said that?' '**Me**.' 'I'm tired.' '**Me** too.'*

1 Circle the correct answer.

▶ *I / Me* don't understand.
1 'Who said that?' 'It was *she / her*.'
2 Tell *we / us* your address.
3 This isn't for you, it's for *he / him*.
4 I don't think *they / them* are here today.
5 'Where's your brother?' 'That's *he / him* over there.'
6 Where are the children? Can you see *they / them*?
7 Ask *she / her* why *she / her* is crying.

2 Put in *he, him, she, her, they* or *them*.

1 'Does your father speak English?' '............... understands a little.'
2 'I'm seeing Lucy and Pete on Tuesday.' 'Oh, give .... my love.'
3 'Mr Carter's here.' 'Ask .... to wait downstairs.'
4 Where are your friends? ....'re very late.
5 'Have you spoken to Mrs Lewis?' 'Not yet. I'm going to speak to .... this evening.'
6 'Where's Ann?' '...............'s in Germany all this week.'

We use ***it, they*** and ***them*** for **things**, including (usually) **countries** and **animals**.

*I like Scotland, but **it**'s cold in winter. She sold her horse because **it** cost too much.*

3 Put in *it, they* or *them*.

1 'Where are my keys?' '..............'re on that chair.'
2 'Where did that cat come from?' '.............. came in through the window.'
3 'What did you think of the film?' '..............'s not very good.'
4 'What shall I do with these letters?' 'Just put .... on the table.'
5 'Can I have John's address?' 'I'll give .... to you this afternoon.'
6 'Did you enjoy your holiday in Ireland?' 'Yes, ...'s a wonderful place.'
7 'Where are your glasses?' 'I've lost ....'
8 'Would you like tickets for the concert?' 'How much do .... cost?'

We use ***it*** to talk about **times, dates, distances** and the **weather**.

***It**'s five o'clock. **It**'s Tuesday. **It**'s December 17th today. **It**'s my birthday.*
***It**'s 20 miles from my house to the centre of Oxford. **It**'s cold today. **It**'s raining.*

4 Write true answers to these questions beginning *It's* …

1 What time is it? It's ....
2 What day is it? ....
3 What's the date? ....
4 How far is it to London? ....

We **don't** usually **leave out** personal pronouns. (For exceptions in spoken English, see page 293.)

Jan arrived in America in 1976. ***He*** *found a job in a clothes shop.* (**NOT** ~~*Found a job*~~ . . .)
*'What languages do you know?' '**I** can speak some German.'* (**NOT** ~~*'Can speak*~~ . . .')
*'Is your room OK?' 'Yes, I like **it**.'* (**NOT** ~~*'Yes, I like.'*~~)

5 Write answers, using *I*, *you* etc.

▶ 'What time is the next train?' (*8.30 / leaves / at*)
It leaves at 8.30. ....

1 'Where's John?' (*has / London / to / moved*)
....

2 'Have you seen my glasses?' (*on / chair / are / that*)
....

3 'What do you think of my new shoes?' (*like*)
....

4 'What's Elisabeth going to do?' (*medicine / study / going to / is*)
....

5 'I'm learning Greek.' 'Is it easy?' (*No / difficult / is*)
....

6 'Where's my bicycle?' (*put / in / the garage*)
....

7 'What do you do at weekends?' (*play / tennis*)
....

8 'Do you like my picture?' (*is / beautiful*)
....

6 GRAMMAR AND VOCABULARY: weather

Make sure you know the adjectives and verbs in the box. Use a dictionary if necessary. Then label the pictures.

ADJECTIVES:	cloudy	cold	foggy ✓	hot	sunny	warm	windy
VERBS:	hail ✓	rain	snow				

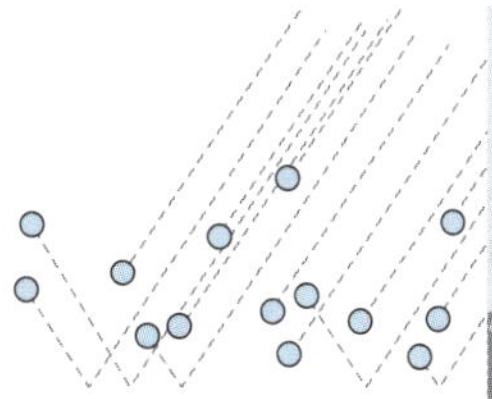

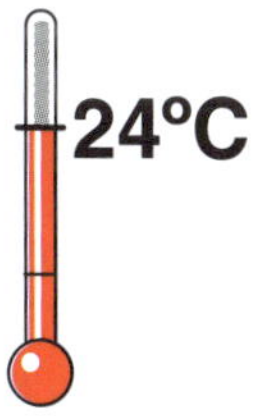

▶ It's hailing. ▶ It's foggy. 1 .... 2 .... 3 ....

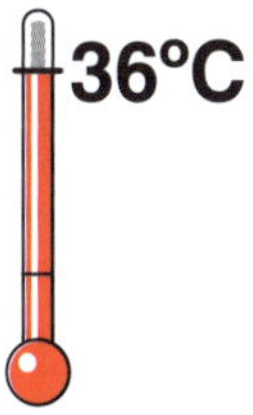

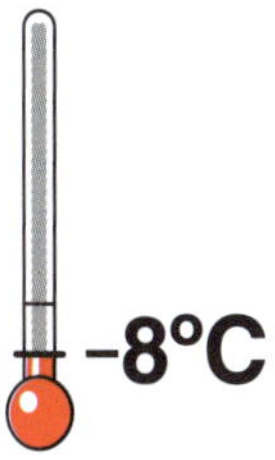

4 .... 5 .... 6 .... 7 .... 8 ....

In some answers, both contracted forms (for example *I'm*, *don't*) and full forms (for example *I am*, *do not*) are possible. Normally both are correct.

possessives: *my, your* etc *This is my coat.*

I	→	***my***	*This is **my** coat.*
you	→	***your***	*That's **your** problem.*
he	→	***his***	*John's visiting **his** mother.*
she	→	***her***	*Ann looks like **her** brothers.*
it	→	***its***	*The club has **its** meetings on Tuesdays.*
we	→	***our***	***Our** friends Joe and Pat are staying with us.*
they	→	***their***	*The children have spent all **their** money.*
who?	→	***whose?***	***Whose** coat is this?*

Possessives **don't change** for singular and **plural**.

***our** friend* ***our** friends* (NOT ~~*ours friends*~~)

Note how we use ***his*** and ***her***: if a **boy** or **man** has something, we use ***his***; if a **girl** or **woman** has something, we use ***her***.

*I saw **John** and **his** sister yesterday.* (NOT … ~~*John and her sister*~~ …)
***Mary** and **her** brother are students.* (NOT ~~*Mary and his brother*~~ …)

We often use **possessives** with **parts of the body** and **clothes**.

*Phil has broken **his arm**.* (NOT ~~*Phil has broken the arm.*~~)
*She stood there with **her eyes** closed and **her hands** in **her pockets**.*

1 Put in the correct possessives.

▶ Would you like to wash ...your... hands?
▶ We're taking ...our... holiday in June.
1 Tina's lost .... keys.
2 Peter says .... wife is ill.
3 .... car is that outside?
4 My bank has changed .... name.
5 I'm going to sell .... motorbike.
6 My students have got .... exam next week.
7 Stephen writes to .... girlfriend every day.
8 Maria lives with .... father in Portugal.
9 Come in and take .... coats off.
10 Robert broke .... leg skiing last winter.
11 'What film did you see?' 'Sorry, I've forgotten .... name.'
12 Elizabeth did well in .... exams.

'Your loving son,'

2 Who sold what to who? Make sentences.

> **AMY**: car → **JAMES**: bike → **CARLOS**: dog → **SARA**: house → **PAT AND SAM**: motorbike → **HARRY**: piano → **ALICE**: coat → **MICHAEL**: camera → **HELEN**: guitar → **MARILYN**: hair dryer → **TOM**: dictionary → **AMY**

▶ Amy sold her car to James.
1 James sold .... to Carlos.
2 Carlos ....
3 ....
4 ....
5 ....
6 ....
7 ....
8 ....
9 ....
10 ....

3 Look at the picture and complete the text.

▶ Anna and her husband Mark went on holiday with 1 .... and 2 .... in 3 .... There's room for six in the van, so Anna invited 4 .... to go with them, but she didn't ask 5 ...., because Mark doesn't get on with Lucy. Mark asked 6 ...., but she said no, because she doesn't like Frank. Then Mark asked 7 ...., but he wasn't free. However, 8 .... was happy to go with them, so everything was OK.

▶ Anna
▶ Anna's husband Mark
1 Mark and Anna's son Joe
2 Mark and Anna's daughter Emma

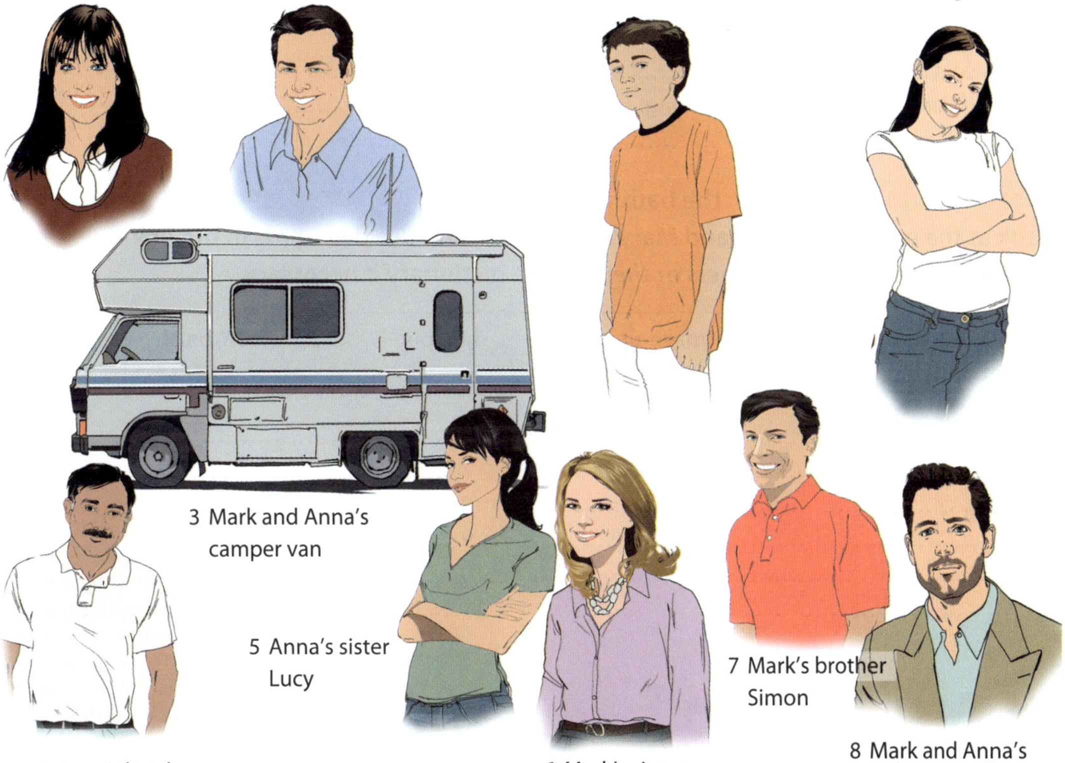

3 Mark and Anna's camper van
4 Anna's brother Frank
5 Anna's sister Lucy
6 Mark's sister Louise
7 Mark's brother Simon
8 Mark and Anna's friend Pete

We **don't** use *a/an, the, this* or *that* **before possessives**.

***my** car* (NOT ~~*the my car*~~) ***this** idea* OR ***my** idea* (NOT ~~*this my idea*~~)

Don't confuse ***its*** (possessive) and ***it's*** (= 'it is' or 'it has' – see page 301). Compare:

*The company had **its** annual meeting yesterday. **It's** losing a lot of money.*

In some answers, both contracted forms (for example *I'm*, *don't*) and full forms (for example *I am*, *do not*) are possible. Normally both are correct.

possessives: *mine, yours* etc *This is mine.*

DETERMINER	PRONOUN
my coat	*mine*
your car	*yours*
his chair	*his*
her book	*hers*

DETERMINER	PRONOUN
its price	---
our house	*ours*
their problem	*theirs*

We use *mine, yours* etc without nouns. Compare:

*That's not **my** coat. This is **mine**.* (NOT ~~*This is the mine.*~~) *Is that **your** car? I thought **yours** was a Ford.*
***Their** garden is much bigger than **ours**.* (NOT ... ~~*ours garden*~~)

We can use the question word ***whose*** with or without nouns.

***Whose** coat is that?* ***Whose** is that coat?*

1 Rewrite the sentences with possessive pronouns.

▶ That's my newspaper. *That's mine.*
1 I prefer our house to their house. I prefer our house to ....
2 Her hair looks better than your hair. Her hair ....
3 Your hair looks terrible. ....
4 That dog looks like our dog. ....
5 That car's not her car. ....
6 This coat isn't my coat. ....
7 My cooking is better than his cooking. ....
8 Is this bike your bike? ....

2 GRAMMAR AND VOCABULARY: the bathroom

Look at the pictures of John and Mary's bathroom, and use the words in the box to make sentences with *his, hers* or *theirs*. Use a dictionary if necessary.

dressing gown	hair dryer	make-up	razor	shampoo	soap	toothbrush
toothbrush	toothpaste	towel	washcloth ✓	washcloth		

▶ *The red washcloth is his.*
1 The .... is not theirs.
2 ....
3 ....
4 ....
5 ....
6 ....
7 ....
8 ....
9 ....
10 ....
11 ....

reflexive pronouns: *myself, yourself* etc

I → ***myself***	*you* → ***yourself***	*he* → ***himself***	*she* → ***herself***	*it* → ***itself***
we → ***ourselves***	*you* → ***yourselves***	*they* → ***themselves***		

We use ***myself, yourself*** etc when an **object** is the **same** person/thing as the **subject**.

I cut myself shaving this morning. (NOT ~~*I cut me*~~ ...)   *We must ask ourselves some questions.*
He tried to kill himself. (Different from *He tried to kill him.*)

1 Circle the correct answer.

1 She doesn't love *him / himself.*
2 She likes looking at *her / herself* in the mirror.
3 Old people often talk to *them / themselves.*
4 I'm going out tonight, so you will all have to cook for *yourself / yourselves.*
5 I like Bill, but I don't understand *him / himself.*

2 Put in *myself, yourself* etc.

1 I'm teaching .... to play the guitar.
2 'Who's John talking to?' ....
3 Get a drink for ....
4 We really enjoyed .... last night.
5 Mary talks about .... all the time.
6 Find chairs for .... and sit down.
7 They just want to make money for ....

We can also use ***myself*** etc to **emphasise** – to say 'that person/thing and nobody/nothing else'.

*It's best if **you** do it **yourself**.*   *I want to speak to **the manager himself**, not his secretary.*

3 Put in *myself, yourself* etc.

1 Did you cut your hair ....?
2 Peter and Ann built their house ....
3 I answer all my letters ....
4 Can you repair this, or must we do it ....?
5 We got a letter from the Queen ....

Note the difference between ***ourselves*** etc and ***each other***.

They're looking at themselves.

They're looking at each other.

4 *Each other* or *-selves*?

1 Henry and Barbara write to .... every week.
2 Joe and Pat have bought a flat for ....
3 Do you and Julia tell .... everything?
4 You'll need photos of .... for your passports.
5 Ruth and I have known .... for years.

GRAMMAR AND VOCABULARY: some common expressions with reflexive pronouns

by myself/yourself etc (= 'alone')   *enjoy myself/yourself* etc   *Take care of yourself.*
Help yourself. (= 'Take what you want.')   *Make yourself comfortable.*

In some answers, both contracted forms (for example *I'm, don't*) and full forms (for example *I am, do not*) are possible. Normally both are correct.

personal pronouns and possessives: more practice

1 Forms. There is one mistake in each column. Find the mistakes in columns 2–5 and correct them.

1	2	3	4	5
I	me	my	mines	myself
you	you	your	yours	yourself
he	him	his	his	himself
she	her	hers	hers	herself
it	it	its	–	itself
we	our	our	ours	ourselves
you	you	your	yours	yourselves
~~its~~ they	them	their	theirs	theirselves

2 Mixed structures. Correct the mistakes.

▶ ~~Her~~ didn't say 'Hello'. ...She...
1 John and her wife have gone to Greece. ....
2 This coat is my. ....
3 Their house is much bigger than our. ....
4 That dog has hurt it's ear. ....
5 'What about this music?' 'I like.' ....
6 There are five miles to the nearest station. ....
7 We are Tuesday. ....
8 Where's the station?' 'He's over there.' ....
9 Their were all late. ....
10 'Did you like France?' 'I thought was wonderful.' ....
11 'Where are your gloves?' 'I've lost its.' ....
12 'Who did that?' 'It was I.' ....
13 'Which girl is your sister?' 'That's she in the red dress.' ....
14 Is cold again today. ....
15 'What's her name?' 'Have forgotten.' ....
16 Lucy broke the leg skiing. ....
17 'What's the date?' 'Is December 17th.' ....
18 Is that the my coat? ....
19 Who's car is this? ....
20 'Who's that?' 'I am.' ....

3 Reflexives and *each other*. Complete the captions.

1 He's talking to ....

2 She's talking to ....

3 They're talking to ....

4 Mixed pronouns. Put in a personal pronoun (*me, you* etc), a reflexive pronoun (*myself, yourself* etc), *each other* or nothing (–).

▶ She looked at ...me............... and I looked at ...her.............. but we didn't say anything.
1 When I'm alone I don't always cook for ....
2 We love .... very much, but we fight all the time.
3 When he looks at .... in the mirror, he gets very depressed.
4 Don't help .... I want to do it by ....
5 Anna and I write to .... every week.
6 The children really enjoyed .... at your party.
7 I'm sorry. I haven't got time to teach .... to cook. You'll have to teach ....
8 'Can we have some coffee?' 'Sure. Help ....'
9 My girlfriend doesn't speak much Italian, and I don't speak much Chinese, so we sometimes have trouble understanding ....
10 Come in and make .... comfortable.

5 Reflexives. Circle the right pronouns.

1 Of all my wife's relations I like *myself / herself* the best. (*Joseph Cook*)

2 Novels are about other people and poems are about *themselves / yourself*. (*Philip Larkin*)

3 An egotist: a person more interested in *himself / yourself* than in me. (*Ambrose Bierce*)

4 'How do you know you're God?' 'Simple. When I pray to Him I find I'm talking to *myself / himself*.' (*Peter Barnes*)

5 We grow neither better nor worse as we get old, but more like *ourselves / themselves*. (*May Lamberton Becker*)

6 You can always get someone to love you – even if you have to do it *ourself / yourself*. (*Tom Masson*)

6 Grammar in a text. Choose words from the boxes to complete the text.

each other	her	his	its	themselves	they	your

My brother and 1 .... girlfriend have known 2 .... for about five years, but 3 ....'ve only been going out together for six months.

he	her	him	she	their	they	we

Before that, he didn't like 4 .... and 5 .... didn't like him, but later 6 .... became good friends, and started going out together.

her	hers	his	its	it's	our	their	they	they're

7 .... both have small flats. His flat is in the town centre, and 8 .... very comfortable. 9 .... is a long way out, and it's not so nice. So they spend most of 10 .... free time at 11 .... place.

he	her	hers	herself	him	himself	its	it's	she's

He works in a garage, and 12 .... a teacher, but she doesn't let 13 .... touch 14 .... car – she looks after it 15 ....

each other	I	my	they	them	their	themselves	they're

I like 16 .... both very much, and I think 17 .... good for 18 ...., so 19 .... hope 20 .... will stay together.

7 Internet exercise. Use a search engine (e.g. Google). Which of these three expressions gets most hits? Can you see why?

"She broke her arm." ....

"She broke the arm." ....

"She broke his arm." ....

pronunciation for grammar → e-book

personal pronouns and possessives: revision test

1 Complete the table.

I	me	my	mine	myself
	you			
he		his		
			hers	
	it		–	
		our		
				yourselves
they				

2 Correct the mistakes.

▶ I ~~him haven't seen~~ today. haven't seen him

1 'Is the soup OK?' 'Yes, I like.' ....
2 There are 20 miles to the shopping centre. ....
3 We are Friday. ....
4 Peter and her sister are in Brazil. ....
5 I like our garden better than their. ....
6 Olivia and Karl are nice. But theirs children! ....
7 Who's is this bag? ....
8 Ann and I write to ourselves every week. ....
9 I really enjoyed at your party. ....
10 I'm teaching me to play the guitar. ....
11 Where's the my bike? ....
12 Is April 1st today. ....
13 James fell off his horse and broke the arm. ....
14 'What's Joe's phone number?' 'Have forgotten.' ....
15 I sat down, made me comfortable, and waited for her to say something. ....

3 Put in a personal pronoun (*me*, *you* etc), a possessive (*my*, *your* etc), a reflexive (*myself*, *yourself* etc), or *each other*.

▶ It is five o'clock.

1 I don't like .... and he doesn't like ....
2 Don't help .... She must do it by ....
3 Oliver and his girlfriend phone .... every day.
4 Thanks for yesterday evening. We really enjoyed ....
5 I like cooking for other people, but I don't much like cooking for ....
6 Let's work together: the work will go much faster if we help ....
7 Hi, Paul. Help .... to coffee. I'll be with .... in a minute.
8 'Will you teach .... the piano?' 'No, sorry, you'll have to teach ....'
9 'Who broke the cup?' 'It wasn't ....'
10 'Which is your mother?' 'That's .... over there by the window.'
11 My parents don't understand ...., and my boyfriend doesn't understand ...., and sometimes I don't understand ....
12 That girl keeps losing .... shoes.
13 Bill's coming this evening with .... three sisters.
14 I don't like looking at photos of ...., because .... always look so old.
15 Mary's mother's really nice, but I don't like .... father much.

In some answers, both contracted forms (for example *I'm*, *don't*) and full forms (for example *I am*, *do not*) are possible. Normally both are correct.

SECTION 14 nouns

grammar summary

Nouns are mostly words for things and people – for example *house, tree, driver, child, water, idea, lesson.* Most nouns can come after *the.*

English nouns can be **countable** (we can say *two houses*) or **uncountable** (we can't say ~~*two waters*~~).
Countable nouns have **plurals** (*houses*), and we can use ***a/an*** with them (*a house, an idea*).
Uncountable nouns have **no plurals**, and we **can't** use ***a/an*** before them.

Some English uncountable nouns are countable in some other languages (like *furniture*).

We can join two nouns:

- with a **possessive *'s* or *s'*** (for example *my* ***brother's wife****, my* ***parents' house***).
- with a **preposition** (for example *a* ***piece of cake***).
- directly one after the other (for example ***chocolate cake****, a* ***shoe shop***).

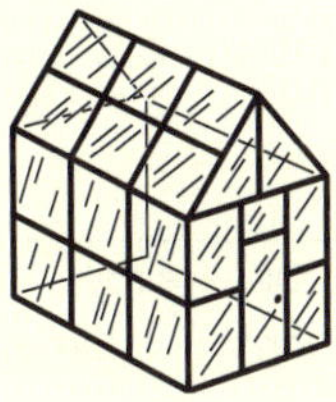

glass house

house key

key ring

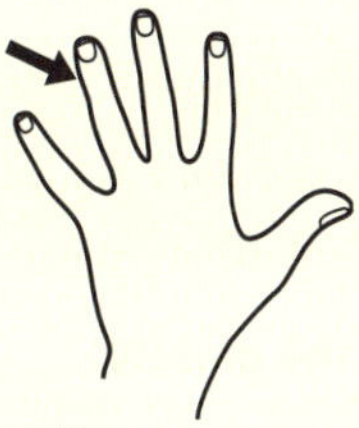

ring finger

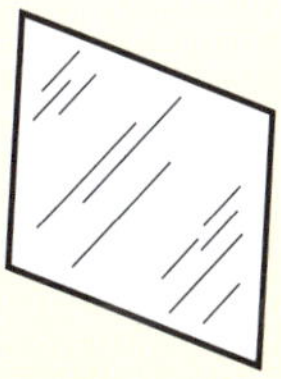

plate glass

number plate

file number

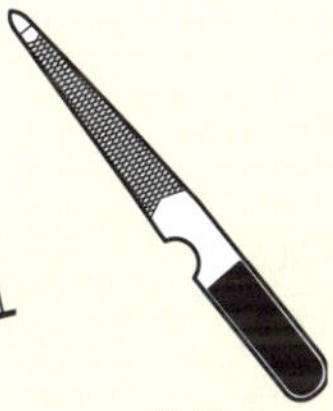

nail file

finger nail

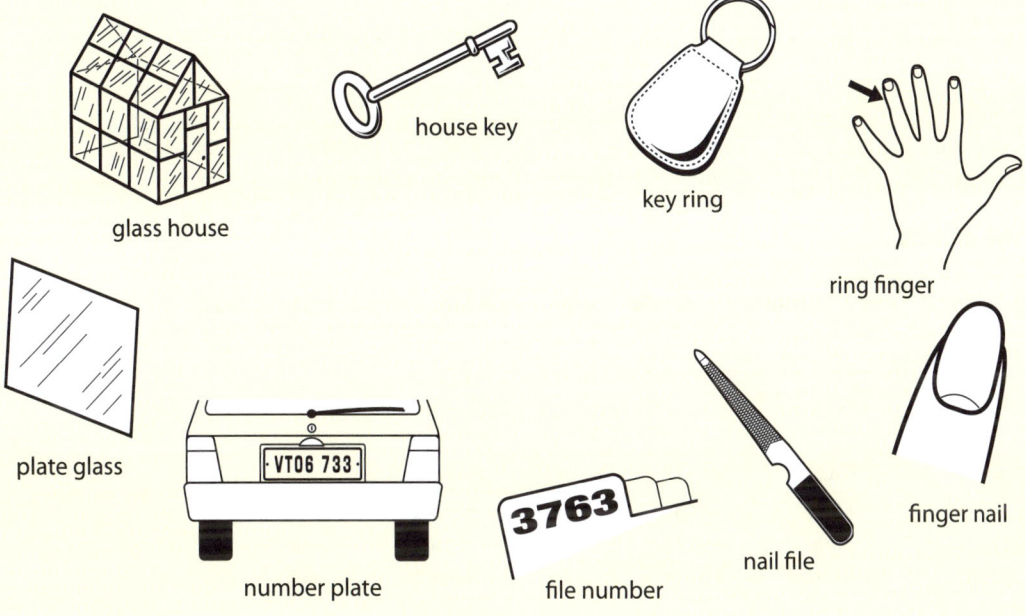

Level 1

singular and plural nouns *cat, cats; box, boxes*

Countable nouns have different forms for **singular** and **plural**.

*one **car*** *four **cars*** *one **day*** *ten **days*** *one **baby*** *four **babies*** *one **child*** *six **children***

HOW TO MAKE PLURALS

- **most nouns: + -s** *book → books* *home → homes* *car → cars*
- ***-s, -sh, -ch, -x*: + *-es*** *bus → buses* *wish → wishes* *church → churches* *fox → foxes*

1 Write the plurals.

apple ✓ boss ✓ box brush cat chair church class dress garden gas glass hotel plane ship table time tree watch wish

+ *-S*: apples ....

+ *-ES*: bosses ....

NOUNS ENDING IN *-Y*

- ***-ay, -ey, -oy, -uy*: + *-s*** *day → days* *monkey → monkeys* *toy → toys*
- ***-by, -dy, -fy, -gy*, etc: *-y* → *-ies*** *baby → babies* *lady → ladies* *lorry → lorries*

2 Write the plurals.

boy ✓ city ✓ copy country family guy holiday key party way

+ *-S*: boys ....

-Y → *-IES*: cities ....

COMMON IRREGULAR PLURALS

mouse → mice	*child → children*	*half → halves*	*shelf → shelves*
foot → feet	*penny → pence*	*knife → knives*	*thief → thieves*
tooth → teeth	*person → people*	*leaf → leaves*	*wife → wives*
man → men		*life → lives*	
woman → women	*potato → potatoes*	*loaf → loaves*	*sheep → sheep*
	tomato → tomatoes	*self → selves*	*fish → fish*

Simple present verbs have different forms after **singular** and **plural** nouns (see page 16).

*This **bus runs** at weekends.* *Most of the **buses run** at weekends.*
*My **brother has** a small flat.* *Both my **brothers have** good jobs.*

3 Put in plural nouns or simple present verbs.

▶ Their homes ...are... in Scotland. (*be*)
1 Our .... play a lot of football. (*child*)
2 Those .... don't look English. (*student*)
3 Some people .... to talk to you. (*want*)
4 Big .... are always dirty. (*city*)
5 Their .... are travelling with them. (*wife*)
6 These knives ....n't cut very well. (*do*)
7 My .... are giving me trouble. (*tooth*)
8 Those .... cost too much. (*watch*)
9 Most .... cry at night. (*baby*)
10 The .... are all wet. (*match*)
11 Who are those ....? (*guy*)
12 My parents .... at home. (*work*)
13 How many .... live here? (*person*)

singular/plural *team, family; jeans, scissors*

Words for **groups of people** can have **singular** or **plural verbs** in British English.
We often use **plural verbs** when we talk about **personal actions** (for example *play, want, think*).

*The **team is/are** playing badly.* *My **family want/wants** me to study.*
*The **government think/thinks** taxes are too low.*

Note the difference between *England* (the country) and *England* (the football team).

***England has** got a new prime minister.* ***England have** got a new manager.*

Police is always **plural**.

*The **police are** looking for a tall 30-year-old woman.* (NOT ~~*The police is looking*~~ …)

1 Group nouns (✓) or not (✗)?

army ..✓.. audience ..✓.. beach ..✗.. class ...... club ...... Communist Party ...... company ......
crowd ...... idea ...... lunch ...... question ...... room ...... school ...... train ......

2 Put the beginnings and ends together, and put in plural verbs from the box.

are have haven't need ✓ play say want

0 The club	A .... her to go to university. ......
1 The company	B only .... classical music. ......
2 Her family	C .... scored a goal this year. ......
3 The orchestra	D .... that they're losing money. ......
4 This team	E ...need... a bigger room for their meetings. ..0..
5 England	F .... asking for information about the accident. ......
6 The police	G .... just lost against Germany. ......

Some nouns are **always plural**. Some common examples:
trousers jeans tights shorts pants pyjamas glasses scissors

***Those** trousers **are** too short.* (NOT ~~*That trouser*~~ …) *Where **are** my glasses?*

3 Complete the sentences. Use the words in the box.

black trousers blue jeans ✓ dark glasses scissors shorts silk pyjamas tights

▶ Every time I see her she's wearing ...blue jeans...........
1 I can't see very well with these ....
2 It's hot today. I'm going to put on ....
3 These .... don't cut very well.
4 You'd better put on your best .... for the interview.
5 She always sleeps in ....
6 I've got a hole in my .... again.

We can also use the expression ***a pair of*** with these nouns.

*There is **a pair of scissors** on your chair.* (NOT … ~~*a scissors*~~ …)
*three **pairs of jeans*** (NOT ~~*three jeans*~~) *two **pairs of pyjamas*** (NOT ~~*two pyjamas*~~)

In some answers, both contracted forms (for example *I'm, don't*) and full forms (for example *I am, do not*) are possible. Normally both are correct.

Level 2

countable and uncountable nouns

Countable nouns are words like *car, book, chair*. They can be **singular** or **plural**.
Uncountable nouns are words like *petrol, rice, water*. They are only **singular**.

1 Circle the uncountable nouns.

cup dog flower guitar love meat music ear oil photo river
salt snow sugar women wool

The following words are **uncountable** in English (but countable in some other languages). They are normally **only singular**. We can use ***some*** with them, but **not *a/an*.** (NOT ~~*a travel*~~, ~~*a furniture*~~)
advice baggage bread furniture hair information knowledge luck
luggage news spaghetti (and *macaroni* etc) *travel work*

*I need **some advice**.* *__This furniture is__ too expensive.*
*His **hair is** very long.* ***Travel teaches** you a lot.*

2 Put *a* with the countable nouns and *some* with the uncountable nouns.

.... bread .... cheque .... baggage .... fridge .... furniture
.... handbag .... holiday .... knowledge .... luck
.... newspaper .... problem .... station .... travel .... work

3 Put in suitable uncountable nouns from the box.

advice	baggage	furniture	hair	information ✓	news	spaghetti	travel	work

▶ Can you give me some ...information... about the school?
1 'Have you got much ....?' 'No, just one small bag.'
2 I live 50 kilometres from my work, so I spend a lot of money on ....
3 This .... isn't very good. You've cooked it for too long.
4 I've stopped reading the papers. The .... is always bad.
5 I don't know what to do. Can you give me some ....?
6 All this .... is from my mother's house.
7 I've got too much .... and not enough free time.
8 I like your .... when it's long like this.

To give a **countable** meaning, we usually use a **longer expression** or a **different word.**
*Can you give me **a piece of advice**?* *Did you have **a good journey**?*

4 Put in words or expressions from the box.

a piece of advice	a piece of baggage ✓	a piece of information
a piece of news	a job	a journey

▶ a suitcase ...a piece of baggage...
1 selling cars ....
2 driving from London to Edinburgh ....
3 'Don't marry him, dear.' ....
4 'The next train leaves at 10.15.' ....
5 'There has been a big train crash.' ....

→ For articles with countable and uncountable nouns, see page 153.

Some words can be countable or uncountable, with **different meanings**.

A light was on in the house. (= 'a lamp') *Light travels at 300,000 km a second.*
I've seen that film three times. *Time goes fast when you're having fun.*
I had a strange experience yesterday. *We need a secretary with experience.*
Three coffees, please. (= 'cups of coffee') *I drink too much coffee.*

5 Look at the pictures and put in descriptions from the box.

a chicken	chicken	a chocolate	chocolate	a glass	glass
an iron	iron	a paper	paper		

1 ....

2 ....

3 ....

4 ....

5 ....

6 ....

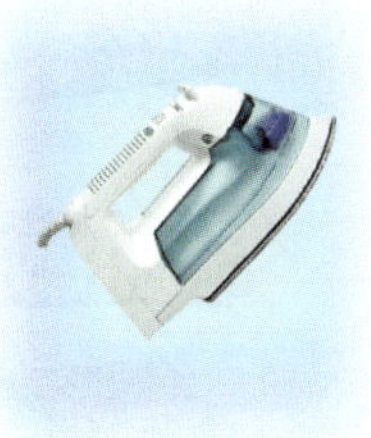
7 ....

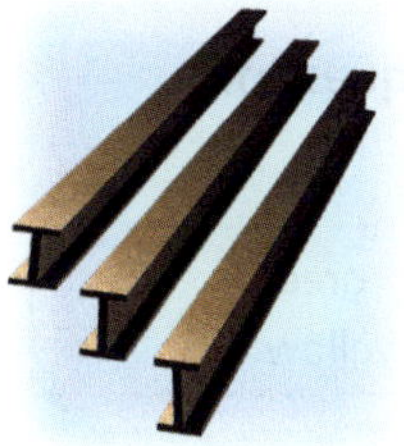
8 ....

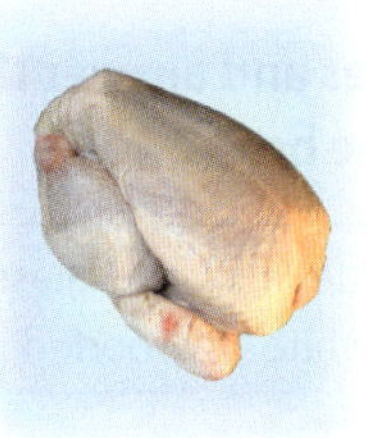
9 ....

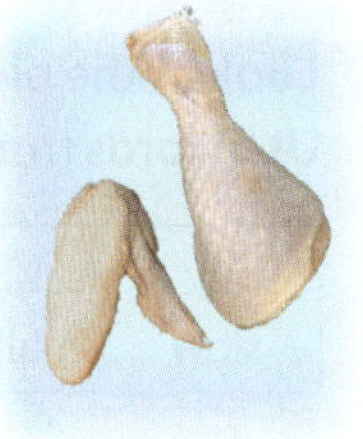
10 ....

6 GRAMMAR AND VOCABULARY: containers

Make sure you know the words in the box. Use a dictionary if necessary. Then use them to complete the descriptions under the pictures.

bag	bottle	box	can	cup	glass	jar	jug	mug	packet

1 a .... of water

2 a .... of water

3 a .... of chocolates

4 a .... of tea

5 a .... of coffee

6 a .... of honey

7 a .... of soup

8 a .... of onions

9 a .... of orange juice

10 a .... of biscuits

one and *ones* *a big one; the ones on the chair*

We often use ***one*** instead of repeating a countable noun.

*'What sort of **car** would you like?' 'A big **one**.'* (= 'A big car.') (NOT ~~*'A big.'*~~)
*That was a great **party**. Let's have another **one** soon.*

The plural is ***ones***.

*'Which are your **gloves**?' 'The **ones** on the chair.'*

1 Complete the sentences with *one(s)*, using words from the box.

another	green ✓	blue	last	new	this	small

▶ I bought a blue shirt and two *green ones.*
1 That shop isn't as good as ....
2 My TV's broken. I must get ....
3 She's finished her apple. She wants ....
4 That bus is the .... tonight.
5 'Another piece of cake?' 'Just a .... '
6 I don't like the red shoes. I prefer the ....

2 Look at the pictures and answer the questions. Use words from the box.

big	black	blue	fast	glass ✓	green	red
slow	small	white	wooden ✓	yellow		

▶ Which table do you prefer? *The glass one.*
OR *The wooden one.*
1 Which house do you prefer? ....
2 Which sweater do you prefer? ....
3 Which car do you prefer? ....
4 Which dog do you prefer? ....
5 Which flower do you prefer? ....

We say ***one***, not ~~*a one*~~, when there is **no adjective**.

*'What sort of cake would you like?' '**One** with a lot of cream.'* (NOT ~~*'A one with ...'*~~)
*'Is there a garage near here?' 'There's **one** in Weston Street.'*

3 Write some true sentences. Use the expressions in the box.

I've already got one.	I haven't got one.	I need one.	I need a new one.
I don't need one.	I'd like one.	I don't want one.	

▶ a computer *I don't need one.*
1 a bicycle ....
2 a fast car ....
3 a camera ....
4 a cup of coffee ....
5 a tennis racket ....
6 a raincoat ....
7 a rich uncle ....

We only use ***one*** for **countable nouns** (see page 198).

*'Would you like some coffee?' 'Yes, **black** (coffee), please.'* (NOT ~~*'Yes, black one ...'*~~)

's and s' possessive: forms *son's, sons', men's*

HOW TO MAKE POSSESSIVE FORMS

- **singular nouns:** + 's *my son's car* *John and Iris's flat* *the cat's leg*
- **most plural nouns:** + ' *those boys' passports* *the babies' toys* *our wives' stories*
- **plurals without s** + 's *most children's poems* *three men's names* *the people's voices*

1 Make possessive forms by adding 's or '.

▶ my mother...'s... nose
▶ my sisters...'... names
1 Alice and John...... house
2 artists...... ideas
3 my dog...... ears
4 those dogs...... ears
5 those men...... faces
6 his girlfriend...... piano
7 their grandchild...... birthday
8 their grandchildren...... school
9 ladies...... hats
10 my aunt and uncle...... shop
11 Patrick...... books
12 a photographer...... job
13 our postman...... cat
14 postmen...... uniforms
15 Joyce...... pen
16 the thief...... bag
17 the thieves...... car
18 that woman...... brother
19 most women...... desks
20 your mum and dad...... bedroom

2 Correct the mistakes and write the correct sentences.

▶ This is the ~~childrens'~~ room. *This is the children's room.*
1 That big building is a girl's school. ....
2 Is this your mothers' office? ....
3 May I speak to the bosses secretary? ....
4 What's Jane and Peters' address? ....
5 This is a picture of my grandparent's wedding. ....
6 Do you know John' new girlfriend? ....
7 She writes for a womens' magazine. ....
8 Is that Roberts' car? ....
9 Let me have Ruth's and Jack phone number. ....
10 What's your wive's job? ....

We can use **more than one** possessive noun together.

***John's mother's** cat* ***Helen's boss's** car* *My **father's secretary's sister's** baby*

3 Write the possessive expressions.

▶ My son has a teacher. She has a husband. *my son's teacher's husband*
1 My sister has a secretary. She has an office ....
2 Jane has children. They have bicycles. ....
3 Rob has a family. They have a holiday flat. ....
4 Olivia has a boyfriend. He has a cat. ....
5 The Prime Minister has a wife. She has a problem. ....
6 Luke has an uncle. He has a farm. ....
7 Mr Patterson has a doctor. She has a car. ....
8 The President has a niece. She has a business. ....
9 Charlotte has a boss. He has a wife. ....
10 The Director has a husband. He has a friend. She has a mother. She has a cousin. ....

In some answers, both contracted forms (for example *I'm, don't*) and full forms (for example *I am, do not*) are possible. Normally both are correct.

's and s' possessive: use *Ian's car; the boss's car*

Possessive nouns with *'s* or *s'* **take the place** of ***the***.

the car that belongs to Ian → *Ian's car* (NOT ~~*Ian's the car*~~) *the shoes that belong to Jo* → *Jo's shoes*

But a possessive noun can have **its own article**.

the car that belongs to the boss → *the boss's car*
the shoes that belong to the children → *the children's shoes*

1 Make *'s* or *s'* possessive structures.

▶ The dog belongs to Joe. Joe's dog
▶ The dog belongs to the postman. the postman's dog
1 The house belongs to Astrid. ....
2 The house belongs to the doctors. ....
3 The book belongs to Oliver and Carla. ....
4 The car belongs to the teacher. ....
5 The money belongs to the girls. ....
6 The money belongs to Susan. ....

2 Change the sentences.

▶ The classes are using the new books. (*the French teachers*)
The French teachers' classes are using the new books.
1 The car is parked in front of the house. (*the builder; Anna*)
.... car is parked in front of .... house.
2 Do you know the address? (*the tall woman*)
....
3 Their bedtime is eight o'clock. (*the children*)
....
4 The brothers are all in the army. (*Alice and Pat*)
....

We use **possessive *'s*** and ***s'*** mostly to talk about people and animals, not things: for example their **possessions, experience, relationships** (family, friends etc), **parts of the body**.

***Ann's** purse* ***Ann's** English lessons* ***Ann's** holiday* ***Ann's** husband* ***Ann's** friend*
***my dad's** book* (NOT ~~*the book of my dad*~~) ***my horse's** ears* (NOT ~~*the ears of my horse*~~)
BUT *the roof **of the house*** (NOT ~~*the house's roof*~~) *the top **of my desk*** (NOT ~~*my desk's top*~~)

3 Write two sentences for each item.

▶ Is the *door* open? (*Paul; the library*)
Is Paul's door open? Is the door of the library open?
1 What's the name? (*your brother; that book*)
....
2 Is there anything in the pockets? (*the children; that coat*)
....
....
3 You can see the church from the window. (*Emma; the living room*)
....
....
4 Why are the arms so dirty? (*John; your chair*)
....
....

With some common **time words**, we add *'s* to say **how long** something takes.

*a **second's** thought*   *a **minute's** silence*

4 Choose a time expression for each sentence. Use the words in the box.

second ✓	minute	hour	day	week	year

▶ 'Who was it?' I asked. There was *a pause* before she answered. ...a second's pause...

1 After university, Les took *a course* to become a teacher. ....

2 Lin had *a holiday* with her mother earlier this year. ....

3 Oxford is nearly 600 km from Edinburgh – that's *a journey*. ....

4 Sita's new job will mean *a drive* to work every morning. ....

5 There was *a wait* while the computer started up. ....

We can use **noun + *'s* or *s'* without another noun**, if the meaning is clear.

*'Whose coat is that?' '**Harry's**.'*   *My hair is dark, but **my children's** is fair.*

We also use **noun + *'s* or *s'* without another noun** for **offices, churches** and **some shops**.

*I bought this at **Sainsbury's**.*   *I hate going to **the dentist's**.*   *She sings at **St. John's**.*

5 Look at the picture. There is some confusion. Complete the sentences as in the example.

▶ The rope is probably ...Texas Joe's...

1 The handbag is probably ....

2 The gun ....

3 The crown ....

4 The big shoes ....

5 The document case ....

We often use **noun + *'s* or *s'* without another noun** to talk about **people's homes**.

*I saw Monica at **June and Barry's** on Friday.*   *Lee is going to **his sister's** next weekend.*

6 Other people's homes: write about two or more things in your past. Use *at ...'s* or *at ...s'*.

...I met my girlfriend at Judy's. I went to my grandparents' for Easter....

....

....

....

In some answers, both contracted forms (for example *I'm, don't*) and full forms (for example *I am, do not*) are possible. Normally both are correct.

Level 2

noun + noun *Milk chocolate is a kind of chocolate.*

We can put one noun before another when we are talking about a **kind** of **thing** or **person**.
The **first noun** is usually **singular**, even if it has a plural meaning.

milk chocolate = a kind of chocolate, with milk in it
chocolate milk = a kind of milk, with chocolate in it
flower shop = shop that sells flowers (NOT *~~flowers shop~~*)
corner shop = a shop on a corner
hotel receptionist = a receptionist in a hotel
history teacher = a teacher who teaches history

1 **Use the words in the box to make noun + noun structures. You can use some of the words more than once.**

army	aspirin	business	corner	email	flower	garden	home	
jazz	kitchen	milk	opera	perfume	police	pop	prison	village

▶ 3 kinds of shop *flower shop, corner shop, village shop*
1 3 kinds of address ....
2 3 kinds of bottle ....
3 3 kinds of singer ....
4 2 kinds of wall ....
5 3 kinds of uniform ....
6 2 kinds of chair ....

2 **Change the expressions in the box to noun + noun structures, and put the beginnings and ends together. Remember: don't make the first noun plural.**

clothes for babies   make-up for eyes ✓   building with offices in it   food for dogs
engineer who works on computers   school of languages   drawer for knives

0	Judy wears too much *eye make-up* to the office	A	but he couldn't repair it. ......
1	They're going to put a big	B	I want to learn Japanese. ......
2	Our dog won't eat ....;	C	– does she think she's at a party? *0*
3	The .... looked at my printer,	D	he only wants fresh meat or fish. ......
4	Do you know of a good ....?	E	when my brother was born. ......
5	My aunt made some lovely	F	at the corner of our street. ......
6	Why are the spoons in the ....?	G	And who put them there? ......

We often use **noun + noun** structures to talk about what things are **made of**.

3 **Write noun + noun names for these.**

▶ soup with chicken in it *chicken soup*
1 a box made of metal ....
2 cakes with chocolate in them ....
3 a fork made of plastic ....
4 soup made of vegetables ....
5 a jacket made of leather ....
6 shirts made of cotton ....
7 a plate made of paper ....
8 salad with tomatoes in it ....
9 a wall made of stones ....

We often use **noun + noun** structures when the second noun is made from a **verb + *er***.

a truck driver = a person who drives a truck   *a hair dryer = a machine for drying hair*

4 What do we call these people or things?

▶ This person drives a bus. ...*a bus driver*...
1 This person manages an office. ....
2 This machine makes coffee. ....
3 This person drinks coffee. ....
4 This person loves animals. ....
5 This stuff cleans floors. ....
6 This person plays tennis. ....
7 This thing opens letters. ....
8 This person smokes cigars. ....
9 This person climbs mountains. ....

NOUN + NOUN STRUCTURE OR *'S / S'* POSSESSIVE STRUCTURE

We mostly use ***'s*** or ***s'*** when the **first noun possesses, experiences** or **has a relationship** with the second noun. We use a **noun + noun** structure for **other kinds of meaning**. So **things** do **not usually** take ***'s / s'***. Compare:

the dog's name (possession: the dog has a name)   *Rita's accident* (experience: Rita had an accident)
Ed's brother (relationship: Ed has a brother)   *Annie's secretary is Ellen's best friend.* (relationships)
BUT *a shoe brush* (the shoe doesn't possess or experience the brush; shoes don't have relationships)

5 Circle the correct answers.

1 Could I borrow your *telephone's book / telephone book* for a minute?
2 Is that your *teacher's book / teacher book*, or is it yours?
3 *Elizabeth's journey / Elizabeth journey* took her to five continents.
4 The *train's journey / train journey* from Huntsville to Victoria was very boring.
5 My *aunt's home / aunt home* is full of beautiful furniture.
6 Our *holiday's home / holiday home* is in the French Alps.
7 My *brother's interview / brother interview* with the president will be on the radio today.
8 I was very nervous about my *job's interview / job interview*.

GRAMMAR AND VOCABULARY: one-word noun + noun structures

Some short **noun + noun** structures are so **common** that we write them as **one word**, for example:
armchair   bathroom   bedroom   bookshop   businessman   businesswoman   hairbrush
handbag   raincoat   postman   postwoman   schoolchild   suitcase   toothbrush   toothpaste

nouns: more practice

1 Countable or uncountable? Put in *a/an* or *some*.

▶ We need ..a.......... new bed.
▶ We need ..some.......... new furniture.
1 Can you give me .... advice?
2 I found .... money in the street this morning.
3 Can you buy .... bread while you're out?
4 I've got .... work to do this evening.
5 I've got .... difficult job to do today.
6 Ann gave me .... good news.
7 I need a taxi, because I've got .... heavy luggage.
8 Did you have .... good journey?
9 I've just had .... good idea.
10 I must give you .... important information.

2 Special plurals. Put in three different plural nouns which have no singular.

1 a pair of .... 2 a pair of .... 3 a pair of ....

3 Singular or plural? Correct (✓) or not (✗)?

1 The team are playing well. ......
2 The police don't usually carry guns in Britain. ......
3 My family have moved to Manchester. ......
4 He buys too much clothes. ......
5 I bought two new blue jeans yesterday. ......
6 People are all different. ......
7 Are those your pyjamas? ......
8 I need a new pair of glasses. ......
9 I don't like that people very much. ......
10 The government are in trouble again. ......

4 Possessive forms. Correct the mistakes.

▶ What's your ~~mothers'~~ phone number? ..mother's..................................
1 That's the Peter's house. ....
2 She writes childrens' books. ....
3 That building is a boy's school. ....
4 This is my fathers office. ....
5 I want to talk to the boss secretary's. ....
6 We're going round to Jane's and Peter place. ....
7 Here's a photo of my parent's wedding. ....
8 Is this the teachers book? ....
9 Johns' friends are all here. ....
10 He only reads mens' magazines. ....

5 Noun + noun. Write shorter descriptions of these people and things.

▶ chocolate with fruit and nuts in it ..fruit and nut chocolate..................
▶ a person who makes toys ..a toy maker..................
1 a shop that sells shoes ....
2 juice taken from oranges ....
3 a jacket made of leather ....
4 a person who drives trains ....
5 a table where you can drink coffee ....
6 a person who cleans windows ....
7 people who read the news (on TV) ....
8 a magazine about computers ....
9 a market in the street ....
10 a watch made of gold ....

6 Noun + noun. What are these people? Put together words from the two boxes and write the descriptions.

bird	bus	butterfly	computer	dog	glass	hockey ✓
maths	mountain	road	tennis			

blower	climber	collector	driver	player ✓	player
programmer	sweeper	teacher	trainer	watcher	

▶ a hockey player

1 ....

2 ....

3 ....

4 ....

5 ....

6 ....

7 ....

8 ....

9 ....

10 ....

7 Grammar in a text. Read the text and circle the correct forms.

In the ▶ *centre of Mappleford / Mappleford centre* there's a large ancient covered market with all sorts of interesting shops: 1 *shops of clothes / clothes shops*, butchers, grocers, jewellers etc etc. But my favourite place in the market is Joe's Café. It's a real 2 *business of family / family business*: Joe, 3 *the wife of Joe / Joe's wife*, his sons, his 4 *son's / sons'* wives, his daughter and his 5 *daughter's / daughters'* boyfriend all work there at different times. It's not luxurious – there are 6 *tables and chairs of plastic / plastic tables and chairs* – but it's excellent value. Joe's Café is the best place in town for a full English breakfast. For a few pounds, you get a big plate of eggs, bacon and sausages, as much toast and butter as you can eat, and an enormous cup of tea. All sorts of people 7 *have / has* breakfast at 8 *Joe / Joe's*, from professors to 9 *drivers of buses / bus drivers / bus's drivers*. When they've all gone off to work, Joe and his family have time for a short rest, and then the café starts filling up with tourists who have come to try Joe's famous 10 *cake of chocolate / chocolate cake*. If you're ever in Mappleford, take my advice and visit Joe's Café.

8 Internet exercise. Checking correctness. Use a search engine (e.g. Google). Which of the following expressions get most hits? So which are correct?

"a heavy baggage" 822 .... "some heavy baggage" 9200 ....

"a coffee table" .... "a table coffee" ....

"the President's birthday" .... "the birthday of the President" ....

"a bus driver" .... "a bus's driver" .... "a driver of bus" ....

"a gold watch" .... "a watch of gold" ....

pronunciation for grammar → e-book

nouns: revision test

1 Write the plurals.

bus	buses	fox	....	journey	....	match	....	book	....
table	....	foot	....	person	....	knife	....	mouse	....
dog	....	day	....	family	....	woman	....	leaf	....
man	....	child	....	car	....	wife	....	baby	....

2 Which nouns can be plural? Write the plural or x.

- ▶ note ...notes...
- ▶ money ...x...
- 1 information ....
- 2 bread ....
- 3 idea ....
- 4 duck ....
- 5 knowledge ....
- 6 journey ....
- 7 furniture ....
- 8 government ....
- 9 class ....
- 10 traffic ....

3 Circle the correct forms.

1 My cousin is a *tennis player / player of tennis / tennis's player*.
2 The police *is / are* looking for a tall thin man.
3 I'm going to have *a sleep of an hour / an hour sleep / an hour's sleep* now.
4 Do you read *woman's / womans' / women's / womens'* magazines?
5 I like travelling to other *countries / countrys / countreys*.
6 'Coffee?' 'Yes, please. *One large / Large one / A large one / A large*.'
7 Could you give me some *information / informations*?
8 England *is / are* leading by 4 goals to 2.
9 My sister works in a *flower shop / flowers shop / shop flower / shop's flower*.
10 I can't find her number in the *phone book / phone's book / book of phone / book of the phone*.

4 Correct the mistakes.

▶ He's bought two new ~~trousers~~. ...pairs of trousers...
1 I like eating chocolate milk. ....
2 My parents lived all their lifes in Dublin. ....
3 I like looking round books shops. ....
4 Who was the people who came to see you? ....
5 Peter is my son's sister. ....
6 I like those gloves. How much are the blue? ....
7 It's a nice jacket, but I'd like a one with pockets. ....
8 You will never be a player of football. ....
9 Marco Polo wrote a book about his journies. ....
10 'Where did you buy it?' 'In the market of street.' ....
11 We spent the weekend at my brother. ....
12 A vet is a doctor of animals. ....
13 The mother of Anna speaks good Spanish. ....
14 My father gave me earrings of silver for my birthday. ....
15 Can I have some oranges juice? ....
16 Birmingham, Liverpool and Manchester are three important citys in England. ....
17 I couldn't open the house's door ....
18 There's the Peter's house ....
19 Do you have the address of Emma? ....
20 I've got a big work to do today. ....

In some answers, both contracted forms (for example *I'm*, *don't*) and full forms (for example *I am*, *do not*) are possible. Normally both are correct.

SECTION 15 adjectives and adverbs

grammar summary

Adjectives are words like ***easy, slow, sorry, important***. They usually tell you more about **people** or **things**. They can go **before nouns**, or **after some verbs** (e.g. ***be, seem, look***).

*an **easy** job* *a **slow** train* *I'm **sorry**.* *This letter looks **important**.*

Adverbs are words like ***easily, slowly, yesterday, there***. Adverbs tell you, for example, **how, when** or **where** something happens.

*I won the game **easily**.* *Please speak **slowly**.* *She arrived **yesterday**.*

Great books for young readers!

DELICIOUSLY CREAMY

'AN UNFORGETTABLE NOVEL'

'A wonderfully funny and moving book'

'Hot socks: the perfect way to warm cold feet and make you feel good'

Level 1

adjectives *a beautiful little girl who was not stupid*

Adjectives go before, not after **nouns**.

a long journey (NOT ~~*a journey long*~~)   *loud music* (NOT ~~*music loud*~~)

Adjectives **don't change** for **singular** and **plural**.

*a **fast** car*   ***fast** cars* (NOT ~~*fasts cars*~~)

Before nouns, we **don't** usually put ***and*** between adjectives.

*a **big bad** wolf* (NOT ~~*a big and bad wolf*~~)

Colour adjectives usually come **after others**.

***beautiful red** apples* (NOT ~~*red beautiful apples*~~)

1 Put in the adjectives and write the story.

One day, a time ago, (*long fine*)	▸ *One fine day, a long time ago* ....
a girl (*beautiful little*)	1 ....
in a coat (*red*)	2 ....
was walking through a forest (*dark*)	3 ....
with a bag (*big*)	4 ....
of apples (*red wonderful*)	5 ....
to see her grandmother. (*old*)	6 ....
Under a tree (*tall green*)	7 ....
she saw a wolf (*big bad*)	8 ....
with teeth. (*white long*)	9 ....

2 Put the words in the correct order and continue the story.

'good little , girl morning', said	1 'Good ....
big the bad wolf.	2 ....
'going you where are	3 ....
that with bag heavy	4 ....
day this fine on?'	5 ....
'going my see to grandmother I'm old'	6 ....
girl the said little.	7 ....
'lives small she in house a	8 ....
new the supermarket near.'	9 ....

3 Put in adjectives from the box to finish the story.

big	friendly	stupid	little

'OK,' said the wolf in a 1 .... voice. 'I'll see you later.' 'I don't think so,' said the 2 .... girl, who was not 3 .... She took a 4 .... pistol out of her bag and shot the wolf dead.

(from an idea by James Thurber)

'I don't think so,' said the little girl.

Adjectives can go after *be, become, get, seem, look* (= 'seem') and *feel*.

The water ***is cold****.* *Everything* ***became clear****.* *It's* ***getting late****.* *You* ***seem tired****.*
She ***looks happy****.* *I* ***feel hot****.*

After these verbs, we put ***and*** **before the last** of two or more adjectives.

He was tall, dark ***and*** *handsome.* (NOT ~~*He was tall, dark, handsome.*~~) *You look well* ***and*** *happy.*

4 Look at the pictures and complete the sentences, using words from the box.

and	and	beautiful	cold	hungry	intelligent	tired

1 She is .... 2 He looks ....

5 Make sentences.

▶ 'Jack / very / tall / be' ..*'Jack's very tall.'*.. 'Yes, he's nearly 2 metres.'
1 'expensive / that / look / car' .... 'No, it's cheap.'
2 'seem / happy / Adele' .... 'She's in love again.'
3 'ill / tired / and / feel / I' .... 'Shall I call the doctor?'
4 dark / very early here in winter / get / it ....
5 getting / my parents / old ....

6 Make sentences with adjectives from the box.

Australian	bad	beautiful	hot ✓	late	rich

▶ This water / not be very / ....*This water isn't very hot.*..
1 'The train / be / ......' .... 'No, it's on time.'
2 'He / look / ......' .... 'No, he's American.'
3 'Your hair / look / ......' .... 'Oh, thanks.'
4 My memory / getting very / ....
5 I want / become ...... / and famous ....

We don't usually use adjectives without nouns.

'Polly's ill.' 'The ***poor girl****.'* (NOT ~~*'The poor.'*~~)

In some answers, both contracted forms (for example *I'm, don't*) and full forms (for example *I am, do not*) are possible. Normally both are correct.

adverbs of manner *He ate quickly.*

ADJECTIVES AND ADVERBS

Adjectives are connected with **nouns** and **pronouns**. They usually tell you more about **people** or **things**. They can go before nouns, or after *be, seem, look* etc (see pages 210–211).
Adverbs are connected with **other words** – for example **verbs**.
Some adverbs tell you **how something happens**. These often end in *-ly*.

*It's an easy **language**.*	*You can **learn** this language easily.*
*The **music** is slow.*	*The pianist **is playing** slowly.*
*Her **ideas** are interesting.*	*She **spoke** interestingly about her ideas.*
***Joe** looked hungry.*	*Joe **ate** hungrily.*

1 Choose an adjective or an adverb.

- ▶ Could I have a ......quick...... word with you? (*quick / quickly*)
- ▶ She walked away ......quickly...... (*quick / quickly*)

1. This is a .... train – it stops everywhere. (*slow / slowly*)
2. He talked very .... about his work. (*interesting / interestingly*)
3. You've cooked the meat .... (*beautiful / beautifully*)
4. I've got an .... job for you. (*easy / easily*)
5. She writes in .... English. (*perfect / perfectly*)
6. I sing very .... (*bad / badly*)
7. I feel .... today. (*happy / happily*)
8. You seem very .... (*angry / angrily*)
9. Anne's a .... swimmer. (*strong / strongly*)
10. Could you talk more .... please? (*quiet / quietly*)

HOW TO MAKE *-LY* ADVERBS

- **usually: adjective + *-ly*** — *quick → quickly*; *real → really* (NOT ~~*realy*~~); *complete → completely*
- ***-y → -ily*** — *easy → easily*; *happy → happily*
- ***-ble → -bly*** — *possible → possibly*

2 Write the adverbs.

▶ wrong ......wrongly......	4 thirsty	8 wonderful ....
1 final	5 probable	9 cold ....
2 sincere	6 usual	10 unhappy ....
3 loud	7 nice	11 comfortable ....

WEST
HAGBOURNE
Please drive slowly

EAST
HAGBOURNE
Please drive carefully

other adverbs *I like sport very much.*

Some **adverbs** tell you **when**, **where** or **how much** something happens.

I'm going away ***tomorrow****.* *We ran* ***downhill****.* *The accident happened* ***there****.*
We don't go out ***much****.* *I watch TV* ***a lot****.* *I play the guitar* ***a bit****.* *He sings* ***a little****.*

These adverbs often come **at the end of a sentence**. They do **not** come **between the verb and the object**.

	VERB	OBJECT	ADVERB	
She	*speaks*	*English*	*well.*	(NOT ~~*She speaks well English.*~~)
They	*make*	*very good bread*	*here.*	(NOT ~~*They make here very good bread.*~~)
I	*bought*	*a lot of clothes*	*yesterday.*	(NOT ~~*I bought yesterday a lot of clothes.*~~)
We	*didn't enjoy*	*the holiday*	*much.*	(NOT ~~*We didn't enjoy much the holiday.*~~)
I	*like*	*sport*	*very much.*	(NOT ~~*I like very much sport.*~~)

1 Make sentences with adverbs from the box. (Different answers are possible.)

carefully clearly correctly perfectly slowly tomorrow much yesterday

▶ soup / cook / the ……*Cook the soup slowly.*…… OR ……*Cook the soup carefully.*……
1 the / read / I / letter ……
2 computer / bought / a / I ……
3 name / your / write ……
4 see / must / the / doctor / you ……
5 languages / speaks / he / four ……
6 the / you / write / address / didn't ……
7 skiing / don't like / I ……
8 speak / and / please (two adverbs) ……

2 Write about six things that you like very much.

1 I like …… very much.
2 ……
3 ……
4 ……
5 ……
6 ……

Adverbs can go before **adjectives**, and before **past participles** (for example *broken, finished*).

terribly sorry (NOT ~~*terrible sorry*~~) ***nearly ready*** ***completely finished***

3 Complete the sentences with words from the box. (Different answers are possible.)

badly beautifully completely extremely happily ✓ nearly terribly very well

▶ Joe and Ann have been ……*happily*…… married for twenty-five years.
1 I'm …… sorry to tell you that we have no more tickets.
2 There's nothing to eat – the fridge is …… empty.
3 The book's …… written but it's not very interesting.
4 After walking all day, David was …… tired.
5 The food here is …… cooked but they don't give you enough.
6 'Is your new house ready yet?' 'No, but it's …… finished.'
7 Languages were …… taught at my school, so I didn't learn much French.
8 I'm …… pleased to tell you that you've passed your exam.

In some answers, both contracted forms (for example *I'm, don't*) and full forms (for example *I am, do not*) are possible. Normally both are correct.

Level 2

adverbs with the verb *often, certainly* etc

Some adverbs, for example ***always*** or ***certainly***, usually go **with the verb**.

how often:	*always*	*often*	*usually*	*sometimes*	*ever*	*hardly ever* (= 'almost never')	*never*
how certainly:	*certainly*	*definitely*	*probably*				
other:	*already*	*also*	*just*	*still*	*even*	*only*	

These **adverbs** go before **most verbs**, but after **auxiliary verbs** (***have***, ***will***, ***can***, ***must*** etc) and after ***am/are/is/was/were***.

BEFORE MOST VERBS

*I **always read** in the evenings.*
*Andy **often goes** to New York.*
*She **hardly ever sees** him.*
*I **certainly like** London.*
*We **only want** to see Barbara.*
*Jack **already knows** Sophie.*

AFTER AUXILIARY VERBS AND *AM* ETC

*I **have always** enjoyed reading.*
*He **can often** get cheap flights.*
*He **is hardly ever** at home.*
*It **will certainly** rain tomorrow.*
*We **are only** here to see Barbara.*
*Jack **has already** met Sophie.*

1 Put the adverbs in the correct places.

▶ I speak French, but people know that I'm English. (*often; always*)
I often speak French, but people always know that I'm English.

1 Jake eats fish. He eats fish for breakfast. (*always; even*)
....

2 Ann plays tennis, but she plays in the evenings. (*often; only*)
....

3 Edward puts tomato sauce on everything. He puts it on ice cream. (*usually; probably*)
....

4 I forget names. I forget faces. (*sometimes; never*)
....

5 Jane gets angry, and she shouts at people. (*hardly ever; never*)
....

6 I get to the station on time, and the train is late. (*always; always*)
....

7 I will phone you tomorrow, and I will write next week. (*definitely; probably*)
....

8 I drink tea. I drink coffee. (*usually; sometimes*)
....

9 Your sister is a good singer. She is a very interesting person. (*certainly; also*)
....

10 My mother is asleep. I think she is ill. (*still; probably*)
....

In **questions**, these adverbs usually go **after auxiliary verb + subject**.

***Do you ever** write poems?* ***Has Mary always** lived here?* ***Are you often** in London?*

2 Put the adverbs in the correct places.

1 Do you play cards? (*often*) ....
2 Have you been to Tibet? (*ever*) ....
3 Are you happy? (*always*) ....
4 Does the boss take a holiday? (*ever*) ....
5 Do you eat in restaurants? (*usually*) ....
6 Is Bethany ill? (*still*) ....

Longer expressions usually go **at the end** of a sentence. Compare:

*She **often** plays tennis.* *She plays tennis **two or three times a week**.*
*She **hardly ever** wins a game.* *She wins a game **once or twice a month**.*
*She **always** practises.* *Does she practise **every afternoon**?*

3 Look at the table and make some sentences with *often*, *once a day* etc.

ACTIVITY	EVA	TOM
goes swimming	1/d*	1/m
plays football	–	3/w
plays tennis	1/w	1/y
goes skiing	5–6/y	–
goes to the theatre	1/w	2–3/y
goes to the cinema	3–4/y	2/m
goes to concerts	–	1/w

*1/d = once a day;
2/m = twice a month; etc

Eva often goes swimming.
Eva goes swimming once a day / every day.
Tom goes to the theatre two or three times a year.
......
......
......
......
......
......
......
......
......
......
......
......
......
......

4 GRAMMAR AND VOCABULARY: *go* with spare-time activities

Look at the pictures, and put the correct numbers with the activities. Use a dictionary if necessary.

IN YOUR SPARE TIME YOU CAN:
go walking ...*6*...
go climbing ......
go swimming ......
go sailing ......
go wind-surfing ......
go skiing ......
go skating ......
go fishing ......
go shopping ......
go to the opera ......
go to the theatre ......
go to concerts ......

5 Write some sentences about your spare-time activities. Use words from Exercises 1–4.

▶ *I never go climbing.*
▶ *I go swimming every day.*
1 ......
2 ......
3 ......
4 ......
5 ......
6 ......
7 ......
8 ......

In some answers, both contracted forms (for example *I'm*, *don't*) and full forms (for example *I am*, *do not*) are possible. Normally both are correct.

interested and *interesting* etc

Interested, bored, excited etc say how **people** feel.
Interesting, *boring*, *exciting* etc describe the **things** (or people) that cause the feelings.

She's very interested in the lessons. (**NOT** ~~*She's very interesting in the lessons.*~~)
The lessons are always interesting. (**NOT** ~~*The lessons are always interested.*~~)
I'm often bored at work, because I've got a boring job.

1 Write these words under the pictures: *interested, interesting, bored, boring*.

1 .... 2 .... 3 .... 4 ....

2 Put in words from the box.

annoyed (= 'a little angry') ✓	annoying	excited	exciting	frightened
frightening	surprised	surprising		

1 Somebody phones you late at night. You are ..*annoyed*.............. He/she is ....
2 A woman hears noises at night. She is .... The noises are ....
3 A family makes .... holiday plans. The children are very ....
4 Your exam mark is very good. This is .... And you are ....

3 Here are the beginnings of five books. Write what you think of the books. Use *very interesting*, *quite interesting*, *not very interesting*, *quite boring* or *very boring*.

1 After King Leofric died in 1342, ...
I think this book is probably ....
2 The moment Olga walked into Alan's office, he realised his life had changed for ever ...
I think ....
3 Since the beginning of history, cats ...
....
4 The man in black had already killed five people that morning. The sixth ...
....
5 *Four billion years ago, our world ...*
....

4 GRAMMAR AND VOCABULARY: adverbs of degree; subjects of study
Make sure you know the words in the box. Use a dictionary if necessary. Then write how interested you are in some of the subjects. You can use *extremely* (= +++), *very*, *quite*, *not very*, *not* or *not at all* (= – – –).

art	biology	economics	history	literature	mathematics	philosophy	physics	politics

I'm extremely interested in .... I'm ....
I'm very bored by ....
I'm not at all ....

fast, hard, hardly, well, friendly, ...

Fast, hard, late, early, daily, weekly and *monthly* are **adjectives** and **adverbs**.

*He's got a **fast** car.* *He drives **fast**.*
*It's **hard** work.* *She works **hard**.*
*The train was **late**.* *Trains are running **late**.*
*I got an **early** flight.* *I went home **early**.*
*It's a **weekly** paper.* *I buy it **weekly**.*

Hardly and *lately* have different meanings from *hard* and *late*.
Hardly = 'almost not'; ***lately*** = 'recently', 'not long ago'

*He **hardly** works these days – maybe one day a week.* *Have you heard from John **lately**?*

Well can be an **adjective** (the opposite of *ill*) or an **adverb** (the opposite of *badly*).

*'How are you?' 'Very **well**, thanks.'* *The team are playing **well**.*

1 These are sentences from real conversations. Put in words from the boxes.

early	hard	hardly	weekly	well

1 And I really understand Italian quite ....
2 You've got no playschool tomorrow so you haven't got to get up ...., have you?
3 Why should I work .... when you never do anything?
4 Departures from the UK are .... mid-morning on Sundays from Dover.
5 She was really, you know, nervous, and .... came out of her flat at all.

2 Choose the best answer.

▶ You look ...well..........., Mike. (*early / lately / well*)
1 Your father read the .... Express when he was alive. (*hardly / Daily / lately*)
2 You haven't seen the window cleaner ...., have you? (*lately / hard / weekly*)
3 I ran as .... as I could, along the Tottenham Court Road. (*early / fast / hardly*)
4 I .... sleep – an hour at a time. (*well / hard / hardly*)
5 I got up .... to finish some work. (*well / hardly / early*)
6 My daughter cooks really .... (*hardly / well / lately*)
7 I went to bed very .... last night. (*late / lately / hardly*)
8 I go to Cambridge .... for a business meeting. (*well / hardly / weekly*)
9 I need a rest. I've been working .... all week. (*lately / hard / hardly*)
10 My grandfather hasn't been very well .... (*early / lately / daily*)

Friendly, lonely, lovely, silly are **adjectives**, not **adverbs**.

*She gave me a **friendly** smile.* (**BUT NOT** ~~*She smiled friendly.*~~)
*He was very **lonely**.* (**BUT NOT** ~~*He walked lonely through the streets.*~~)
*Her voice is **lovely**.* (**BUT NOT** ~~*She sings lovely.*~~) *Don't be **silly**.*

There are no adverbs ~~*friendlily*~~, ~~*lovelily*~~ etc. Instead, we use other words or expressions.

*She spoke **in a friendly way**.* *She sings **beautifully**.*

3 Correct (✓) or not (✗)?

1 He spoke very friendly, but I didn't like him. ......
2 You have a lovely smile. ......
3 He's not stupid, but he sometimes talks really silly. ......
4 He doesn't speak English very well, but he writes it lovely. ......
5 I gave her a friendly look, but she turned away. ......

In some answers, both contracted forms (for example *I'm, don't*) and full forms (for example *I am, do not*) are possible. Normally both are correct.

adjectives and adverbs: more practice

1 Word order.

Where do the adjectives and adverbs go?

▶ She's a ∧ cook. (*good*)

1 She was driving a fast car. (*red*)
2 She speaks Chinese. (*perfect*)
3 She speaks Chinese. (*perfectly*)
4 I lost my keys. (*yesterday*)
5 I've got a meeting tomorrow. (*very important*)
6 Anna read Peter's letter. (*slowly*)
7 Tim plays the piano. (*brilliantly*)
8 Lucy is unhappy. (*terribly*)
9 They make very good ice cream. (*here*)
10 She's been unmarried for 15 years. (*happily*)

2 Adjective or adverb?

Circle the correct answers.

1 You are making a *terrible / terribly* mistake.
2 She walked up the steps *slow / slowly*.
3 It was raining very *hard / hardly* when I got up.
4 The boss is a really *friend / friendly* person.
5 I cook very *bad / badly*.
6 Amelia looks very *unhappy / unhappily*.
7 I'm *extreme / extremely* sorry I arrived so *late / lately*.
8 I drove very *careful / carefully* on the snow.
9 I was *late / lately* because of a problem with the trains.
10 I've *complete / completely* forgotten his name.
11 Your hair looks *beautiful / beautifully*.
12 He doesn't work very *hard / hardly*.
13 I can't understand her. She talks very *unclear / unclearly*.
14 The President spoke in *perfect / perfectly* French.
15 This letter isn't very *good / well* written.

4 Adjective or adverb? **Choose the correct words for the caption.**

'*Be careful / Be carefully*, these plates are *extreme / extremely* dirty.'

3 Adverbs with the verb. **Write sentences about yourself.**

1 I often ....
2 I never ....
3 I am sometimes ....
4 I usually ....
5 I have often ....
6 I have never ....
7 I have always ....
8 I am certainly ....
9 I will probably ....
10 I will definitely ....

5 Mixed structures. These sentences are all wrong. Can you correct the mistakes?

▶ She was wearing ~~a red beautiful coat~~. *a beautiful red coat*

1 There are films interestings on TV tonight. ....
2 There's a good and cheap restaurant in Dover St. ....
3 He's tall, dark, good-looking. ....
4 I am very interesting in the lessons. ....
5 I like very much this music. ....
6 'Emma's got appendicitis.' 'The poor!' ....
7 I'm terrible sorry! ....
8 I lost yesterday my glasses. ....
9 She smiled happy when I walked in. ....
10 I often have thought of changing my job. ....
11 There were some difficults questions in the test. ....
12 The boss always talks to us friendly. ....
13 My mother speaks very well Arabic. ....
14 You look beautifully in that dress. ....
15 You're walking too fastly for me. ....
16 Please drive careful. ....
17 The manager welcomed us in perfectly English. ....
18 John always is ready to help people. ....
19 We speak usually Spanish together. ....
20 I worked hardly, but I failed the exam. ....

6 Grammar in a text. Put in adjectives or adverbs from the box.

daily	early ✓	fast	friendly	hard	hardly	late	lonely	silly

I don't like getting up ▶ *early* so I usually stay in bed too long, and then have to eat breakfast very 1 .... and run for my train. On the train I read the 2 .... paper, because after I get to work there's no more time for reading. The boss is nice, but she makes us work very 3 ...., and I often have to stay 4 .... to finish everything. There's a nice new secretary in the office. I 5 .... know her, but she always gives me a 6 .... smile when I arrive. She hasn't lived here long. Perhaps it's a 7 .... idea, but I wonder if she's 8 .... I think I'll ask her out.

7 GRAMMAR AND VOCABULARY: nouns and adjectives. Find the answers. Use a dictionary to help you. Different answers are possible.

a bed	a light	apples	children	coffee	hair	holidays	milk	skin	water ✓	water

▶ It can be cold, warm or hot. *water*
1 It can be strong or weak. ....
2 It can be deep or shallow. ....
3 They can be long or short. ....
4 It can be dark or fair. ....
5 It can be bright or dim. ....
6 It can be hard or soft. ....
7 It can be rough or smooth. ....
8 It can be fresh or sour. ....
9 They can be sweet or sour. ....
10 They can be quiet or noisy. ....

8 Internet exercise. Use a search engine (e.g. Google) to find some simple sentences with *hard* and some with *hardly*. Write three of each.

1 ....
2 ....
3 ....
4 ....
5 ....
6 ....

pronunciation for grammar → e-book

adjectives and adverbs: revision test

1 Write the adverbs.

quick ....quickly.... real .... complete .... possible ....
happy .... nice .... easy .... beautiful ....
probable .... usual .... incredible ....
unhappy .... right .... sincere .... hungry ....
careful .... perfect .... warm .... angry ....
comprehensible .... slow ....

2 Where do the adjectives and adverbs go?

▶ It's a /day. (*nice*)
1 I saw a good film. (*yesterday*)
2 Andy can help you. (*definitely*)
3 You speak Russian. (*very well*)
4 She smiles. (*never*)
5 Alice had some ideas. (*really interesting*)
6 They sell very good clothes. (*here*)
7 I have been to Norway. (*never*)
8 Karl plays the violin. (*very badly*)
9 I have paid. (*already*)
10 He was wearing a new suit. (*blue*)
11 We see Annie and Seb. (*often*)
12 Emma read the report. (*slowly*)
13 Judy and Simon are late. (*always*)
14 You are right. (*probably*)
15 I go to the cinema. (*hardly ever*)

3 Correct (✓) or not (✗)?

▶ I had a headache very bad. ..✗..
▶ Read this now. ..✓..
1 She makes wonderfully soup. ......
2 I spoke to them very slow and clear. ......
3 It snowed very hard yesterday. ......
4 That secretary isn't very friendly. ......
5 I sing terribly bad. ......
6 Your baby looks really happy. ......
7 I'm sorry I got here so lately. ......
8 Fill in this form very carefully. ......
9 I complete forgot to phone Paul. ......
10 She studied very hardly for the exam. ......
11 Everybody spoke perfect English. ......
12 This fish isn't very well cooked. ......
13 They asked some difficults questions. ......
14 Do you know a hotel good and cheap? ......
15 I never have understood maths. ......

4 These sentences are all wrong. Can you correct the mistakes?

▶ He was wearing ~~black old boots~~. ....old black boots....
1 He's short, fat, stupid-looking. ....
2 We usually are at home on Saturdays. ....
3 I am boring in the science lessons. ....
4 People never will stop fighting. ....
5 I listen always to the news at breakfast. ....
6 'Jenny's in hospital.' 'The poor!' ....
7 We often have been to India. ....
8 We're terrible late. ....
9 They stood up slow when we walked in. ....
10 The weather already is getting better. ....
11 Never you tell me what you are thinking. ....
12 Your hair looks beautifully today. ....
13 John probably has forgotten my name again. ....
14 I don't like you driving so fastly. ....
15 Please speak slow. ....

In some answers, both contracted forms (for example *I'm*, *don't*) and full forms (for example *I am*, *do not*) are possible. Normally both are correct.

SECTION 16 comparison

grammar summary

We can **compare** people and things with each other using ***as … as, -er than*** or ***more … than***.

*Joe's **as tall as** me.* *Jane's **taller than** me.* *She works **more carefully than** me.*

We can use ***-est*** or ***most*** to compare people and things with **all of their group**.

*John is the **oldest** of Mary's children.* *Nasima's the **most intelligent** person in the class.*

We use ***-er*** and ***-est*** with **shorter adjectives** and some **short adverbs**; we use ***more*** and ***most*** with **other adjectives and adverbs.**

London's wildest nightclub

For smaller kitchens,

the smallest **dishwasher** in the world

'Best sports car of the year'
– it's bigger, lighter, stronger and faster.

We can make your car go **faster**.

100% Organic Soup
Nothing could be more comforting

The world's longest running musical:
Les Misérables

The finest vegetables
you've ever tasted

The sooner you come to us, the sooner you'll find the job you want.

30% CHEAPER

20% FASTER

50% BETTER

Level 2

comparative and superlative adjectives: forms

Comparative adjectives are forms like ***colder, more famous***.
Superlative adjectives are forms like ***coldest, most famous***.

- **most short (one-syllable) adjectives:** + *-er, -est* — *old* → *older, oldest*
- **short adjectives ending in *-e*:** + *-r, -st* — *nice* → *nicer, nicest*

1 Write the comparative and superlative adjectives.

▶ cold ...colder, coldest...
▶ late ...later, latest...
1 green ....
2 safe ....
3 rich ....
4 small ....
5 strange ....
6 fine ....
7 high ....
8 wide ....
9 near ....
10 white ....

- **short adjectives ending in one vowel + one consonant:**
  double consonant + *-er, -est* — *fat* → *fatter, fattest* — *thin* → *thinner, thinnest*
  BUT **don't double *w*:** — *low* → *lower, lowest*

2 Write the comparative and superlative adjectives.

▶ red ...redder, reddest...
▶ slow ...slower, slowest...
1 big ....
2 hot ....
3 new ....
4 wet ....
5 slim ....

- **two-syllable adjectives ending in *-y*:** *y* → *i* + *-er, -est* — *happy* → *happier, happiest*

3 Write the comparative and superlative adjectives.

▶ friendly ...friendlier, friendliest...
1 lazy ....
2 hungry ....
3 sleepy ....
4 angry ....
5 dirty ....

- **most other longer adjectives:** + *more, most* — *hopeful* → *more hopeful, most hopeful*

4 Write the comparative and superlative adjectives.

▶ famous ...more famous, most famous...
1 careful ....
2 beautiful ....
3 intelligent ....
4 dangerous ....
5 important ....
6 boring ....
7 interested ....

- **irregular adjectives:** *good* → ***better, best*** — *bad* → ***worse, worst***
  far → ***further, furthest*** OR ***farther, farthest***

5 Put in irregular comparative adjectives.

▶ I know that my handwriting is bad, but Jenny's is ...worse...
1 I'm so tired. Is the bus stop much ....?
2 I don't enjoy train travel here, but I do in France – the trains are .... there.
3 'How's your toothache today?' 'It's ....' 'You should see a dentist.'

comparative or superlative?

We use **comparatives** to compare people and things with **other people and things**.

***A** is **bigger than B**.* *__A__ is __bigger than__ __B__ and __c__.* ***John** is a **more careful** driver **than Robin**.*

◄ *Dawn is tall.*

◄ *Dawn is **taller than** Leah.* ►

◄ *Dawn is **taller than** all the other players.* ►

We use **superlatives** (usually with *the*) to compare people and things with **all of the group that they are in**.

***A** is **the biggest** of the three letters **A**, **B** and **c**.*

***John** is **the most careful** driver **in the family**.*

◄ *Dawn is **the tallest** player in the team.*

1 Circle the correct answer.

► Dawn is *older / the oldest* than all of her sisters. (older)
► Leah is *taller / the tallest* person in her family. (the tallest)
1 All of the players are nice, but Sarah is certainly *the nicer / the nicest*.
2 This is *the better / the best* women's basketball team in the country.
3 Basketballs are *more expensive / the most expensive* than footballs.
4 Ice hockey is a *more dangerous / most dangerous* sport than basketball or tennis.
5 Of all the sports in the Olympics, which sport is *more dangerous? / the most dangerous*?
6 A basketball court is usually *bigger / the biggest* than a tennis court.
7 Which is *the faster / the fastest* game? Not chess.
8 Which is the *more / most* expensive game? Poker?

2 Choose a comparative or a superlative. Remember to use *the* before the superlatives.

► 'The Marriage of Figaro' is ...the most beautiful... of all Mozart's operas. (*beautiful*)
► My new car is ...faster... than my old one. (*fast*)
1 My mother and her sisters are all .... than their children. (*short*)
2 I think Annie is .... person in our class. (*intelligent*)
3 Let's meet in the library – it's .... than all the other rooms. (*quiet*)
4 My bedroom is .... room in the house. (*cold*)
5 A 3-year-old's voice is .... than 200 people in a busy restaurant. (*loud*)
6 Brazil is .... South American country. (*big*)
7 My computer is much .... than me. (*intelligent*)
8 Which is .... thing to study? (*boring*)

In some answers, both contracted forms (for example *I'm, don't*) and full forms (for example *I am, do not*) are possible. Normally both are correct.

comparatives: use *brighter than the moon*

We use ***than* after comparative** adjectives.

*Russia is **bigger than** China.* (**NOT** … ~~*that China.*~~) *Rob and Tina are **older than** Emma.*

1 Compare each pair of things in the box. Write two sentences for each pair. More than one answer may be possible.

COMPARE: the sun and the moon ✓ dogs and cats train travel and air travel the Sahara and the Himalayas English and Chinese Canada and Ireland
ADJECTIVES: big bright ✓ cheap cold easy difficult fast friendly hot intelligent small ✓ small

▶ *The sun is brighter than the moon.*
▶ *The moon is smaller than the sun.*
1 ....
2 ....
3 ....
4 ....
5 ....
6 ....
7 ....
8 ....
9 ....
10 ....

2 Use comparative adjectives with … *than all the other* …

▶ Alaska's area is 1,518,700km². No other US state is so large.
Alaska is larger than all the other US states.

1 The Amazon is 6,670km long. No other river in South America is so long.
....

2 Blue whales can weigh 120 tonnes. No other whales are so heavy.
....

3 Mont Blanc is 4,807m high. No other mountain in the Alps is so high.
....

4 Cheetahs can run at 110km/h. No other big cats are so fast.
....

5 The Atacama desert has no rain. No other deserts are so dry.
....

6 Redwoods can grow up to 110 metres. No other trees are so tall.
....

whales

big cats

With comparatives, we can say … ***than I am / than you are / than John is*** etc.
But in informal **spoken English**, we usually prefer … ***than me/you/him/her/it/us/them***.

3 Write two endings for each sentence: one with *than me, than you* etc and one with *than I am, than you are* etc.

▶ Tariq was angry, but I was angrier than him. / than he was.
1 John's very careful with money, but Maria ……………………
2 I'm hungry, but you must be ……………………
3 You're not very short. Tony's ……………………
4 We're excited, but our children ……………………
5 My girlfriend is so beautiful. No other woman ……………………

We can use ***a lot / a bit*** (more conversational) or ***much / a little*** before comparatives.

*Your cooking is **much better** than my sister's.* (NOT … ~~very better~~… AND NOT … ~~too better~~ …)
*This book is **a lot more interesting** than that one.* *You sound **a bit happier** today.*

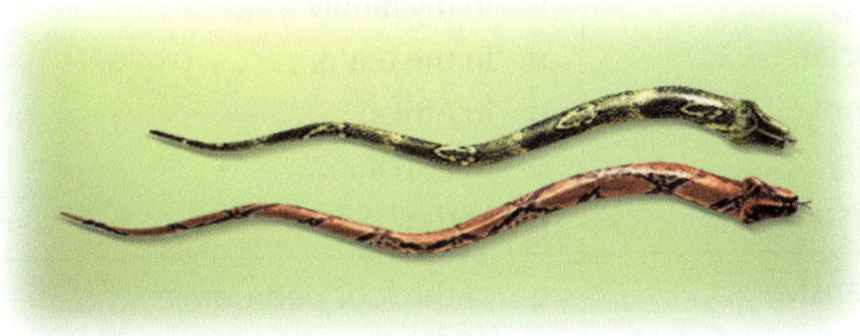
a bit longer

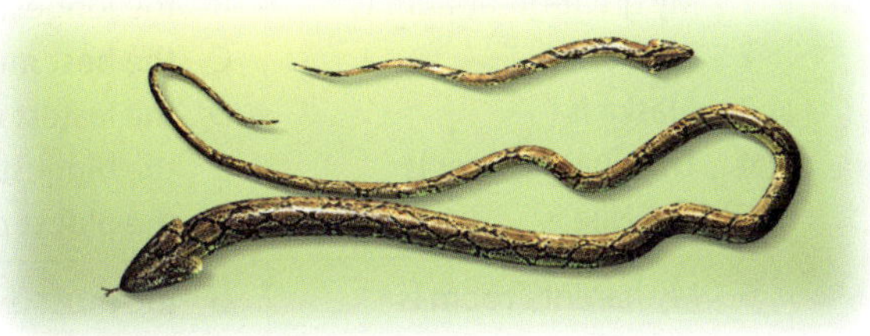
much longer

4 Use the table. Write sentences about Mark and Simon with *a bit / a little* and *a lot / much* with the adjectives from the box.

short ✓ / tall	old / young	rich	fast / slow	comfortable	quiet / noisy

	How tall?	How old?	How rich?
Mark	1m95	35	€900,000/year
Simon	1m85	36	€250,000/year

	How fast?	How comfortable?	How quiet?
Mark's car	190km/h	★★★	★★
Simon's car	130km/h	★★	★★★★★

▶ Simon is a bit (OR a little) shorter than Mark.
1 ……………………
2 ……………………
3 ……………………
4 ……………………
5 ……………………
6 ……………………
7 ……………………
8 ……………………
9 ……………………

Simon Mark

We can use ***more than*** and ***less than*** without adjectives.

*Liz spent **more than** a week's pay on that dress.* *It took us **less than** ten minutes to get home.*

superlatives *the highest mountain in the world*

After **superlatives**, we normally use ***in*** before the names of **places**.

*Everest is the **highest** mountain **in the world**.* (**NOT** … ~~of the world.~~)
*Jamal is the **most intelligent** person **in the office**.*
*Sirius is the **brightest** star **in the sky**.*

After **superlatives**, we also use ***in*** before **singular** words for **groups** of people.

*Sam is the **youngest** player **in the orchestra**.*
*Wilkins is the **oldest** minister **in this government**.*

In most **other cases**, we use ***of*** after superlatives.

*Anna's the **tallest of** the three sisters.* *This is the **shortest** day **of** the year.*

1 Put the beginnings, middles and ends together.

0 Jonathan is	A the biggest state ……	k in the group. ……
1 My great-great-aunt is	B the longest river ……	l in my family. ……
2 London is	C the best musician ……	m in the team. ..o..
3 Alaska is	D the fastest runner ..o..	n in Africa. ……
4 The guitar player is	E the biggest city ……	o in Britain. ……
5 The Nile is	F the oldest person ……	p in the USA. ……
6 My parents' room is	G the most expensive ……	q of the four bedrooms. ……
7 The Mercedes is	H the longest day ……	r of the five girls. ……
8 Sarah is	I the youngest ……	s of the three cars. ……
9 June 21st is	J the biggest ……	t of the year. ……

2 Write sentences with superlatives.

▶ In my job, Friday / busy day / week
In my job, Friday is the busiest day of the week.

1 In the 1970s, the Beatles / rich musicians / world
……………………………………………………

2 Eric says that Eleanor / good singer / group
……………………………………………………

3 When I was a child, my father / tall man / our town
……………………………………………………

4 In this country, February / cold month / year
……………………………………………………

5 Who / old / your three aunts?
……………………………………………………

6 Helen is very intelligent, but she / quiet person / my class
……………………………………………………

7 Which / good / these three bikes / ?
……………………………………………………

8 Which / big city / Argentina / ?
……………………………………………………

> There is so much good in the worst of us,
> and so much bad in the best of us.
> (*Author unknown*)

comparison of adverbs *More slowly, please.*

Level 2

To make the **comparative** of **most adverbs:** ***more*** + **adverb** (... ***than***)

*Can you speak **more quietly**, please?* *I'm working **more slowly** today **than** yesterday.*
*Angela writes **more clearly than** Ellie.*

1 Write sentences with comparative adverbs and *than*.

▶ Jacob drives / dangerously / Sam
Jacob drives more dangerously than Sam.

1 Lee talks to people / politely / Ben
....

2 Liam works / carefully / John
....

3 Simon goes swimming / often / Karen
....

4 My car runs / quietly / my sister's car
....

5 Annie talks / slowly / Rob
....

6 Olivia thinks / clearly / most people
....

7 Jack dresses / expensively / me
....

8 I live / cheaply / my friends
....

Some short adverbs have comparatives with **-*er***, like adjectives. Examples: ***early***, ***late***, ***fast***, ***hard***, ***high***, ***long***, ***near*** and ***soon***.

*I got to the station **earlier** than Mary.* *Bill lives **nearer** to school than Pete, so he gets up **later**.*

Irregular comparatives:	*well* → ***better***	*badly* → ***worse***	*far* → ***further/farther***
	little → ***less***	*a lot / much* → ***more***	

*My mother drives **better** than my father.* *He sings badly, but I sing **worse**.*
*She talks **less** than he does, but she thinks **more**.* *I live **further** from the centre than you.*

2 Use the comparatives of the adverbs in the box to complete the advice.

early	fast	hard ✓	high	late	little	long	much	near

▶ 'I want to earn more money.' 'Work harder.'
1 'I want to eat my breakfast slowly in the morning.' 'Get up ....'
2 'I want to get more sleep.' 'Get up ....'
3 'I want to be stronger.' 'Exercise ....'
4 'I hate driving to work.' 'Live .... to your work and walk.'
5 'I get a lot of headaches.' 'Try to worry ....'
6 'I'm afraid I'm going to miss the train.' 'Walk ....'
7 'I'm no good at basketball.' 'Practise jumping ....'
8 'I want to learn everything there is.' 'Live ....'

Sentences with **superlative adverbs** (for example *John drives **the most dangerously***) are **not very common**.

In some answers, both contracted forms (for example *I'm*, *don't*) and full forms (for example *I am*, *do not*) are possible. Normally both are correct.

(not) as … as *Your hands are as cold as ice.*

We use ***(not) as … as*** to say that people and things are **(not) the same** in some way.

*I don't think Tom is going to be **as tall as** his sister.* *Your hands are **as cold as** ice.*
*Can you read this for me? My eyes **aren't as good as** yours.*

1 Read the sentences and decide: which picture is Jenny and which picture is Cassie?

Jenny isn't as old as Cassie.
Jenny's hands aren't as small as Cassie's.
Cassie's hair isn't as long as Jenny's.
Jenny isn't as fair as Cassie.

Picture A is ....   Picture B is ....

Now write some more sentences about Jenny and Cassie with *not as … as*.

1 slim ....
2 tall ....
3 skirt / long ....
4 bag / big ....
5 coat / heavy ....
6 glass / big ....

With ***as … as***, we can say ***… as I am / as you are / as John is*** etc. But in informal **spoken** English, we usually prefer ***… as me/you/him/her/it/us/them***.

2 Change the sentences in two ways, but keep the same meaning.

▶ Nicole's prettier than her sister. *Nicole's sister isn't as pretty as her.*
Nicole's sister isn't as pretty as she is.

1 You're nicer than the other doctor. The other doctor ....
....
2 He's more interesting than his boss. ....
....
3 I'm slimmer than my mother. ....
....
4 We're more careful than the Browns. ....
....

We can put **just**, **nearly**, **not quite** and **half**, **twice**, **three times** etc **before as … as.**

*He's **just as** handsome **as** his brother.* *My hair is **not quite as** fair **as** my sister's hair.*
*The twins are **nearly as** tall **as** their mother.* *Brazil is **half as** big **as** Russia.*

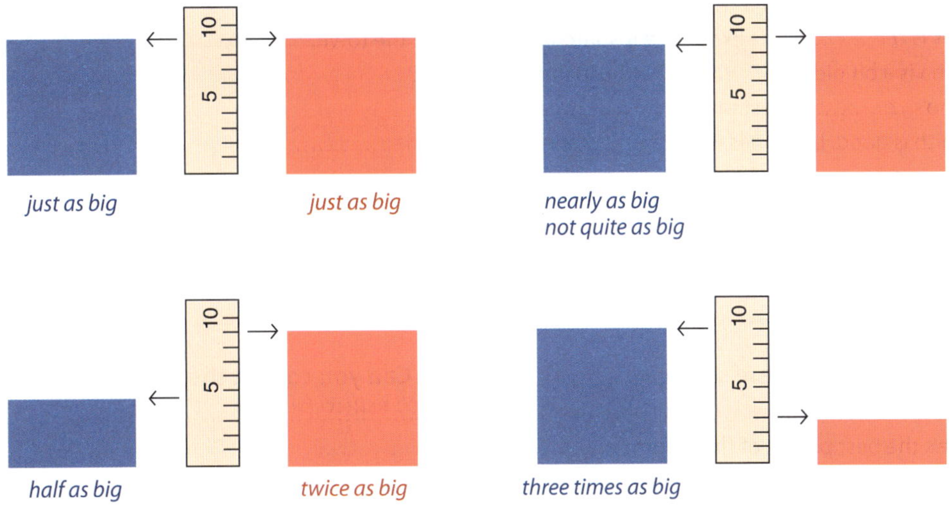

just as big just as big nearly as big
 not quite as big

half as big twice as big three times as big

③ **Think of a member of your family. Compare yourself to him or her, using *as … as* and some of the words and expressions from the box. Write five sentences.**

BEFORE AS:	just	nearly	not quite	half	twice	three times	*etc*	
ADJECTIVES:	dark	fair	friendly	handsome	happy	intelligent	kind	nice
	old	pretty	quiet	short	slim	tall		

▶ *I'm nearly as tall as Grace.*
▶ *I'm not quite as tall as her.*
1 ...
2 ...

3 ..
4 ..
5 ..
6 ..

We can use **as much as** and **as many as** with **nouns.**

*Deborah doesn't work **as many hours as** I do, but she makes just **as much money as** me.*

④ **Make sentences with *as … as* or *not as … as*, and some of the expressions from Exercise 3.**
▶ Alice has $200 and Matt has $100. *Alice has twice as much money as Matt.*
1 Eric has 20 cousins, and Tony has 10. Eric ..
..

2 Ben eats 3 sandwiches every day; Jo eats 1. ...
..

3 Helen has 23 computer games and Adrian has 25.
..

4 Liz drinks 6 cups of coffee a day; Chris drinks 12.
..

5 Mike has 600 books, and David has 600 too. ..
..

6 Rebecca only has a little free time; Fred has a lot.
..

In some answers, both contracted forms (for example *I'm*, *don't*) and full
forms (for example *I am*, *do not*) are possible. Normally both are correct.

comparison: more practice

1 Mixed structures. Put in the correct words.

1 I'm not .... tall .... my sister.
2 This is the .... expensive restaurant .... the town.
3 Anna is a bit older .... her husband.
4 Who's .... best player .... the family?
5 Smith is good, but Jones is .... and Ericsson is the ....
6 Please drive .... slowly.
7 How much fruit can I have? Take .... much .... you want.
8 Texas is bigger .... France.
9 You're .... beautiful than I ....
10 A metre is more .... a centimetre and .... than a kilometre.

2 Mixed structures. These sentences are all wrong (✗). Can you correct the mistakes?

▶ You're the ~~beautifullest~~ woman I have ever seen. most beautiful
1 She's the best pianist of the world. ....
2 My sister is much taller that me. ....
3 Katie is the more beautiful person here. ....
4 Please drive slowlier. ....
5 This is the more expensive hotel in London. ....
6 You drive much faster of me. ....
7 My hands are cold like ice. ....
8 James is much older as his wife. ....
9 Everest is more high than Mount Fuji. ....
10 We all sing badly, but I'm the worse. ....
11 My sister is the intelligentest person in the family. ....
12 I'm happyer this year than last year. ....
13 Tokyo is the biggest city of Japan. ....
14 Robert is the youngest from the three children. ....
15 Sunday is best day of the week. ....

3 Mixed structures. Look at the pictures and make sentences.

A £17, 999
Maximum speed 120km/h

B £62, 999
Maximum speed 200km/h

C £24, 300
Maximum speed 150km/h

▶ B / fast / A B is faster than A.
1 B / fast / C ....
2 A / fast / B A is not as ....
3 C / fast / B ....
4 B / fast B is the ....
5 C / expensive / A ....
6 A / expensive / B ....
7 B / expensive B is the ....
8 B / big / C ....
9 C / big / A ....
10 C / big ....

4 GRAMMAR AND VOCABULARY: time. **Make sure you know the words in the box. Use a dictionary if necessary. Then answer the questions, using *more* and *less*.**

century	day	decade	hour	minute	month	second	week	year

▸ How much is a minute? More than a second and less than an hour.
1 How much is a decade? ....
2 How much is a month? ....
3 How much is a week? ....
4 How much is an hour? ....
5 How much is a day? ....
6 How much is a year? ....

5 Grammar in a text. **Read the text carefully, and then answer the questions.**

John lives in Birmingham. He is a bus driver. He is very interested in history. He is taller than Tom, and better-looking, but he doesn't have as much money as Tom. Tom works in an import-export firm in Liverpool. He collects antique furniture. He is deeply in love with Julia. He's much older than she is, but not as tall as she is, and he's really not very good-looking. Julia's friend Hannah lives in Birmingham, near her cousin Pete. She's exactly as old as he is, and they're both very interested in information technology. Pete runs a very successful computer business. He has much more money than Tom, but not nearly as much as Hannah. He has dark hair and blue eyes, and he's better looking than Tom, but not as tall as Tom. Pete and John are old friends. They often play tennis together. John is twice as old as Pete (he's nearly as old as Tom), but he usually wins when he and Pete play. They are both deeply in love with Julia. Julia works in a travel agency. She likes fast cars, travel, horse-riding and fashionable clothes. She often goes on holiday with Hannah. Hannah usually pays for the holidays, because Julia doesn't have as much money as Hannah. Hannah is taller than Julia, (but not as tall as John) and very beautiful. Hannah is deeply in love with the tallest of the three men. Julia is deeply in love with the oldest.

1 Who is Hannah in love with? ....
2 Who is Julia in love with? ....
3 Who is the richest of the five people? ....

6 ***Than, that* or *as*? Complete the caption.**

'There, dear! I think we've left the world a better place .... we found it!'

7 Internet exercise. **Use a search engine (e.g. Google). Which of the following gets most hits?**

"beautifuller" 8,100
"more beautiful" 5,880,000
"more happy" ....
"happier" ....
"older that" ....
"older than" ....
"the highest mountain of Britain" ....
"the highest mountain in Britain" ....
"the best player of the team" ....
"the best player in the team" ....

comparison: revision test

1 Write the comparatives and superlatives.

▶ tall ....taller, tallest....
1 interesting ....
2 thin ....
3 cheap ....
4 easy ....
5 bad ....
6 beautiful ....
7 lazy ....
8 far ....
9 good ....
10 old ....
11 fat ....
12 happy ....
13 late ....
14 hot ....
15 slow ....
16 big ....
17 expensive ....
18 dirty ....
19 important ....
20 strong ....

2 Put in *as*, *than* or *that*.

1 My feet are .... cold .... ice.
2 She looks older .... her sister.
3 I think .... he's Chinese.
4 Alice is much stronger .... her brother.
5 Can't you eat faster .... that?
6 He's as funny .... toothache.
7 The car .... I saw was too small.
8 The cat seems worse .... yesterday.
9 It's not as cold .... last week.
10 She's got a more interesting job .... me.

3 Put in the correct words.

1 A kilogram is less .... a tonne and .... than a gram.
2 Jake is bad at languages, but he's not as bad as I ....
3 I get up early, at 6.30; George gets up ...., at 6.15, and Pam is the ...., at 6.00.
4 Please speak .... slowly.
5 Karl is .... oldest player .... the team.
6 'How many people can I invite?' '........ many .... you like.'
7 We stayed in the .... expensive hotel .... the city.
8 She's not .... nice .... her brother.
9 Siberia is bigger .... Europe.
10 Phil is a bad teacher, and Annie is .... and Douglas is the ....

4 These sentences are all wrong. Can you correct the mistakes?

▶ He's the ~~intelligentest~~ man I have ever met. ....most intelligent....
1 Which is the highest mountain of Europe? ....
2 We all play badly, but I'm the worse. ....
3 Julie has the more interesting job in our office. ....
4 Your house is much nicer as ours. ....
5 Please walk quicklier. ....
6 His eyes are hard like stones. ....
7 London is more big than Paris. ....
8 My sister is the beautifullest of the three girls. ....
9 Paul is the oldest from the three children. ....
10 Monday is worst day of the week. ....

In some answers, both contracted forms (for example *I'm*, *don't*) and full forms (for example *I am*, *do not*) are possible. Normally both are correct.

SECTION 17 conjunctions

grammar summary

after	*although*	*and*	*as soon as*	*because*	*before*	*but*	*so*	*until*	*when*	*while*

both ... and *either ... or* *neither ... nor* (For *if*, see Section 18.)
(If necessary, use a dictionary to check the meanings of these conjunctions.)

We use **conjunctions** to **join** sentences together.

*I went to Germany **because** Emma was there.* *We went home **after** the concert finished.*
*I phoned **as soon as** I got the news.*

Some conjunctions (and the words that follow them) can go in **two places**.

*I cleaned my room **before I went out**.* ***Before I went out**, I cleaned my room.*

We use **present tenses** to talk about the **future** with **time-conjunctions**.

*I'll phone you **when I arrive**.* *Let's wait here **until somebody comes**.*
*She'll pay you **as soon as she has** the money.*

We can use ***and*** to join sentences, shorter expressions or single words. We **don't** need to **repeat unnecessary words** with ***and***.

*I went downstairs **and (I)** opened the door.* *I've got friends in Canada **and (in)** Australia.*
*Could I have a knife **and (a)** fork?*

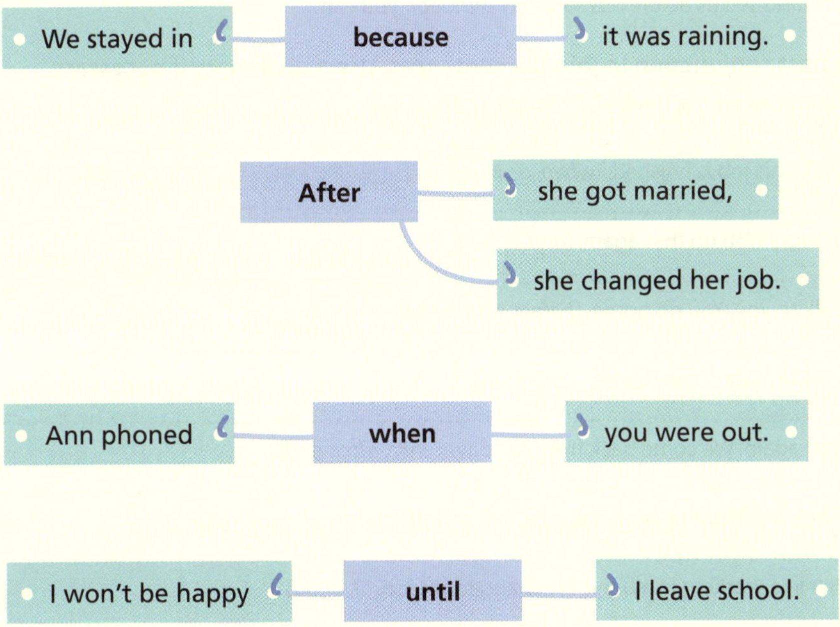

conjunctions: introduction *and, but, because …*

Conjunctions are words like ***and, but, because, although, if, while, so, until***.
We use conjunctions to **join sentences together**.

It was cold	***and***	*I wanted to go home.*
I like him	***but***	*I don't like her.*
He got up	***although***	*he was ill.*
I didn't buy it	***because***	*it was too expensive.*
I'll phone you	***if***	*the train is late.*
Andrew called	***while***	*you were out.*
It was raining	***so***	*I took my umbrella.*
I waited	***until***	*Mary was ready.*
Let's go out	***as soon as***	*Peter arrives.*

1 Circle the best conjunction.

▶ I'll phone you *although / so / when* I arrive.

1 The party was boring, *although / because / so* I went home.
2 The weather was nice, *although / or / until* it was a bit cold.
3 She speaks good French, *after / because / but* she has a strong English accent.
4 I enjoyed my month in Argentina, *although / and / but* I learnt a lot of Spanish.
5 I'll tell you my plans *because / so / while* we're having lunch.
6 I helped him *after / because / or* he was a good friend.
7 I'll wait here with you *as soon as / until* your train leaves.
8 Let's talk about the future *while / because / or* we're walking.
9 You can pay me now *or / so / because* I can wait until next week.
10 Please come and see us *before / as soon as / although* you can.

2 Choose the best conjunction to join the sentences. Use a dictionary if necessary.

▶ I lived in Liverpool. I left school. (*if, although, until*)
I lived in Liverpool until I left school.

1 We'll be glad. This job is finished. (*when, or, while*)
....
2 I'll be very angry. You do that again. (*and, if, but*)
....
3 I'd like to talk to you. You go home. (*before, and, although*)
....
4 Sue watched TV. John came home. (*if, until, or*)
....
5 We'll see you again. We come back from holiday. (*while, after, and*)
....
6 I like her. She's a difficult person. (*because, before, although*)
....
7 Henry didn't like working in a bank. He changed his job. (*if, or, so*)
....
8 They think they can do what they like. They're rich. (*because, although, until*)
....
9 I want to stop working. I'm 50. (*if, before, and*)
....
10 You look beautiful. You're smiling. (*or, so, when*)
....

position of conjunctions *If you need help, ask me.*

When we use **conjunctions**, there are often **two possibilities**.

1 **Start** with the conjunction (and the part that follows it).	2 Put the conjunction **between** the two parts of the sentence.
CONJUNCTION bbbbb, aaaaa	Aaaaa(,) CONJUNCTION bbbbb
IF you need help, please ask me.	*Please ask me IF you need help.*
WHEN you are in London, phone us.	*Phone us WHEN you are in London.*
ALTHOUGH it was raining, I went out.	*I went out, ALTHOUGH it was raining hard.*
AS SOON AS she could, she went to bed.	*She went to bed AS SOON AS she could.*

Note that we often put **commas** (,) in sentences with conjunctions, especially in longer sentences.
We **usually** use a **comma** if we **start** with the conjunction.

1 Put these sentences together in two ways.

▶ I enjoyed the film. The beginning was boring. (*although*)
I enjoyed the film, although the beginning was boring.
Although the beginning was boring, I enjoyed the film.

1 I put on two sweaters. It was very cold. (*because*)
....
....

2 I'm going to work in Australia. I leave school. (*when*)
....
....

3 I go and see Felix. I want to talk to somebody. (*if*)
....
....

4 Ann made coffee. Bill fried some eggs. (*while*)
....
....

5 I was interested in the conversation. I didn't understand everything. (*although*)
....
....

6 We went to a restaurant. There was no food in the house. (*because*)
....
....

7 We'll have a big party. John comes home. (*when*)
....
....

8 I stayed with friends. My parents were travelling. (*while*)
....
....

9 I go for long walks at the weekend. The weather's fine. (*if*)
....
....

10 Come and see us. You arrive in Scotland. (*as soon as*)
....
....

NOTE: *and*, *but*, *or* and *so* always come **between** the two parts of the sentence.

In some answers, both contracted forms (for example *I'm*, *don't*) and full forms (for example *I am*, *do not*) are possible. Normally both are correct.

Level 2

tenses with time conjunctions *I'll see you before you go.*

We use the **simple present** with a **future** meaning after ***before, after, while, until, when*** and ***as soon as***.

I'll see you ***before*** *you* ***go***. (NOT … ~~*before you will go.*~~) *We'll talk about it* ***after I get*** *back.*
You can use my car ***while I'm*** *in Ireland.* *Don't move* ***until I tell*** *you.*
He'll phone ***when*** *he* ***gets home***. (NOT … ~~*when he will get home.*~~)
We'll start the party ***as soon as*** *Alice* ***arrives***.

1 Put in verbs from the box. Use the simple present.

arrive	be	finish	get	go	hear	leave	make	open ✓	stop	write

▶ Wait here until Jane ..*opens*.. the door.
1 Call me as soon as you .... about the exam.
2 Can you hold the baby while I .... coffee?
3 What's John going to do when he .... school?
4 Give my love to Sue when you .... to her.
5 I'll cook supper after I .... back from the gym.
6 I'm going to travel round the world before I .... 60.
7 I'm not going out until the rain ....
8 Will you stay in while I .... shopping?
9 We'll call you as soon as we .... in Paris.
10 We'll go for a drink after the class ....

2 Put in verbs from the box (simple present or *will*).

come	find	get	give ✓	help	look after	look	start	stop	tell	travel

▶ I ..*'ll give*.. you my address before I say goodbye.
1 Lisa's going to live here until she .... a job.
2 We're going to look after Sue's flat while she .... round America.
3 I .... you to clean the flat after I get back from work.
4 We're early – we've got half an hour before the lesson ....
5 I .... you the price as soon as I know myself.
6 Can I go and see Maggie while you .... the kids?
7 When I get time, I .... for a new place to live.
8 Mum's going to move to Scotland after she .... work.
9 I'll bring you a present when I .... home.
10 Things .... worse before they get better.

3 Write five or more sentences about yourself, using some of the beginnings in the box.

When I leave school, I'll … When I finish university, I'll … When I get married, I'll …
When I have children, I'll … When my children leave home, I'll … When I stop work, I'll …
When I have time, I'll … When I'm 20/30/40/50/60/70/80/90/100, I'll …

1 ....
2 ....
3 ....
4 ....
5 ....
6 ....
7 ....

→ For tenses with *if* see page 245.

because and *so*; *although* and *but*

We can say **why** things happen with ***because*** or ***so*** (but **not both**).

Because *Sue was tired, she went to bed. / Sue went to bed* ***because*** *she was tired.*
OR *Sue was tired,* ***so*** *she went to bed.* (**BUT NOT** ~~*Because Sue was tired, so she went to bed.*~~)

We usually put a **comma** (,) before *so*. For more about commas with conjunctions, see page 235.

1 Join the sentences with *because* (twice) and with *so*.

▶ He passed the exam. He had a good teacher.
Because he had a good teacher, he passed the exam.
He passed the exam because he had a good teacher.
He had a good teacher, so he passed the exam.

1 I changed my hotel. The rooms were dirty.
....
....
....

2 The taxi was late. We missed the train.
....
....
....

3 I didn't like the film. I walked out of the cinema.
....
....
....

We can say that things are **not as we expect** with ***although*** or ***but*** (but **not both**).

Although *Pete was tired, he didn't go to bed. / Pete didn't go to bed,* ***although*** *he was tired.*
OR *Pete was tired,* ***but*** *he didn't go to bed.* (**BUT NOT** ~~*Although Pete was tired, but he didn't go to bed.*~~)

We usually put **commas** before ***although*** and ***but***.

2 Join the sentences with *although* (twice) and with *but*.

▶ She passed the exam. She had a bad teacher.
Although she had a bad teacher, she passed the exam.
She passed the exam, although she had a bad teacher.
She had a bad teacher, but she passed the exam.

1 I felt ill. I went on working.
....
....
....

2 She was very kind. I didn't like her.
....
....
....

3 He's a big man. He doesn't eat much.
....
....
....

In some answers, both contracted forms (for example *I'm, don't*) and full forms (for example *I am, do not*) are possible. Normally both are correct.

and *I speak Russian, English and Swahili.*

We can use ***and*** to **join** sentences, shorter expressions or single words.

*Sylvia won the first game **and** Pete won the second.*
*'What's she interested in?' 'Scottish dancing **and** mountain climbing.'*
*'What shall we have for supper?' 'Fish **and** chips.'*

In lists, we usually put ***and*** between the **last two things**, and **commas** (,) between the **others**.

*We need soap, bread, orange juice, **tomatoes and sugar**.*
*She was beautiful, **intelligent and kind**.* (NOT ... ~~*beautiful, intelligent, kind.*~~)

1 Write the sentences using *and* and commas.

▶ She speaks (*French German Japanese Arabic*).
She speaks French, German, Japanese and Arabic.

1 My company has offices in (*London Tokyo New York Cairo*).
....

2 I've invited (*Paul Alexandra Eric Luke Janet*).
....

3 I'll be here on (*Tuesday Thursday Friday Sunday*).
....

4 She's got (*five cats two dogs a horse a rabbit*).
....

5 He plays (*golf rugby hockey badminton*).
....

6 She (*addressed stamped posted*) the letter.
....

When we use ***and***, we do **not** usually **repeat unnecessary words**.

*She sings and **she** plays the violin.*	→	*She sings and plays the violin.*
*He plays tennis and **he plays** badminton.*	→	*He plays tennis and badminton.*
*They have offices in Britain and **in** America.*	→	*They have offices in Britain and America.*
*We stayed with my brother and **my** sister.*	→	*We stayed with my brother and sister.*
*The house and **the** garden were full of people.*	→	*The house and garden were full of people.*
*I've been to Greece and **I've been to** Turkey.*	→	*I've been to Greece and Turkey.*
*I washed **my shirt** and **I** dried my shirt.*	→	*I washed and dried my shirt.*

2 Cross out the unnecessary words, and put in commas if necessary.

▶ I speak Russian, ~~and I speak~~ English and ~~I speak~~ Swahili.

1 She has painted the kitchen and she has painted the living room and she has painted the dining room.
2 Bob was wearing a pink shirt and Bob was wearing blue jeans and Bob was wearing white trainers.
3 Can you give me a knife and can you give me a fork and can you give me a spoon, please?
4 Many people speak English in India and many people speak English in Singapore and many people speak English in South Africa.
5 I've written six letters and I've posted six letters this morning.

We use ***or*** in similar ways.

*You can come with me **or** wait here.* *I don't speak German, French **or** Spanish.*

double conjunctions *both … and; (n)either … (n)or*

We can make ***and*** more emphatic ('stronger') by using ***both … and***.

*He's **both** a top sportsman **and** a famous writer.* *She **both** sings **and** dances.*

We can make ***or*** more emphatic by using ***either … or***.

*You can **either** come with me now **or** find your own way home.*
*We have time to see **either** the museum **or** the cathedral, but not both.*

Neither … nor means *'not one and not the other'*.

*The lessons were **neither** interesting **nor** useful.* *He speaks **neither** English **nor** French.*

1 Make sentences with *both … and*, *either … or* or *neither … nor*.

▶ She speaks (*Chinese* + *Japanese* +)
She speaks both Chinese and Japanese.

▶ You can have (*coffee / tea*)
You can have either coffee or tea.

▶ I can (*draw* – *sing* –)
I can neither draw nor sing.

1 I think that she's (*Scottish / Irish*)
....

2 I'd like to work with (*animals / children*)
....

3 He did well in (*mathematics* + *history* +)
....

4 This car is (*fast* – *comfortable* –)
....

5 She (*looked at me* – *said anything* –)
....

6 I've got problems (*at home* + *in my job* +)
....

7 You can (*stay here / go home*)
....

8 I like (*theatre* + *cinema* +)
....

9 She speaks (*English* – *French* –)
....

10 I don't understand (*politics / economics*)
....

2 Write some true sentences about yourself.

1 I can both ....
2 I can neither ....
3 I like both ....
4 I don't like either ....
5 I haven't got either ....
6 ....

In some answers, both contracted forms (for example *I'm, don't*) and full forms (for example *I am, do not*) are possible. Normally both are correct.

conjunctions: more practice

1 Tenses with time conjunctions. Put in the simple present or *will* . . . .

▶ I ...'ll phone... you when I ...arrive... (*phone; arrive*)

1 I think I .... some tea before I .... to bed. (*have; go*)
2 I .... here until your father .... (*wait; arrive*)
3 When you .... again, Ann .... here. (*come; be*)
4 We .... sorry when Rachel .... back home. (*be; go*)
5 After we .... home I .... something for supper. (*get; cook*)
6 We .... your tickets as soon as we .... the money. (*send; receive*)
7 I .... very busy until the exams .... over. (*be; be*)
8 Before I .... to Tokyo, I .... some Japanese lessons. (*go; take*)
9 As soon as the rain ...., I .... shopping. (*stop; go*)
10 We .... breakfast after Luke .... (*have; get up*)

2 Position of conjunctions. Put these sentences together in two ways.

▶ The weather's good. I go fishing at weekends. (*if*)
...If the weather's good, I go fishing at weekends...
...I go fishing at weekends if the weather's good...

1 The teacher was ill. The children had a holiday. (*because*)
....
....

2 I was in China. I made a lot of friends. (*when*)
....
....

3 They built the new road. It was difficult to get to our village. (*until*)
....
....

4 Jessica wrote three letters. Dylan never answered. (*although*)
....
....

5 I phoned him. The work was finished. (*as soon as*)
....
....

3 Double conjunctions. Make sentences with *both* . . . *and*, *either* . . . *or* or *neither* . . . *nor*.

1 I (*swim* [+] *play tennis* [+]). ....
2 He (*lives / works*) in Birmingham. ....
3 My father speaks (*Greek* [-] *French* [-]). ....
4 She likes (*pop music* [-] *jazz* [-]). ....
5 You can have (*orange juice / water*). ....
6 I can (*sing* [-] *dance* [-]). ....
7 He's (*Scottish / Irish*). ....
8 He's studying (*physics* [+] *biology* [+]). ....
9 This sofa is (*nice-looking* [-] *comfortable* [-]). ....
10 Anna (*looked at Henry* [-] *spoke to him* [-]). ....

4 Grammar in a text. Put conjunctions from the box into the text.

although	although	and	and	and	because	because	before	so	until	when

Andy Probert was bored at school, 1 .... he left 2 .... he was sixteen 3 .... got a job in a travel agency. He did not stay there very long, 4 .... he liked the work. He decided to move 5 .... the pay was very low 6 .... the hours were too long. His next job was in an import-export company. He liked that much better 7 .... he travelled to America a lot 8 .... the work was very well paid. He worked there for three years, 9 .... he really understood the business; then he started his own company. Now he is doing very well, 10 .... the work is sometimes very hard. He says he wants to make enough money to stop working 11 .... he is 50.

5 GRAMMAR AND VOCABULARY: musical instruments. Look at the table and make sure you know the names of the instruments. Then make sentences. Put *the* with the names of the instruments.

▶ (*Steve, guitar, piano*) Steve plays both the guitar and the piano.
▶ (*Joanna, David, cello*) Neither Joanna nor David plays the cello.
1 (*Karl, trombone, saxophone*) ....
2 (*Melanie, cello, drums*) ....
3 (*Steve, Karen, violin*) ....
4 (*Joanna, Charles, guitar*) ....
5 (*Karen, piano, trumpet*) ....
6 (*Sophie, guitar, trumpet*) ....
7 (*Charles, Steve, saxophone*) ....
8 (*Sophie, Steve, trumpet*) ....

	cello	drums	trombone	guitar	piano	saxophone	trumpet	violin
Joanna	✗	✗	✓	✓	✓	✓	✓	✓
Karl	✓	✓	✗	✓	✓	✗	✓	✓
David	✗	✓	✓	✗	✓	✓	✓	✓
Steve	✓	✓	✓	✓	✓	✓	✗	✗
Melanie	✓	✓	✗	✓	✗	✓	✓	✓
Sophie	✓	✓	✓	✗	✓	✓	✗	✓
Karen	✓	✓	✓	✓	✓	✗	✓	✗
Charles	✓	✗	✓	✓	✗	✓	✓	✓

6 Internet exercise. Use a search engine (e.g. Google). Which of the following gets most hits?

"as soon as we will arrive" 9
"until it will stop" ....
"after they will finish" ....
"before I will arrive" ....
"while I will be there" ....

"as soon as we arrive" 24,600
"until it stops." ....
"after they finish" ....
"before I arrive" ....
"while I am there" ....

pronunciation for grammar → e-book

conjunctions: revision test

1 Choose the right conjunctions and put the sentences together.

▶ I was tired. I went to bed. (*while, so, after*)
I was tired, so I went to bed.

1 I'm going to do some gardening. It gets dark. (*because, but, until*)
....

2 I couldn't read. It was too dark. (*although, because, so*)
....

3 The food wasn't very good. He ate everything. (*so, but, because*)
....

4 The lesson finished early. We went for a walk. (*but, until, so*)
....

5 I got his letter. I went round to see him. (*after, although, while*)
....

6 Jane gets up. She makes coffee. (*as soon as, until, although*)
....

7 You can't have any more coffee. There isn't any more. (*so, because, why*)
....

8 I didn't go to work. The buses weren't running. (*because, although, as soon as*)
....

9 The buses weren't running. I didn't go to work. (*until, so, as soon as*)
....

10 The phone always rings. I'm having a bath. (*while, until, so*)
....

11 I can't tell you the decision. I know myself. (*as soon as, while, until*)
....

12 He didn't work very hard. He passed all his exams. (*so, but, because*)
....

13 The holiday was over. I had to start working very hard. (*when, until*)
....

14 Andrew saw Zoë. He fell madly in love with her. (*as soon as, until, but*)
....

15 I left school. I worked as a taxi driver. (*until, after, while*)
....

2 Correct the mistakes.

▶ You can either stay here ~~either~~ come with me. ..or..........

1 He plays neither the piano nor he plays the guitar. ....
2 Although the train was late, but I got there in time. ....
3 The house was small, cold, dirty. ....
4 Although it was raining, went out. ....
5 After Jake will get here, we'll all go swimming. ....
6 Because it was cold, so I put on a coat. ....
7 You can either come in my car or either walk home. ....
8 I need a knife and I need a fork. ....
9 Although I would like to help you, but I don't have time. ....
10 I play both classical music and I play jazz. ....
11 I'll change my job as soon as I'll find another one. ....
12 Will you still love me when I'll be old? ....

In some answers, both contracted forms (for example *I'm, don't*) and full forms (for example *I am, do not*) are possible. Normally both are correct.

SECTION 18 *if*

grammar summary

Most tenses are possible in sentences with ***if***.

*He **won't come** tomorrow if he **came** yesterday.*
*If that **was** Mary, why **didn't** she **stop** and say hello?*
*If you**'ve been** to Paris, you**'ve seen** the Eiffel Tower.*
*Oil **floats** if you **pour** it on water.*
*If you**'re** happy, **I'm** happy.*

Note the following **three important structures**:

- **present tenses for future:**
  With ***if***, we use **present** tenses to talk about the future.
  *I'll phone you **if I have** time.* (NOT ~~*... if I will have time.*~~)
- ***if* + past, ... *would* ...**
  We can use **past** tenses with ***if*** to show that something is **not real** or **not probable now**. (We normally use ***would*** in the other part of the sentence.)
  ***If** I **had** more money, I **would buy** a car now.*
- ***if* + past perfect, ... *would have* ...**
  To talk about **unreal past** events – things that did not happen – we use ***if* + past perfect**. (We normally use ***would have* + past participle** in the other part of the sentence.)
  *I'm sorry you had all those problems. If you **had asked** me, I **would have helped** you.*

These three structures are often called 'first', 'second' and 'third conditional'.
The structure with two present tenses (e.g. *If you're happy, I'm happy*) is sometimes called 'zero conditional', for no very good reason.

We can use ***unless*** to mean 'if not', 'except if'.

*You can't come in **unless** you have a ticket.* (= ' if you don't have a ticket.')

If you were the only girl in the world,
and I were the only boy . . .
(*Song by Clifford Grey, British songwriter, born 1937*)

If you can find something that everyone agrees on, it's wrong.
(*Mo Udall, American politician, 1922–1998*)

If God did not exist, it would be necessary to invent him.
(*Voltaire, French writer, 1694–1788*)

If the automobile had followed the same development cycle as the computer, a Rolls-Royce would today cost $100, get a million miles per gallon, and explode once a year, killing everyone inside.
(*Robert X. Cringely, InfoWorld magazine*)

If you can keep your head when all about you are losing theirs, . . . you'll be a man, my son.
(*Rudyard Kipling, British short-story writer, novelist and poet, 1865–1936*)

If you can keep your head when all about you are losing theirs, you just don't know what's going on.
(*British Army saying*)

If one morning I walked on top of the water across the Potomac River, the headline that afternoon would read "President Can't Swim".
(*Lyndon B. Johnson, American politician, 1908–1973 – President 1963–1969*)

If the human mind was simple enough to understand, we'd be too simple to understand it.
(*Emerson Pugh, American writer on technology*)

if: position; *unless*

An *if*-clause can come at the beginning or end of a sentence. When it comes first, it is often separated by a comma (,).

If I have time, *I'll clean up the garden.* *I'll clean up the garden* ***if I have time.***

1 Use *if* to put these sentences together in two ways.

▶ Joe works at Brown's. He probably knows Annie.
If Joe works at Brown's, he probably knows Annie.
Joe probably knows Annie if he works at Brown's.

1 I can't sleep. I get up and read.
....
....

2 You take books from my room. Please tell me.
....
....

3 You're hungry. Why don't you cook some soup?
....
....

4 She's been travelling all day. She must be tired
....
....

5 We catch the first train. We can be in London by 9.00.
....
....

We can use ***unless*** to mean **'if ... not', 'except if'**.

You can't come in ***unless*** *you have a ticket.* (= 'You can't come in if you don't have a ticket.')
Unless *I'm very tired, I go to bed about midnight.* (= 'Except if I'm very tired ...')

2 Rewrite these sentences with *unless*.

▶ Children can't go in if they are not with an adult.
Children can't go in unless they are with an adult.

▶ If you don't give me my money, I'm going to the police.
Unless you give me my money, I'm going to the police.

1 You can't park here if you don't live in this street.
....

2 If you are not over 15, you can't see this film.
....

3 I don't drive fast except if I'm really late.
....

4 If I'm not going fishing, I get up late on Sundays.
....

5 We usually go for a walk after supper if there isn't a good film on TV.
....

6 I see my mother at weekends if I'm not travelling.
....

7 If it's not raining, I play tennis most evenings.
....

8 I can't help you if you don't tell me the truth.
....

if: future *I'll phone you if I hear from Alice.*

Most tenses are possible in sentences with *if*. But after *if*, we normally use a **present tense** to talk about the **future**.

***If** it **is** sunny tomorrow, we'll eat in the garden.* *I'll phone you **if** I **hear** from Alice.*
*I'll be sorry **if** I **don't pass** this exam.*

1 Choose the best verb to complete the sentence.

- ▶ I'll buy you a sweater if I ..find.......... a nice one. (*find*, *hold*, *pay*)
- ▶ If it rains, we ..'ll have.......... the party indoors. (*think*, *play*, *have*)

1 I'll be glad if I .... a letter from Jack tomorrow. (*expect*, *get*, *decide*)
2 Olivia .... back your bike if she remembers. (*come*, *bring*, *sell*)
3 If you like, I .... you Japanese lessons. (*bring*, *hold*, *give*)
4 If Alex ...., tell him I'm out. (*phone*, *stop*, *write*)
5 We'll stop and see you in Dublin if we .... time. (*give*, *think*, *have*)
6 I'll give you £100 if you .... smoking. (*stay*, *stop*, *break*)
7 I .... very surprised if Angela marries Jack. (*be*, *stand*, *find*)
8 If you sing, I ...., I promise. (*not learn*, *not laugh*, *not drive*)
9 If you cook lunch, I .... supper. (*eat*, *drink*, *cook*)
10 The government will do what it likes if nobody .... it. (*stop*, *speak*, *find*)

2 Put in the correct verb forms.

- ▶ If it ..rains.........., we ..'ll have.......... the party inside. (*rain*; *have*)

1 I .... happy if I .... my exam. (*be*; *pass*)
2 If you .... now, you .... the train. (*leave*; *catch*)
3 John says he .... as a taxi-driver if he .... money. (*work*; *need*)
4 If I .... free tomorrow evening, I .... you on Friday. (*not be*; *see*)
5 Mary .... Chinese next year if she .... time. (*study*; *have*)
6 I .... you to the station if I .... find my car keys. (*drive*; *can*)
7 If he .... her, he .... a happy life. (*marry*; *not have*)
8 .... you .... work if the doctor .... you that you must? (*stop*; *tell*)
9 If you .... to your father very politely, ... he .... us his car? (*talk*; *lend*)

3 Make sentences with *if*.

I'm afraid the bus will be late.

- ▶ (→ get to work late again) ..If the bus is late, I'll get to work late again.........
- ▶ (→ lose my job) ..If I get to work late again, I'll lose my job.........

1 (→ not find another job) If I lose my job, ...
....
2 (→ lose my flat) ....
3 (→ move back to my parents' house) ....
4 (→ get very bored) ....
5 (→ go swimming every day) ....
6 (→ look very good) ....
7 (→ meet interesting people) ....
8 (→ go to lots of parties) ....
9 (→ have a wonderful time) ....

In some answers, both contracted forms (for example *I'm*, *don't*) and full forms (for example *I am*, *do not*) are possible. Normally both are correct.

not real / not probable *If dogs could talk, …*

We use ***if*** + **past tense** + ***would*** to talk about things that are **not real or not probable** now.

IF + PAST TENSE	*WOULD* + INFINITIVE (WITHOUT *TO*)
*If I **had** a million dollars,*	*I **would build** a big swimming pool.*
*If you **were** the President,*	*what **would** you **do**?*
*If dogs **could** talk,*	*they **would tell** some interesting stories.*
*If he **didn't travel** so much,*	*he**'d have** more money.*

Contractions (see page 301): *I would* → *I'd, you would* → *you'd* etc

1 Put in the correct forms of the correct verbs.

▶ If people ...had... four arms, life ...would be... easier. (*have; be*)
▶ This ...would be... a nice country if it ...didn't rain... so much. (*not rain; be*)
1 If my cat .... open the fridge, it .... all my food. (*can; eat*)
2 If Lily and Jack .... here, they .... what to do. (*know; be*)
3 If I .... the answer, I .... you. (*know; tell*)
4 If your boss .... you to work on Sunday, ... you .... it? (*do; ask*)
5 If you .... read people's thoughts, what .... you ....? (*can; do*)
6 I .... a car if I .... enough money. (*buy; have*)
7 If I .... you to marry me, what .... you ....? (*say; ask*)
8 Alex .... his work on time if he .... so much. (*finish; not talk*)
9 I .... Chinese if I .... more time. (*have; study*)
10 If the programmes .... better, I .... more TV. (*be; watch*)

2 Make sentences beginning with *if*.

▶ My parents don't live near here, so I don't see them at weekends.
If my parents lived near here, I would see them at weekends.
1 We won't play cards because Jane and Peter aren't here.
If Jane ....
2 We haven't got enough money, so we won't buy a new car.
....
3 Fred doesn't answer letters, so I don't write to him.
....
4 I won't take your photo because I can't find my camera.
....
5 I don't enjoy opera because I can't understand the words.
....
6 I don't like Carola because she talks about herself all the time.
....
7 I haven't got a dog, so I don't go for walks.
....

3 What would you do if you had a free year and a lot of money? Write three or more sentences.

travel round the world	study	go to	(*other answers*)

1 If I ....
2 ....
3 ....

If I were you, ...

We sometimes use ***were*** instead of *was* after *if*. This is usually rather **formal**.

*If I **were** taller I would play basketball.* *If John **were** here, he would know what to do.*

We often say ***If I were you, I would / I'd ...***, when we want to give people **advice**.

***If I were you, I'd** get a new car.* ***I wouldn't** stand there **if I were you**.*

1 Write sentences with *if I were you*, using the expressions in the box.

call the police at once	fly	not sell it	join a club	see a doctor ✓	take a holiday

▶ 'I feel ill.' If I were you, I'd see a doctor.
1 'I'm really tired.' ....
2 'I haven't got any friends.' ....
3 'Shall I take the train to Scotland?' ....
4 'Somebody has stolen my car.' ....
5 'Otto wants to buy my motorbike.' ....

2 John Baker has won a lot of money in the lottery. His family and friends are giving him advice. Look at the pictures and use the words in the box to complete the sentences.

buy a sports car	buy a house ✓	give the money away	have a big party
put the money in the bank	start a business	stop work	travel round the world

▶ JOHN'S GIRLFRIEND: If I were you, I'd buy a house.
1 HIS MOTHER: ....
2 HIS FATHER: ....
3 HIS BROTHER: ....
4 HIS GRANDMOTHER: ....
5 HIS SISTER: ....
6 HIS FRIEND JOE: ....
7 HIS FRIEND STEPHANIE: ....

Level 2

If I go ..., I will ...; If I went ..., I would ...

The difference between ***if I go*** and ***if I went*** (for example) is **not** a difference of **time**.
We can use both ***if I go/see*** **etc** and ***if I went/saw*** **etc** to talk about the **present or future**.
With *if*, a **past tense** does not mean 'past time'; it means '**not real**' **or** '**not probable**'.

PROBABLE/POSSIBLE	NOT REAL/NOT PROBABLE
*If I **go** to London, I'll visit Tony.* *If I **see** Ann, I'll give her your address.*	*If I **went** to the moon, I would take a lot of photos.* *If I **saw** the Prime Minister, I would say 'hello'.*

1 Choose the best sentence-beginning.

▶ If I *live / lived* to be 75, ... (*live* circled)
1 If I *live / lived* to be 175, ...
2 If dogs *can / could* talk, ...
3 If I *go / went* shopping next week, ...
4 If Switzerland *starts / started* a war against Australia, ...
5 If the government *gives / gave* everybody a month's holiday with pay, ...
6 If you *need / needed* help one day, ...
7 If everybody *gives / gave* 10% of their money to poor countries, ...
8 If everybody *thinks / thought* the same as me, ...
9 If I *am / was* the most intelligent person in the world, ...
10 If prices *go / went* up next year, ...

2 Choose the best way to continue the sentences.

▶ I'm not going to open the window. If I *open / opened* the window, it *will / would* be too noisy. (*opened*, *would* circled)
▶ Maybe I'll open a window. But if I *open / opened* a window, it *will / would* be very noisy. (*open*, *will* circled)
1 I'm going to get up early tomorrow. If I *have / had* time, *I'll / 'd* walk to work.
2 If I *have / had* time, I *'ll / 'd* walk to work, but it's just not possible.
3 'I may get a job in Germany.' 'If you *get / got* it, what *will / would* your boyfriend say?'
4 'There's a job in Germany, but I don't think I'll get it.' 'If you *get / got* it, what *will / would* your boyfriend say?'
5 We never leave food on the table. If we *do / did*, the cat *will / would* eat it.
6 'Shall I put this on the table?' 'If you *do / did*, the cat *will / would* eat it.'
7 I'll probably go to university. But if I *go / went*, I *won't / wouldn't* earn any money for three years.
8 I'm not going to go to university. If I *go / went* to university, I *won't / wouldn't* earn any money for three years.
9 Maybe Jenny will marry Phil. But if she *does / did*, I'm afraid she *won't / wouldn't* be happy.
10 Phil isn't going to marry Jenny. Because if he *does / did*, he *will / would* have a terrible time with her.

3 Complete the sentences with your own ideas.

1 If I live to be 90, ...
2 If I lived to be 190, ...
3 If I learn more English, ...
4 If I learnt 20 languages, ...
5 If I go to New York, ...
6 If I went to the moon, ...

unreal past *If A had happened, B would have happened.*

We can use ***if*** to talk about **unreal past** events – things that **didn't happen**.
We use the **past perfect** and ***would have*** + **past participle.**

IF + PAST PERFECT	*WOULD HAVE* + PAST PARTICIPLE
If the weather had been better,	*we would have gone to the sea.* (But it wasn't, so we didn't.)
If you had asked me,	*I would have helped you.* (But you didn't, so I didn't.)
If Mary had seen you,	*what would you have said?* (But she didn't.)
If she hadn't gone skiing,	*she wouldn't have fallen and broken her leg.* (But she did.)

1 Put in the correct verb forms.

1 If I .... here yesterday, I would have come to see you. (*be*)
2 If Joe .... harder, he would have passed his exams. (*work*)
3 If you .... a map with you, you wouldn't have got lost. (*take*)
4 We would have won the game if we .... so badly. (*not play*)
5 If I had gone to university, I .... medicine and become a doctor. (*study*)
6 .... you .... if you had driven more slowly? (*crash*)
7 You .... badly if you hadn't drunk all that coffee. (*not sleep*)
8 If you .... on holiday with us, you .... a wonderful time. (*come*; *have*)
9 If my car .... I .... here at 8 o'clock. (*not break down*; *be*)
10 .... you .... harder at school last year if you .... the teachers? (*study*; *like*)
11 She .... married if she .... to leave home. (*not get*; *not want*)
12 .... you .... me if I .... you? (*help*; *ask*)

2 Getting up early is bad for you. Read the text in the box and make sentences.

> get up early → catch the 8.15 train → sit by a beautiful foreign woman → fall in love and marry her → go to live in her country → work in her father's diamond business → become very rich → go into politics → die in a revolution

► *If I had got up early, I would have caught the 8.15 train.*
1 If I had caught ....
....
2 ....
.... and married her.
3 ....
....
4 ....
....
5 ....
....
6 ....
....
7 ....
....

In some answers, both contracted forms (for example *I'm, don't*) and full forms (for example *I am, do not*) are possible. Normally both are correct.

if: more practice

1 Probable/possible or not real / not possible. Put the beginnings and ends together. (Different answers are possible.).

0 If I had a lot of money,	A I would give it all to you. ..0..
1 If you ask me nicely,	B I'll break my leg. ......
2 If the news was always good,	C nobody would believe them. ......
3 If we go to the country,	D I'll dance all night. ......
4 If we go skiing,	E I'll wear my new bikini. ......
5 If everybody spoke English,	F it would be a disaster. ......
6 If I come to your party,	G I'll make you a cup of tea. ......
7 If everybody was telepathic,	H newspapers wouldn't have many pages. ......
8 If politicians told the truth,	I they might say some interesting things. ......
9 If we go swimming,	J I'll take my bicycle. ......
10 If animals could talk,	K international communication would be much easier. ......

2 Probable/possible or not real / not possible. Choose the best ways to continue the sentences.

▶ I think I'll study medicine. But I know if I *do / did* that, I*'ll / 'd* have to work very hard.
▶ She's a very generous person. If she *wins / won* the lottery, she *will / would* give it all away.

1 I'm not going to buy a car. If I *buy / bought* a car I *will / would* spend all my money on it.
2 I really must go and see Sandra. But if I *go / went* and *see / saw* her, I*'ll / 'd* have to talk to her stupid brother.
3 My parents live a long way away. If they *live / lived* nearer, I *will / would* see them more often.
4 We're going to stay at home this evening. If we *go / went* out, we *won't / wouldn't* do anything interesting.
5 Those exams are difficult. Unless you *start / started* working harder, you *won't / wouldn't* pass.
6 The United Moderate Anarchist Party will probably win the election. And if they *win / won*, the country *will / would* be in deep trouble.
7 I'm glad Marion isn't going to marry Jack. Because if she *marries / married* him she *will / would* be very unhappy.
8 Maybe I'll take you to London with me. But if I *take / took* you, you*'ll / 'd* have to pay for your ticket.
9 If it *rains / rained* again tomorrow, I *won't / wouldn't* go cycling.
10 Dylan never tells the truth. And if he *does / did*, I *won't / wouldn't* believe him.

3 Grammar in a text. Put in the missing words.

The laws of work

1. If anything can go wrong, it .... go wrong.
2. If a job looks easy, it's difficult. If it .... difficult, ... impossible.
3. If you think a job will take two hours, it .... take four days. If you think it .... take four days, it .... eight weeks. And so on.
4. If you throw something away, you .... need it the next day.
5. If you do what everybody wants you to do, somebody .... like it.
6. If you explain so clearly that nobody can misunderstand, somebody ....

4 Unreal past. Put in the correct verb forms.

1 If I .... coffee last night, I .... better. (*not drink*; *sleep*)
2 If my parents .... more money, I .... to university after I left school. (*have*; *go*)
3 Jessica .... to Brazil last year if she .... Pete. (*go*; *not meet*)
4 If I .... ill last week, I .... to Ireland. (*not be*; *go*)
5 I .... the bus if I .... (*catch*; *run*)
6 If he .... smoking, he .... longer. (*stop*; *live*)
7 I .... you for help unless I .... it. (*not ask*; *need*)
8 Yesterday .... a better day if I .... in bed. (*be*; *stay*)
9 I .... a sweater if I .... it was going to be so cold. (*wear*; *know*)
10 If we .... time we .... to see Uncle Pete. (*have*; *go*)

5 Unreal past. Read the text and complete the chain of *if*-sentences.

HOT WEATHER IS GOOD FOR YOU

It was hot, so my mother opened the door. A cat came in and ate her supper, so she went to the shop to buy food. In the shop she saw an advertisement for a secretary. So she got a new job, and met my father. I'm glad it was a hot day!

If it hadn't been hot, my mother wouldn't have opened the door. If she hadn't opened the door, the cat .... her supper. If the cat ....
....
....
....
....
....

6 GRAMMAR AND VOCABULARY: names of languages

Anna is going to work in another country next year. See if you can make sentences with the correct language names. Use a dictionary if necessary.

Arabic	Chinese ✓	Dutch	German	Greek	Portuguese	Swahili

▶ (*China*) If she goes to China, she will have to learn Chinese.
1 (*Egypt*) If she ....
2 (*Brazil*) ....
3 (*Holland*) ....
4 (*Kenya*) ....
5 (*Greece*) ....
6 (*Austria*) ....

7 Internet exercise. Use a search engine (e.g. Google) to find out which of the following are more common.

"unless I buy" 104,000
"if I were you" ....
"if she knew" ....
"if we go" ....
"if they had said" ....

"unless I will buy" 6
"if I was you" ....
"if she would know" ....
"if we will go" ....
"if they would have said" ....

pronunciation for grammar → e-book

if: revision test

1 Put in the correct verb forms.

▶ I'm sure John ..will help.. you if you ask him. (*help*)
▶ I would be very happy if I ..had.. more friends. (*have*)
1 If you .... your glasses, you would see much better. (*clean*)
2 If Peter lives in Little Compton, he probably .... my friend Jack. (*know*)
3 I .... and see you tomorrow if I have time. (*come*)
4 If she spoke more slowly, perhaps I .... her. (*understand*)
5 If you .... at 12.00, you will arrive at 3.20. (*leave*)
6 I .... my car unless I needed money. (*not sell*)
7 If you .... so far away, it would be easier for us to see each other. (*not live*)
8 I .... this letter for you if I can find my dictionary. (*translate*)
9 If I .... you very nicely, will you make me some coffee? (*ask*)
10 If water .... very cold, it becomes ice. (*get*)

2 Five of sentences 1–10 have mistakes. Find them and correct them.

▶ I usually get up and watch TV if I can't sleep. ..Correct..
▶ I wouldn't do that if I ~~would be~~ you. ..were..
1 I'll be very happy if I'll pass the exam. ....
2 If she's from Russia, she probably speaks Russian. ....
3 If he would eat more, he wouldn't be so thin. ....
4 If I don't see you today, I see you next week. ....
5 I'll come and see you on Wednesday if I have time. ....
6 If we left early tomorrow morning, we would arrive before 12.00. ....
7 Unless he doesn't work harder, he won't pass his exams. ....
8 If it doesn't rain tomorrow, I'll play tennis with James. ....
9 We'll go and see Max and Chris if we'll be in Berlin. ....
10 I would get a better job if I could find one. ....

3 Unreal past. Put in the correct verb forms.

1 If I .... Michael, I .... what to do. (*not ask*; *not know*)
2 If Alex .... in London yesterday I .... to see him. (*be*; *go*)
3 I'm sorry. I .... that if I .... that your mother was listening. (*not say*; *know*)
4 It .... better if you .... nothing when the policeman stopped you. (*be*; *say*)
5 If I .... on that bus, I .... my girlfriend. (*not get*; *not meet*)
6 Lucy .... if we .... her to hospital when she started feeling ill. (*die*; *not take*)
7 If I .... so tired last night, I .... out. (*not be*; *go*)
8 If I .... what my father wanted, I .... medicine. (*do*; *study*)
9 Mark .... skiing last winter if he .... enough money. (*go*; *have*)
10 If you .... me yesterday, I .... in deep trouble. (*not help*; *be*)

In some answers, both contracted forms (for example *I'm*, *don't*) and full forms (for example *I am*, *do not*) are possible. Normally both are correct.

SECTION 19 relative pronouns

grammar summary

who	(whom)	which	that	what

We use **relative pronouns** to **join sentences** to **nouns**.

The man was Welsh. (*He*) *won the prize.* *The man* (*who*) *won the prize was Welsh.*

We use ***who*** for **people** and ***which*** for **things**. We can also use ***that*** for **people and things**.

There's ***the man who/that*** *sold me my bike.* *She said* ***a word which/that*** *I didn't hear.*

We often leave out **object pronouns**, but not subject pronouns.

Do you remember those photos (***which/that***) *I showed you?*

The photos ***which/that*** *show the beach are beautiful.* (**NOT** ~~*The photos show the beach*~~ ...)

Prepositions can often go **in two places**.

The woman ***about whom*** *we were* ***talking*** *walked into the room.* (formal)

The woman ***that*** *we were* ***talking about*** *walked into the room.* (conversational)

We can use ***what*** to mean **'the thing(s) which'**.

The children always eat ***what*** *I cook.*

art·ist /ˈɑːtɪst; *NAmE* ˈɑːrt-/ *noun* **1** a person who creates works of art, especially paintings or drawings: *an exhibition of work by contemporary British artists* ◇ *a graphic artist* ◇ *a make-up artist* ◇ *Police have issued an artist's impression of her attacker.* ◇ (*figurative*) *Whoever made this cake is a real artist.* ➲ COLLOCATIONS at ART **2** (*especially BrE* **ar·tiste** /ɑːˈtiːst; *NAmE* ɑːrˈt-/) a professional entertainer such as a singer, a dancer or an actor: *a recording/solo artist*

bee /biː/ *noun* **1** a black and yellow flying insect that can sting. Bees live in large groups and make HONEY (= a sweet sticky substance that is good to eat): *a swarm of bees* ◇ *a bee sting* ◇ *Bees were buzzing in the clover.* ➲ see also BEEHIVE, BEESWAX, BUMBLEBEE, QUEEN BEE **2** (*NAmE*) a meeting in a group where people combine work, competition and pleasure: *a sewing bee* ➲ see also SPELLING BEE IDM **the ˌbee's ˈknees** (*informal*) an excellent person or thing: *She thinks she's the bee's knees* (= she has a very high opinion of herself). **have a ˈbee in your bonnet (about sth)** (*informal*) to think or talk about sth all the time and to think that it is very important ➲ more at BIRD, BUSY *adj.*

build·er /ˈbɪldə(r)/ *noun* **1** a person or company whose job is to build or repair houses or other buildings **2** (usually in compounds) a person or thing that builds, creates or develops sth: *a shipbuilder* ◇ *a confidence builder* ➲ see also BODYBUILDER

burg·lar /ˈbɜːɡlə(r); *NAmE* ˈbɜːrɡ-/ *noun* a person who enters a building illegally in order to steal

bus /bʌs/ *noun, verb* ■ *noun* (*pl.* **buses**, *US* also **busses**) **1** a large road vehicle that carries passengers, especially one that travels along a fixed route and stops regularly to let people get on and off: *Shall we walk or go* ***by bus***? ◇ *A regular bus service connects the train station with the town centre.* ◇ *a* ***bus company/driver*** ◇ *a school bus* ➲ VISUAL VOCAB page V46 ➲ compare COACH ➲ see also BUS LANE, BUS SHELTER, BUS STATION, BUS STOP, MINIBUS, TROLLEYBUS **2** (*computing*) a set of wires that carries information from one part of a computer system to another ■ *verb* (**-s-** or **-ss-**) **1 ~ sb (from/to...)** to transport sb by bus: *We were bussed from the airport to our hotel.* **2 ~ sb** (*NAmE*) to transport young people by bus to another area so that students of different races can be educated together **3 ~ sth** (*NAmE*) to take the dirty plates, etc. off the tables in a restaurant, as a job

cheese /tʃiːz/ *noun* **1** [U, C] a type of food made from milk that can be either soft or hard and is usually white or yellow in colour; a particular type of this food: *Cheddar cheese* ◇ *goat's cheese* (= made from the milk of a GOAT) ◇ *a* ***cheese sandwich/salad*** ◇ *a* ***chunk/piece/slice of cheese*** ◇ *a selection of French cheeses* ◇ *a cheese knife* (= a knife with a special curved blade with two points on the end, used for cutting and picking up pieces of cheese) ➲ VISUAL VOCAB page V19

plant /plɑːnt; *NAmE* plænt/ *noun, verb* ■ *noun* ▸ LIVING THING **1** [C] a living thing that grows in the earth and usually has a STEM, leaves and roots, especially one that is smaller than a tree or bush: *All plants need light and water.* ◇ ***flowering/garden/indoor plants*** ◇ *a tomato/potato plant* ◇ *the animal and plant life of the area* ➲ COLLOCATIONS at LIFE ➲ VISUAL VOCAB page V9 ➲ see also BEDDING PLANT, HOUSE PLANT, POT PLANT, RUBBER PLANT

sau·cer /ˈsɔːsə(r)/ *noun* a small shallow round dish that a cup stands on; an object that is shaped like this: *cups and saucers* ➲ VISUAL VOCAB page V19 ➲ see also FLYING SAUCER

(*Oxford Advanced Learner's Dictionary, 8th edition, 2010*)

relative *who* and *which* *the keys which I lost*

We can use **sentences** to describe **nouns**.
To join sentences to nouns, we use **relative pronouns**: ***who*** (for **people**) and ***which*** (for **things**).

*The man plays golf. **He** lives at No 10.* → *The man **who** lives at No 10 plays golf.*

*The letter is for me. You saw **it**.* → *The letter **which** you saw is for me.*

*I like the girl. **She** works with Ann.* → *I like the girl **who** works with Ann.*

*I've got those books. You wanted **them**.* → *I've got those books **which** you wanted.*

1 Put in *who* or *which*.

1 The people .... live downstairs are Irish.
2 The shop .... sells that good bread is closed today.
3 The dictionary .... I bought yesterday isn't very good.
4 That cheese .... you like comes from Scotland.
5 Do you know the girls .... are standing by the window?
6 I can't find the key .... opens this door.
7 I've lost the earrings .... Harry gave me.
8 The police are looking for three men .... robbed the National Bank yesterday.
9 We know the woman .... teaches French at Jane's school.
10 Here's a word .... I don't understand.
11 Are those the shoes .... Tracy has just bought?
12 I had just one teacher .... was really good.

We use ***who*** or ***which*** **instead of** *he, him, she, it* etc. **Don't** use **both**.

*The woman **who** ~~she~~ teaches me French is ill.* *Here's the address **which** you wanted ~~it~~.*

2 Circle the correct answer.

1 There's the man who *took / he took* your coat.
2 Do you know the people who *live / they live* next door?
3 I like that woman; *she is / is* very kind.
4 I've found the keys which I *lost / lost them*.
5 Do you like the new dress which I *bought / bought it* yesterday?
6 The car which *is parked / it is parked* outside belongs to Susan.
7 This is a new kind of knife: *cuts / it cuts* everything.
8 The poems which Mark *writes / writes them* are very hard to understand.
9 We've got three children who *make / they make* a lot of noise.
10 What did you do with the sweater which *I lent you / I lent you it*?

The man who makes no mistakes
does not usually make anything.
(*E J Phelps*)

3 Look at the picture and the information, and write sentences with *who*.

▶ The man and woman who live in flat 8 are from Scotland.

1 ....

2 ....

3 ....

4 ....

5 ....

6 ....

7 ....

FLAT	INFORMATION
1	play loud music all night
2	broke her leg skiing
3	play golf all day
4	haven't got much money
5	has three children
6	drives a Rolls-Royce
7	are hiding from the police
8	are from Scotland

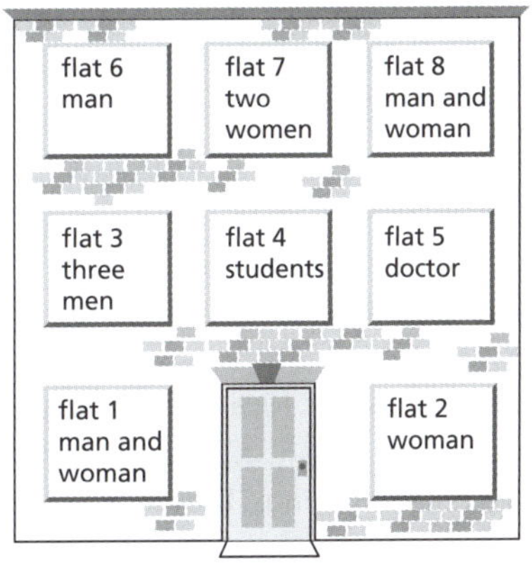

4 Join the sentences in the place marked *. Change *he*, *it* etc to *who* or *which*.

▶ Most of the people* speak German. They live in Austria.
Most of the people who live in Austria speak German.

▶ I know a shop*. It sells really good meat.
I know a shop which sells really good meat.

1 The bus* isn't running today. It goes to Oxford.
....

2 Yesterday I met a man*. He works with your brother.
....

3 The child* was ill. She didn't come to the party.
....

4 Can you pick up the papers*? They are lying on the floor.
....

5 The eggs* were bad. I bought them yesterday.
....

6 Here's the book*. You asked me to buy it for you.
....

7 I don't like the man*. He is going out with my sister.
....

We can use ***whom*** for people when the relative pronoun is the **object** of the following verb.

I've just got a postcard from a woman ***whom*** *I met on holiday last year.* (I met the woman.)

But *whom* is formal and unusual. In spoken English, we more often use ***that*** (see page 256), ***who*** or **nothing** (see page 257).

I've just got a postcard from ***a woman who/that I met*** *on holiday last year.*
OR *I've just got a postcard from* ***a woman I met*** *on holiday last year.*

In some answers, both contracted forms (for example *I'm*, *don't*) and full forms (for example *I am*, *do not*) are possible. Normally both are correct.

relative *that* *a bird that can't fly*

We can use ***that*** instead of *who* or *which*.

*The man **that** lives at number 8 is getting married.* *You haven't drunk the tea **that** I made for you.*

1 Join the sentences in the place marked *, using *that*.

▶ I'd like to speak to the person*. She wrote this letter.
I'd like to speak to the person that wrote this letter.

▶ The tomatoes* are all bad. I bought them yesterday.
The tomatoes that I bought yesterday are all bad.

1 Joe's got a motorbike*. It can do 200 km an hour.
....

2 Is that the computer*? It doesn't work.
....

3 Those are the trousers*. I use them for gardening.
....

4 A man* wants to marry my sister. He lives in New York.
....

5 The doctors* all said different things. They looked at my leg.
....

6 The flowers* are beautiful. You gave them to Aunt Sarah.
....

7 The children* have gone on holiday. They play football with Paul.
....

2 GRAMMAR AND VOCABULARY: things that fly

Write descriptions with *that*. Use a dictionary if necessary.

can fly straight up | flies at night and hears very well | can't fly | doesn't have an engine | eats small animals and birds | can fly to the moon | makes honey ✓ | doesn't make honey and can bite you

▶ an insect that makes honey.

1 an insect ....

2 a bird ....

3 a bird ....

4 an animal ....

5 a machine ....

6 a plane ....

7 a thing ....

▶ bee

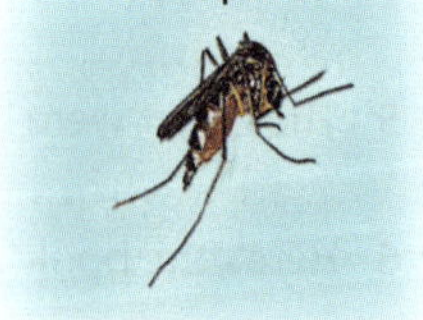

1 mosquito

2 penguin

3 eagle

4 bat

5 helicopter

6 glider

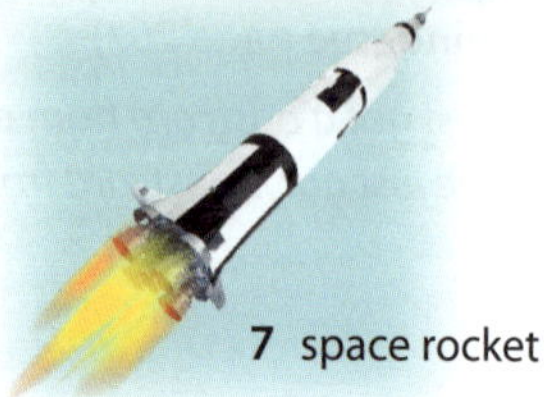

7 space rocket

leaving out relative pronouns *the car (that) you bought*

When a **relative pronoun** (*who/which/that*) is the **object** of the following verb, we often **leave it out**.
But we **can't leave out** a relative pronoun when it is the **subject** of the following verb.

*(I phoned **a man**.)*
*The man **that** I phoned spoke Spanish.*
→ *The man I phoned spoke Spanish.*
*The train **that** you want leaves at 10.00.*
→ *The train you want leaves at 10.00.*

*(**A man** phoned me.)*
*The man **that** phoned me spoke Greek.*
(NOT ~~*The man phoned me spoke Greek.*~~)
*The train **that** stops at York goes at 8.00.*
(NOT ~~*The train stops at York goes at 8.00.*~~)

1 Is the relative pronoun the subject (S) or object (O) of the following verb?

▶ the woman who wrote this letter S
▶ the film that I saw O
1 the languages that she spoke ......
2 a woman who helped me ......
3 the sweater which I wore ......
4 a man who(m) I helped ......
5 the weather that we have had ......
6 a machine that makes paper ......
7 that car which you bought ......
8 the man who cuts my hair ......

2 Look at Exercise 1. Find the expressions with object relative pronouns and rewrite them without *who(m)*, *which* or *that*.

▶ the film I saw
1 ......
2 ......
3 ......
4 ......
5 ......

3 Join the sentences in the place marked * without using *who*, *which* or *that*.

▶ The cup of coffee* is on the table. You wanted it.
The cup of coffee you wanted is on the table.
1 I'm working for a man*. I've known him for twenty years.
......
2 They played a lot of music*. I didn't like it.
......
3 The campsite* was very dirty. We found it.
......
4 I'm going on holiday with some people*. I know them.
......
5 That book* is very good. You gave it to me.
......
6 The ring* belonged to her grandmother. She lost it.
......
7 I'm driving a car*. I bought it 15 years ago.
......
8 The papers* are on the table. You wanted them.
......

4 Write three sentences beginning *Everybody I know …*

▶ Everybody I know likes rock music.
1 ......
2 ......
3 ......

In some answers, both contracted forms (for example *I'm, don't*) and full forms (for example *I am, do not*) are possible. Normally both are correct.

prepositions *the man that she works for*

Some **verbs** have **prepositions** with them (see page 141) – for example ***look at, listen to***.
When **relative pronouns** are the **objects** of these verbs, there are **two possibilities:**

- **keep the preposition with the verb (more informal; we can leave out *who(m)/which/that*.)**

*The woman smiled. I was **looking at her**. → The woman (whom/that) I was **looking at** smiled.*
*The flat was dirty. He **lived in it**. → The flat he **lived in** was dirty.*

- **put the preposition before *whom/which* (very formal)**

*The woman **at whom** I was **looking** smiled.*
*The flat **in which** he **lived** was dirty.*

1 Change these expressions to make them more conversational. Use *that*.

▶ a boy with whom I went to school ...a boy that I went to school with...
1 the girl about whom I was talking ....
2 the people for whom I work ....
3 the house in which I live ....
4 the music to which you are listening ....
5 the bus on which I go to work ....

2 Rewrite the expressions from Exercise 1, but leave out *that*.

▶ ...a boy I went to school with...
1 ....
2 ....
3 ....
4 ....
5 ....

3 Look at the information about Helen, and then make sentences (like the example) about the people in her life.

Helen lives in a big flat with a friend called Ruby. She works for a man called Eric. At weekends she plays tennis with a woman called Monica. Sometimes she reads to an 80-year-old woman called Karen, or babysits for people called Emily and Jack. She is in love with a man called Tom.

▶ Ruby is ...the friend she lives with....
1 Eric is ....
2 Monica is ....
3 Karen is ....
4 Emily and Jack are ....
5 Tom is ....

4 Now write sentences (like the example) about Helen's birthday presents.

For Helen's birthday, Ruby gave her a handbag, Eric gave her chocolates, Monica gave her a clock, Karen gave her theatre tickets, Emily and Jack gave her a picture, and Tom gave her flowers and earrings.

▶ The friend she lives ...with gave her a handbag....
1 The man she works ....
2 The woman ....
3 The 80-year-old woman ....
4 The people ....
5 The man ....

relative *what* *It was just what I wanted.*

We can use ***what*** to mean **'the thing(s) which/that'** or **'anything that'**.

*Have you got **what** you need for your journey?* (='... the things that you need ...')
*I'm sorry about **what** happened.* *'Can I have something to eat?' 'Take **what** you like.'*

We use ***what*** with a **singular** verb.

***What** I bought **was** mostly very cheap.* (NOT ~~*What I bought were*~~ ...)

1 Change the words *in italics* to *what*.

▶ *The things that* she said weren't true.
What she said wasn't true.

1 *The things that* he did made everybody angry.

....

2 Take *anything that* you want.

....

3 Soap – that's *the thing that* I forgot to pack!

....

4 She gave me a watch. It was just *the thing that* I wanted.

....

5 That child does *anything that* he likes.

....

6 *The things that* I read in the paper make me unhappy.

....

7 Don't tell me *things that* I know already.

....

8 *The thing that* I like best in life is doing nothing.

....

2 Write a sentence beginning *What I need is ...*

....

We use ***that***, not *what*, after ***anything, something, nothing, everything, all*** and ***the only thing***.

*You can take **anything that** you want.* (NOT ... ~~*anything what you want.*~~)
*The shop had **nothing that** I wanted.* ***All that** I could do was stand and watch.*
*Money is **the only thing** in the world **that** matters to him.*

3 Put in *that* or *what*.

1 I believe everything .... she says.
2 .... she did surprised everybody.
3 I can't give you .... you want.
4 He said nothing .... was important.
5 I can't eat .... I like.
6 .... you need is a holiday.
7 I can't eat everything .... I like.
8 The only thing .... I forgot was toothpaste.
9 Ask Peter – he'll tell you .... you need to know.
10 She said something .... was very helpful.

In some answers, both contracted forms (for example *I'm, don't*) and full forms (for example *I am, do not*) are possible. Normally both are correct.

relative pronouns: more practice

1 Use of *who* and *which*. Join the sentences in the place marked *, using *who* or *which*.

▶ Yesterday I saw a film.* You would like it.
Yesterday I saw a film which you would like.

1 I know a man.* He writes film music.

2 The bus* got to London twenty minutes late. I took it.

3 We have friends*. They live in Chicago.

4 The car* isn't very good. I bought it last month.

5 We stayed in a hotel*. It had a beautiful garden.

6 I didn't like the man*. My sister married him.

7 The people* weren't very interesting. They were at the party.

8 Tim uses long words*. I can't understand them.

9 The computer* crashes every five minutes. I'm using it.

10 The woman* is terribly nice. She works in the flower shop.

2 Use of *that*. Join the sentences in the place marked *, using *that*.

1 The tickets* were very expensive. I got them.

2 These are the scissors*. I use them for cutting paper.

3 The woman* is from Brazil. She gives me tennis lessons.

4 The man* is always very friendly. He lives next door.

5 I'm spending the day with some people*. I know them.

6 What did you do with the money*? We collected it.

7 People* are called linguists. They study languages.

8 We've got a cat*. It brings dead rats into the house.

9 The oranges* are all bad. You bought them.

10 Why did you throw away the soup*? I cooked it.

3 Leaving out *who, which* or *that*. Rewrite the words *in italics* without relative pronouns if it's possible. If not, write 'No change'.

▶ Where's *the book which I was reading?* ......the book I was reading......
▶ *The people who live next door* are German. ......No change......
1 *The clock that I bought* doesn't work. ....
2 I didn't like *the film which I saw* last night. ....
3 Here's *the letter that came* for you. ....
4 It was *a journey that took* twelve hours. ....
5 He was *a man that I really disliked*. ....
6 I had *an experience which changed my life*. ....
7 What happened to *that dog which you had*? ....
8 I know *a woman who speaks eight languages*. ....
9 Do you know *anybody who can play* the trumpet? ....
10 Did you see *those earrings that I bought* for Helen? ....

4 Grammar in a text. Cross out *that* if it can be left out.

'How was that hotel ~~that~~ I suggested?' 'That hotel! The rooms that they put us in were like cupboards, the beds that they gave us were much too small, and the extra blankets that we asked for never arrived. The 'full English breakfast' that they served was uneatable, and the 'French champagne' that we ordered at dinner was undrinkable. And that brochure that you showed me was full of lies. The 'view of the sea' that they talked about was a view of the car park, and the gym that they advertised wasn't there. And then, the bill that we got at the end was unbelievable. Never again!'

5 Position of prepositions. Make these expressions more conversational.

▶ a boy ~~to whom~~ I talked ....to....
1 the book at which I was looking ....
2 the people for whom I work ....
3 the hotel in which we stayed ....
4 the place to which I drove ....
5 those people to whom we were talking ....
6 the train on which we travelled ....
7 some people with whom I work ....
8 the place about which I was telling you ....
9 the pen with which I write ....
10 the small village in which my mother lives ....

6 GRAMMAR AND VOCABULARY: jewellery
Read the text and complete the sentences. Use a dictionary if necessary.

Anna, Naomi, Sally, Jane, Jessica and Thalia have all got rich boyfriends. For Christmas, Anna wanted a gold watch, Naomi wanted a diamond brooch, Sally wanted sapphire earrings, Jane wanted a pearl necklace, Jessica wanted a ruby ring and Thalia wanted a silver bracelet. But:

▶ Anna got a diamond brooch, so ......Anna got what Naomi wanted......
1 Naomi got a ruby ring, so ....
2 Sally got a silver bracelet, so ....
3 Jane got a gold watch, so ....
4 Jessica got a pearl necklace, so ....
5 Thalia got sapphire earrings, so ....

7 Internet exercise. Use a search engine (e.g. Google) to find five simple sentences beginning "Everybody I know likes ...". Write one yourself.

1 Everybody I know likes ....
2 ....
3 ....
4 ....
5 ....
6 (*Your sentence*) ....

pronunciation for grammar → e-book

relative pronouns: revision test

1 Which answer is right: A, B or both?

▶ The people ... play loud music very late. (A) who live downstairs B live downstairs
▶ I don't much like the music .... (A) they play (B) that they play
1 The girls ... gave me flowers for my birthday. A with whom I work B that I work with
2 I don't want a phone ... more intelligent than me. A that is B is
3 Where's the paper ... ? A that you wrote the address on B that you wrote the address on it
4 I like people ... laugh at themselves. A can B who can
5 ... she said made me very angry. A What B That what
6 Yesterday everything ... was wrong. There are days like that. A I did B that I did
7 'What do you call a thing that ... bottles?' 'A bottle-opener.' A opens B it opens
8 There are the keys .... A I was looking for B that I was looking for
9 The train ... was very uncomfortable. A in which we travelled B which we travelled in
10 There's a shop near here ... open all night. A that stays B which stays
11 I've found the shoes .... A that I lost B that I lost them
12 Do you know anybody ... Russian? A who speaks B speaks
13 She married a man ... on holiday. A she met B that she met
14 The woman ... wanted to speak to James. A phoned B who phoned
15 Who were those people that you ... ? A were talking to B were talking to them

2 Six of sentences 1–15 have mistakes. Find them and correct them.

▶ The people ~~which~~ live next door have got five children. *who*
▶ Do you know a shop which sells good cheese? *Correct*
1 I didn't understand the language which she was speaking. ....
2 We stayed in a hotel who had a beautiful garden. ....
3 I didn't understand the language she was speaking. ....
4 Is the book you're reading interesting? ....
5 I didn't understand the language that she was speaking. ....
6 The woman came to dinner stayed very late. ....
7 A vet is a doctor who works with animals. ....
8 I didn't like the man which my sister married. ....
9 Did I tell you about the film which we saw last night? ....
10 Eric said a word which I couldn't understand it. ....
11 I'm spending the day with some people I know. ....
12 People what live in London are called 'Londoners'. ....
13 There's the man I was telling you about. ....
14 The train I came home on was an hour late. ....
15 I don't like people that you can't relax with them. ....

3 Put in *that* or *what*.

1 I like everything .... you cook.
2 Nobody rememers everything .... they do.
3 .... I said shocked everybody.
4 The only thing .... I need is a toothpaste.
5 They couldn't give me .... I asked for.
6 I learnt nothing .... was useful.
7 Peter will tell you .... you have to do.
8 I can't wear .... I like at work.
9 .... you need is a long holiday.
10 Amy said something .... was interesting.

In some answers, both contracted forms (for example *I'm*, *don't*) and full forms (for example *I am*, *do not*) are possible. Normally both are correct.

SECTION 20 indirect speech

grammar summary

When we tell people **what somebody said or thought**, we often use **indirect speech**.

Tenses, here-and-now words (like ***this, here, today***) and **pronouns** (like ***I, you***) may **change** in indirect speech. This is because the time, place and speaker may be different.

*'I really **like** it **here**.'* *Bill said that **he** really **liked** it **there**.*

We often **leave out *that***, especially after common verbs like ***say*** and ***think***.

*Bill **said** he really liked it there.*

Indirect questions have a **different structure** from direct questions.

*'What **is your phone number**?'* *He asked me what **my phone number was**.*

***'Do you like** cherries?'* *She asked me **if I liked** cherries.*

We can use **object + infinitive** (with *to*) after ***ask*** and ***tell***.

*I **asked him to make** some coffee.* *She **told the children not to make** a noise.*

PROMISES, PROMISES

'You said I was beautiful.'
'You are more beautiful every day.'
'You said you loved me.'
'And it's true. I love you. Deeply. Passionately.'
'You told me you would love me for ever.'
'And I will. For ever and ever.'
'You said you would never look at another woman.'
'I have never looked at another woman. I shut my eyes when one comes close.'
'You told me you were rich.'
'We have a solid gold bath with diamond taps.'
'You told me you wanted children.'
'We have thirteen children.'
'You said you could cook.'
'I cook you a magnificent five-course dinner every night.'
'You told me you would bring me a cup of tea in bed every morning.'
'You get a cup of tea in bed every morning. With biscuits and the newspaper.'
'You said you could play the saxophone.'
'I am a world-famous saxophonist.'
'You promised that you would take me to Hawaii.'
'We have just come back from three months in Hawaii.'
'You said you would mend the dishwasher.'
'Sorry. I forgot.'
'You see. I can't believe a word you say.'

Level 2

tenses and pronouns *Bill said he was really happy.*

When we tell people **what somebody said or thought,** we often use **indirect speech.**
Tenses and **pronouns** (*I, you* etc) **change** in indirect speech if the **time** and **speaker change.**
For example, **present** tenses become **past**; ***I*** may become ***he*** or ***she***; ***my*** may become ***his*** or ***her***.

SOMEBODY SAID/THOUGHT	INDIRECT SPEECH
*'**I'm** happy.'*	*Bill said **that he was** happy.* (NOT ~~*Bill said that I'm happy.*~~)
*'I **have** a problem.'*	*I thought that I **had** a problem.* (NOT ~~*I thought that I have a problem.*~~)
*'She **likes me**.'*	*He knew **that** she **liked him**.*
*'**My** feet **are** cold.'*	*She said **her** feet **were** cold.*

We often **leave out *that***, especially after common verbs like ***say, think***.

*Bill **said** he was really happy.* *I **thought** it was a great party.*

1 Put in the correct pronouns (*I* etc) or possessives (*my* etc).

▶ 'She likes me.' He knew she liked ...him....

1 'I speak French.' He said .... spoke French.
2 'I'm sorry.' She said .... was sorry.
3 'Kate phoned me.' She said Kate had phoned ....
4 'We want our money.' They said .... wanted .... money.
5 'I'm tired.' He said .... was tired.
6 'I can't help you.' She told me she couldn't help ....
7 'We're leaving.' They said .... were leaving.
8 'I've lost my coat.' He said .... had lost .... coat.
9 'I like my job.' She told me .... liked .... job.
10 'Where are our tickets?' They asked where .... tickets were.

Note the difference between ***say*** and ***tell***.
Tell must have a **personal object**: we ***tell somebody*** *something*.

*She **told me** I was late.* (NOT ~~*She told I was late.*~~)
*They **told Anna** the wrong time.* (NOT ~~*They told the wrong time to Anna.*~~)

Say doesn't need a personal object: we ***say something*** (*to somebody*).

*She **said** I was late.* (NOT ~~*She said me I was late.*~~)
*I **said** nothing to the police.* (NOT ~~*I said the police nothing.*~~)

2 Circle the correct answer.

1 I *said / told* the driver I wanted to stop.
2 My mother *said / told* there was a letter for me.
3 Everybody *said / told* I looked beautiful.
4 Why did you *say / tell* the lessons were expensive?
5 Ross *said / told* the waiter he couldn't pay.
6 I didn't *say / tell* Peter that I was going away.
7 Nobody *said / told* me that the shop was closed.
8 Mia *said / told* that she would wait at the bus stop.

TENSE CHANGES

When we tell people what somebody **said in the past**, there is a **time difference**.
(For example, somebody said something on Sunday, and I tell you about it on Monday.)
Because of this, **tenses usually change as follows:**

DIRECT SPEECH ON SUNDAY	TENSE CHANGE	INDIRECT SPEECH ON MONDAY
*The children **are** in Ireland.* *My TV **isn't** working.*	*AM/ARE/IS → WAS/WERE*	*Karen said her children **were** in Ireland.* *He said his TV **wasn't** working.*
*I **have** a meeting at 4.00.* *Sue **has** passed her exam.*	*HAVE/HAS → HAD*	*She said she **had** a meeting at 4.00.* *Sally told me Sue **had** passed her exam.*
*I **will** probably be late.*	*WILL → WOULD*	*I thought I **would** probably be late.*
*You **can** have three tickets.*	*CAN → COULD*	*The man said I **could** have three tickets.*
*It **doesn't** matter, Martin.*	*DO/DOES → DID*	*I told Martin it **didn't** matter.*
*The train **leaves** at 6.00.* *We all **speak** English.*	SIMPLE PRESENT → SIMPLE PAST	*The timetable said the train **left** at 6.00.* *She said they all **spoke** English.*
*I **forgot** my keys.*	SIMPLE PAST → PAST PERFECT	*He said he **had forgotten** his keys.*

3 Rewrite the sentences in indirect speech, changing the tenses. Begin *He/She/They said* …

▶ SALLY: 'I'm tired.' *She said (that) she was tired.*
1 ANNA: 'My sister needs a car.' ....
2 DANIEL: 'I have to phone Andrew.' ....
3 MARY: 'Nobody wants to help me.' ....
4 HELEN: 'The radio doesn't work.' ....
5 BEN: 'I will be in Paris in July.' ....
6 MIKE: 'I like the red sweater.' ....
7 DAVID: 'I can't swim.' ....
8 ALICE: 'My parents are travelling.' ....
9 MARIA: 'The lessons are very good.' ....
10 BRAD AND AMY: 'We haven't heard from Joseph.' ....

4 Look at the picture to see what John thought when he was small. Write his thoughts in indirect speech.

He thought animals could talk.
....

ANIMALS CAN TALK.
CATS HAVE NINE LIVES.
MY FATHER KNOWS EVERYTHING.
SPAGHETTI GROWS ON TREES.
THE TEACHER LIVES IN THE SCHOOL.
I WILL BE RICH ONE DAY.
MY MOTHER HAS ALWAYS BEEN OLD.

5 What did you think when you were small? Write three or more sentences.

1 ....
2 ....
3 ....
4 ....
5 ....

In some answers, both contracted forms (for example *I'm*, *don't*) and full forms (for example *I am*, *do not*) are possible. Normally both are correct.

Level 2

indirect questions *She asked him what his name was.*

Indirect questions have a **different word order** from direct questions, and no question marks: ~~???~~

DIRECT QUESTION:	*Monica said, 'Where **is John**?'*	*I said, 'When **can you** come?'*
INDIRECT QUESTION:	*Monica asked where **John was**.* (**NOT** ~~*Monica asked where was John?*~~)	*I asked when **she could** come.*

We **don't** use ***do*** in indirect questions.

DIRECT QUESTION:	*'What **do** you **want**?'*	*'Where **does** Andrew **live**?'*
INDIRECT QUESTION:	*She asked me what I **wanted**.* (**NOT** ~~*She asked me what did I want.*~~)	*I asked him where Andrew **lived**.*

1 A policewoman stopped a driver in London and asked him some questions. Write the questions in indirect speech.

▶ 'What is your name?' She asked him what his name was.

1 'Where do you live?' ....

2 'Where do you work?' ....

3 'Where are you going?' ....

4 'Where have you been?' ....

5 'What is the number of your car?' ....

....

6 'Why are you driving on the right?' ....

....

With indirect ***yes/no*** questions we use ***if*** or ***whether***. They mean the same.

DIRECT QUESTION:	***Do you know** Tim?*	***Are you** French?*
INDIRECT QUESTION:	*He asked me **if/whether I knew** Tim.*	*She asked **if/whether I was** French.*

2 The policewoman asked some more questions. Write them in indirect speech with *if* or *whether*.

▶ 'Are you British?' She asked him if he was British.

1 'Is it your car?' She asked him whether ....

2 'Do you have a driving licence?' ....

3 'Do you have it with you?' ....

4 'Do you always drive with the door open?' ....

....

5 'Are you listening to me?' ....

3 These are some questions from a job interview. Write them in indirect speech.

▶ 'How old are you?' They asked him how old he was.

1 'Are you married?' ....

2 'Do you have children?' ....

3 'Where have you worked before?' ....

4 'Why do you want to change your job?' ....

....

5 'Can you speak any foreign languages?' ....

....

6 'What exams have you passed?' ....

....

present reporting verbs *She says she comes from London.*

Level 2

After **present** verbs (for example *she **says**, I **think***) we **don't change** the tenses.

DIRECT SPEECH: *'Well, yes, I **come** from London.' 'Funny – you **have** a Scottish accent.'*

INDIRECT SPEECH: *She says she **comes** from London, but I think she **has** a Scottish accent.*

1 Complete the indirect speech sentences.

- ▶ 'I'm Irish.' He says *he's Irish.*
- ▶ 'Where is Peter?' She wants to know *where Peter is.*
- ▶ 'Did John phone?' I don't know *if John phoned.*
1. 'We live in Greece.' They say ……
2. 'I went to Belfast yesterday.' She says ……
3. 'I've been ill.' He says ……
4. 'It's going to rain.' She thinks ……
5. 'I'll ask my sister.' She says ……
6. 'We're going to be rich.' They believe ……
7. 'Is lunch ready?' He wants to know ……
8. 'Where did I put my keys?' I don't remember ……
9. 'I'm getting a cold.' I think ……
10. 'This is the right answer.' I know ……

We can ask questions politely by saying *Do you know …?* or *Can you tell me …?* + **indirect question.**

Where does she live? → *Do you know **where she lives**?* *Is he at home?* → *Can you tell me **if he's at home**?*

2 Rewrite the questions.

- ▶ What does this word mean? Do you know *what this word means?*
- ▶ Is there a lesson today? Can you tell me *if there's a lesson today?*
1. Where can I buy tickets? Can you ……
2. How much does it cost? Do ……
3. Has John phoned? Can ……
4. Must I pay now? Can ……
5. Does Maria like steak? Can ……
6. Where did I park the car? Do ……

We can also use **indirect questions** in answers.

*Sorry, I don't know **where she lives**.* *I can't remember **if he's married**.*

3 Don't give the answers! But write sentences beginning *I know, I don't know, I'd like to know, I don't want to know, I don't care* or *I can't remember*.

- ▶ Who built the Eiffel Tower? *I know who built the Eiffel Tower.*
1. What languages do Irish people speak? ……
2. What do elephants eat? ……
3. Does the British Museum open on Christmas Day? ……
4. Was King William II a tall man? ……
5. Do birds dream? ……

In some answers, both contracted forms (for example *I'm, don't*) and full forms (for example *I am, do not*) are possible. Normally both are correct.

here and *now* → *there* and *then*

When we tell people what somebody said, we may have to **change** words like ***here, this, today*** and ***now***. This is because the **place and time have changed** since the words were spoken.

BILL IN IRELAND IN DECEMBER	JOE IN LONDON IN MARCH
*I like it **here**.*	*Bill said he liked it **there / in Ireland**.*
*I'm going fishing **this** week.*	*He said he was going fishing **that** week.*
*I'm not working **today**.*	*He said he wasn't working **that day**.*
*What do you want to do **now**?*	*He asked what I wanted to do **then/next**.*

1 Match the direct and indirect speech expressions.

DIRECT SPEECH: *'here* and *now'* words		INDIRECT SPEECH: *'there* and *then'* words	
0 here	5 today	A that day	F the next day ......
1 now	6 tonight	B that night	G there ..0..
2 this	7 last week	C that	H the week before ......
3 tomorrow	8 next week	D the day before	I then ......
4 yesterday		E the next week	

2 A friend of yours said these sentences a month ago in another country. Now you are telling somebody what she said. Complete the sentences with the correct '*there* and *then*' words.

- ▶ 'I'm not happy here.' — She said she wasn't happy ...there....................
- 1 'I hate this place.' — She said she hated ....
- 2 'I left home last week.' — She said she had left home ....
- 3 'I wrote to my father yesterday.' — She said she had written to her father ....
- 4 'Are you leaving today?' — She asked me if I was leaving ....
- 5 'Where will you be tonight?' — She asked where I would be ....
- 6 'I'll phone you tomorrow.' — She said she would phone me ....

3 Another friend of yours said these sentences two weeks ago in another town. Now you are telling somebody what he said. Write the sentences with the correct tenses and '*there* and *then*' words.

- ▶ 'I'm really happy here.' ...He said he was really happy there.........................
- 1 'I love this place.' ....
- 2 'I saw a great film yesterday.' ....
- 3 'I'm going to another party tonight.' ....
....
- 4 'Do you want to play tennis tomorrow?' ....
....
- 5 'My girlfriend will be here next week.' ....
....

infinitives *She told me to get out.*

We use ***ask*** or ***tell*** **+ object + infinitive** (with *to*), to say what people **want(ed) us to do.**

DIRECT SPEECH	INDIRECT SPEECH
*'**Please close** the door.'*	*She **asked me to close** the door.*
*'**Could you phone** Angela?'*	*I **asked John to phone** Angela.*
*'**Get out!**'*	*She **told me to get out**.*
*'**Don't worry.**'*	*The doctor **always tells her not to worry**.*

1 Write past indirect speech sentences.

▶ **MARK** Peter, could you close the window? (*ask*)
Mark asked Peter to close the window.

▶ **THE TEACHER:** Andrew, don't talk so loud. (*tell*)
The teacher told Andrew not to talk so loud.

1 **DAVE:** Sandra, please give me your phone number. (*ask*)
....

2 **THE BOSS:** James, I'd like you to work late. (*tell*)
....

3 **JUDY:** Kim, please don't tell Karen about Ryan. (*ask*)
....

4 **MR SANDERS:** Fred, please don't smoke in my car. (*ask*)
....

5 **THE GENERAL:** Colonel Walker, take 100 men and cross the river. (*tell*)
....

6 **ANNA:** Polly, you mustn't study so hard. (*tell*)
....

2 Joe left home for university. His family gave him lots of advice. Look at the picture and complete the sentences.

▶ His mother told him to write every week.
▶ His grandmother told him not to forget to brush his teeth.
1 His girlfriend told .... every day.
2 His mother .... clean.
3 His father .... hard.
4 His sister .... parties.
5 His brother .... exercise.
6 His mother .... every day.
7 His father .... late.
8 His brother .... with money.
9 His sister .... for money.
10 His grandmother .... properly.

We can use infinitives after *how, what, when* etc.

*I don't know **how to cook** fish.* *She asked me **what to write**.* *Tell me **when to pay**.*

3 Write two sentences about yourself.

1 I know how to ....
2 I don't know how to ....

In some answers, both contracted forms (for example *I'm, don't*) and full forms (for example *I am, do not*) are possible. Normally both are correct.

indirect speech: more practice

1 Indirect questions. Yesterday morning Peter asked his mother hundreds of questions. Here are some of them. Report them using indirect speech.

▶ 'Why do cats have tails?' He asked her why cats had tails.

▶ 'Will I get all your money when you die?' He asked her if he would get all her money when she died.

1 'Can I have ice cream for breakfast?' ……

2 'Why do the stars only come out at night?' ……

3 'Why does Daddy have to work?' ……

4 'Where is God?' ……

5 'Will I be taller than you one day?' ……

6 'Do you believe in Father Christmas?' ……

7 'Is Scotland in London?' ……

8 'When will I be rich?' ……

9 'Why don't French people speak English?' ……

10 'How big is the universe?' ……

2 Infinitives. Yesterday morning Peter's mother told him to do hundreds of things. Here are some of them. Report them using "She told him".

▶ Say 'Please'. She told him to say 'Please'.

▶ Don't ask so many questions. She told him not to ask so many questions.

1 Wash your hands before breakfast. ……

2 Don't eat with your mouth open. ……

3 Eat everything on your plate. ……

4 Don't talk with your mouth full. ……

5 Make your bed. ……

6 Clean your room. ……

7 Polish your shoes. ……

8 Put on a clean shirt. ……

9 Don't shout at your sister. ……

10 Don't be late for school. ……

3 *What to...* etc. Write sentences beginning *John doesn't know*.

▶ 'What should I tell Ann?' John doesn't know what to tell Ann.

1 'How do I phone New York?' ……

2 'Where do I pay?' ……

3 'When do I start work?' ……

4 'How do I switch the computer on?' ……

5 'Where shall I put my coat?' ……

6 'How much must I pay?' ……

7 'What should I study?' ……

4 Grammar in a text. Read the letter and then complete the report.

Dear all,

Sorry I haven't written for a few weeks. I've been too busy. I'm having a great time; I'm going to parties every night. I'm doing a bit of work too. We had an exam last week. I hope I'll get good marks.

I only have one shirt – I've lost the others. Mum, can you buy me six more? And I can't find my raincoat. Is it at home?

My room here isn't very nice – I'll have to look for a better one. And the food here in college isn't much good, so I'm living on hamburgers. I've spent nearly all my money. Dad, can you send some more?

Can you give me Aunt Ellen's address? And I haven't heard from Sarah. Where is she living? And does Jasper want to come and spend two or three days down here with me?

That's all for now. Love to everybody.

Joe

In his letter Joe ▶ said he was sorry that he ▶ hadn't written for a few weeks. It was because he 1 ………… too busy. He 2 ………… his family that he 3 ………… a great time, but he 4 ………… some work too. He said he 5 ………… an exam 6 ………… week …………, and he hoped he 7 ………… get good marks.

Joe 8 ………… that he only 9 ………… one shirt, because he 10 ………… the others. He asked his mother 11 ………… him six more. And he asked 12 ………… his raincoat 13 ………… at home.

His room 14 ………… not very nice, he said, so he 15 ………… have to look for a better one. And because of the bad college food he 16 ………… on hamburgers.

He said he 17 ………… nearly all his money, and asked his father 18 ………… him some more. Joe also asked his family 19 ………… him his Aunt Ellen's address. And he 20 ………… them that he 21 ………… from Sarah, and asked 22 ………… she 23 …………

At the end of the letter, Joe asked 24 ………… Jasper 25 ………… to go and spend a few days with him.

5 Internet exercise. Use a search engine (e.g. Google) to find some simple sentences beginning *"We don't know what/where/when/how"* + infinitive. Write some of them. (Note that *why* + infinitive is very unusual.)

1 …………
2 …………
3 …………
4 …………

indirect speech: revision test

1 Put in *said* or *told*.

1 The newspaper .... it would snow at the weekend.
2 Everybody .... me I would pass the exam, but I didn't.
3 I .... the driver I knew the way.
4 My father .... he was feeling tired because of working at weekends.
5 Everybody .... Emma looked ill, but she was fine.
6 Luke .... the doctor he had a lot of trouble sleeping.
7 I .... my mother I wasn't coming home before Saturday.
8 Nobody .... me that the school was closed.
9 Rachel .... that she would be back by one o'clock.
10 You never .... me that you loved me.

2 Correct (✓) or not (✗)?

▶ I knew that I will see her again. ..✗..
▶ Andrew told me he hated his brother's wife. ..✓..
1 Leo phoned me on Sunday and said he went to a great party yesterday. ......
2 I said that I was sorry, but that I'm really tired. ......
3 I knew I would forget her name in a few days. ......
4 You told me I like the new car. ......
5 Jack said he had to phone Karl that evening. ......
6 Lucy said that nobody likes her. ......
7 I thought the TV didn't work, but I was wrong. ......
8 Maggie said she would see me soon, but I never saw her again. ......
9 I saw Carola in January and she told me I was unhappy just now. ......
10 Shakespeare told his wife that you don't understand my work. ......

3 Nine of sentences 1–15 have mistakes. Find them and correct them.

▶ Do you remember what time the play starts? ..Correct..
▶ John asked ~~how did I feel~~. ..how I felt..
1 I asked what the time was. ....
2 I didn't know if I was late. ....
3 A man asked me where was the post office. ....
4 Do you know when is arriving Jane? ....
5 I didn't know whether I was late. ....
6 Do you know where all those people work? ....
7 Can you say me what the time is? ....
8 The policeman asked me where I am going. ....
9 The children wanted to know was I English. ....
10 I asked him what he wanted? ....
11 I don't know what does this word mean. ....
12 Nobody understood what Sophie wants. ....
13 I'd like to know what you are thinking. ....
14 Please tell me what you want. ....
15 I don't know why did she say that. ....

In some answers, both contracted forms (for example *I'm*, *don't*) and full forms (for example *I am*, *do not*) are possible. Normally both are correct.

SECTION 21 prepositions

grammar summary

above across against along at behind between by down during
for from in in front of into near off on opposite out of over
past round through to under until/till up

Some prepositions are difficult, because they have more than one meaning. (A preposition in one language often has several different translations into another language.)

In this section, we explain and practise the most important prepositions: those that we use to talk about **time, place** and **movement**.

→ For *since* and *for*, see page 65.

→ For the place of prepositions in questions, see page 111; with relative pronouns, see page 258.

→ For *-ing* forms after prepositions, see page 132.

→ For verbs followed by prepositions, see page 141.

→ For lists of common expressions with prepositions, see pages 305–306.

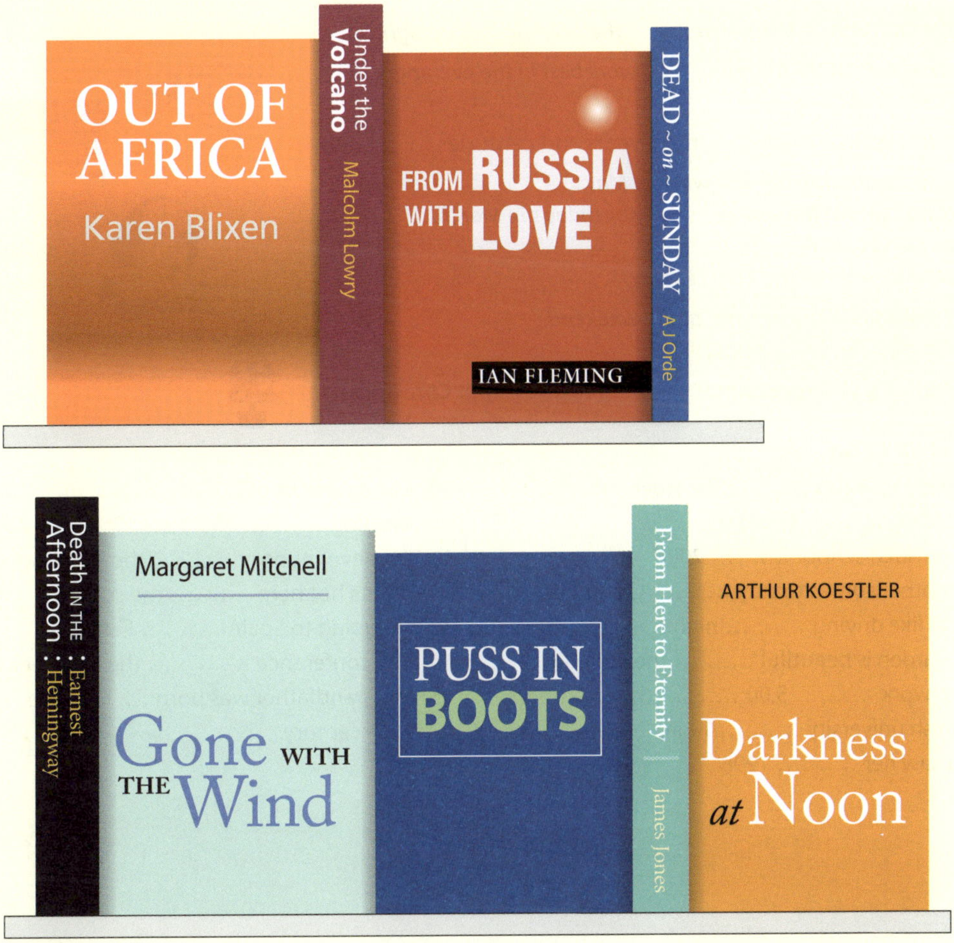

at, in and *on* (time)

We use ***at*** with **clock times.**

*I'll see you **at 4.15.*** *The plane leaves **at six.*** *Call me **at lunchtime.***

But we say ***What time***...?, **NOT USUALLY** *At what time ...?*

***What time** is the film?*

We use ***on*** with **days, dates** and expressions like ***Monday morning*** and ***Friday afternoon***.

*I'll be at home **on Tuesday.*** *We get up late **on Sundays.***
*The meeting's **on June 23rd.*** *I'm always sleepy **on Monday mornings.***
*I had to work **on Christmas Day.***

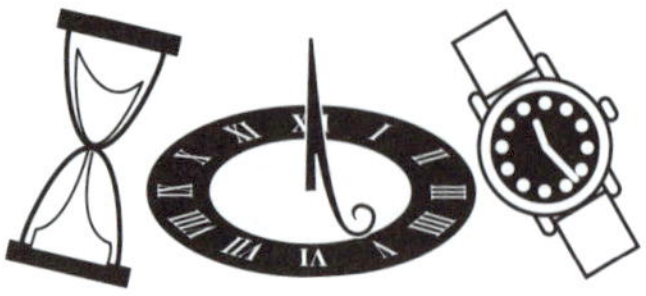

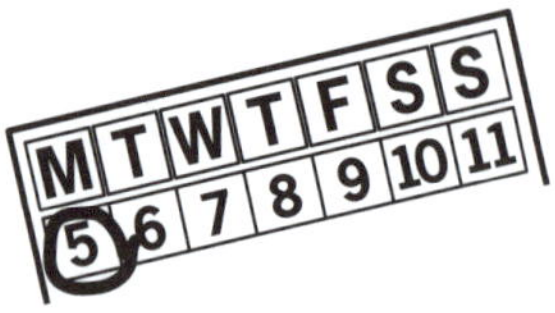

1 Put in *at* or *on*.

1 What are you doing .... Saturday?
2 Can you wake me .... 6.30?
3 The classes start .... September 8th.
4 I'll be in late .... Tuesday morning.
5 I have my guitar lessons .... 10.00 .... Wednesdays.
6 She arrived .... Easter Monday.
7 My job starts .... April 17th.
8 Can we meet .... lunchtime .... Tuesday?
9 I'll be home .... 5.00.
10 I'll see you .... Friday evening.
11 She always phones .... midnight.
12 I was born .... March 21st.

We say ***in the morning, in the afternoon, in the evening**, but **at night.***

*She was born at 6.16 **in the morning.*** *I work best **in the evening.***
*This street is very quiet **at night.***

We use ***in*** with **weeks, seasons, months, years** and **centuries.**

*We're going to Denmark **in the first week** of May.*
*I always get unhappy **in the winter.*** *My birthday's **in March.***
*Shakespeare died **in 1616.***
*There were terrible wars **in the 17th century.***

We say ***at Christmas, at Easter*** and ***at the weekend.***
(American English ***on** the weekend*)

*What are you doing **at the weekend?*** *Did you go away **at Christmas?***

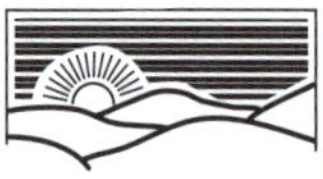

William Shakespeare 1564–1616

2 Put in *in, at* or *on*.

1 We went to Wales .... the weekend.
2 I go skiing .... February.
3 She finished school .... 2006.
4 My mother comes to stay .... Christmas.
5 I don't like driving .... night.
6 Our garden is beautiful .... the spring.
7 I stop work .... 5.00 .... the afternoon.
8 I'll finish university .... June.
9 I last saw her .... 1998.
10 Carola was born .... 8.25 .... the evening .... Thursday 17th April 2000.
11 I'm never hungry .... the morning.
12 It gets hot here .... the summer.
13 I'm going to Spain .... Easter.
14 The conference is .... the last week of May.
15 My grandfather was born .... the 19th century.

We **don't** use **prepositions** before common expressions with ***this, next, last*** and ***every***.

*What are you doing **this afternoon**?* *Goodbye. See you **next week**.*
*Theo was here **last Tuesday**.* *We go on holiday to the same place **every year.***

3 Today is Wednesday March 16th 2011. Rewrite the sentences using *this, next, last* and *every*.

▶ I met her in 2010. I met her last year.
1 I'll see you on March 23rd. ....
2 It rained non-stop from March 7th to March 13th. ....
3 Business was bad in February 2011. ....
4 Shall we go out on March 16th in the evening? ....
5 We're going to America in April 2011. ....
6 Ann had a car crash on March 9th. ....
7 I'm going to change my job in 2012. ....
8 My holiday is in August 2011, 2012, 2013, 2014, 2015 etc. ....
9 I've spent too much money already in March. ....
10 The new school will be open in March 2012. ....

To say **how long** it takes to **finish** something, we use ***in***.

*They built our house **in three months**.* *Your soup will be ready **in ten minutes**.*

4 My Australian friend Sheila is saving money because she wants to buy a sports car. She is saving $1 a day, starting tomorrow.

▶ When will she have $2 in her savings account? In two days.
1 When will she have $5? ....
2 When will she have $7? In a ....
3 When will she have $14? ....
4 When will she have $30? ....
5 When will she have $365? ....
6 The car costs $36,500. When will she have it? ....

GRAMMAR AND VOCABULARY: dates

WE WRITE	WE SAY
1999	nineteen ninety-nine
17(th) March 2011	the seventeenth of March, two thousand and eleven
OR March 17(th) 2011	March the seventeenth, two thousand and eleven
OR 17.3.(20)11	
OR 17/3/(20)11	
American English: 3.17.2011	March (the) seventeenth, two thousand (and) eleven

5 Say these dates:

1 *21.3.1999* 2 *14 February 1960* 3 *July 28 1846* 4 *6/5/03* 5 *May 9 1984* 6 *17 December 2012*

In some answers, both contracted forms (for example *I'm, don't*) and full forms (for example *I am, do not*) are possible. Normally both are correct.

from … to, until and *by*

We use ***till*** (informal) or ***until*** to say when an action or situation **ends**.

*I'll be in London **till** Thursday.* *We played football **until** 5 o'clock.*

1 Complete the sentences with *until* or *till* and expressions from the box.

the age of 14	July	lunchtime	six o'clock in the morning ✓	Saturday	the end

▶ It was a great party. We danced until six o'clock in the morning.
1 I'm going to have a sandwich now. I can't wait ……
2 Granny's coming on Monday for a few days. She's going to stay ……
3 When I was young, you had to go to school ……
4 I didn't like the film, so I didn't stay ……
5 I'm doing a three-month computer course; it goes on ……

We can give the **beginning** and **end** of an action or situation with ***from … to/until/till***.

*I worked **from 8.00 to 6.00** yesterday.* *We'll be away **from July 16 until/till August 4**.*

2 Make sentences about John's Sunday morning with *to, till* or *until*.

▶ read paper 7.30 – 8.00 He read the paper from 7.30 to 8.00.
OR He read the paper from 7.30 until/till 8.00.
1 washed car 8.00 – 9.00 ……
2 talked to woman next door 9.00 – 9.15 ……
……
3 played tennis 10.00 – 11.00 ……
4 talked to friends 11.00 – 11.30 ……
5 went for a walk 11.30 – 12.45 ……

3 Write two sentences with *from … to/till/until* about things you did yesterday.

1 ……
2 ……

We use ***by*** (= '**not later than**') to say that something happens **at** or **before** a certain moment.

UNTIL
*You can keep the car **until Sunday**.*

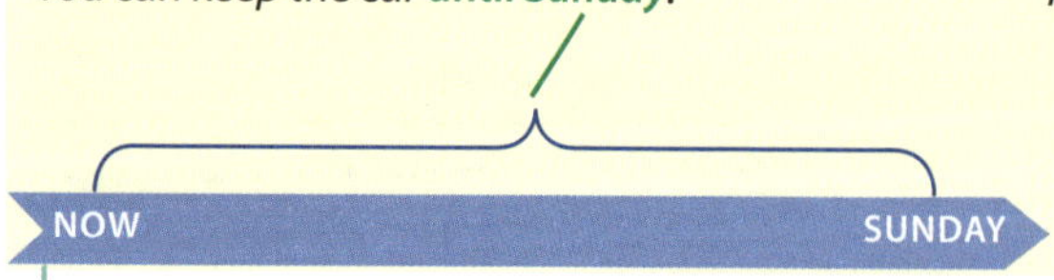

BY
*You really must bring it back **by 12.00 on Sunday**.*

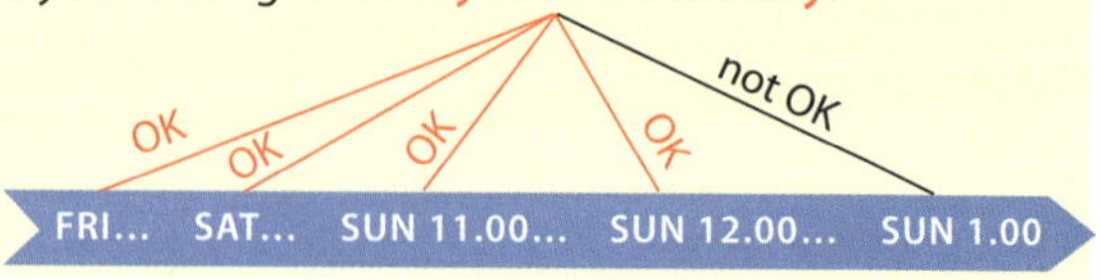

4 Put in *by* or *until*.

1 This book must go back to the library …… Tuesday.
2 The film goes on …… 9.30.
3 Can you finish painting the room …… Friday?
4 If I give you this coat to clean, can you do it …… tomorrow?
5 I must find some money …… the end of the week.
6 Can you wait for my answer …… tonight?

for, during and *while*

For + **period** tells you **how long**. ***During*** tells you **when**.

*The journey lasted **for three days**.* *There was a rainstorm **during the night**.*
*I slept **for 20 minutes during the lesson**.*

1 Put in *for* or *during*.

1 I lived in Mexico .... six years.
2 I got a headache .... the examination.
3 We visited Kyoto .... our holiday in Japan.
4 The electricity went off .... two hours .... the afternoon.
5 Alex and his wife met .... the war.
6 Could I talk to you .... a few minutes?
7 I usually get a lot of phone calls .... the morning.
8 She and her boyfriend have been together .... a long time.

During is a **preposition**: we use ***during* + noun**.
While is a **conjunction**: we use ***while* + subject + verb** (often past progressive - see page 52).

*They got into the house **during the night**.* *They got into the house **while I was asleep**.*
*He got ill **during the journey**.* *He got ill **while he was travelling**.*

2 Change the expressions.

▶ during the meal (*I / eat*) while I was eating
▶ while I was travelling (*journey*) during the journey
1 during the game (*they / play*) ....
2 while we were listening (*lesson*) ....
3 while they were fighting (*war*) ....
4 during her lesson (*she / teach*) ....
5 during his speech (*he / speak*) ....
6 during the conversation (*they / talk*) ....
7 while she was in hospital (*illness*) ....
8 during the snowstorm (*it / snow*) ....

3 GRAMMAR AND VOCABULARY: useful expressions with *for*

Look at the expressions in the box, and choose suitable ones to complete the sentences. Different answers are possible.

for a moment	for a minute or two	for a few minutes	for an hour or so (= 'about an hour')		
for a couple of hours	for a long time	for ages	for years and years	for ever	for life

1 They waited ...., but the bus didn't come.
2 I will love you ....
3 Could I talk to you ....?
4 I played tennis .... and then went home.
5 I went to sleep .... during the opera.
6 She usually stops work at 11 o'clock .... and has a cup of coffee.
7 I often watch TV .... before I go to bed.
8 They put him in prison ....

In some answers, both contracted forms (for example *I'm, don't*) and full forms (for example *I am, do not*) are possible. Normally both are correct.

in and *on* (place)

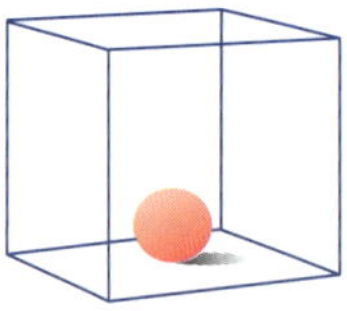

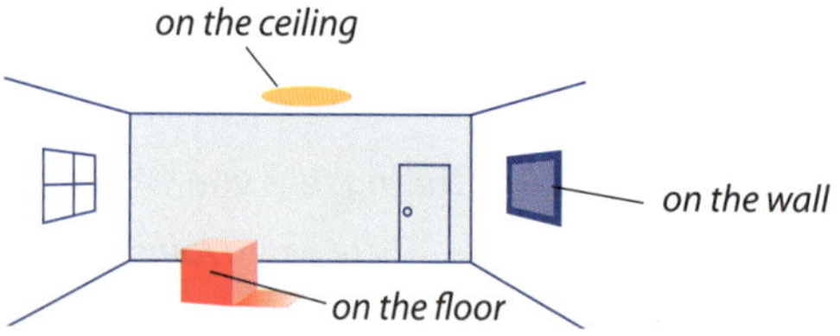

We use *in* with **3-dimensional spaces** like boxes, rooms, towns or countries.
We use **on** with **2-dimensional surfaces** like floors, tables, walls or ceilings.

'Where's Joe?' 'In the kitchen.' *There's nothing in the fridge.* *Tara's in Poland.*
Why are all those papers on the floor? *The church has wonderful paintings on the ceiling.*
She had photos of all her family on the wall.

People are *in* **clothes**. Clothes and jewellery (earrings etc) are *on* **people**.

Who is the man in the grey suit? *That sweater looks good on you.* *She had a ring on every finger.*

1 Put in *in* or *on*.

1 .... a bath 2 .... a roof 3 .... a tree 4 .... a table 5 .... a cup

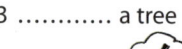

6 .... her arm 7 .... a plate 8 .... your head 9 .... your head 10 .... a door

We say *in a book*, *in the newspaper*, *in a story* (**BUT** *on a page*); *in a street*.

Is there anything interesting in the paper? *Her photo is on page 4.* *They live in Park Street.*

2 Put in words from the boxes with *in* or *on*.

children's stories ✓	her first finger	my diary	the office	the roof of the car	the cupboard

▶ *In children's stories,* .... animals can talk.
1 'Are you free next Tuesday?' 'Just a minute. I'll look ....'
2 Is Sandra .... today?
3 She had a wonderful diamond ring ....
4 'Where's the salt?' ....
5 The cat likes to sleep ....

a little village	his T-shirt	my pocket	a piece of paper	the wall	your car

6 Don't leave your keys .... when you get out.
7 .... it said 'Aberdeen University Football Club'.
8 She had pictures of pop singers .... in her room.
9 They live .... near Belfast.
10 I wrote her address .... and put it ....

Note that we say *in a car* **BUT** *on a bus/train/plane/ship*.

Granny arrived in a taxi, as usual. *I'm leaving on the 4.15 train.*

at (place)

I'll meet you ***at*** *the cinema.*

Operator	TE	GW
LONDON Paddington	1743	1803
Ealing Broadway	...	...
Slough	1800	1822
Maidenhead	...	...
Twyford	...	...
Reading... *dep*	1820	1838
Tilehurst	...	...
Pangbourne	...	...
Goring & Streatley	...	...
Wallingford		
Cholsey	...	...
Didcot Parkway... *arr*	1835	153

The train stops ***at*** *Slough, Reading and Didcot.*

We often use ***at*** to show **where something happens** – for example, with **meeting places** or **points on a journey**.

I'll see you this evening ***at Sarah's house****.* *You have to change planes* ***at Karachi****.*
I saw Linda waiting ***at the bus stop****.* *Turn left* ***at the next corner****.*

We often use ***at*** with words for **things that people do**, or the **places where they do them**.

at *a football match* ***at*** *breakfast, lunch etc* ***at*** *a restaurant* ***at*** *work* ***at*** *the office*
at *the theatre* ***at*** *the cinema* ***at*** *the station* ***at*** *a party* ***at*** *(the) college/university*

1 Put in words from the box with *at*.

a Chinese restaurant	a theatre	Birmingham	breakfast	the cinema	the crossroads
the hotel bar	the party	the station	the traffic lights ✓	work	

▶ Paul crashed his car because he didn't stop *at the traffic lights.*
1 Are there any good films .... this week?
2 Her train was terribly late – I spent hours waiting ....
3 Will you be .... at Mike's house on Saturday?
4 We had a really good meal .... in Park Street last night.
5 I saw my first Shakespeare play .... in a small town in Ireland.
6 The boss doesn't let us take personal phone calls ....
7 Helen never says anything .... because she's still asleep.
8 There isn't a direct train. You change ....
9 I'll meet you downstairs .... at 6.00.
10 'Where's the car park?' 'Turn right ....

We often use ***at*** with ***the top, the bottom, the side, the beginning*** and ***the end***.

My room's ***at the top*** *of the house.* *Begin* ***at the beginning****.*

2 Put in *at the top, at the bottom* etc.

1 Their house is down .... of the hill.
2 I never have any money .... of the month.
3 I stopped for a minute .... of the stairs to have a rest.
4 The best fruit is always .... of the tree, where you can't get it.
5 Maria wasn't there .... of the lesson; she came in late.

Sometimes ***in*** and ***at*** are **both possible**. We prefer ***at*** when we are thinking about **the activity** – what we do in the place – and ***in*** when we think about the **place itself**.

We ***had lunch at*** *the station restaurant. It was very hot* ***in the big dining room****.*

→ For expressions with no article like *at breakfast*, *at work*, see page 162.

In some answers, both contracted forms (for example *I'm*, *don't*) and full forms (for example *I am*, *do not*) are possible. Normally both are correct.

other prepositions of place

above	against	behind	between	by	in front of	near	opposite	under

Anna is sitting ***between*** *Tim and John.*

Come and sit ***by*** *me.*

We camped ***by*** *the lake.*

Montreal is in eastern Canada, ***near*** *Ottawa.*

I left my bicycle ***against*** *the shop window.*

Joe's car is parked ***in front of*** *our house.*
There's a bus stop ***opposite*** *our house.*

Lucy is ***in front of*** *Beth.*
Beth is ***behind*** *Lucy.*

Andy is ***opposite*** *Mike.*

The dog is hiding ***under*** *the table.*

The plane is flying ***above*** *the clouds.*

1 Choose the correct prepositions.

▶ I usually sit ....by........ a window in class, so I can look out if I get bored. (*behind, by, in front of*)

1 There was a big bird flying high up .... the trees. (*above, against, opposite*)

2 They live in a beautiful old house .... a river. (*above, by, under*)

3 There's a big clock .... the door of the station. (*above, against, between*)

4 I sat down .... Marion and looked into her eyes. (*above, behind, by*)

5 You can park your car .... the house. (*against, behind, between*)

6 I'll meet you at the station .... the clock. (*against, between, under*)

7 The door wouldn't stay shut, so I put a chair .... it. (*above, against, near*)

2 Put in the correct prepositions.

1 She put the money at the bottom of her suitcase, ... her clothes.

2 Our house is .... a bank and a supermarket, and just .... the police station.

3 Please don't put your bicycle .... our wall.

4 Sorry we're late – we were driving .... a slow bus all the way.

5 I work in a small town .... Birmingham.

6 In the theatre I couldn't see anything because there was a very tall man .... me.

7 We usually have lunch in a little café .... the school, about five minutes' walk away.

3 Look at the picture and choose the correct prepositions.

▶ *above* / *near* the travel agent

1 *opposite* / *in front* of the National Bank

2 *against* / *between* the two women

3 *above* / *behind* the child

4 *near* / *by* the travel agent

5 *in front of* / *behind* the restaurant

6 *opposite* / *under* the car

7 *against* / *opposite* the window

8 *behind* / *between* the banks

9 *by* / *opposite* the supermarket

prepositions of movement

across	*along*	*down*	*into*	*off*	*over*	*out of*	*past*	*round*	*through*	*under*	*up*

1 Write the expressions under the correct photos. Use a dictionary if necessary.

across the river along the yellow line down the mountain into the water
off the bike over the fence out of the shop past the café
round the corner through the gate under the bridge up the steps

1 ....

2 ....

3 ....

4 ....

5 ....

6 ....

7 ....

8 ....

9 ....

10 ....

11 ....

12 ....

2 Cross out the words that are wrong.

▶ across *the road* / ~~*the church*~~
1 along *the corner / the road*
2 up *the mountain / the table*
3 down *the church / the stairs*
4 over *the corner / the wall*
5 into *the bank / the bridge*
6 round *the corner / the road*
7 through *the door / the railway line*
8 off *the police station / the table*
9 out of *the church / the stairs*
10 under *the bridge / the people*
11 past *the floor / the bank*
12 across *the river / the wall*

3 Choose the correct prepositions and put them in the correct places.

▶ I went ...up............ the stairs and ...along........ the passage. (*along, into, out of, up*)
1 Mrs Andrews got .... the taxi and ran .... Oxford Street. (*along, round, out of, over*)
2 Alice walked .... the steps to the river and .... the bridge. (*along, down, through, over*)
3 He walked slowly .... the road for a few minutes, then he stopped and went .... a small door .... a garden. (*across, along, into, through*)
4 Mandy went .... the stairs and .... her office, took a letter .... the table and started to read it. (*into, off, out of, over, up*)
5 Go .... the supermarket, ... the railway bridge, ... the first corner, and the police station is on your right. (*along, down, past, round, under*)
6 As soon as I got .... the boat I went straight .... the town centre to do some shopping. (*into, off, out of, past, through*)
7 I got .... bed, walked .... the bedroom, and looked .... the window. It was raining again. (*across, into, out of, out of, under*)
8 It takes three hours to walk .... the mountain, but you can get .... it in two. (*across, down, over, round, up*)

We use ***to*** for **movement**, and ***at*** or ***in*** for **position** – where somebody/something is (see pages 278–279).

*I went **to** the bus stop to meet Helen.* *I waited **at** the bus stop for twenty minutes.*

We can use ***from*** … with ***to*** …

*He took five days to cycle **from** London **to** Edinburgh.*

We ***get to*** a place, but we ***arrive at*** a place, or ***arrive in*** a big place (NOT ~~*arrive to*~~).

*It took three hours to **get to** Cambridge.* *I was tired when I **arrived at** the station.*
*We **arrived in** London very early in the morning.*

4 Put in *from, to, at* or *in*.

1 Let's go .... the country this weekend.
2 She spends hours .... the bathroom.
3 Shall we drive .... Scotland or go by train?
4 We flew directly .... Berlin .... Tokyo.
5 What time do we arrive .... Paris?
6 After six days' walking, they got .... a river.
7 I saw Annie standing .... the bus stop.
8 When we arrived .... her house she had already left.
9 Are there tigers .... Africa?
10 It takes me about half an hour to get .... work.

5 Write a few sentences about a journey that you have made, using *from, to, at* and *in*.

....
....
....
....
....

NOTE: we get ***into*** and ***out of*** *cars* BUT ***on(to)*** and ***off*** *buses/trains/planes/ships*.

In some answers, both contracted forms (for example *I'm, don't*) and full forms (for example *I am, do not*) are possible. Normally both are correct.

prepositions: more practice

1 Time. Circle the correct prepositions.

1 He phoned *on / in* Friday.
2 The party is *at / on* June 18th.
3 Are you at home *at / on* Christmas?
4 I'll be here *during / for* two months.
5 We get up late *in / on* Sunday mornings.
6 I often watch TV *in / at* night.
7 The film ends *on / at* 9.45.
8 You can't learn English *in / by* a month.
9 Hannah's birthday is *on / in* May.
10 What are you doing *on / at* Thursday?
11 Bring my bike back *until / by* Friday.
12 I'll work *for / until* 8.00 this evening.
13 I couldn't sleep *for / during* the night.
14 Stay here *while / during* I go shopping.
15 I play tennis *at / in* the weekend.

2 Expressions without prepositions. Today is Saturday August 13th 2011. Rewrite the expressions in *italics* using *this*, *next*, *last* and *every*.

▶ I finished university *in 2010.* ....last year....
1 Joanne had a party *on Saturday August 6th.* ....
2 I'm going to buy a new car *in 2012.* ....
3 My holiday is *in September 2011, 2012, 2013, 2014 etc.* ....
4 I've already bought too many clothes *in August.* ....
5 It was really hot *from August 1st to August 7th.* ....
6 Shall we go and see a film *on August 14th in the evening?* ....
7 I'll be away on *Saturday August 20th.* ....
8 My brother was ill *in July 2011.* ....
9 We're going camping *in September 2011.* ....
10 The new station will be ready *in August 2012.* ....

3 Movement. Cross out the wrong words.

▶ across *the river* / ~~*the bank*~~
1 along *the church / the road*
2 down *the police station / the mountain*
3 into *the church / the table*
4 off *the corner / the table*
5 out of *the church / the wall*
6 up *the mountain / the floor*
7 over *the door / the wall*
8 past *the floor / the church*
9 round *the corner / the railway line*
10 through *the door / the table*

4 Place and movement. Put in suitable prepositions.

▶ He sat ....by/near.... the window, and looked out from time to time.
1 C comes .... B and D in the alphabet.
2 I couldn't see the plane, because it was high .... the clouds.
3 I had to wait a long time at the post office, because the woman .... me wanted a lot of different things.
4 There's a garage on the other side of the street just .... our house.
5 Please don't put bicycles .... the shop window.
6 He turned round and walked away .... the trees.
7 We cycled .... a little road .... the river for about five kilometres.
8 Ann came .... the church and walked slowly .... the square.
9 I got .... the bus and went .... the bank.
10 'Where's the swimming pool?' 'Drive .... the police station, ... the railway bridge and .... the corner, and you'll see it on your left.'

5 Place and movement. Write the opposites.

- ▶ on the train ..off the train..........
- 1 into the church ....
- 2 off the bus ....
- 3 down the stairs ....
- 4 over the bridge ....
- 5 out of the river ....
- 6 in front of the door ....
- 7 at the top of the stairs ....
- 8 up the mountain ....
- 9 behind the police station ....
- 10 at the beginning ....

6 Dates. Write these dates as you would say them.

- ▶ 2006 ..two thousand and six..........
- ▶ 17th March ..the seventeenth of March..........
  OR ..March the seventeenth..........
- 1 23rd April ....
- 2 1st September ....
- 3 5th August, 2010 ....
- 4 March 2, 1980 ....
- 5 10.1.02 ....
- 6 3/4/08 ....
- 7 October 4th ....
- 8 21st March, 1936 ....
- 9 Oct 22, 2006 ....
- 10 1/1/01 ....

7 GRAMMAR AND VOCABULARY: duration. Put in suitable expressions from the box. (Different answers are possible.)

for a couple of hours
for a few minutes
for a long time
for a moment
for an hour or so
for ever
for life
for years and years

- ▶ I feel as if I've known you ..for ever..........
- 1 I need to speak to you ....
- 2 The terrorists were sent to prison ....
- 3 We haven't seen Peter ....
- 4 I'm going to rest ....
- 5 It's been raining ....
- 6 I usually play tennis .... on Sundays.
- 7 We've lived in the same house ....
- 8 Can you help me ....?
- 9 She went to sleep on the train just ....
- 10 I'm going out into the garden ....

8 Grammar in a text. Choose the correct prepositions.

Dear Louise

I'm glad you can come 1 *on / in* Friday. You asked how to get to our house. It's very easy. Get 2 *in / on* a No. 16 bus 3 *opposite / along* the police station, and get 4 *off / out* at the fourth stop just 5 *above / by* the new supermarket. Then walk 6 *off / along* Boston Street for about 300 metres, turn right 7 *at / on* the traffic lights, keep straight on 8 *along / under* the railway bridge, go 9 *through / up* the hill past the church, 10 *round / across* the corner by the pub, then 11 *down / off* the hill and 12 *under / across* the main road. That takes you into South Park. Walk 13 *along / through* the park and 14 *out of / off* the other side, turn left 15 *round / in front of* the school, and you'll find yourself 16 *on / in* Green Road. Our house is the fourth on the left, just 17 *out of / by* the old railway station. You can't miss it.

Love, Judy.

9 Internet exercise. Use a search engine (e.g. Google) to find simple sentences with the expressions in the box. Write some of them.

"across the river" "along the road" "out of the church" "off the table" "up the mountain" "over the wall" "round the corner"

....

....

....

pronunciation for grammar → e-book

prepositions: revision test

1 Put in the correct words.

1 Let's go to Cardiff .... Tuesday. (*in, at, while, on*)
2 The bridge .... the river is closed. (*along, over, up, through*)
3 The next meeting is .... December 8th. (*on, at, in, by*)
4 What do you usually do .... the weekend? (*on, at, in, by*)
5 Max fell .... his bike and broke his leg. (*down, on, out of, off*)
6 I need your answer .... (*in, by, at, until*) Friday.
7 I'm not free now, but I can talk to you .... half an hour. (*in, for, by, until*)
8 I slept .... two hours this afternoon. (*in, by, for, during*)
9 The quickest way to our house is .... the park. (*along, through, in, over*)
10 Let's go for a walk .... the sun's shining. (*while, during, for, along*)

2 Put in suitable prepositions. (More than one may be possible.)

1 I'm going to put this picture .... my bedroom wall.
2 I'll be away .... June 1st .... July 15th.
3 Olivia lived in Cairo .... three years.
4 I didn't work very hard .... my time at university.
5 It says .... the newspaper that there will be snow.
6 Does this bus stop .... the railway station?
7 Your father's photo is .... page 16.
8 We're leaving .... the 10.40 train.
9 I always wear this ring .... my little finger.
10 Write your name .... the top of the page.
11 Can you clean this suit .... 4 o'clock?
12 A lot of people travel for a year .... school and university.
13 Pete met his girlfriend .... a party.
14 I'll be ready to go .... ten minutes.
15 I like walking .... the river.

3 All these sentences are wrong. Correct the mistakes.

▶ I'll see you ~~at~~ Tuesday. ...*on*...................................
1 She talked non-stop during three hours. ....
2 Please let me have all the information until Saturday. ....
3 Anna walked slowly out the room and down the stairs. ....
4 There's a pub on the other side of the road in front of our house. ....
5 Do you think you can swim through this river? ....
6 There's a strange insect in the ceiling. ....
7 It took a long time to drive over the town to the church. ....
8 I'll see you on next Monday. ....
9 Did you stay at home on Christmas? ....
10 We have to get down the bus at the next stop. ....

In some answers, both contracted forms (for example *I'm, don't*) and full forms (for example *I am, do not*) are possible. Normally both are correct.

SECTION 22 spoken grammar

grammar summary

We often **leave words out** if the meaning is clear. This is particularly common in **spoken English**.

It often happens **after auxiliary verbs.**

She said she would phone, but she ***didn't**.* (= '… she didn't phone.')
I'll finish the work as soon as I ***can**.* (= '… as soon as I can finish the work.')

There are several common kinds of **short spoken sentence** made with **subject + auxiliary verb**:

- **question tags:** *You're from Scotland,* ***aren't you?***
- **short answers:** *'Did you see Patrick?'* ***'No, I didn't.'***
- **reply questions:** *'I've got a headache.'* ***'Have you?*** *I am sorry.'*
- ***so do I, nor can I*** **etc:** *'I was really cold on that bus.'* ***'So was I.'***

We also often **leave out infinitives** (and other words) **after *to*.**

I've never seen the Taj Mahal, but I'd like ***to**.* (= '… I'd like to see the Taj Mahal.')

And we may **leave out small words** (pronouns, articles, auxiliary verbs) **at the beginning of sentences.**

Don't know. (= '**I** don't know.') *Train's late.* (= '**The** train's late.')
Been waiting long? (= '**Have you** been waiting long?')

'Forgotten your key again, George?'

'It's all coming back to me now.
We were married once, weren't we?'

'Seen John?'

'Cold, isn't it?'

'Need any help?'

'Nor do I.'

'Don't think so.'

'No, we haven't.'

'Can't understand a word.'

'DO THEY?'

question tags *This music isn't very good, is it?*

Question tags are short questions that can follow sentences, especially in **spoken English**.
We make question tags with **auxiliary verb** (*have, can* etc) or ***be*** + **pronoun** (*I, you* etc).
We use question tags to **ask if something is true**, or to **ask people to agree** with us.

*You haven't got my keys, **have you?*** *Louise will be here tomorrow, **won't she?***
*This music isn't very good, **is it?*** *That child can run fast, **can't he?***

Question tags are usually **negative** (−) after **affirmative** (+) sentences, and **not negative** after **negative** sentences. We **don't** put question tags **after questions**.

It is warm, isn't it? *It isn't cold, is it?* (BUT NOT ~~*Is it cold, isn't it?*~~)

Negative tags are usually **contracted** (see page 301) – for example ***isn't it?*** (NOT USUALLY *is it not?*)
The negative tag for *I am* is ***aren't I?*** (see page 301)

*I'm late, **aren't I?***

1 Question tag or nothing (–)? Circle the correct form.

▶ I'm late , *am I? / , aren't I? / – ?*
▶ You can't swim *, can you? / , can't you? / – ?*
▶ Has Anna phoned , *has she? / , hasn't she? / – ?*
1 You'll be here tomorrow *, will you? / , won't you? / – ?*
2 The postman hasn't come *, has he? / , hasn't he? / – ?*
3 Are you ready *, are you? / , aren't you? / – ?*
4 It's dark in here *, is it? / , isn't it? / – ?*
5 He can't speak Greek *, can he? / , can't he? / – ?*
6 The train's late *, is it? / , isn't it? / – ?*
7 The food wasn't bad, *was it? / , wasn't it? / – ?*
8 Have you done it *, have you / , haven't you? / – ?*
9 I'm too early *, amn't I? / , aren't I?/ – ?*

If the sentence has an **auxiliary verb** or ***be***, we use this in the question tag.

*You **would** like coffee, **wouldn't** you?* *I'**m** not talking too fast, **am** I?*
*Sally **doesn't** eat meat, **does** she?* *You **aren't** angry with me, **are** you?*

If there is **no auxiliary verb**, we use ***do/does/did*** in the tag.

*They **went** to Spain, **didn't** they?* *The lesson **starts** at 6.00, **doesn't** it?*

2 Here are some sentences from real conversations. Put in the question tags.

▶ You're playing football tomorrow, aren't you?
1 That's the answer, ……………………
2 We're seeing Rebecca again tomorrow, ……………………
3 She's a lovely baby, ……………………
4 You'll be OK, ……………………, Roger?
5 Your brother can tell us that, ……………………
6 Isabel likes brown bread, ……………………
7 This house gets hot in summer, ……………………

3 Here are some negative sentences. Put in the question tags.

▶ They weren't at home, were they?
1 But he's not at school now, ……………………
2 You can't remember anything, ……………………
3 They don't use much electricity, ……………………
4 She doesn't look happy, ……………………
5 Those flowers don't need much water, ……………………
6 That kid hasn't done any work, ……………………

We can use ***there*** as a **subject** in question tags.

*There's a letter for me, **isn't there**?* *There weren't any problems, **were there**?*

Level 2

4 Put in the question tags.

1 There was a phone call for me, ...
2 There are six more lessons this year, ...
3 There's a meeting this afternoon, ...
4 There hasn't been any snow this year, ...
5 There weren't many people at the party, ...

5 Put in the correct question tags.

1 You don't know Alicia, ... (*do you?, don't you?, are you?*)
2 Polly's looking well, ... (*doesn't she?, isn't she?, is she?*)
3 It's really cold today, ... (*isn't it?, isn't there, doesn't it?*)
4 You can't hear what she's saying, ... (*is she?, can you?, can't you?*)
5 You'd like a drink, ... (*wouldn't you?, don't you?, you would?*)
6 They don't listen, ... (*are they?, aren't they, do they?*)
7 Carola's been away, ... (*isn't she?, wasn't she?, hasn't she?*)
8 I'm at the right address, ... (*am I?, aren't I?, amn't I?*)
9 There's a problem, ... (*isn't there?, isn't it?, is it?*)
10 You like chocolate, ... (*like you, aren't you?, don't you?*)

6 Change these questions into statements with question tags.

▸ Do you work at Smith's? *You work at Smith's, don't you?*
1 Have they lived in France? They've ....
2 Did they all go home early? ....
3 Did it rain all last week? ....
4 Does her brother write for the newspapers? ....
....
5 Do I need a visa? ....
6 Would you like a holiday? ....
7 Was the train late? ....
8 Did Sarah forget your birthday? ....
9 Was there a letter for me? ....
10 Am I in time for lunch? ....

If a tag asks **a real question**, we say it with a **rising** intonation: the music of the voice goes up.
If a tag just asks for **agreement**, we use a **falling** intonation: the voice goes down.

We're meeting in Oxford, aren't we? *Nice day,* isn't it?

7 Try to pronounce these tags.

1 The lesson begins at twelve, doesn't it?
2 Your sister's gone to America, hasn't she?
3 Bill's a good singer, isn't he?
4 It's cold, isn't it?
5 You're from Scotland, aren't you?
6 She looks good in red, doesn't she?

In some answers, both contracted forms (for example *I'm, don't*) and full forms (for example *I am, do not*) are possible. Normally both are correct.

short answers *Yes, I have. No, they didn't.*

To answer just *'Yes'* or *'No'* can be **impolite**.
We often prefer answers with **pronoun** (***I, you*** etc) + ***be*** or **auxiliary verb** (*have, can* etc).
The auxiliary verb in the **answer** is usually the **same** as the one in the **question**.

*'**Are** you ready?' 'Yes, I **am**.'* *'**Have** you phoned home?' 'Yes, I **have**.'*
*'**Can** Ellie speak Spanish?' 'No, she **can't**.'* *'**Did** you watch the match?' 'No, I **didn't**.'*

Note that the negative of *I am* is ***I'm not***.

*'Are you happy?' 'No, **I'm not**.* (NOT ~~*No, I amn't.*~~)

Negative (−) short answers are usually **contracted** (see page 301): ***can't, didn't*** etc.
Affirmative (+) short answers are **not contracted**: we **don't** say ~~*Yes, I'm*~~ or ~~*Yes, she's*~~, for example.

1 Write short answers to these questions.

▶ 'Do you like jazz?' 'Yes, I do.'
▶ 'Are you coming home?' 'No, I'm not.'
1 'Is it raining?' 'No, ...'
2 'Has Joe phoned?' 'No, ...'
3 'Do the children understand?' 'Yes, ...'
4 'Is this your coat?' 'No, ...'
5 'Does your brother like sport?' 'No, ...'
6 'Do you want tickets?' 'Yes, ...'
7 'Would your mother like coffee?' 'No thanks, ...'
8 'Was the film interesting?' 'No, ...'
9 'Are you ready?' 'No, I'm afraid ....'

2 Give your own personal short answers to these questions.

▶ 'Do you like coffee?' Yes, I do. / No, I don't.
1 'Are you thinking in English now?' ....
2 'Do you live in a town?' ....
3 'Do you speak French?' ....
4 'Is it raining now?' ....
5 'Is your English getting better?' ....
6 'Have you been to New York?' ....
7 'Did you watch TV yesterday?' ....
8 'Can you swim?' ....
9 'Are you tired?' ....

We can use short answers to **agree** or **disagree** with things that people say.

'It's hot today.' ***'Yes, it is.'*** *'You didn't buy bread.'* ***'Yes, I did.'*** *'The train's late.'* ***'No, it isn't.'***

If there is **no auxiliary verb**, we use ***do/does/did*** in the short answer.

*'Her hair **looks** nice.' 'Yes, it **does**.'*

3 Write short answers to agree or disagree.

1 'You're early.' 'No, ...'
2 'It's cold.' 'Yes, ...'
3 'She sings really well.' 'Yes, ...'
4 'The lesson starts at 5.00.' 'No, ...'
5 'Simon didn't phone.' 'Yes, ...'
6 'He made a mistake.' 'Yes, ...'

4 GRAMMAR AND VOCABULARY: things that people can do

Give true answers with *Yes, I can* or *No, I can't*.

1 Can you knit? ....
2 Can you cook? ....
3 Can you skate? ....
4 Can you repair cars? ....
5 Can you dive? ....
6 Can you draw? ....
7 Can you sing? ....
8 Can you ride a horse? ....

reply questions *Oh, yes? Did they really?*

In conversation, we often ask **short questions** (auxiliary verb + pronoun) **to show interest.**

*'I've just had a letter from Eric.' '**Have you?**' 'Yes. He says he's coming back …'*

These '**reply questions**' are not really questions: they mean 'Oh, yes? That's interesting.'
Some more examples:

*'John's getting married.' '**Is he** really? Who to?'*
*'Anna and Peter had a lovely time in Greece.' '**Did they?**' 'Yes. They went …'*

We answer **negative** sentences with **negative** reply questions.

*'I can't see very well with these glasses.' '**Can't you?** Maybe you should get new ones.'*

1 Choose the correct reply questions.

▶ 'Your mother hasn't phoned.' *'Has she? / Hasn't she?* I wonder why not.'
1 'I've just got married.' *'Have you? / Haven't you?* Congratulations.'
2 'William had an accident last week' *'Has he? / Did he?* Is he OK?'
3 'There's a strange bird on the roof.' *'Is it? / Is there?* Let me look.'
4 'I can't understand this.' *'Can you? / Can't you?* Let me help you.'
5 'This coffee doesn't taste very nice.' *'Doesn't it? / Does it?* I'm sorry.'
6 'Your sister's in trouble with the police.' *'Is she? / Isn't she?* Oh, dear. Not again!'
7 'The children want computers for Christmas.' *'Do they? / Don't they?* They think I'm made of money.'
8 'The students don't like your lessons.' *'Don't they? / Aren't they?* Well, I don't like them either.'

2 Put the beginnings and ends together, and put in reply questions.

0 'Oliver didn't eat much.'	A Didn't he? Perhaps he's ill.' 0
1 'I don't like this bread at all.'	B '.................. I hope they're having a good time.' ......
2 'The Smiths are in America.'	C '.................. I'll get a different kind next time.' ......
3 'My French is getting very bad.'	D '.................. When's he going to bring it back?' ......
4 'Ryan's taken the car.'	E '.................. I'll have a look at them.' ......
5 'I can't understand these papers.'	F '.................. You need to go to France.' ......

3 GRAMMAR AND VOCABULARY: showing our feelings

**Complete the sentences with reply questions and expressions from the box.
Use a dictionary if necessary. Different answers are possible.**

Congratulations!	Good luck!	I am sorry.	I don't believe it. ✓	Say 'hello' to him/her for me.
That's interesting.	That's terrible.	That's a surprise.	What a nuisance!	What a pity!

▶ 'The Swiss have declared war on America.' 'Have they? I don't believe it.'
1 'I've just passed my exams.' ....
2 'I'm seeing Katie next week.' ....
3 'My job interview is tomorrow.' ....
4 'Some trees can live for thousands of years.' ....
5 'Lewis didn't get into university.' ....
6 'My computer has crashed again.' ....
7 'I don't feel well.' ....
8 'Andy and Paula are getting married.' ....
9 'I haven't got enough money to buy food.' ....

In some answers, both contracted forms (for example *I'm, don't*) and full forms (for example *I am, do not*) are possible. Normally both are correct.

revision of spoken question and answer structures

QUESTION TAGS	SHORT ANSWERS	REPLY QUESTIONS
*It is …, **isn't it?***	*'Are you …?' **'No, I'm not.'***	*'I'm …' **'Are you?'***
*I am …, **aren't I?***	*'Has she …?' **'Yes, she has.'***	*'He's …' **'Has he?'***
*She has …, **hasn't she?***	*'Do they …?' **'Yes, they do.'***	*'They like …' **'Do they?'***
*They like …, **don't they?***	*'Are we …?' **'No, we aren't.'***	*'We're …' **'Are we?'***
*We aren't …, **are we?***	*'He wasn't …' **'No, he wasn't.'***	*'She wasn't …' **'Wasn't she?'***
*He didn't …, **did he?***	*'She didn't …' **'Yes, she did.'***	*'He didn't …' **'Didn't he?'***

1 Circle the best expression.

▶ Jemima can't sing at all, *can she? / she can't.*

1 'I'm worried about Peter.' *'You are?' / 'Are you?' / 'Aren't you?'*
2 *'Joe didn't phone yesterday.' / 'Joe phoned yesterday.'* 'Didn't he?'
3 *'I'm feeling ill.' / 'I'm not feeling well.'* 'Are you?'
4 *'Does John need help?' / 'John needs help.'* 'Does he?'
5 *Do you remember David, / You don't remember David,* do you?
6 'I've got a headache.' *'You haven't.' / 'You have.' / 'Have you?'*
7 They can stay with us, *they can't? / can't they? / can they?*

2 Read the conversation, and put in question tags (QT), short answers (SA) or reply questions (RQ).

QT 'Hello, Carol. Lovely day, ▶ isn't it?'
SA '▶ Yes, it is. How are you?'
'Well, I've got a problem.'
RQ '▶ Have you? What's the matter?'
QT 'You remember my brother's boy Theo, 1 ……………………'
SA; QT '2 …………………… He went to Australia, 3 ……………………'
SA 'No, 4 …………………… He went to Canada. Anyway, he's coming back to England.'
RQ '5 …………………… That's nice.'
'Well, yes, but he wants to stay with me.'
RQ 'Oh, 6 …………………… Is that the problem?'
SA '7 …………………… I'm not very happy about it.'
RQ; QT '8 …………………… Why? You like Theo, 9 ……………………'
SA '10 …………………… – very much.'
QT 'And you've got a lot of room in that big house, 11 ……………………'
SA '12 …………………… But would you like to have a young man living in your house all the time?'
'No, I suppose not.'
'Well, I don't know what to do. I'm really very worried.'
RQ '13 …………………… Would you like some advice?'
SA '14 ……………………'
'Tell him the truth. Say you like him a lot, but you don't want people in your house.'
QT 'I can't say that, 15 ……………………'
SA '16 …………………… He'll understand. I'm sure of it.'
RQ '17 …………………… I don't know. Anyway, I'll think about it. Thanks.'

leaving out words *Don't know if she has.*

We often use just an **auxiliary verb instead of repeating a longer expression**, if the meaning is clear. This happens in question tags, short answers and reply questions (see pages 288–291), and in other sentences too.

*'Get up!' 'I **am**.'* (= 'I am getting up.') *Come round tomorrow evening, if you **can**.*
*I haven't seen that film, but my brother **has**.* (NOT … ~~*but my brother has seen.*~~)

We use ***do/does/did*** if there is no other auxiliary verb to repeat.

*David said he knew the address, but he **didn't** really.*

1 Make these sentences more natural by crossing out unnecessary words.

▶ You said it wasn't raining, but it is ~~raining~~.
1 He thinks I don't understand, but I do understand.
2 'You'd better eat something.' 'I have eaten something.'
3 Alice said she would lend me her car, but I don't think she will lend me her car.
4 Eric was sure he would pass his exam. I hope he has passed his exam.
5 'Will you write to me every day?' 'Of course I will write to you every day.'
6 I can't help you today, but I can help you tomorrow.

We often use ***to*** **instead of a longer expression**, if the meaning is clear.

*'Would you like to stay with us next weekend?' 'I'd love **to**.'* (= 'I'd love to stay with you.')
*I don't play tennis, but I used **to**.* *'Are you going to Scotland this summer?' 'We hope **to**.'*

2 Complete the sentences, using the words in the box with *to*.

I'd like	It's starting	I'm trying ✓	I used	she didn't want	Sorry, I forgot	They hope

▶ 'Can't you go faster?' *I'm trying to.*
1 'Are Cathy and Dave getting married this year?' ....
2 I asked her to dance, but ....
3 I've never learnt to ski, but ....
4 I don't speak German very well now, but ....
5 'Did you remember to phone Liz?' ....
6 'Is it raining?' ....

In conversation, people may **leave out 'small words'** (for example pronouns, articles, auxiliary verbs) **at the beginnings of sentences.**

Must go now. *Can't help you, sorry.* *Don't know.* *Car's not going well.*
Seen Billy? (= 'Have you seen Billy?') *Nobody here.* (= 'There's nobody here.')

3 Write the complete sentences.

1 Couldn't understand what he wanted from me. ....
2 Doesn't know what she's doing. ....
3 Bus is late again. ....
4 Speak French? ....
5 Haven't seen them. ....
6 Don't think so. ....

→ For sentences where we leave out *that*, see pages 257 and 264.

In some answers, both contracted forms (for example *I'm, don't*) and full forms (for example *I am, do not*) are possible. Normally both are correct.

Level 2

so am I; nor do I etc

To say that A is/does the same as B, we can use **so + *be* or auxiliary verb** (*have, can* etc) **+ subject** (note the word order).

'I'm hungry.' 'So am I.' (NOT ~~*So I am.*~~) *Sue's stopped her lessons, and* ***so has George****.*

If there is **no auxiliary verb** to repeat, we use ***do/does/did***.

'My brother works in the theatre.' 'So does my cousin.'

1 Complete the sentences, using *so*.

▶ 'My job's boring.' (+ *mine*) 'So is mine.'
▶ 'My room gets very cold at night.' (+ *mine*) 'So does mine.'
1 'Anna is very interested in history.' (+ *Alice*) ....
2 'My grandfather plays golf all day.' (+ *my father*) ....
3 'I can swim under water.' (+ *I*) ....
4 'Peter wants a bicycle for Christmas.' (+ *Carla*) ....
5 'Joe has just got married.' (+ *Edward*) ....

In **negative** sentences we use **neither or nor + auxiliary verb + subject**.

'I'm not working today.' 'Neither am I.' 'Mary can't drive.' 'Nor can Pat.'
Bill doesn't like the boss, and ***neither does Jan****.*

2 Complete the sentences, using *neither/nor*.

▶ Max didn't play very well, and (- *the others*) nor did the others. OR neither did the others.
1 The soup wasn't very good, and (- *the meat*) ....
2 'Rob hasn't phoned yet.' (- *Gemma*) ....
3 'This dictionary doesn't show pronunciation.' (- *this one*) ....
4 'I can't cook.' (- *I*) ....
5 His parents won't help him, and (- *his friends*) ....

We can use short sentences (**subject + auxiliary verb**) to say that **A is not the same as B**.

'I'm not going to school today.' 'I am.' Some people don't like modern art, but ***I do****.*
'I like this music.' 'I don't.' The food was cheap, but ***the drinks weren't****.*

3 Complete the sentences with expressions from the box, to say that things are not the same.

her second one	her sister	my car	my father ✓	our dog
the back door	the green ones ✓	the train		

▶ 'My father works too hard.' 'My father doesn't.'
▶ 'The red apples aren't very sweet.' 'The green ones are.'
1 'My car doesn't use a lot of petrol.' ....
2 'Mary has passed all her exams.' 'Yes, but ....
3 Most dogs can swim, but ....
4 'The bus takes a long time to get to London.' ....
5 The front door wasn't open, but ....
6 'Her first book didn't sell very well.' ....

4 Look at the table and write sentences.

	LIKES DANCING	HAS BEEN TO AMERICA	PLAYS TENNIS	CAN SKI	IS TALL	LAUGHS A LOT
ERIC	✓	✗	✓	✓	✗	✓
JULIE	✓	✓	✗	✗	✗	✓
PAUL	✗	✗	✗	✓	✗	✗
DAN	✓	✓	✓	✓	✓	✓
DENISE	✗	✓	✗	✗	✓	✗
RACHEL	✓	✓	✗	✗	✓	✓

▶ *(Eric, Dan, dancing)* Eric likes dancing, and so does Dan.
▶ *(Julie, Rachel, ski)* Julie can't ski, and nor can Rachel.
▶ *(Julie, Denise, laugh)* Julie laughs a lot, but Denise doesn't.
▶ *(Eric, Julie, America)* Eric hasn't been to America, but Julie has.
1 *(Eric, Dan, tennis)* ....
2 *(Julie, Denise, tall)* ....
3 *(Denise, Paul, laugh)* ....
4 *(Dan, Rachel, ski)* ....
5 *(Julie, Denise, America)* ....
6 *(Eric, Paul, tall)* ....
7 *(Julie, Dan, tennis)* ....
8 *(Paul, Rachel, dancing)* ....

5 Here are some facts about Mike and Katy. Are you the same as them, or different? Write your answers, using *So am I, Neither/Nor do I, I have, I can't* etc.

▶ Katy has got blue eyes. So have I. **OR** I haven't.
▶ Mike doesn't like fish. I do. **OR** Nor do I.
1 Katy is interested in politics. ....
2 Mike has been to Texas. ....
3 Katy can sing. ....
4 Mike likes old music. ....
5 Katy speaks French. ....
6 Katy isn't very tall. ....
7 Mike hasn't got much hair. ....
8 Katy can't drink milk. ....
9 Mike doesn't like hot weather. ....
10 Mike doesn't understand computers. ....

We can also use ***too*** or ***not either*** to say that **A is/does the same as B.**

*'I'm hungry.' 'I am **too**.'*   *Lucy hasn't written, and Carol has**n't either**.*

In informal conversation we often say ***Me too*** instead of ***So do I, I do too*** etc.

*'I've got a headache.' '**Me too**.'* (NOT ~~*I also.*~~)

In some answers, both contracted forms (for example *I'm, don't*) and full forms (for example *I am, do not*) are possible. Normally both are correct.

SPOKEN GRAMMAR **295**

spoken grammar: more practice

1 Short answers. Complete the conversations.

▶ 'Do you like swimming?' ...'Yes, I do.'...
1 'Was Emma at home when you went to see her?' 'No, ...'
2 'Does Tom play a musical instrument?' 'Yes, ...'
3 'Would your sister like some coffee or tea?' 'No thanks, ...'
4 'The plane arrives at 6.45, I think.' 'No, ...'
5 'Can you work next Saturday?' 'Yes, ...'
6 'Have you written to Felicia?' 'No, ...'
7 'John wants to be a doctor.' 'No, ...'
8 'Did Carol phone this morning?' 'Yes, ...'
9 'Will the children be in this evening?' 'No, ...'
10 'Do you understand what I'm saying?' 'Yes, ...'

2 Reply questions. Complete the conversations with reply questions and expressions from the box. (Different answers are possible.)

Congratulations!	Good luck!	I am sorry. ✓	I am sorry.	I don't believe it!
Say 'hello' to him for me.	That's interesting.	That's terrible.	That's a surprise.	
What a nuisance!	What a pity!			

▶ 'I didn't get that job that I wanted.' ...'Didn't you? I am sorry.'...
1 'I'm seeing James on Tuesday.' ....
2 'I've got excellent results in my exams.' ....
3 'Scotland has declared its independence.' ....
4 'I've got an important interview tomorrow.' ....
5 'Light takes four years to travel here from the nearest star.' ....
....
6 'Anna and Peter are getting divorced.' ....
7 'My car has been stolen.' ....
8 'I feel ill.' ....
9 'Tim has decided to become a ballet dancer.' ....
10 'I can't come to your party.' ....

3 *So am I* etc. Complete the sentences with *So am I, Nor/Neither do I*, etc.

▶ Arthur has gone home, and (+ *Jane*) ...so has Jane....
▶ Oliver can't run very well and (− *Susan*) ...neither can Susan....
1 Dogs don't eat tomatoes, and (− *cats*) ....
2 The 3.45 train hasn't arrived yet, and (− *the 3.15*) ....
3 'I wasn't happy at school.' (− *I*) ....
4 Ken didn't come to the lesson, and (− *Sally*) ....
5 Roger likes travelling, and (+ *his brother*) ....
6 The meat is cold, and (+ *the potatoes*) ....
7 Natasha doesn't speak Russian, and (− *her brother*) ....
8 Our friends were late, and (+ *we*) ....
9 'We don't know why Teresa is unhappy.' (− *her parents*) ....
10 'I'll try to help Robert.' (+ *I*) ....

4 Leaving out words. Make these sentences more natural by crossing out unnecessary words.

▶ You said you weren't crying, but you were ~~crying~~.
1 She says I don't love her, but I do love her.
2 'You should phone Aunt Lucy.' 'I have phoned Aunt Lucy.'
3 Henry thought that he would get rich fast, but I don't think he will get rich fast.
4 'Help me.' 'I'm trying to help you.'
5 'Will you forget me?' 'Of course I won't forget you.'
6 Jasper can sing, but I can't sing.
7 Andrew has asked me to go out with him, but I don't want to go out with him.
8 She's finished breakfast, but I haven't finished breakfast.
9 'You broke that window.' 'No, I didn't break that window.'
10 I haven't been to America yet, but I hope to go to America soon.

5 Leaving out words. Write the complete sentences.

▶ Been shopping? Have you been shopping?
▶ Car won't start. The car won't start.
1 Don't know why. ……
2 Seen my mother today? ……
3 Don't think so. ……
4 Sorry, can't come in here. ……
5 Want some help? ……
6 Know what I think? ……
7 Can't understand a word. ……
8 House is cold. ……
9 Raining again. ……
10 Lost my keys. ……

6 GRAMMAR AND VOCABULARY: things from the office. What would you ask if you were not sure of the names of the things in the pictures?

▶ It's a stapler, isn't it?
1 They're ……
2 ……
3 ……
4 ……
5 ……
6 ……

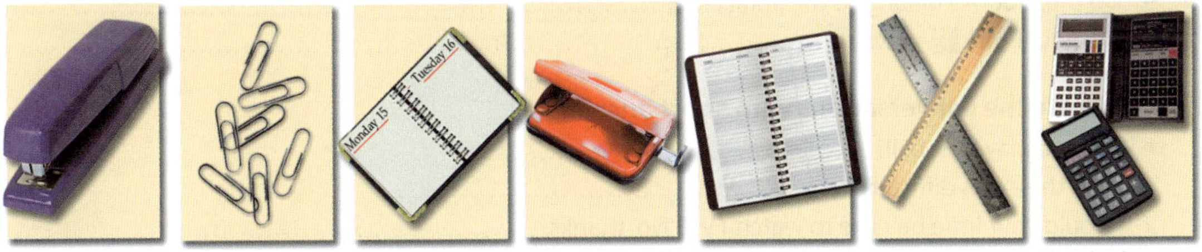

▶ stapler 1 paper clips 2 diary 3 hole-punch 4 address book 5 rulers 6 calculators

7 Internet exercise. Use a search engine (e.g. Google) to find some simple sentences with the expressions in the box. Write some of them.

"and so is" "and so are" "and so has" "and so have" "and so does" "and so do"
"and neither is" "and neither are" "and neither has" "and neither have"
"and neither does" "and neither do"

……
……
……
……

pronunciation for grammar → e-book

spoken grammar: revision test

1 Correct (✓) or not (✗)?

▶ Daniela looks like you, looksn't she? ..✗..
▶ You're Scottish, aren't you? ..✓..
1 We didn't give you our address, did we? ......
2 You can't speak Spanish, do you? ......
3 There's a problem, isn't it? ......
4 Jane doesn't smoke, doesn't she? ......
5 You'll be at home tonight, won't you? ......
6 Is today the 31st, is it? ......
7 Peter and Annie are getting married, aren't they? ......
8 Maggie wasn't here yesterday, was she? ......
9 I'm playing tomorrow, amn't I? ......
10 You haven't seen Pat anywhere, did you? ......

2 Put in the question tags.

▶ It's a nice day, ..isn't it?..
1 You can play the piano, ...
2 Lily will be here tomorrow, ...
3 You haven't got the keys, ...
4 Stephen likes fishing, ...
5 There wasn't much rain in the night, ...
6 Petra went back home, ...
7 George doesn't play golf, ...
8 Dinner's ready, ...
9 It's not raining, ...
10 You won't be late, ...
11 Philip and Rachel have got married, ...
12 The papers haven't arrived, ...
13 I'm late, ...
14 All the trains stop at Oxford, ...
15 That letter didn't arrive, ...

3 Change these questions into affirmative (+) or negative (−) statements with question tags.

▶ Do you live in Dublin? + ..You live in Dublin, don't you?..
▶ Do you know my friend Adrian? − ..You don't know my friend Adrian, do you?..
1 Have they gone home? − They haven't ....
2 Do we need tickets? + ...
3 Would you like some more coffee? + ...
4 Was Mike away yesterday? + ...
5 Did Angela tell you her news? − ....
6 Can Sophie play the piano? − ....
7 Will there be room for everybody? + ...
8 Does your father eat meat? − ....
9 Do these books belong to the library? − ....
10 Are you tired? + ...

4 Complete the conversations with short answers.

▶ 'Do you play baseball?' ..'Yes, I do.'..
1 'Was the exam difficult?' 'No, ...'
2 'Would your little boy like to watch TV?' 'No, thanks, ...'
3 'The lesson starts at 10.00.' 'No, ...'
4 'Did the post come this morning?' 'Yes, ...'
5 'Will it rain today?' 'No, ...'

5 Complete the conversations with reply questions.

▶ 'I've just passed my exam.' ..'Have you?.. Congratulations!'
1 'Joe and Suzy moved to London in March.' '.......... I didn't know.'
2 'I won't be here next week.' '.......... Then come and see us the week after.'
3 'I need some help.' '.......... I'll see what I can do.'
4 'The dog has brought a dead rat into the house.' '.......... Well, could you throw it out, please?'
5 'You didn't lock the door last night.' '.......... That was stupid of me.'

In some answers, both contracted forms (for example *I'm*, *don't*) and full forms (for example *I am*, *do not*) are possible. Normally both are correct.

appendix 1 common irregular verbs

(These are the most common irregular verbs. For a complete list, see a good dictionary.)

INFINITIVE	SIMPLE PAST	PAST PARTICIPLE	INFINITIVE	SIMPLE PAST	PAST PARTICIPLE
be	was/were	been	let	let	let
become	became	become	lie	lay	lain
begin	began	begun	lose	lost	lost
break	broke	broken	make	made	made
bring	brought	brought	mean	meant	meant
build	built	built	meet	met	met
buy	bought	bought	pay	paid	paid
catch	caught	caught	put	put	put
choose	chose	chosen	read /ri:d/	read /red/	read /red/
come	came	come	ride	rode	ridden
cost	cost	cost	run	ran	run
cut	cut	cut	say	said	said
do	did	done	see	saw	seen
draw	drew	drawn	sell	sold	sold
dream	dreamt/dreamed	dreamt/dreamed	send	sent	sent
drink	drank	drunk	show	showed	shown
drive	drove	driven	shut	shut	shut
eat	ate	eaten	sing	sang	sung
fall	fell	fallen	sit	sat	sat
feel	felt	felt	sleep	slept	slept
fight	fought	fought	speak	spoke	spoken
find	found	found	spell	spelt	spelt
fly	flew	flown	spend	spent	spent
forget	forgot	forgotten	stand	stood	stood
get	got	got	steal	stole	stolen
give	gave	given	swim	swam	swum
go	went	gone/been	take	took	taken
have	had	had	teach	taught	taught
hear	heard	heard	tell	told	told
hit	hit	hit	think	thought	thought
hold	held	held	throw	threw	thrown
keep	kept	kept	understand	understood	understood
know	knew	known	wake	woke	woken
lead	led	led	wear	wore	worn
learn	learnt/learned	learnt/learned	win	won	won
leave	left	left	write	wrote	written
lend	lent	lent			

appendix 2 active and passive verb forms

	ACTIVE		PASSIVE: TENSE OF *BE* + PAST PARTICIPLE	
INFINITIVE	*(to) watch*	*(to) write*	*(to) be watched*	*(to) be written*
-ING FORM	*watching*	*writing*	*being watched*	*being written*
SIMPLE PRESENT	*I watch*	*I write*	*I am watched*	*It is written*
PRESENT PROGRESSIVE	*I am watching*	*I am writing*	*I am being watched*	*It is being written*
SIMPLE PAST	*I watched*	*I wrote*	*I was watched*	*It was written*
PAST PROGRESSIVE	*I was watching*	*I was writing*	*I was being watched*	*It was being written*
PRESENT PERFECT	*I have watched*	*I have written*	*I have been watched*	*It has been written*
PAST PERFECT	*I had watched*	*I had written*	*I had been watched*	*It had been written*
WILL FUTURE	*I will watch*	*I will write*	*I will be watched*	*It will be written*
GOING TO FUTURE	*I am going to watch*	*I am going to write*	*I am going to be watched*	*It is going to be written*
MODAL VERBS	*I can watch*	*I can write*	*I can be watched*	*It can be written*
	I must watch	*I must write*	*I must be watched*	*It must be written*
	I should watch	*I should write*	*I should be watched*	*It should be written*
	etc	etc	etc	etc

→ For the use of the different tenses, see Sections 2–5.

→ For the use of passives, see Section 7.

→ For the spelling of *-ing* forms, see page 23.

→ For the spelling of third-person present forms (*writes*, *watches*, *sits*, *goes* etc), see page 16.

appendix 3 capital letters (A, B, C etc)

We use CAPITAL LETTERS to begin the names of **people, places, nationalities, languages, days, months** and **holidays**.

Abraham Lincoln *New York* *American* *Arabic* *Thursday* *September* *Christmas*

We also use CAPITAL LETTERS for the most important words in the titles of **books**, **films** etc.

War and Peace *Gone with the Wind*

And we use a CAPITAL LETTER for the **first word in a sentence**, and for the pronoun ***I***.

*Yesterday **I** went for a long bike ride.*

appendix 4 contractions

Contractions like ***he's***, ***isn't*** show the pronunciation of **informal speech**.
They are common and correct in **informal writing** (for example, friendly letters), but are unusual in formal writing.

AFFIRMATIVE (+) CONTRACTIONS: PRONOUN + *'M, 'RE, 'S, 'VE, 'D, 'LL*	NEGATIVE (-) CONTRACTIONS: *BE, HAVE* OR OTHER AUXILIARY + *N'T*	
I am → I'm	*are not → aren't*	*shall not → shan't*
we are → we're	*is not → isn't*	*would not → wouldn't*
she is → she's	*have not → haven't*	*should not → shouldn't*
he has → he's	*has not → hasn't*	*cannot → can't*
I have → I've	*had not → hadn't*	*could not → couldn't*
you had → you'd	*do not → don't*	*might not → mightn't*
you would → you'd	*does not → doesn't*	*must not → mustn't*
they will → they'll	*did not → didn't*	*need not → needn't*
	will not → won't	

- With *be*, two negative forms are common: *you're not / you aren't, she's not / she isn't*, etc. With *have, had, will* and *would*, the forms with ***n't*** are more common: we usually say *I haven't, I hadn't* etc, NOT *I've not, I'd not* etc.
- There is no contraction ~~*amn't*~~, BUT *am not* → ***aren't*** in **questions**.
  *I'm late, **aren't** I?* (BUT *I'm not late*, NOT ~~*I aren't late.*~~)
- The contraction *'s* (= *is* or *has*) can be written after pronouns, nouns, question words, *here* and *there*.
  It's late. *Your mother's gone home.* *Mary's got a headache.*
  How's Joe these days? *Here's your money.* *There's the telephone.*
- We don't use affirmative (+) contractions at the ends of sentences.
  *'You're early.' 'Yes, **we are**.'* (NOT ~~*Yes, we're.*~~)
  *'I think she's gone home.' 'Yes, I think **she has**.'* (NOT ... ~~*I think she's.*~~)
- Negative (-) contractions are possible at the ends of sentences.
  'It's raining.' 'No, it isn't.'
- Don't confuse *it's* (= *it is/has*) with *its* (possessive – see page 188).
  *The cat isn't hungry. **It's** only eaten half of **its** food.*
- Don't confuse *who's* (= *who is/has*) with *whose*.
  ***Who's** the woman in the green coat?* ***Whose** car is that?*
- In very informal speech, *going to, want to* and *got to* are often pronounced like *gonna, wanna* and *gotta*. They are sometimes written like this, especially in American English.

appendix 5 punctuation

This section summarises the most important rules of punctuation.

the basic sentence

We don't put commas (,,,) between the basic parts of a sentence (**subject** and **verb**, **verb** and **object** etc).

My brother has found a really good job.

(**NOT** ~~*My brother, has found a really good job.*~~

OR ~~*My brother has found, a really good job.*~~)

before the basic sentence

If we put **long adverbial expressions** (saying *when*, *where* etc) before the basic sentence, we often use a comma (,). Compare:

Last year *he followed a business studies course in Edinburgh.*

Between January 2010 and March 2011*, he followed a business studies course in Edinburgh.*

after the basic sentence

We don't usually use commas when **adverbial expressions** come **after** the basic sentence.

He followed a business studies course in Edinburgh ***between January 2010 and March 2011****.*

inside the basic sentence

When adverbial expressions come **between** parts of the basic sentence, we usually put commas before and after them.

She has, in the six months since she started her music studies, made remarkable progress.

noun phrases

We don't usually separate a noun from the adjectives or other expressions that go with it.

those very nice people (**NOT** ~~*those very nice, people*~~)

those very nice people in the flat downstairs (**NOT** ~~*those very nice people, in the flat downstairs*~~)

those very nice people who invited us to their party

(**NOT** ~~*those very nice people, who invited us to their party*~~)

sentences with conjunctions

We often put **commas** in sentences with conjunctions, especially in longer sentences. (See page 219.) Compare:

Everything will be different ***when*** *Mr Harris leaves.*

Everything will be very different after April next year, ***when*** *Mr Harris leaves.*

We **usually** use a **comma** if we **start** with the conjunction.

When *Mr Harris leaves, everything will be different.*

indirect speech

We **don't put commas** after verbs of saying, thinking etc in **indirect speech**.

Jamie ***says that*** *he has a problem.* (**NOT** ~~*Jamie says, that*~~ ...)

I don't ***know what*** *I was going to tell the police.* (**NOT** ~~*I don't know, what*~~ ...)

We **don't put question marks** (?) in **indirect questions**.

I ***asked why*** *he was late.* (**NOT** ~~*I asked why he was late?*~~)

a useful rule: no comma before *that*

We **don't put commas** before ***that*** (conjunction or relative pronoun).

I ***know that*** *she married* ***a man that*** *worked for her father.*

between separate sentences
Between separate sentences (with no conjunction), we use a full stop (.) or a semi-colon (;), but **not a comma**.
Compare:
*Robert phoned**, and** he asked to speak to the manager.* (comma and conjunction)
*Robert phoned**.** He asked to speak to the manager.*
OR *Robert phoned**;** he asked to speak to the manager.*
BUT NOT ~~*Robert phoned, he asked to speak to the manager.*~~

lists
We use commas to separate the different things in a list (but not before *and*).
*She gave presents to her brothers, her sister, her sister's husband, her secretary **and** all of her colleagues.*

abbreviations (short forms of words)
We use full stops after some abbreviations, like *e.g.* (meaning 'for example'). *Mr* and *Mrs* have full stops in American English, but not usually in British English.
*Some British cities have beautiful cathedrals**, e.g.** Salisbury.*
*Everybody liked **Mr** Carter.*

quotation marks ('…' or "…")
Quotation marks are used to show direct speech (somebody's actual words).
*His father said, **'Do what you want.'*** (**NOT** *<Do what you want>* **OR** *– Do want your want.*)

figures
We use commas after thousands and millions, and full stops in decimal fractions.
*€ 5**,**500**,**000* (= 'five million, five hundred thousand euros')
*€ 5**.**5m* (= 'five and a half million euros')

apostrophes (')
For apostrophes in contractions (e.g. *isn't*), see Appendix 4. For apostrophes in possessives (e.g. *John's*), see page 201.

appendix 6 word order

This section summarises the most important rules of word order that you can find in other parts of the book.

sentences

The basic word order of English sentences is **SUBJECT – VERB – OBJECT**.
I play the piano. (**NOT** ~~*I the piano play.*~~)

questions

In questions we usually put an auxiliary verb before the subject.
Did you *see the news last night?* (**NOT** ~~*Saw you the news*~~ *...?*) ***Can you*** *swim?*
For more details, see Section 8, pages 103–111.
This does not usually happen with **indirect questions**.
She asked me ***where I lived.*** (**NOT** ~~*She asked me where did I live.*~~)
For more details, see page 266.

adjectives

Adjectives usually go before, not after, nouns.
an ***interesting film*** (**NOT** ~~*a film interesting*~~)
Adjectives can go after *be*, *seem* and similar verbs.
I think she ***is tired.***
For more details, see Section 15, pages 209–211.

adverbs

Different adverbs can go in different places in a sentence.
Yesterday *I got up at 6.00.* *I've* ***just*** *seen a rabbit.* *You're driving very* ***slowly.***
They do **not** usually go **between the verb and the object**.
I ***bought a bike yesterday.*** (**NOT** ~~*I bought yesterday a bike.*~~)
She speaks ***Spanish very well.*** (**NOT** ~~*She speaks very well Spanish.*~~)
For more details, see Section 15, pages 212–215.

prepositions

Prepositions often go **at the ends of questions**, especially in spoken English.
Who did you go ***with****?* *What did you do that* ***for****?*
For more details, see Section 8, page 111.
Prepositions can also go **at the ends of relative clauses**, especially in spoken English.
There's the man ***that I told you about.*** *The train* ***that I usually travel on*** *wasn't running.*
For more details, see Section 19, page 258.

phrasal verbs

The objects of **phrasal verbs** (but not prepositional verbs) can often go **between the two parts of the verb**.
I ***turned the light out.*** (**OR** *I turned* ***out the light.***)
Pronoun objects always go between the two parts of a phrasal verb.
I ***turned it out.*** (**NOT** ~~*I turned out it.*~~)
For more details, see Section 10, pages 142–143.

ago

Ago **follows** an expression of **time**.
We arrived ***two hours ago.*** (**NOT** ... ~~*ago two hours*~~)

enough

Enough usually goes **before nouns** but **after adjectives and adverbs**.
Have you got ***enough soup****?* (**NOT** ... ~~*soup enough?*~~)
Is the soup ***hot enough****?* (**NOT** ... ~~*enough hot?*~~) *I didn't get up* ***early enough.***

appendix 7 expressions with prepositions

prepositions after verbs, adjectives and nouns

We use prepositions (*at, in* etc) after some verbs, adjectives and nouns.
This is a list of the most common examples.

afraid of
*She's **afraid of** dogs.*

agree with
*I don't **agree with** you.*

angry about something
*We're all **angry about** the new working hours.*

angry with somebody
*Mary's very **angry with** you.*

arrive at/in a place
*I usually **arrive at** school at 8.30.*
*What time do we **arrive in** London?*

ask for
*If you want anything, just **ask for** it.*

bad at
*I'm **bad at** games.*

believe in (= 'believe that something is real')
*Do you **believe in** ghosts?*

belong to
*This book **belongs to** me.*

depend on
*We may arrive late this evening. It **depends on** the traffic.*

different from/to
*You're **different from** (OR **to**) your sister.*

difficulty in doing something
*I have a lot of **difficulty in** understanding her.*

discuss something with somebody
*We **discussed** our plans **with** the manager.*

divide into
*I **divided** the cake **into** four parts.*

dream about something or somebody;
dream of doing something
*I often **dream about** horses.*
*When I was young, I **dreamt of** becoming a pilot.*

dressed in
*She was **dressed** completely **in** black.*

example of
*Can you show me an **example of** your work?*

explain something to somebody
*Can you **explain** this word **to** me?*

get into/out of a car;
get on(to)/off a bus, train, plane, ship
*I picked up my case and **got into** the taxi.*
*She **got off** the bus at the wrong stop.*

get to a place
*How do you **get to** Southport from here?*

good at
*He's **good at** tennis.*

happen to
*What's **happened to** Alice? She's an hour late.*

the idea of doing something
*We had **the idea of** starting a small business.*

interested in
*Are you **interested in** animals?*

kind to
*They have always been very **kind to** me.*

laugh at
*Please don't **laugh at** my French pronunciation.*

listen to
*I like to **listen to** music while I'm working.*

look after children etc
*Can you **look after** the children for half an hour?*

look at
***Look at** that wonderful old car!*

look for (= 'try to find')
*'What are you **looking for**?' 'My keys.'*

married to
*He's **married to** Jane Gordon, the novelist.*

nice to
*You weren't very **nice to** my mother.*

pay somebody for something; pay a bill
*Have you **paid** John **for** the tickets?*
*I forgot to **pay** the electricity bill.*

pleased with
*We are very **pleased with** his work.*

polite to
*It's best to be **polite to** policemen.*

reason for
*What was the **reason for** his change of plans?*

smile at
*In this job you have to **smile at** people all day.*

talk about
*Were you **talking about** me?*

thank somebody for
***Thank** you **for** waiting.*

think about/of
*I **think about** you all the time.*
*We're **thinking of** going to America.*

translate into/from
*I've got to **translate** this letter **from** French **into** German.*

typical of
*She went out without saying 'Thank you'. That's just **typical of** her.*

wait for
*I **waited for** her for half an hour, and then went home.*

write to
*We **write to** each other every week.* (**BUT** *We phone each other ...* – no preposition)

wrong with
*What's **wrong with** the car?*

→ For more about prepositions, see Section 21.
→ For more about prepositions with verbs, see page 141.

common expressions beginning with prepositions

***at** a party* ***at** the cinema* ***at** the theatre*
***at** the top* ***at** the bottom* ***at** the side*
***at** the beginning* ***at** the end of something* ***in** the end* (= 'finally', 'after a long time')

***by** car/bus/train* etc (**BUT** ***on** foot*)
*a book **by** Dickens* *an opera **by** Mozart*

***for** example*

***in** a raincoat/dress/hat*
***in** the rain/snow*
***in** the sky* ***in** the world*
***in** a picture*
***in** the middle*
***in** a loud/quiet voice*
*write **in** pen/pencil*
***in** my opinion*
***in** time* (= 'not late') ***on** time* (= 'at just the right time; not late or early')

***on** the phone* ***on** the radio* ***on** TV*
***on** page 22*

→ For expressions without articles like *in hospital, at university*, see page 162.

appendix 8 word problems

This section tells you about some words that are difficult to use correctly. We explain some other word problems in other sections of the book: see the Index.

after We **don't** usually say ***and after***, *X happened*. We prefer ***afterwards*** or ***after that***.
*We had a pizza, and **afterwards / after that** we went skating.* (NOT … ~~*and after, we went*~~ …)

ago ***Ago*** goes **after** a time expression. Compare *ago* with *for* and *since* (see page 65).
*It's August 1st. I came here **three months ago**. I've lived here **for three months, since May**.*

another is one word.
*Would you like **another** glass?* (NOT … ~~*an other glass.*~~)

as and *like* (similarity) To say that things are **similar**, we normally use ***like***. But before **subject + verb**, we prefer ***as*** in a formal style.
*Your sister looks **like you**.*   *Pronounce it **like I do*** (informal) / ***as I do*** (formal).

as, not *like* (jobs) To talk about the **jobs** that people or things do, use ***as***, not *like*.
*He's working **as** a waiter.* (NOT ~~*He's working like a waiter.*~~)   *I used my shoe **as** a hammer.*

born We say that somebody ***is/was born*** (passive).
*I **was born** in London.*   *Thousands of deaf children **are born** every year.*

do and *make* Common expressions with ***do*** and ***make***:
***do** work, a job, shopping, washing, ironing, business; **do** something, nothing, anything, everything*
***make** a suggestion, a decision, a phone call, a noise, a journey, a mistake, money, a bed, a fire, love*

do + …ing Common expressions:
***do** the shopping; **do** some (a lot of / a bit of) walking, swimming, reading, climbing, sailing, skiing*

else We use ***else*** to mean ***other*** after ***something, anything, somebody, nobody*** etc.
***Something else** to drink?*   ***Nobody else** cooks like you.*

ever is used mostly in **questions**, or with **present perfect + superlative**.
*Do you **ever** play golf?*   *Have you **ever** been to Ireland?*
*This is the best film I've **ever** seen.*   *She says he's the nicest boy she's **ever** met.*

explain is **not** used with **two objects** (see page 144).
Can you explain this word to me? (NOT ~~*Can you explain me this word?*~~)

forget see *remember*.

hear and *listen to* We can **hear** something **without trying**. When we **listen to** something, we **want** to hear it.
*Suddenly **I heard** a noise in the garden.*   ***Are** you **listening to** me?* (NOT … ~~*listening me?*~~)

We often use ***can*** with ***hear***.
*I **could hear** Mary and John talking in the kitchen.*

home We **leave out *to*** before ***home***.
*Well, goodnight, I'm going **home**.* (BUT *Is anybody **at home**?*)

hope We often use ***so*** and ***not*** after ***hope***.
*'Is David coming tomorrow?' 'I **hope so**.'*   *'Do you think it will rain?' 'I **hope not**.'*

if and *when* We use ***if*** for things that **may happen**, and ***when*** for things that **will happen**.
***If** I live to be 100 …*   ***If** it rains today …*   ***When** I die …*   ***When** it gets dark …*

just has several meanings: 1) ***right now***   2) ***a short time ago*** (with present perfect, see page 64)
3) ***exactly***   4) ***really***   5) ***only***
1) *I'll phone you later. We're **just** having lunch.*   2) *Aunt Daphne has **just** arrived.*   3) *It's **just** four o'clock.*
4) *I **just** love your dress.*   5) *'Put those chocolates down!' 'I was **just** looking at them, Mum.'*

let and *make* If I **let** you do something, I say that you **can** do it. If I **make** you do it, I say that you **must**. After ***let*** and ***make***, we use **object + infinitive without *to***.
*Her parents **let** her go to the party. But they **made** her come home at midnight.*

***remember* and *forget* + infinitive (with *to*)** look towards the **future**: things that one **has to do**.
***remember* and *forget* + *-ing* form** look back to the **past**: things that one **has done**.

*I must **remember to buy** bread.* *She always **forgets to close** the door.*
*I **remember seeing** the Queen when I was six.* *I'll never **forget meeting** you.*

same We normally use ***the*** with ***same***; and we say ***the same as*** … (**NOT** ~~*the same like*~~ …).

*We had **the same** idea.* (**NOT** … ~~*a same idea*~~ **OR** … ~~*same idea*~~) *Her shoes are **the same as** mine.*

see* and *hear* + object + infinitive (without *to*)/…*ing If you **see/hear somebody do something**, you see/hear a **complete action**. If you **see/hear somebody doing something**, they are **in the middle** of doing it.

*I **saw her go** into John's house.* *I **heard her play** Beethoven's violin concerto on the radio.*
*I looked up and **saw Leo talking** to Zoe.* *I walked past Anna's room and **heard her crying**.*

see, look* and *watch We can **see** something **without trying**. When we **look at** something, we **want** to see it.

I saw Bill in the supermarket yesterday. *Look at that bird!* (**NOT** ~~*Look that bird!*~~)

We often use ***can*** with ***see***.

*On the left of the photo you **can see** my grandmother.*

We **watch** things that **move, change** or **happen**.

*We **watch** TV most evenings.* *Did you **watch** the football match?*
*The police are **watching** him to see where he goes.*

so* and *such We use ***so*** + **adjective without a noun**, and ***such*** when **there is a noun**.

so** kind* ***so** big* ***such** kind **people ***such** a big **mistake*** ***such** a **fool***

still, yet* and *already We use ***still*** to say that something **is continuing**; ***yet*** to **ask** if it **has happened** (or to say it **hasn't**); ***already*** to say it **has happened earlier** than we expected.

*Granny's **still** on the phone.* *'Has the postman come **yet**?' 'No, not **yet**.'*
*I've **already** spent the week's money, and it's only Tuesday.*

than, as* and *that Use ***than*** after **comparatives** (see page 223); ***as*** in the structure ***as … as*** (see page 228); ***that*** after ***say***, ***think*** etc and as a **relative pronoun** (see page 256).

*She's **taller than** me.* *It's **as cold as** ice.* *The boss **says that** you're right.*
*Who's the woman **that** just came in?*

think We often use ***so*** after ***think***. **Don't** use an **infinitive** after ***think***.

*'Are you coming to the party?' 'I **think so**.'* *'Is it raining?' 'I don't **think so**.'*
*I'm **thinking of going** to America.* (**NOT** ~~*I'm thinking to go*~~ …)

try After ***try*** we can use an **infinitive** (with ***to***) or an ***-ing*** form. We prefer an **infinitive** when we are talking about **trying difficult things**.

***Try to stop** smoking – it's bad for you.* *'It's really hot in here.' '**Try opening** a window.'*

very* and *too ***Too*** means '**more than we want**'; ***very*** doesn't.

*'It's very warm today.' 'Yes, a bit **too warm** for me.' 'Oh, it's OK for me.'*

wait We often use ***wait for*** with **object** + **infinitive** (with ***to***).

*I'm **waiting for the postman to come**.*

which?* and *what? We prefer ***which*** when we are choosing between a **small number** of things, and ***what*** when there is a **wider choice**.

*'I'd like a pair of those shoes.' '**Which** ones – the blue or the red? And **what** size?'*

whom In a very **formal** style, we use ***whom*** as an **object** in questions and relative clauses.

***Whom** did they elect?* *With **whom** did she go?* *She hated the man for **whom** she worked.*

In an **informal** style, ***who*** is more normal in questions, and ***that*** (or nothing) in relatives.

***Who** did they elect?* ***Who** did she go with?* *She hated the man (**that**) she worked for.*

why* and *because ***Why* asks for** a reason. ***Because* gives** a reason.

*'**Why** are you late?' '**Because** I missed the train.'*

answer key

page 2

1 1 are 2 is 3 are 4 am 5 are 6 is 7 am

2 1 We're all tired. 2 They're here. 3 I'm sorry.
4 My name's Peter. 5 You're early.
6 The shop's closed. 7 She's at home.

3 1 Is Marie from Paris? 2 Are we very late?
3 Is John in bed? 4 Is the boss here?
5 Is your car fast? 6 Is Luke here?
7 Are we all ready? 8 Am I early?
9 Are they at home? 10 Are you happy?
11 Is Joe married? 12 Is this your house?
13 Is that Jane?

4 1 What's 2 Where are 3 Who's 4 When are
5 Why are 6 How's 7 Where's 8 Who are
9 How are 10 When's

page 3

5 1 she's not ill. / she isn't ill.
2 they're not in London. / they aren't in London.
3 you're not too tall. / you aren't too tall.
4 we're not very late. / we aren't very late.
5 it's not hot. / it isn't hot.
6 I'm not at university.
7 he's not very nice. / he isn't very nice.
8 she's not in her office. / she isn't in her office.
9 it's not mine. / it isn't mine.
10 it's not very fast. / it isn't very fast.

6 1 He is thirsty. 2 She is cold. 3 They are hot.
4 It is cold.

7 1 right. 2 size 3 colour 4 interested
5 wrong 6 thirsty. 7 hot 8 cold
9 old 10 hungry.

page 4

1 1 were; was 2 was; were 3 were
4 was; were 5 was; were 6 were; was
7 was; was 8 were; was

2 1 Was the party good?
2 Were the people interesting?
3 Was your father a teacher?
4 Was everybody late?
5 When was your driving test?
6 Where were you on Tuesday?
7 Why were all the windows open?
8 Was John's brother at school with you?

3 1 weren't late. 2 wasn't a teacher.
3 wasn't with Anna 4 weren't well
5 weren't in England 6 wasn't good
7 weren't in their hotel 8 wasn't warm

page 5

1 It will be hot in Rio. It will be warm in Paris.
It will be cold in London. It will be very cold in Moscow.

2 1 I won't be sorry.
2 It will be hot.
3 We will be at home.
4 The shops won't be closed.
5 He won't be in Scotland.
6 Lisa won't be at school.

3 1 When will your father be in England?
2 Will Ann be at the party with John?
3 Will everybody be here at 8.00?
4 Will the train be late again?
5 When will Joe and Mary be in the office?
6 Will the weather be good tomorrow?
7 Where will you be on Tuesday?

page 6

2 1 Is there a doctor here?
2 Are there any trains to London from this station?
3 Was there a special price for students?
4 Were there any mistakes in my letter?
5 Is there much money in your bank account?
6 How many students are there in your class?
7 Were there many children at the swimming pool?
8 How many people were there at the party?

In these answers, we usually give **either** contracted forms (for example *I'm, don't*) **or** full forms (for example *I am, do not*). Normally both are correct.

page 7

1 1 there will be sun 2 There will be two new students 3 There will be ten people 4 there will be (enough) food 5 There will be fish 6 There will be (a new) hospital 7 There will be trouble 8 There will be (a lot of) flowers

2 1 There will not be a meeting tomorrow. 2 There will not be any trains on Sunday. 3 There will not be any buses at 4 o'clock in the morning. 4 If you get up late tomorrow, there will not be any breakfast. 5 There will not be anybody at home tomorrow evening. 6 There will not be any children at the party. 7 There will not be a French lesson on Monday evening. 8 There will not be time to have lunch today.

3 1 Will there be trains? 2 Will there be computers? 3 Will there be good food? 4 Will there be different countries? 5 Will there be governments? 6 Will there be a lot of problems?

page 8

1 1 My father 2 we all 3 have 4 has 5 Paul 6 have 7 has 8 Susie and Mick

3 1 have a garden. 2 Do they have any children? 3 Does Peter have a cold? 4 My aunt doesn't have a dog. 5 Does Monica have any brothers or sisters? 6 I don't have enough money. 7 Does Laura have a boyfriend? 8 Why do you have two cars?

page 9

1 1 She didn't have a computer. 2 She had very fair hair. 3 She didn't have lots of friends. 4 She didn't have many nice clothes. 5 Did she have her own room?

3 1 He will have a job. 2 He won't have a bicycle. 3 He will have a car. 4 Will he have a house? 5 Will he have a girlfriend? 6 He won't have old clothes. 7 He will have a suit. 8 Will he have a guitar?

page 10

1 1 had dinner 2 has coffee 3 have a baby 4 have a shower 5 have toast 6 have a game

2 1 do you have lunch 2 She didn't have a good trip. 3 didn't have a shower. 4 Did you have a good flight? 5 'Did you have a good game?' 6 I don't have coffee

page 11

1 1 He's got two brothers. 2 He hasn't got a car. 3 He's got three dogs. 4 He's got a dictionary. 5 He hasn't got long hair. 6 He hasn't got any sisters.

3 1 Have they got a big garden? 2 Has Beth got a good job? 3 Has Tom got a big car? 4 Have they got a plane? 5 Have they got any horses?

page 12

1 1 They weren't ready. 2 We're all here. 3 I'm not a student. 4 Where's your house? 5 She won't be late. 6 You've got my keys. 7 I haven't got much time. 8 Franz doesn't live here.

2 1 Tom is late. 2 I will not have time. 3 Anna is hungry. 4 He does not have a car. 5 She has got two sisters. 6 She is right. 7 Emma has got beautiful eyes. 8 There is a letter for you.

3 1 Is he from Beijing? No, he's not / he isn't from Beijing. 2 Was he in bed? No, he wasn't in bed. 3 Will we be very late? No, we won't be very late. 4 Is it very big? No, it's not / it isn't very big. 5 Were they at university? No, they weren't at university. 6 Was she in her office? No, she wasn't in her office. 7 Will they have coffee? No, they won't have coffee. 8 Are they happy? No, they're not / they aren't happy.

4 1 do 2 Does 3 does 4 Do 5 do 6 does 7 do 8 Does

5 1 there will be 2 Is there 3 There was 4 are there 5 there weren't 6 Were there 7 There are 8 There won't be 9 Was there 10 Will there be

page 13

7 1 is 2 is 3 are 4 has 5 was 6 were not 7 did not have 8 was 9 is 10 has 11 has 12 is 13 is 14 is 15 has 16 does not have 17 has 18 is 19 has 20 has

8 1 true 2 false 3 true 4 true 5 false 6 true 7 false 8 false 9 false 10 true

page 14

1 1 Where 2 I 3 Are 4 has 5 is 6 am 7 won't 8 am 9 is 10 is 11 have 12 Does 13 Have 14 Will you be 15 I'm not 16 How 17 have 18 will be 19 have 20 are

2 1 ✓, ✗, ✓, ✓ 2 ✗ 3 ✗ 4 ✓ 5 ✗ 6 ✗ 7 ✓ 8 ✗ 9 ✓ 10 ✗

3 1 Is there a taxi outside? 2 Has Chris got a headache? 3 Joe doesn't have a car.
4 Did Ann have a meeting yesterday?
5 I didn't have coffee for breakfast.
6 Will there be an English lesson tomorrow?
7 I'm not hungry. 8 Petra hasn't got a new car.
9 Did she have a nice time at the party?
10 Has the house got a big garden?

4 1 Is Rosemary from London? 2 Will we be early? 3 Was Sarah at home? 4 Does Karim have / Has Karim got a cold? 5 Is your car fast? 6 Will the manager be in America? 7 Were Tim and Anna students? 8 What time will you have lunch today? 9 Will you be here tomorrow? 10 Were those people American?

page 16

1 + -*S*: cooks, drinks, lives, reads, runs, smokes, stands, starts, writes + -es: fetches, fixes, misses, pushes, touches, watches, wishes

2 + -*S*: enjoys, plays, stays, tries
-*Y* > -*IES*: copies, fries, marries, studies

3 1 I live in that house. 2 Kim works in a bank. 3 Claire plays the violin very badly. 4 Those children come from Scotland. 5 You look very young.

4 1 The boss 2 I 3 Bread 4 Andy 5 Sophy and Ian 6 You 7 Our cat 8 That child 9 All those buses 10 My father

page 17

1 1 play 2 speaks 3 ask 4 goes 5 make 6 forget 7 listen 8 lives 9 watch 10 get

2 1 thinks; knows 2 studies 3 tries 4 wear 5 washes 6 work 7 says 8 sits 9 watches 10 want

page 18

1 1 You do not speak very good Chinese.
2 Bill / He does not play the guitar very well.
3 We do not agree about holidays.
4 George and Andrew do not live near me.
5 My father / He does not write poetry.
6 Barbara / She does not live in London.
7 Henry / He does not like parties.

2 1 doesn't stop at Cardiff. 2 I don't like pop music. 3 He / Peter doesn't remember faces very well. 4 We don't know his wife. 5 She / Alice doesn't teach mathematics. 6 They / The children don't play hockey on Mondays. 7 They / The shops don't open on Sunday afternoons.

3 1 Our cat doesn't / does not like fish.
2 Melinda doesn't / does not speak Russian.
3 I don't / do not remember your phone number.
4 Oranges don't / do not grow in Britain.
5 The postman doesn't / does not come on Sundays.
6 We don't / do not play much tennis.

page 19

4 1 don't like 2 doesn't speak
3 don't remember 4 don't know
5 doesn't want 6 don't want 7 doesn't work
8 don't think

page 20

1 1 Does 2 Do 3 Do 4 Does
5 Does 6 Do

In these answers, we usually give **either** contracted forms (for example *I'm, don't*) **or** full forms (for example *I am, do not*). Normally both are correct.

2 1 Does the Oxford bus stop here?
2 Do the teachers know her?
3 Do you play the piano?
4 Does John work in a restaurant?
5 Does this train stop at York?
6 Do we need more eggs?
7 Does Fatima like parties?
8 Does Peter speak Spanish well?

3 1 your children 2 the lesson 3 you
4 the holiday 5 those women 6 you

page 21

4 1 Where do 2 What does 3 When do
4 Why does 5 How many … does 6 How do

5 1 What do you want? 2 What does this word mean? 3 What time does the film start?
4 How much do those shoes cost? 5 Why does she need money? 6 How does this camera work? 7 Where do you buy your meat?
8 Who do you want to see?

6 1 How do you spell that? 2 What do you do?
3 What does this word mean? / How do you pronounce this word? 4 What time does the train arrive? 5 How much does it cost / do they cost? 6 Do you know Anna? 7 How do you do? 8 What time does the film start?

page 22

1 1 does 2 My cats 3 doesn't 4 stops
5 do English people 6 open 7 your holiday start 8 play 9 That café 10 say

2 1 I don't like getting up early.
2 Do you want something to drink?
3 Dan plays football on Saturdays.
4 Do you remember her phone number?
5 That clock doesn't work.
6 She often flies to Paris on business.
7 It doesn't rain much here in summer.
8 Do elephants eat meat?
9 Does he think he can sing?
10 We need a new car.

page 23

1 1 are talking 2 is eating 3 is cooking
4 am not enjoying 5 am reading
6 is not raining 7 are not listening
8 am feeling 9 is not going 10 are learning

2 cleaning, coming, dying, enjoying, going, living, making, playing, singing, starting, washing, writing

3 getting, feeling, putting, hitting, jumping, raining, robbing, shopping, shouting, sitting, slimming, dreaming, standing, talking, turning, answering, opening, visiting, forgetting

page 24

1 1 The baby's crying again.
2 It's snowing hard.
3 You're looking very beautiful today.
4 Your coffee's getting cold.
5 I'm playing a lot of football this year.
6 We're waiting for a phone call.
7 Chris and Helen are spending a week in France.

2 1 She's washing 2 She's brushing
3 She's listening 4 She's drinking
5 She's reading 6 She's brushing
7 She's reading 8 She's opening
9 She's going

page 25

1 1 He's not / He isn't listening to me. 2 I'm not working today. 3 It's not / It isn't raining now.
4 She's not / She isn't wearing a coat. 5 John's students aren't learning very much. 6 We're not / We aren't enjoying this film. 7 You're not / You aren't eating much these days. 8 I'm not expecting to pass the exam. 9 My computer's not / My computer isn't working. 10 I'm not playing much tennis these days.

2 1 he's not / he isn't playing well today.
2 they're not / they aren't living in London.
3 it's not / it isn't running well.
4 I'm not enjoying it.
5 the sun's not / the sun isn't shining.
6 I'm not studying at university.
7 she's not / she isn't singing just now.
8 I'm not sleeping well these days.
9 we're not / we aren't having a good time.
10 I'm not crying because of you.

3 1 The train's not/ The train isn't moving. 2 The children aren't listening. 3 It's not / It isn't raining. 4 The cat's not / The cat isn't eating.
5 John's not / John isn't working.

page 26

1 1 Are you waiting for somebody? 2 Is your boyfriend enjoying the concert? 3 Are those men taking our car? 4 Are you talking to me? 5 Is it snowing? 6 Are we going too fast? 7 Is your computer working? 8 Are you reading that newspaper? 9 Is the bus coming? 10 Is somebody cooking lunch?

2 1 '… what is he writing?' 2 'Why is it stopping?' 3 'What are they studying?' 4 'What game are they playing?' 5 '… Where are you going?' 6 'Who is she telephoning?' 7 'What is it/he/she eating?' 8 'Where is she working?' 9 'What are you cooking?' 10 'Where are you living?'

3 1 Where are you going now? 2 Why is Anne crying? 3 What/Why is he writing? 4 Who/Why are you telephoning? 5 Where are they living? 6 Where/Why is your brother studying English? 7 What/Why are you cooking? 8 Why are those people looking at me? 9 What is the dog eating? 10 What are the children doing?

page 27

1
1 Are you getting up?
2 It's raining again.
3 You aren't / You're not listening.
4 Where are you going?
5 Am I talking too fast?
6 I'm not enjoying this film.
7 Why are those people laughing at me?
8 I'm not cooking this for you.
9 What are you drinking?
10 The baby's eating the newspaper.

2
1 Peter's trying to save money.
2 Why are those children crying?
3 Are your friends playing football this afternoon?
4 She's not / She isn't looking very well today.
5 I think she's making a big mistake.
6 You're not / You aren't wearing your usual glasses.
7 I'm starting to learn Spanish.
8 Is the 10.15 train running today?
9 David's not / David isn't living with his parents any more.
10 What are you doing in my room?

3 1 is snowing 2 is looking 3 is wearing 4 is not wearing 5 is walking 6 are looking 7 are trying 8 are stopping 9 is returning 10 is kissing 11 is (he) saying

page 28

1 SIMPLE PRESENT: nearly always, on Fridays, very often, when I'm tired
PRESENT PROGRESSIVE: just now, these days, this afternoon, today

2
1 eat; is not eating grass.
2 fly; plane is not flying.
3 rains; it is not raining.
4 works; he/John is not working hard
5 plays; she/Ann is not playing tennis
6 speaks; he/John is not speaking English now.
7 drives; he/Bill is not driving a bus now.
8 sells; this shop / it is not selling books now.
9 plays; is not playing the piano now.
10 writes; he/Simon is not writing poetry now.
11 chase; dog is not chasing cats now.

page 29

3 1 is she working 2 Does it rain 3 don't speak 4 is getting 5 Do you play 6 are you writing 7 She's coming 8 I'm going 9 boils 10 Is that water boiling 11 Is the bus coming 12 talks; never listens. 13 He writes 14 it's getting 15 do you see your parents 16 He's coming back 17 Does John drive 18 'm waiting for 19 are you looking 20 do you like.

page 30

1 1 What does this word mean? 2 Rob doesn't want to see the doctor. 3 She loves me. 4 Peter seems tired. 5 We don't need a new car. 6 Do you know that man? 7 I hate this cold weather. 8 Do you like this music? 9 I don't remember her address. 10 Do you understand this letter?

2 1 don't understand. 2 prefer 3 like 4 Do (we) need 5 doesn't matter. 6 hope 7 don't remember 8 Do (you) believe 9 don't know 10 Do (you) think 11 see. 12 do (you) mean 13 love 14 hates

In these answers, we usually give **either** contracted forms (for example *I'm, don't*) **or** full forms (for example *I am, do not*). Normally both are correct.

page 31

3 1 'I don't understand.' 2 'I see.' 3 'I hope not.' 4 'I think so.' 5 'I don't think so.' 6 'I don't know.' 7 'I know.' 8 'It depends.' 9 'It doesn't matter.' 10 'I don't remember.' 11 'I don't mind.' 12 'I hope so.' 13 'I don't think so.' 14 'I hope not.' 15 'I think so.'

page 32

1 1 What 2 When 3 Where 4 How many 5 What time 6 How much 7 Why 8 How

2 1 What language do Brazilians speak? 2 Felix drives fast cars. 3 Annemarie doesn't read newspapers. 4 My two brothers both work in London. 5 Dogs don't eat vegetables. 6 Maria doesn't play the piano. 7 Does Peter work at weekends? 8 My husband cooks very well. 9 Roger wants to work with animals. 10 Does this bus go to Belfast?

4 1 ✓ 2 ✗ 3 ✗ 4 ✓ 5 ✗ 6 ✗ 7 ✗ 8 ✓ 9 ✓ 10 ✓

page 33

5 1 looks after 2 gets up 3 has 4 goes 5 likes 6 likes 7 does not like 8 lives 9 works 10 does not want 11 is not working 12 is sitting 13 is reading 14 is crying 15 want 16 do not want 17 does not know 18 loves 19 is doing 20 do you think

6 *(possible answers)*
Cathy is wearing a black skirt, a red blouse, a green cardigan, black boots and a raincoat. She is not wearing a hat. Sandra is wearing a long green dress, a black coat, black shoes, and a black hat. She is not wearing glasses. David is wearing a blue shirt with a pink tie, a grey suit, a black belt, black shoes and glasses. He is not wearing a coat. *(Other answers are possible.)*

page 34

1 catches, costs, does, enjoys, flies, has, hopes, knows, lives, mixes, passes, plays, stands, teaches, thinks, tries, washes, wears, wishes, works

2 beginning, crying, dying, enjoying, flying, forgetting, getting, happening, holding, hoping, learning, looking, making, opening, playing, sending, sitting, sleeping, stopping, taking

3 1 Do you work in London? 2 I don't like pop music. 3 Where does James live? 4 Do you want some coffee? 5 It rains a lot here. / It rains here a lot. 6 I wash my car every week. 7 Luke doesn't speak Spanish. 8 Do all your friends play football? 9 I don't wear a suit to the office. 10 How do you make spaghetti carbonara?

4 1 My sister is travelling in Spain. 2 Alice isn't looking very happy. 3 Why is the baby crying? 4 Are you waiting for the bus? 5 I'm not playing much tennis these days. 6 Tim's wearing a very nice raincoat. 7 Are you talking about me? 8 You're walking too slowly. 9 What's that child eating? 10 I'm not enjoying this concert.

5 1 ✓ 2 ✗ 3 ✗ 4 ✓ 5 ✓ 6 ✗ 7 ✓ 8 ✗ 9 ✓ 10 ✓ 11 ✓ 12 ✗ 13 ✓ 14 ✗ 15 ✗

page 36

1 1 The woman is going to have breakfast. 2 He is going to read a letter. 3 She is going to play the piano. 4 The cars are going to crash. 5 He is going to drink coffee. 6 The ball is going to break the window.

2 1 Is Jane going to change her school?
2 Where are you going to put that picture?
3 What are you going to buy for Felix's birthday?
4 Is Ethan going to play football tomorrow?
5 When are you going to stop smoking?
6 Is Alice going to go to university?
7 Are you going to phone the police?
8 Is your mother going to come and stay with us?
9 Is she going to buy that coat?
10 What are you going to tell the boss?

page 37

3 1 I'm going to stay in a nice hotel.
2 I'm going to swim a lot.
3 I'm not going to do any work.
4 I'm going to take photos.
5 I'm not going to read English newspapers.
6 I'm going to learn some Italian.
7 I'm not going to write postcards.
8 I'm not going to visit museums.

4 1 How are you going to get to London?
2 When is Monica going to come and see us?
3 It's not going to snow.
4 I'm going to cook fish for lunch.
5 When are you going to see the doctor?
6 Angela is going to marry her secretary.
7 Is John going to call this evening?
8 I'm going to stop playing poker.
9 Everybody is going to watch the football match.
10 Sally is not going to get the job.

page 38

1 1 I'm not playing baseball tomorrow.
2 I'm not going to Canada next year.
3 We're staying with Paul and Lucy next week.
4 Are you working this evening?
5 What time are your friends arriving?
6 My company is moving to Scotland next year.
7 How is your mother travelling to France?
8 I'm seeing the dentist on Thursday.
9 I'm going to a concert tonight.
10 Gary is not marrying Cathy after all.

2 1 No, he's seeing John Parker on Sunday morning.
2 No, he's going to the Birmingham office by train.
3 No, he's having lunch with Stewart on Tuesday.
4 No, he's going to the theatre on Wednesday evening.
5 No, his new secretary is starting on Thursday. OR No, he's going to Berlin on Friday.
6 No, he's going to Phil and Monica's wedding on Saturday.

3 1 Where are you going? 2 Why are you going there? 3 How long are you staying? 4 Are you staying in one place? 5 Are you staying with friends? 6 How are you travelling? 7 Are you taking the dog? 8 Who is going with you? 9 When are you coming back?

page 39

1 1 The class will begin at 9.30. 2 They'll be home soon. 3 The examination will be difficult. 4 We'll walk to the party. 5 She will not speak to me. 6 John will answer your questions. 7 Emily will be ten years old on Sunday.

2 1 What time will tomorrow evening's concert start? 2 When will you and the family get back from Paris? 3 Will you be here tomorrow? 4 Will you and your mother be here tomorrow? 5 Where will you be this evening? 6 Will the children have enough money for the journey? 7 How soon will you know the answer?

3 1 won't be; will she be 2 won't have; Will you have 3 won't find; will I find 4 won't go; will they go? 5 won't get; will he get? 6 won't be; will it be 7 won't know; will you know

page 40

1 1 'll wash 2 'll do 3 won't start 4 'll tell 5 won't stop 6 'll go shopping. 7 'll help 8 won't open.

3 1 A 2 B 3 A 4 A 5 B 6 A 7 B 8 B

page 41

1 1 The next lesson starts at 2.00.
2 This term ends on March 12th.
3 When does the concert finish?
4 We don't have a lesson next Thursday.
5 Does this bus stop at the post office?
6 The play starts at 8.00.
7 What time do you arrive in Rome?
8 The banks close at 3.00 tomorrow.
9 The next train stops at every station.
10 When do the school holidays start?

2 1 will be; pass 2 leave; will catch 3 will work; needs 4 'm not / won't be; will see 5 will study; stops 6 will drive; find 7 marries; will change 8 Will (you) stop; tells 9 talk; will (he) listen 10 will phone; get

page 42

1 1 He's going to write a letter.
2 She's going to play the violin.
3 They're going to get on a bus.
4 The car's going to crash.
5 He's going to sing.
6 He's going to go skiing.
7 They're going to start running.
8 He's going to go swimming.
9 They're going to have dinner.
10 She's going to drink a glass of water.

In these answers, we usually give **either** contracted forms (for example *I'm, don't*) **or** full forms (for example *I am, do not*). Normally both are correct.

2 1 She's seeing her bank manager on Monday.
2 She's seeing her doctor on Tuesday.
3 She's seeing her dentist on Wednesday.
4 She's seeing her accountant on Thursday.
5 She's seeing her solicitor on Friday.

3 1 'll start 2 will change 3 won't snow
4 'll go to sleep soon. 5 'll tell

page 43

4 1 I'm going to stop smoking. 2 I'm seeing Andrew tonight. 3 It's not going to rain.
4 Peter's going to marry his boss. 5 Oliver won't pass his exams. 6 You'll like this film. 7 What time does the bus from London arrive? 8 I'm not using the car tomorrow. 9 I'm going to cook steak this evening. 10 How are you going to travel to Ireland? 11 I'll phone you when I get home. 12 Are you working on Saturday?
13 Will you need a room for the night? 14 Are you going to write to your father? 15 We won't have enough money for a good holiday.
16 Where will I find the key? 17 Will you go to university after you leave school? 18 John and Sylvia are staying with us next week. 19 When are you going to have a haircut? 20 Are you going to get up soon?

5 1 old house 2 'll come to 3 bridge
4 'll come to 5 'll see 6 house
7 'll recognise 8 door 9 apple trees.
10 'll find 11 key 12 'll have 13 great time.

page 44

1 1 I'll 2 She'll 3 It won't 4 They're going to
5 They'll 6 They won't 7 She's not going to OR She isn't going to 8 I'm not going to

2 1 ✗ 2 ✓ 3 ✗ 4 ✗ 5 ✓ 6 ✓ 7 ✓ 8 ✓
9 ✗ 10 ✗

3 1 The concert is tonight. 2 Will I 3 will move
4 are not 5 am going 6 won't 7 I'll phone … I get 8 will give 9 are you 10 will the meeting be

4 1 Is Melanie seeing Martin on Monday? Tessa isn't / Tessa's not seeing Tom on Tuesday.
2 Is Mr Andrews going to study Arabic in Algiers? Mrs Roberts is not going to study Russian in Rome.
3 Will Derek cook duck for Dorothy? Sally won't cook spaghetti for Sam.
4 Is Harry going to take a holiday in Hungary? Steve is not going to study in Siberia.
5 Is Oliver travelling to Oslo in October? Monica is not travelling to Madagascar in May.

page 46

1 arrived, changed, cooked, hated, lived, passed, shaved, watched

2 stayed, studied, cried, annoyed, carried, hurried, prayed

3 shopped, rained, started, robbed, slimmed, jumped, shouted, slipped, fitted, turned, visited, regretted, developed, galloped, opened, answered, referred

page 47

1 1 I forgot my girlfriend's birthday on Monday.
2 That's a really good book. I read it last year.
3 When we were children we always spoke French at home.
4 I didn't like my piano teacher, so I stopped my lessons last week.
5 Where did you learn to speak Spanish so well?

3 1 stood 2 heard 3 opened 4 came
5 did not see 6 said 7 took 8 gave
9 held 10 did not read 11 said
12 did not speak 13 wrote 14 ran 15 turned

page 48

1 1 worked 2 know 3 feel 4 came 5 see
6 write 7 arrive 8 like

2 1 We didn't speak Arabic. 2 He / My uncle didn't teach science. 3 He / Bill didn't cook the fish. 4 I didn't take my father (to the mountains). 5 We didn't tell the police everything. 6 I didn't write to my brother.
7 I didn't like the music. 8 We didn't know her phone number.

3 1 he changed his shirt. 2 she didn't answer the others. 3 he didn't go to her house. 4 I brought some chocolates. 5 she bought a very nice dress. 6 I didn't eat the meat. 7 we didn't keep the letters. 8 they spoke German. 9 he didn't shave at weekends.

page 49

1 1 bring 2 start 3 saw 4 began 5 break 6 leave 7 speak 8 keep 9 learnt 10 forgot 11 come 12 say

2 1 did she remember it? 2 did you pay the others? 3 did you like the film? 4 did he play well? 5 did you give them any money? 6 did she write to her mother? 7 did he learn English? 8 did she get up early enough? 9 did you shut the front door? 10 did they take the dog? 11 did she feel OK yesterday? 12 did he forget the address as well?

3 1 Where did he go? 2 What did he buy? 3 Who did she marry? 4 What did she break? 5 Where did he stay? 6 What did he study? 7 Where did he study? 8 What did she write? 9 Who did she hear? 10 What did he understand? 11 What did she forget? 12 Where did she go (on holiday)?

page 50

1 1 I learnt a lot of Latin. 2 I didn't remember to buy the milk. 3 I didn't speak to her mother. 4 'Did he phone this morning?' 5 I took the train. 6 did you go to Malaysia? 7 it didn't stop at Glasgow. 8 'They saw two films.' 9 'Did you eat my chocolates too?' 10 I didn't study enough.

2 1 Where did they go? 2 Why did they give him it / a bicycle? 3 What did she say? 4 What did they buy? 5 Who did you invite? 6 What did she drop? 7 Who did he beat? 8 Why did he write (to the police)? 9 Who did she ask (to marry her)? 10 When did he live there / in India?

3 did you remember

page 51

1 1 were dancing. 2 was cooking supper. 3 was driving home. 4 was not watching TV.

2 1 What was she writing? 2 Where was he shopping? 3 What was she cooking? 4 Why were they crying? 5 Were they driving to Scotland?

page 52

1 1 was having 2 watched 3 was watching 4 worked 5 were studying 6 drove 7 walked 8 was working 9 studied 10 was talking

2 1 we were playing cards. 2 he wasn't talking. 3 it was snowing. 4 she wasn't walking 5 were you doing 6 were they talking about me? 7 were you driving 8 wasn't expecting 9 was doing 10 weren't running

page 53

3 1 was reading; jumped 2 met; was travelling 3 broke; was skiing 4 was shopping; stole 5 phoned; was working 6 stopped; was driving 7 heard; was having 8 went; was watching 9 was washing up; broke 10 cut; was working 11 left; was snowing 12 opened; were talking 13 rang; was cooking 14 heard; was working

4 1 ✗ 2 ✓ 3 ✓ 4 ✗ 5 ✗ 6 ✓ 7 ✓ 8 ✗

5 1 were singing. 2 were waiting 3 opened 4 drove 5 turned 6 started 7 turned 8 was passing 9 ran 10 pulled

page 54

1
1 What did all those people want?
2 Did all your brothers send you birthday cards?
3 The baby ate some toothpaste this morning.
4 The teacher didn't answer my question.
5 I lost my keys again yesterday.
6 Did anybody phone while I was out?
7 The Prime Minister told us that things were getting better.
8 My friends and I did not believe the Prime Minister.
9 Richard didn't give me a birthday present.
10 What time did you get up today?

2 1 we were watching TV. 2 he wasn't reading (it). 3 were they speaking English? 4 what were the children doing? 5 I wasn't expecting her. 6 I don't know what I was doing 7 it was snowing again. 8 the trains were not running. 9 How fast were you driving 10 he was standing

In these answers, we usually give **either** contracted forms (for example *I'm, don't*) **or** full forms (for example *I am, do not*). Normally both are correct.

page 55

3 1 went; was raining. 2 read 3 Did (you) watch 4 walked; were talking 5 was swimming 6 looked; was talking; was listening. 7 rang; was having 8 was lying 9 did (you) go 10 met; was travelling

4 1 looked 2 was raining 3 washed 4 got dressed 5 gave 6 made 7 didn't eat 8 went 9 waited 10 didn't arrive 11 walked 12 was walking 13 arrived 14 was working 15 was talking 16 came in 17 told 18 didn't make 19 sat down 20 started

5
1 Mozart composed 'The Marriage of Figaro'.
2 Leonardo da Vinci painted the 'Mona Lisa'.
3 Shah Jehan built the Taj Mahal.
4 Alfred Nobel invented dynamite.
5 Sergei Eisenstein directed 'Ivan the Terrible'.
6 Gustave Eiffel built the Eiffel Tower.
7 Edmund Hillary and Tenzing Norgay first climbed Mount Everest.
8 Marie Curie discovered radium.
9 John Lennon and Paul McCartney wrote the song 'Help'.
10 The novelist Jane Austen wrote 'Pride and Prejudice'.

page 56

1 became, began, broke, brought, bought, changed, cried, developed, felt, went, hoped, left, liked, paid, started, stayed, stopped, watched, wrote, worked

2 1 stopped 2 visited 3 making 4 feel 5 spoke 6 tell 7 like 8 see 9 phoned; was going 10 played

3 1 worked 2 was working; met 3 lost; was shopping 4 listened to 5 was cleaning; stopped 6 burnt; was cooking 7 was reading; came 8 lived 9 was studying; got 10 caught; was running

4 1 drove 2 I studied 3 were you crying 4 beginning; went 5 paid; left 6 shopping; stole 7 rang 8 opened 9 did you get up 10 I lost; was walking

page 58

2 1 She has forgotten my address. 2 I have made a mistake. 3 You have not shut the door. 4 Alan has worked very hard. 5 I have not heard from Mary. 6 John has not learnt anything. 7 I have broken a cup. 8 We have bought a new car. 9 The rain has stopped. 10 I have not seen a newspaper today.

page 59

3 1 Have we paid? 2 Has Tim phoned? 3 Have you heard the news? 4 Have the dogs come back? 5 What has Barbara told the police? 6 Why have Andy and Sarah brought the children? 7 What have you said to Mike? 8 Why has everybody stopped talking? 9 Have you seen Martin anywhere? 10 Who has taken my coat? 11 What has happened? 12 Where has my brother gone? 13 Why has Peter closed the window? 14 Has Judith passed her exam? 15 Has the postman come?

4 Have you seen a lady without me? No, sorry, I haven't seen your ball. OR No, I haven't seen your ball, sorry.

page 60

1 1 PROBABLY NOT 2 YES 3 DON'T KNOW 4 YES 5 DON'T KNOW 6 YES 7 NO 8 DON'T KNOW 9 DON'T KNOW 10 NO

2 1 never travelled 2 studied 3 has lost 4 met 5 've bought 6 left 7 've told 8 've made 9 've forgotten 10 built

page 61

3 1 has sent 2 have bought 3 have cut 4 has stopped 5 has given 6 have sold 7 have eaten 8 have found 9 have passed 10 have broken

4 1 … because she has lost her keys. 2 … 'Yes, his girlfriend has left him.' 3 … 'Sorry. I know him, but I have forgotten his name.' 4 … 'No, I've seen it.' 5 … 'I think she's gone to Ireland.' 6 … 'Sorry, I've lent it to Maria.' 7 Luis has found a new job. He's working in a bank now. 8 … 'We can't. It's closed.' 9 … 'Yes, she's changed her hair-style.'

5 1 gone 2 been 3 been
4 gone 5 been 6 gone

page 62

1 1 a few days ago, last week, then, yesterday, when, in 1990

2 1 ✗ 2 ✗ 3 ✓ 4 ✗ 5 ✗ 6 ✗ 7 ✓
8 ✗ 9 ✓ 10 ✗ 11 ✗ 12 ✓
13 ✗ 14 ✗ 15 ✓ 16 ✗

3 1 Have you ever written a poem?
2 I have never climbed a mountain.
3 Has Charles spoken to you today?
4 Clara hasn't told me her new address.
5 Have you ever lost your memory?
6 We haven't played football this year.
7 Alex has never written to me.
8 Have you seen Henry this week?
9 My father has never driven a car.
10 Has the cat had anything to eat today?
11 Have you finished those letters?
12 I haven't paid for the lessons this month.
13 Sally has had a baby.
14 Lucy hasn't phoned today.
15 Has Corinne come back from India?
16 It has stopped raining.
17 Has the postman come this morning?
18 We have eaten everything in the house.

page 63

4 1 Joe has changed his job twice this year.
2 How often has she asked you for money?
3 I have often tried to stop smoking.
4 Tom has phoned me six times this week.
5 My father has met the Prime Minister twice.
6 The police have questioned Annie more than once.
7 I have only played rugby once in my life.
8 My brother has often helped me in my work.
9 Nobody has ever understood her.
10 I have never wanted to go to the moon.

5 1 Have you ever been 2 have never read
3 has won 4 won 5 never went 6 this year
7 stayed 8 yesterday 9 have never seen
10 did John phone

page 64

1 1 have already paid. 2 has already left.
3 has already got up. 4 have already cooked (chicken). 5 has already finished.

2 1 Has my sister phoned yet?
2 the postman hasn't come yet.
3 Bill hasn't found a job yet.
4 Have you finished that book yet?
5 I haven't started work yet.
6 Have you had supper yet?

3 1 I have just looked at the floor.
2 I have just thought about my home.
3 I have just moved my feet.
4 I have just put my hand on my head.

4 1 She has already written three letters.
2 She has just telephoned her mother.
3 She has already cleaned the kitchen.
4 She hasn't read the newspaper yet.
5 She has just made some toast.
6 She hasn't listened to the radio yet.

page 65

1 1 for 2 since 3 since 4 for 5 since
6 since 7 for 8 for 9 since 10 since
11 for 12 since

4 1 How long have you known Mike?
2 How long have you been a student?
3 How long has your brother been a doctor?
4 How long has Andrew had that dog?
5 How long have David and Elizabeth been together?

page 66

1 1 Mary has been painting the house for four days.
2 We have been driving for four hours.
3 Anna has been working at Smiths since January.
4 Joseph has been building boats for 20 years.
5 We've been waiting for the bus since 8.30.
6 Prices have been going up since last year.
7 We've been camping since July 20th.
8 My father has been teaching for 40 years.
9 It's been snowing for 12 hours.
10 The team has/have been training together for three months.

In these answers, we usually give **either** contracted forms (for example *I'm, don't*) **or** full forms (for example *I am, do not*). Normally both are correct.

page 67

3 1 ✓ 2 ✗ 3 ✓ 4 ✗ 5 ✓ 6 ✗ 7 ✗ 8 ✓ 9 ✗ 10 ✓

4 1 She has been playing the piano. 2 He has been playing football. 3 She has been teaching. 4 He has been writing letters. 5 She has been swimming.

page 68

1 1 had worked 2 had not rained. 3 had happened? 4 had seen 5 had not got 6 had they been? 7 had paid 8 had not done

2 1 understood; had got 2 didn't play; had hurt 3 had looked; started 4 had never travelled; went 5 arrived; had already closed 6 didn't have; had paid

page 69

3 1 got; had eaten 2 met; had been 3 started; remembered; had not closed 4 found; had not opened 5 had already told; bought

4
1 When George had eaten all the chocolate biscuits, he started eating the lemon ones.
2 When I had turned off the lights in the office, I locked the door and left.
3 I borrowed Karen's newspaper when she had read it.
4 Mark had a long hot shower when he had done his exercises.
5 When Barry had phoned his mother with the good news, he went to bed.

page 70

1
1 Have all those people gone home?
2 Peter hasn't told us everything.
3 Has the postman been?
4 Has Pat spoken to Robert?
5 Tim and Angela haven't bought a house.
6 Has Emma's boyfriend forgotten her birthday?
7 Has Monica been working in London all this week?
8 I haven't phoned Joseph.
9 Have Robert and Sally moved to Ireland?
10 We haven't been working all day.

2 1 YES 2 WE DON'T KNOW 3 YES 4 WE DON'T KNOW 5 WE DON'T KNOW 6 YES 7 NO 8 YES 9 WE DON'T KNOW 10 YES

3
1 Why has everybody already gone home?
2 How long has Anna been learning Chinese?
3 Why did George close the door?
4 Where have Sue and Jeanne gone on holiday?
5 When did the President visit Russia?
6 How long has Jan's father been travelling in Wales?
7 What has happened?
8 How long has Joe been working in Spain?
9 Where did Mary study medicine?
10 Who has taken my/your bicycle?

page 71

4 1 saw; knew; had met 2 did not have; had bought 3 had already started; arrived. 4 broke; had forgotten 5 met 6 forgot; had said. 7 had gone 8 had finished; went 9 found; had bought 10 closed; had left

5 1 had 2 spent 3 lost 4 did not pass 5 happened 6 has been 7 has changed 8 have bought 9 has opened 10 have passed

6 1 swept 2 made 3 polished 4 washed 5 ironed 6 washed up 7 put 8 tidied 9 did 10 Have you swept 11 Have you made 12 Have you polished 13 Have you washed 14 ironed 15 Have you washed up 16 put 17 Have you tidied 18 haven't done

page 72

1 broken, brought, come, drunk, eaten, forgotten, given, left, made, stood, stayed, stopped, taken, thought, tried

2 1 began 2 broken 3 come 4 knew 5 drunk 6 ate 7 fell 8 forgotten 9 given 10 taken

3 1 We've known; for 2 I've been working 3 has gone; did she leave? 4 has already lost; lost 5 Have you ever driven 6 has never had 7 Have you seen 8 started; eight weeks ago 9 I've been; for 10 have you known

4 1 did (Mike) lose 2 has been eating 3 has just had 4 has been snowing 5 studied 6 have just passed 7 have you known 8 Have (you ever) written 9 lost 10 have not started

page 74

1 1 to be 2 be 3 pass 4 to get 5 be 6 to speak

2 1 likes 2 may 3 must 4 works 5 should 6 seems 7 might 8 wants

3 1 Can he ski? 2 Can he play poker? 3 She mustn't sing. 4 He may not go this week. 5 She can't visit us on Sunday.

page 75

1 1 must write 2 must hurry 3 must stop 4 must pay 5 must study 6 must speak 7 must go

2 1 … I must phone her tonight.
2 … I must go back and get it.
3 … My mother made it. You must have a piece.
4 … You must see it. It's a cinema classic.
5 … I must get up early.
6 … You must give me your phone number.
7 … We must go for a walk this weekend.

3 1 Must I pay any money? 2 Must I come to this room? 3 Must I write in ink? 4 Must I sit in my usual place? 5 Must I answer every question? 6 Must I work without a dictionary? 7 Must I stay if I finish early?

page 76

1 1 has to wear 2 have to read 3 has to like 4 have to have 5 has to be 6 have to do 7 has to have 8 has to know 9 have to know 10 has to practise

2 1 … 'Do we have to finish it today?' 2 … 'Do I/we have to stay until the end?' 3 … 'Do they have to speak Spanish?' 4 … 'Do I have to tell you now?' 5 … 'So do I have to babysit?' 6 … 'Do I have to pay it all now?' 7 … 'Does he have to travel a lot?'

page 77

1 1 You mustn't wash 2 You mustn't play 3 You mustn't let 4 You mustn't smoke 5 You mustn't play 6 You mustn't make

2 1 You don't have to make breakfast for me; I'll just have coffee. 2 You don't have to make lunch for me; I'll have lunch in the canteen. 3 You don't have to drive me to the station; I can walk. 4 You don't have to give me your newspaper; I'll buy The Times at the station. 5 You don't have to post those letters; Cathy's going to the post office. 6 You don't have to speak French; everybody here understands English.

3 1 mustn't 2 don't have to 3 mustn't 4 don't have to 5 don't have to 6 mustn't 7 mustn't 8 don't have to 9 don't have to 10 mustn't 11 mustn't 12 don't have to

page 78

1 1 He didn't have to learn Russian. 2 He had to learn maths. 3 He didn't have to learn music. 4 He had to play football. 5 He didn't have to write poems. 6 He had to write stories.

2 1 Did Adam have to pay for his lessons? 2 Did Tina have to take an exam last year? 3 Did Joe and Sue have to wait a long time for a train? 4 Did you have to show your passport at the airport? 5 Did the children have to walk home? 6 Did Peter have to cook supper?

3 1 'll have to get 2 won't have to go 3 Will (you) have to learn 4 'll have to play 5 'll have to ask 6 won't have to work 7 Will (she) have to get 8 'll have to tell

page 79

1 1 should keep 2 should learn 3 shouldn't believe 4 should eat 5 shouldn't smoke 6 should tell 7 shouldn't play 8 shouldn't read 9 shouldn't drive 10 should(n't) (always) say

2 1 'What time should I arrive?' 2 Who should I phone 3 'What should I wear?' 4 'Where should I sit?' 5 Where should I put 6 What time should I wake

In these answers, we usually give **either** contracted forms (for example *I'm, don't*) **or** full forms (for example *I am, do not*). Normally both are correct.

3 1 must 2 should/must 3 should 4 must 5 must 6 must 7 should

page 80

1 1 He can't play tennis, but he can play baseball.
2 He can play the piano, but he can't play the violin.
3 He can't remember names, but he can remember faces.
4 He can eat oranges, but he can't eat cherries.

2 1 Can he cook? 2 Can she speak Spanish? 3 How much can they pay? 4 Can you drive a bus? 5 Can you wear red? 6 Can you see the sea? 7 Can you read music? 8 What can he do? 9 Can you eat butter? 10 Can she talk?

page 81

1 1 could name 2 could count 3 could read 4 could not write 5 could tell 6 could remember 7 could not walk

3 1 Little Tim will be able to talk soon.
2 I will be able to pay you next week.
3 I hope that I will be able to go to America one day.
4 The doctor will be able to see you tomorrow.
5 We will be able to buy a car next year.

page 82

1 1 It may not rain. 2 We may buy a car. 3 Joe may not be at home. 4 Anna may need help. 5 The baby may be hungry. 6 I may not change my job. 7 She may be married. 8 He may not want to talk to you. 9 You may not be right. 10 I may not be here tomorrow.

2 1 … 'Perhaps. I may not have enough money.'
2 … 'Not sure. They may stay at home.'
3 … 'It's early. He may not be out of bed yet.
4 … 'Yes. I think it may snow.'
5 … 'We may go round to Sophie's place.'
6 … 'No. I may decide to study physics.'
7 … 'I don't know. I may give him a sweater.'

page 83

3 1 may not 2 can't 3 may not 4 can't 5 can't 6 may not 7 may not 8 may not 9 can't 10 may not

4 1 might find 2 might send 3 might fall 4 might make 5 might buy

5 1 might not finish 2 might miss 3 might give 4 might not believe 5 might not pass 6 might not know 7 might be 8 might have to 9 might not have 10 might not

page 84

1 1 Can I have a glass of water (, please)?
2 Can I use your pencil (, please)?
3 Can I have some more coffee (, please)?
4 Can I put my coat here (, please)?
5 Can I have some bread (, please)?
6 Can I look at those photos (, please)?

2 1 Could I use your calculator, please?
2 Could I leave early today, please?
3 Could I take your photo, please?
4 Could I borrow your newspaper, please?
5 Could I turn on the TV, please?
6 Could I open a window, please?

3 1 The children can play in the garden.
2 Tell the boys that they can eat the cake in the kitchen.
3 If you're cold, you can turn on the heating.
4 If you're bored, you can watch television.
5 Only teachers can park in this car park.

page 85

4 1 You can't smoke here. 2 You can't take photos here. 3 You can't cycle here.
4 You can't use mobile phones here.

5 1 Can I make a cup of tea for you / make you a cup of tea? 2 Can I help you? 3 Can I drive you to the station? 4 Can I get some aspirins for you / get you some aspirins?

6 1 may not talk 2 may not leave 3 may use 4 may take 5 may leave 6 may use 7 may do

page 86

1 1 pass 2 clean 3 tell 4 drive 5 hold 6 babysit 7 lend 8 put 9 speak / drive 10 wait

2 1 Can you open the door?
2 Could you give me an envelope?
3 Can you pass me the sugar?
4 Could you watch my children for a minute?
5 Could you tell me the time?
6 Could you possibly change some dollars for me?
7 Can you wait outside?
8 Could you possibly translate this letter for me?
9 Can you come back tomorrow?
10 Could you say it in English?

3 'Miss Ellis, could you come in here and pass me my coffee?'

page 87

1 1 What shall I buy for Sandra's birthday? 2 When shall I phone you? 3 Shall I pay now? 4 Shall I clean the bathroom? 5 How many tickets shall I buy? 6 Where shall I leave the car? 7 What time shall I come this evening? 8 Shall I shut the windows? 9 When shall I go shopping? 10 Shall I get your coat?

2 1 Shall we go out this evening? 2 Shall we have a game of cards? 3 How shall we travel to London? 4 What shall we do at the weekend? 5 Where shall we go on holiday? 6 Shall we look for a hotel? 7 What time shall we meet Peter? 8 How much bread shall we buy? 9 Shall we have a party? 10 When shall we have the next meeting?

3 1 Shall I post your letters? 2 Shall I do your shopping? 3 Shall I make your bed? 4 Shall I read to you? 5 Shall I drive you to the station? 6 Shall I make you a cup of tea? 7 Shall I clean your car? 8 Shall I phone your secretary? 9 Shall I cut your hair? 10 Shall I bring you an aspirin?

page 88

1 1 I'd like a black T-shirt, please. 2 Would you like an aspirin? 3 Would you like the newspaper? 4 I'd like an ice cream, please. 5 Would you like some more toast? 6 I'd like a receipt, please.

3 1 Would 2 Yes, please. 3 like 4 Would 5 'd like 6 Yes, I do. 7 would like 8 don't 9 wouldn't 10 'd like.

page 89

1 1 Most people used to travel on foot or on horses.
2 Most people didn't use to go to school.
3 Most people didn't use to learn to read.
4 Most people used to cook on wood fires.
5 Most people didn't use to live very long.
6 Most people used to work very long hours.

2 1 Emily used to study German. Now she studies French. 2 Paul used to live in London. Now he lives in Glasgow. 3 Grace used to read a lot. Now she watches TV. 4 Dan used to be a driver. Now he's a hairdresser. 5 Alice used to drink coffee. Now she drinks tea. 6 Peter used to have lots of girlfriends. Now he's married.

3 1 Did you use to have dark hair? 2 Did you use to play football? 3 Where did you use to work? 4 Did you use to enjoy your work? 5 Did you use to go to a lot of parties?

page 90

1 1 Can he swim?
2 Must she go immediately?
3 but he may not go this week.
4 She doesn't have to work on Thursday evening.
5 Can he play hockey?
6 Should she see the secretary today?
7 She couldn't read when she was three.
8 Would he like it now?
9 but we might not take the children.
10 I must not go to sleep.

2 1 I will be able to speak French 2 Everybody had to fill in a big form 3 Everybody will have to fill in a big form 4 Will you be able to play the guitar 5 Did you have to wear a tie 6 John couldn't read very well 7 We won't be able to buy a car 8 I had to see the doctor 9 Everybody will be able to say what they think 10 couldn't sing; won't be able to sing

In these answers, we usually give **either** contracted forms (for example *I'm, don't*) **or** full forms (for example *I am, do not*). Normally both are correct.

3 1 … You should make her a cup of tea.
2 … You should take more exercise.
3 … You should tell her you love her.
4 … You should give her a saucer of milk.
5 … You should change your shampoo.
6 … You shouldn't go to bed so late.
7 … You shouldn't tell her.
8 … You shouldn't buy so many electronic gadgets.
9 … You should practise your service.
10 … You should buy a new one.
11 … You should buy some new clothes.
12 … You should study grammar.

page 91

4 *(possible answers)*
1 Could I have a cup of coffee? 2 May I take a photograph of you? 3 Could you close the door, please, John? 4 Could you possibly help me? 5 Can you give me that newspaper, please? 6 Could you clean my bicycle, please? 7 Could I possibly borrow some money from you? 8 Can I use your phone? 9 Could you hold this, please? 10 Could you wash all my clothes before tomorrow, please?
(Other answers are possible.)

5 1 With a scanner you can make copies.
2 With a freezer you can keep food very cold.
3 With a washing machine you can wash clothes.
4 With a fridge you can keep food cool.
5 With a mobile phone you can make phone calls.
6 With a dishwasher you can wash plates, cups etc.
7 With a camera you can take photos.

6 1 She might be a pilot. 2 He might be a businessman. 3 She might be an opera singer. 4 He might be a politician. 5 She might be a lawyer. 6 He might be a chef. 7 She might be a gardener.

page 92

1 1 ✗ 2 ✗ 3 ✗ 4 ✓ 5 ✓ 6 ✗ 7 ✓ 8 ✓ 9 ✗ 10 ✗

2 1 must 2 shouldn't 3 must not 4 should 5 don't have to 6 have to 7 don't have to 8 may not 9 can't 10 should

3 1 You must phone Martin. 2 Ann might be here this evening. 3 You don't have to wait. 4 People shouldn't watch TV all the time. 5 Shall I open a window? 6 People should cooperate. 7 John used to smoke. 8 It may rain. 9 Alan can speak Spanish. 10 Can you help me?

4 1 can; can't 2 must 3 must 4 may; can; can't

page 94

1 1 B 2 E 3 H 4 C 5 F 6 G 7 D

2 1 is spoken 2 studied 3 spent 4 was broken 5 are made 6 was written 7 will be opened 8 was driving; was stopped 9 was built 10 had

page 95

1 1 is 2 is 3 am 4 Are 5 is 6 is 7 are 8 Are

2 1 is written 2 are watched 3 are sold 4 is known 5 is pronounced 6 is spoken 7 is played 8 are cleaned

3 1 is not spelt; is it spelt? 2 is not seen; is it seen? 3 is not pronounced; is it pronounced? 4 are not found; are they found? 5 is not paid; is she paid?

page 96

1 1 will be opened 2 will be spoken 3 will be finished 4 will be cleaned 5 will be sent

2 1 won't be taken; will they be taken 2 won't be built; will it be built? 3 won't be spoken; will be spoken?

page 97

1 1 was 2 were 3 were 4 were 5 was 6 was

2 1 were taken 2 were left 3 was cleaned 4 were met 5 was told 6 was sent

3 1 was not educated; was he educated?
2 were not posted; were they posted?
3 was not cooked; was it cooked?
4 was not made; was it made?
5 was not paid; was it paid?

page 98

1 1 it's being cleaned. 2 she's being interviewed 3 My watch is being repaired. 4 I'm being sent 5 my hair is being cut. 6 we are being followed 7 The engine is being repaired. 8 It's being rebuilt. 9 he is being watched 10 it is being painted.

2 1 Bills are being paid. 2 Coffee is being made. 3 Drinks are being served. 4 Food is being prepared. 5 Baggage is being brought down. 6 Money is being changed. 7 New guests are being welcomed. 8 Reservations are being taken. 9 Phones are being answered. 10 Rooms are being cleaned.

page 99

1 1 has been arrested 2 has been bought
3 has been killed 4 have been found
5 has been chosen 6 has been closed.
7 has been stolen. 8 have been asked
9 have been lost. 10 has been invited

2 1 It's never been ridden. 2 It's never been worn. 3 It's never been opened.
4 It's never been used. 5 It's never been played.

page 100

1 1 is made 2 were killed 3 will be done 4 is spoken 5 was made 6 were examined 7 is cleaned 8 will be informed 9 will be opened 10 are found

2 *(possible answers)*
Baggage is not being brought down. Bills are not being paid. Coffee is not being made. Drinks are not being served. Food is not being prepared. Money is not being changed.
New guests are not being welcomed.
Reservations are not being taken.
Rooms are not being cleaned.
Telephones are not being answered.

3 *(possible answers)*
Arriving passengers are being met. Boarding passes are being printed. Cars are being parked. Departures are being announced. Passports are being checked. Reservations are being made. Tickets are being sold.

page 101

4 1 are being followed. 2 has been stolen.
3 is being repaired. 4 have been moved.
5 have been sent 6 are (you) being interviewed? 7 have/has been arrested
8 have/has not been arrested; are being watched.
9 is being rebuilt. 10 has been asked

5 1 are covered 2 are spent 3 walk
4 do not eat 5 are left 6 sleep 7 are made
8 is not known 9 live 10 are cut down

page 102

1 1 posted 2 weren't paid 3 speaks
4 isn't pronounced 5 will be built 6 is being cleaned 7 have been invited 8 is made
9 is spoken 10 broke

2 1 ✗ 2 ✗ 3 ✗ 4 ✓ 5 ✓ 6 ✗
7 ✗ 8 ✓ 9 ✗ 10 ✓

3 1 has been moved. 2 will be opened
3 has been taken. 4 is being washed.
5 will be told 6 has been stolen.
7 was made 8 is spoken 9 are cleaned
10 have been asked 11 was killed.
12 will be done 13 will (the match) be played
14 have been stolen 15 were sent
16 is made 17 was hit; was broken
18 is being translated 19 has been found
20 will be finished

page 104

1 1 Are you tired?
2 Is he at home?
3 Must you go now?
4 Can they speak Spanish?
5 Will Derek be here tomorrow?
6 Will Aunt Ruth arrive by train?
7 Has she forgotten her keys?
8 Is your sister playing tennis?
9 Would you like some coffee?
10 Has your secretary gone home?

2 1 Do you drink coffee at bedtime?
2 Do you like classical music?
3 Do you know my friend Andrew?
4 Did you go skiing last winter?
5 Do you work in London?
6 Do you live in a flat or a house?
7 Do you watch a lot of TV?
8 Did you remember to buy bread?
9 Did you see Barbara last weekend?
10 Do you play tennis?

page 105

3 1 Does she speak Arabic?
2 Does she know Mr Peters?
3 Does she work at home?
4 Did she live in Birmingham?
5 Did she go home last week?
6 Does she play the piano?
7 Does she ride horses?
8 Does she like working with children?
9 Did she travel a lot last year?
10 Does she drive to work?

4 1 C 2 B 3 A 4 B 5 B 6 A 7 A 8 C

5 1 Did the police catch the drug dealers?
2 Have Lucy and Felicia come back from holiday?
3 When do English children start school?
4 What is that man doing in the garden? OR What is that man in the garden doing?
5 Are the buses running next week?
6 Has the film started?
7 Has John's letter arrived yet?
8 Is Alicia working today?
9 Does Paul know your girlfriend?
10 Why is Kate crying?

page 106

1 1 'Why are you here?' 2 'Where have you been today?' 3 'When are you going to Glasgow?' 4 'How do you like Scotland?' 5 'How did you come here?' 6 'Why did you come by car?' 7 'Where do you live?' 8 'When are you leaving?' 9 'When will we see you again?'

2 1 How far is 2 How tall is 3 How fast was 4 How often do 5 How big is 6 How long did 7 How well do

page 107

3 1 C What colour 2 D What sort/kind of 3 B What size 4 F What colour 5 H What sort/kind of 6 E What time 7 G What size

4 1 'What's your new girlfriend like?'
2 'What are you new neighbours like?'
3 'What's your new car like?'
4 'What's your new house like?'
5 'What's your new job like?'
6 'What's your new school like?'

page 108

1 1 plays 2 made 3 did she marry? 4 does this word mean? 5 did you say? 6 told

2 1 How many people came to her party?
2 Which train did Peter catch?
3 Which bus goes to the station?
4 How many languages does Douglas speak?
5 What sort of music does Alice like?
6 What sort of music keeps the baby quiet?

3 1 Alice. 2 Who loves Ann? Pete. 3 Who does Ann love? Joe. 4 Who loves Alice? Fred. 5 Who does Joe love? Mary. 6 Who does Pete love? Ann. 7 Who loves Pete? Nobody/No one.

page 109

5 1 (a) What did Melissa buy? (b) Who bought a coat?
2 (a) What did the bus hit? (b) What hit that tree?
3 (a) Who lost the office keys? (b) What did Rose lose?
4 (a) What does Paul teach? (b) Who teaches Arabic?
5 (a) Who hates computers? (b) What does Mike hate?

6 1 Who first reached the North Pole? 2 Who wrote War and Peace? 3 Who built the Great Wall of China? 4 Who painted Sunflowers?

page 110

1 1 Is your sister Caroline talking to the police?
2 Do all the people here understand Spanish?
3 Did most of the football team play well?
4 Is the man at the table in the corner asleep?

2 1 How much does a ticket for Saturday's concert cost? 2 What time does the film about skiing in New Zealand start? 3 What does the second word in the first sentence mean? 4 Why does the man in the flat downstairs want to change his job?

3 1 Why are all those people laughing? 2 What is that big black dog eating? 3 Is everybody in your family going to Scotland for Christmas? 4 What game are those children playing? 5 Where are Lola and her friends studying? 6 Are those people over there speaking French?

page 111

1 1 to 2 from 3 about 4 about 5 in 6 from 7 with 8 for 9 to 10 with 11 to 12 on

2 1 'What are you thinking about?' 2 'Who does Alice work for?' 3 'Who/What were you talking about?' 4 'What are you interested in?' 5 'What are you looking at?' 6 'Who did you stay with?' 7 'Who do you work with?' 8 'What did you spend the money on?' 9 'What was the film about?' 10 'Where can I get tickets from?'

3 1 What 2 Who 3 What 4 Who 5 Who 6 What 7 to 8 for 9 Where 10 What 11 to 12 for

page 112

1 1 Milk's not red. / Milk isn't red. 2 The children aren't at home. 3 Max hasn't been to Egypt. 4 You mustn't give this letter / it to her mother. 5 I won't be in the office tomorrow. 6 I couldn't swim when I was two years old. 7 We weren't in Birmingham yesterday. 8 I'm not English.

page 113

4 1 Shakespeare didn't live in New York. 2 Phone books don't tell you about words. 3 The earth doesn't go round the moon. 4 Most Algerians don't speak Russian. 5 Cookers don't keep food cold. 6 The Second World War didn't end in 1955. 7 John doesn't know my sister.

6 1 don't 2 wasn't 3 doesn't 4 haven't 5 aren't 6 won't 7 didn't/couldn't 8 didn't/couldn't 9 hasn't 10 'm not

page 114

1 1 not 2 not 3 no 4 not 5 no 6 not 7 not 8 Not 9 no 10 not

2 1 There are no newspapers. 2 There's no time. 3 There were no letters. 4 I saw no light. 5 He gave no answer.

page 115

1 1 Nobody lives in that house. 2 I'll never understand my dog. 3 The children told me nothing. 4 I have no money. 5 I could hardly see the road.

2 1 I saw nobody. 2 We had no trouble. 3 My parents never go out. 4 I looked for the dog, but it was nowhere in the house. 5 I ate nothing yesterday. 6 It hardly rained for three months. 7 Nobody spoke.

3 1 My grandmother never drives fast. 2 Andrew doesn't play the guitar. 3 When she talked, I understood nothing. 4 I don't like Ann's new shoes. 5 Nothing happened this morning. 6 There's nowhere to sit down in the station. 7 I hardly watch TV. 8 Nobody wants to play tennis.

page 116

1 1 Who cooked dinner? 2 What did Julia cook? 3 What hit Joe? 4 Who did the ball hit? 5 What does Sarah play? 6 Who plays the guitar? 7 How many languages does Beth speak? 8 Who speaks eight languages? 9 Who ate Mum's breakfast? 10 What did Dad eat?

2 1 Who did you go with? 2 Who are you writing to? 3 Who did you buy it for? 4 Who is the letter from? 5 What were you talking about? 6 What did you carry it in? 7 How much did you sell your car for? 8 What did she hit him with? 9 Who did you send the flowers to? 10 Where does she come from?

In these answers, we usually give **either** contracted forms (for example *I'm, don't*) **or** full forms (for example *I am, do not*). Normally both are correct.

3 1 Why are all those people looking at me? 2 Did Anna and Oscar have lunch together yesterday? 3 Does that man in the dark coat work for the government? 4 Is/Are the football team playing in Scotland next Saturday? 5 What are those children doing in the garden? 6 What does the first word in this sentence mean? 7 Are Tom and his sister staying at your house this week? 8 When are Emma's teacher and her class going to Paris? 9 What did that strange woman say to you? 10 When did/will Mary and Phil get married?

page 117

4 1 My father never eats meat. 2 Peter doesn't like jazz. 3 There's nothing to do in this town. 4 I understood nothing. 5 Sally doesn't play the piano. 6 I hardly go to the cinema. 7 Nothing happened. 8 Nobody wants to talk to you. 9 I've got no money. 10 I haven't got enough money.

6 1 Adult grizzly bears can't climb trees. 3 Tigers don't live in Africa. 4 The first people didn't hunt dinosaurs. 5 Spiders aren't insects. 6 Cats can't see when there is no light.

page 118

1 1 live 2 Are all your friends coming … 3 Correct. 4 Do you play 5 are you 6 Correct. 7 Correct. 8 can I 9 told you 10 phone 11 I don't speak 12 anywhere 13 not 14 Correct. 15 What are you looking at? 16 Correct. 17 anything 18 not 19 helped 20 not

2 1 Who 2 Why 3 Where 4 How old 5 What colour 6 How tall 7 What sort/kind of 8 How fast 9 What size 10 What … like

3 1 Kelly/She isn't at work. 2 I haven't forgotten your face. 3 Peter/He doesn't drive taxis. 4 We didn't go to Portugal. 5 You mustn't use that one. 6 Henry/He doesn't eat meat. 7 These people / They don't play soccer. 8 Luke/He didn't break his leg. 9 I won't be at home in the afternoon. 10 Elisabeth/She doesn't read books.

4 1 Have she and her sisters been to America? 2 Do she and her sisters like dancing? 3 Can she and her sisters swim? 4 Will she and her sisters be here tomorrow? 5 Did she and her sisters go to the party yesterday? 6 Have she and her sisters ever studied history? 7 Can she and her sisters drive? 8 Did she and her sisters phone last night? 9 Were she and her sisters talking to Philip when you saw them? 10 Will she and her sisters get married soon?

page 120

1 1 – 2 to 3 – 4 – 5 –; to 6 –; to 7 to 8 to

2 1 to learn 2 help 3 see 4 buy 5 to hear 6 to go 7 send 8 stop

3 1 not to have 2 not to break 3 not to go to sleep 4 not to make 5 not to have 6 not to talk 7 not to wake 8 not to tell 9 not to see 10 not to play

page 121

1 1 to drive 2 to catch 3 to ask for 4 to wait for 5 to meet 6 to buy 7 to finish 8 to learn 9 to hear 10 to relax.

2 1 to clean 2 to buy 3 to get 4 to open 5 to tell 6 to earn 7 to go 8 to wish 9 to make 10 to get up

3 1 E to cut 2 F to see 3 B to buy 4 C to open 5 D to dry

page 122

1 1 refuse to 2 start to 3 promise to 4 expect to 5 try to 6 decide to 7 want to 8 learn to 9 plan to 10 need to 11 forget to 12 seem to 13 begin to 14 continue to 15 prefer to

page 123

2 1 needs to 2 agreed to 3 decided to 4 tried to 5 learnt to 6 promised to 7 forgot to 8 refused to 9 want to 10 started to 11 prefers to 12 continued to 13 hopes to 14 seemed to 15 began to

page 124

1
1 Sarah would like John to cook (tonight).
2 The policeman wants the man to move his car.
3 Helen's mother wants her to wash her face.
4 Bill would like Andy to help him.
5 Roger would like Karen to lend him some money.
6 Jessie wants Peter to be quiet for a minute.
7 David would like Alice to have dinner with him.
8 Mike would like the government to put more money into schools.
9 Lucy wants Bill to stop playing that terrible music.
10 Mary would like Gordon to make the bed for once.

2
1 Her boss wants her to work harder.
2 Her little brother wants her to buy him a bicycle.
3 Her dog wants her to take him for a walk.
4 Her boyfriend wants her to go to America with him.
5 Her friend Martha wants her to lend her a blue dress.
6 Her guitar teacher wants her to buy a better guitar.
7 Her mother wants her to spend every weekend at home.
8 Her sister wants her to go to Russia with her.
9 The people downstairs want her to stop playing loud music at night.
10 Her father wants her to study economics.

page 125

3 1 I didn't tell Alan to go home. 2 I asked Fred to be quiet. 3 Do you expect her to phone? 4 I helped Joe to carry the books. 5 The policewoman told me to show her my driving licence. 6 Ann helped me to finish the work. 7 I asked the shop assistant to help me. 8 I need you to stay with me. 9 I expect her to pass her exam. 10 I need some people to help with the party.

4 1 His father wanted him to get rich. 2 His sister Isabel wanted him to be good at sport. 3 His brother Andy wanted him to go to university. 4 His sister Nicole didn't want him to go to university. 5 His brother Henry wanted him to be a racing driver. 6 His grandmother wanted him to be a doctor. 7 His friend Anthony wanted him to have an easy life. 8 His maths teacher wanted him to study maths. 9 His literature teacher wanted him to study literature. 10 His music teacher didn't want him to study music.

page 126

1
1 It wasn't necessary to phone John.
2 It's impossible to understand that woman.
3 It's nice to stay in bed late on Sundays.
4 It's sometimes difficult to say 'No'.
5 It was easy to make our children happy.
6 It's sometimes dangerous to tell the truth.
7 It's expensive to eat out in restaurants.
8 It's almost impossible to learn a foreign language perfectly.
9 It's nice to travel.
10 It was good to visit my parents.

2 1 It was nice to have 2 It was interesting to see 3 it was a bit hard to understand 4 It was very easy to make 5 It was expensive to eat 6 it was dangerous to swim 7 it was impossible to be

page 127

4 *(our answers)*
1 It's important to practise grammar.
2 It's important not to translate everything.
3 It's important to read a lot.
4 It's important to read things that interest you.
5 It's not important to have perfect pronunciation.
6 It's important to have good enough pronunciation.
7 It's important not to make too many mistakes.
8 It's not necessary to speak without mistakes.
9 It's important to practise listening to English.
10 It's important to know 3,000 – 5,000 words.
11 It's not necessary to know 50,000 words.
12 It's important to have a good English-English dictionary.
13 It's important to have a good bilingual dictionary.

page 128

1 1 to meet 2 to see 3 sorry 4 afraid 5 to have 6 to find 7 surprised 8 pleased 9 to leave 10 happy

2 1 Eleanor's silly to listen to Mark. 2 Elizabeth was wrong to take the train without a ticket. 3 I was stupid to sit on my glasses. 4 I was wrong to wash a white shirt with a red one. 5 You're silly to believe Luke. 6 You're right to eat a good breakfast. 7 You were crazy to lend money to Chris. 8 I was stupid to think the new Prime Minister was a good man. 9 Rebecca was wrong to tell Peter she loved him. 10 I was right to stay in bed until lunchtime.

In these answers, we usually give **either** contracted forms (for example *I'm, don't*) **or** full forms (for example *I am, do not*). Normally both are correct.

page 129

1 1 is old enough to work 2 isn't old enough to leave 3 isn't old enough to leave 4 is old enough to leave 5 isn't old enough to 6 is old enough to change 7 is old enough to drive

2 1 He's not tall enough to play basketball. 2 She's not old enough to vote. 3 I'm not strong enough to open this bottle. 4 My French is good enough to read a newspaper. 5 He isn't old enough to go out by himself. 6 He's intelligent enough to do well at university.

3 1 Helen's too ill to work. 2 My grandfather's too old to travel. 3 I'm too bored to listen any longer. 4 Cara's too hot to play tennis. 5 I'm too hungry to work. 6 I'm too tired to drive. 7 I was too afraid to move. 8 Molly was too ill last week to go to school. OR ... too ill to go to school last week. 9 Our dog's too fat to run. 10 My mother's too deaf to understand what people say.

page 130

1 1 homework to do. 2 letters to post? 3 film to watch 4 dress to wear 5 shopping to do 6 friend to see

2 1 anything to wear. 2 somewhere to work. 3 nothing to do 4 nobody/no one to teach. 5 something to finish. 6 nowhere to go. 7 somebody/someone to love. 8 anywhere to stay 9 somebody/someone/anybody/anyone to help 10 something to carry.

page 131

1 1 Skiing; reading. 2 Flying; going by train. 3 Eating; washing. 4 Speaking; writing OR Writing; speaking. 5 Understanding; listening. 6 Shopping; shaving. 7 Working; resting. 8 Smoking; driving.

4 2 NO CAMPING 3 NO SMOKING 4 NO CYCLING 5 NO FISHING

page 132

1 1 C 2 E 3 D 4 B 5 I 6 J 7 G 8 H 9 F

2 1 hearing 2 smoking 3 going 4 watching 5 washing 6 closing 7 working 8 getting 9 skiing 10 asking.

page 133

3 1 Bob is quite good at running, but not very good at cycling. 2 Sue is not very good at drawing, but very good at running. 3 Mark is quite good at swimming, and very good at running. 4 Bob is bad at swimming, but quite good at singing. 5 Jane is very good at running, and quite good at cycling. 6 Mark is not very good at singing, but quite good at drawing. 7 Jane is not very good at drawing, but quite good at singing. 8 Sue is quite good at singing, and very good at swimming.

5 1 Ellie stayed awake by drinking lots of coffee. 2 Paul drank three glasses of water without stopping. 3 Charles woke us up by turning the TV on. 4 You can find out the meaning of a word by using a dictionary. 5 Mike paid for his new house without borrowing any money. 6 Helen lost her driving licence by driving too fast, too often. 7 Carl did all his homework without asking for any help. 8 Teresa cooks all her food without using any salt.

page 134

1 1 taking 2 eating 3 shopping 4 driving 5 stopping 6 working

2 1 They've just finished playing tennis. 2 All that week, it kept raining. 3 It's just stopped snowing. 4 He's given up smoking. 5 He can't help thinking of/about Annie. 6 They're going shopping. 7 She's practising writing.

page 135

3 1 washing 2 watching 3 working 4 playing 5 wearing 6 studying 7 watching 8 shopping 9 cooking; eating

page 136

1 1 I was surprised to find a cat in my bed. 2 She was wrong to leave her job. 3 I've got no money to buy a car. 4 I was crazy to give Peter money. 5 We were glad to say goodbye to Aunt Emma. 6 I was sorry not to have time to phone you. 7 I was too tired to work. 8 Here are some letters to post. 9 I've got no time to wash the dishes. 10 I need something to drink.

2 1 D to learn 2 E to watch 3 F to stop 4 B to make 5 C to keep 6 H to pay 7 I to cut 8 J to impress 9 K to catch 10 G to look for

page 137

4 1 sorry to say 2 unhappy to think 3 happy not to have 4 pleased to find 5 surprised to find 6 happy to be 7 pleased to see

5 1 They want me to buy a bike. 2 They want me to buy a plane. 3 They want me to buy a yacht. 4 They want me to buy a motorboat. 5 They want me to buy a motorbike.

page 138

1 1 to work 2 to see 3 smoking. 4 driving 5 to buy 6 to talk 7 sending 8 talking. 9 to come 10 speaking.

2 1 Correct. 2 not to have 3 to learn 4 Correct. 5 by taking 6 smoking 7 Correct. 8 to go 9 Correct. 10 Correct. 11 you to pay 12 Correct. 13 to get 14 eating 15 changing 16 Correct. 17 to see 18 Correct. 19 not to forget 20 Correct.

3
1 Anna wants Beth to look after the children.
2 Joe wants Jack to lend him money.
3 Peter's mother wants him to clean his room.
4 Sam wants Joe to go shopping.
5 Tom would like Sarah to pass the newspaper.
6 Mike's parents would like him to study medicine.
7 The boss would like Emma to answer the phone.
8 Mary doesn't want Jack to look at her like that.
9 Harry doesn't want Jim to say anything to the police.
10 Maria's mother doesn't want her to fall in love with a pop singer.

page 140

1 1 get (some) money 2 got into 3 got (a long) letter 4 Get out 5 get wet. 6 get cold. 7 get off 8 get (really) hungry 9 get(ting) tired 10 gets dark

2 1 got burnt. 2 getting divorced. 3 got broken 4 get undressed 5 gets lost. 6 get stolen. 7 get dressed 8 get changed. 9 get invited 10 got married

page 141

1 1 A laugh 2 C wait 3 B ask 4 E belong 5 J listen 6 H Look 7 G think 8 F talks 9 I happened

2 1 believe in; belong to; happen to; laugh at; listen to; look at; talk about; think about; wait for

3 1 for 2 at 3 to 4 after 5 for 6 for 7 about 8 to 9 for 10 about 11 into 12 on 13 to 14 in 15 on 16 – 17 in 18 out of 19 at 20 off

page 142

1 1 wake/get 2 go 3 round. 4 on. 5 back 6 up! 7 lie 8 Go

2 1 up 2 down 3 back

page 143

3 1 on 2 on 3 down 4 off 5 down 6 back 7 up 8 look 9 pick 10 give 11 let 12 fill 13 take 14 Break

4 1 Could you turn the TV down? Could you turn it down? 2 You can throw the potatoes away. You can throw them away. 3 Why don't you take your glasses off? Why don't you take them off?
4 Please put that knife down. Please put it down.
5 Shall I fill your glass up? Shall I fill it up?
6 I'll switch the heating on. I'll switch it on.

In these answers, we usually give **either** contracted forms (for example *I'm, don't*) **or** full forms (for example *I am, do not*). Normally both are correct.

page 144

1 1 I lent my bicycle to Joe yesterday.
2 I often read Lucy stories.
3 Carol teaches maths to small children.
4 Ruth showed the others the photo.
5 Amanda often gives flowers to her mother.
6 Could you buy me a newspaper?
7 I found my parents a hotel room.
8 Pass Mr Andrews this paper.
9 Luke has written Joy a letter.
10 I want to get Peter a good watch.

2 1 Sally gave Fred a book. 2 Fred gave Annie flowers. 3 Annie gave Luke a picture.
4 Luke gave Mary a sweater. 5 Mary gave Joe a camera.

3 1 find 2 Give; give 3 buy

page 145

1 1 has his tyres checked 2 has his oil changed
3 has his car repaired 4 has his shoes cleaned
5 has his gardening done 6 has his letters typed

2 1 She should have it repaired. 2 He should have them cleaned. 3 They should have it repaired. 4 He should have it cut. 5 They should have it serviced. 6 She should have them checked. 7 He should have it repaired.
8 He should have it checked.

page 146

1 1 B 2 D 3 C

2 1 turn 2 go 3 turn 4 take 5 turn

3 1 Hurry up! 2 Be careful. 3 Help!
4 Have a good holiday. 5 Sleep well.
6 Don't forget 7 Wait for me! 8 Have some more 9 Follow me 10 Don't worry.
11 Come in; sit down; make yourself at home.

page 147

1 1 Let's not go for a walk. 2 Let's play tennis.
3 Let's play cards. 4 Let's go swimming.
5 Let's not go swimming. 6 Let's go skiing.
7 Let's watch TV. 8 Let's go to France/Paris.

2 1 Athens. 2 to Copenhagen. 3 go to Vienna.
4 'Let's go to Prague.' 5 'Let's go to Warsaw.'
6 'Let's go to Moscow.' 7 'Let's go to Marrakesh.'
8 'Let's go to Istanbul.' 9 'Let's go to Bangkok.'
10 'Let's go to Beijing.' 11 'Let's go to Mexico City.' 12 'Let's go to Rio.'

page 148

1 1 up 2 round 3 fill 4 turn 5 on 6 Put
7 up 8 back. 9 Go 10 wake/get

2 1 Could you wash the cups up? Could you wash them up? 2 You can throw those papers away. You can throw them away. 3 Why don't you take off your coat? Why don't you take it off?
4 You need to fill this form in. You need to fill it in.
5 Please bring back my bicycle. Please bring it back. 6 Let me fill your glass up. Let me fill it up.
7 Please put that gun down. Please put it down.
8 I'll switch on the TV. I'll switch it on.
9 Can you cut the onions up? Can you cut them up? 10 Pick up your coat. Pick it up.

3 1 Alice sent €500 to her sister. 2 Sarah bought the children ice creams. 3 Let's send a postcard to Granny. 4 Ruth showed the others the photo.
5 I gave the secretary some flowers. 6 Can you find me John's address? 7 I found Aunt Patsy a hotel. 8 Take Mrs Lewis these papers.
9 I've given all the information to George.
10 I want to buy my sister a nice present.

page 149

4 1 Come 2 worry. 3 Have 4 out! 5 Make
6 Help 7 Sleep 8 Follow 9 Have 10 forget

5 1 Pick 2 Hold 3 Put 4 Let 5 fetch
6 continue 7 throw 8 Get 9 Open
10 Get 11 Kneel 12 blow 13 Drink
14 remove 15 Telephone 16 Find

page 150

1 1 A, B, D 2 E 3 A, D 4 A, C 5 C 6 A
7 B, C 8 C, D 9 A, C 10 A, B, C, D

2 1 to 2 at 3 for 4 about 5 for 6 for
7 after 8 – 9 for 10 on 11 to 12 in
13 to 14 at 15 to 16 – 17 to 18 –; on
19 about 20 from

page 152

1 1 a 2 an 3 a 4 a 5 an 6 a 7 an 8 a

2 1 an old friend 2 a big apple 3 an unhappy child 4 an early train 5 a rich uncle 6 an easy job 7 a hard exercise 8 a European language 9 a small book

4 1 an envelope 2 A calculator 3 a torch. 4 a hammer. 5 A knife 6 An alarm clock

page 153

1 1 children PC; flower SC; love U; meat U; mountains PC; music U; nose SC; oil U; photos PC; piano SC; river SC; snow U; songs PC; table SC; windows PC

2 1 – 2 an 3 –; – 4 – 5 – 6 a 7 – 8 an 9 a 10 –; –

3 1 cotton or wool 2 metal, plastic and glass (and perhaps leather) 3 brick, wood, metal and glass (and perhaps stone) 4 cotton or silk or wool 5 wood or metal or glass or plastic (or perhaps stone)

4 1 a 2 one 3 a 4 one 5 a 6 one

page 154

1 1 the 2 the 3 an 4 a; a 5 the 6 a; the 7 the 8 the 9 The 10 a 11 the 12 the; the

2 1 F a 2 D the 3 B the 4 C the 5 A a

page 155

3 1 a 2 a 3 An 4 The 5 the 6 The 7 the 8 a 9 the 10 the 11 the

4 1 This is a mouse. It's the smallest animal in the group. 2 This is a monkey. It's the most intelligent animal in the group. 3 This is an eagle. It's the fastest bird in the group. 4 This is a parrot. It's the only blue and yellow bird in the group. 5 This is a pigeon. It's the smallest bird in the group. 6 This is a spider. It's the only creature with eight legs in the group. 7 This is an ant. It's the only creature with six legs in the group. 8 This is a snake. It's the only creature with no legs in the group. 9 This is a frog. It's the only green creature in the group.

page 156

1 1 He's a cook. 2 He's a builder. 3 She's a driver. 4 He's a teacher. 5 She's a photographer. 6 She's a dentist. 7 He's a hairdresser. 8 She's a musician. 9 He's a shop assistant.

3 1 A bag is a container. 2 A hammer is a tool. 3 A piano is an instrument. 4 A bus is a vehicle. 5 A screwdriver is a tool. 6 A guitar is an instrument. 7 A box is a container. 8 A hotel is a building.

page 157

1 1 a long neck. 2 big ears. 3 a loud voice. 4 a big beard. 5 dark hair.

2 A 1 a 2 – 3 a 4 –
B 1 a 2 a 3 – 4 – 5 – 6 a 7 a

page 158

2 1 Books 2 the books 3 English people 4 The flowers 5 Life 6 the words 7 The food 8 Water; ice 9 the windows

3 1 drivers 2 money 3 understand; understand 4 think 5 think 6 things; things

page 160

1 1 Spanish; Peru. 2 Uncle Eric; Lake Superior. 3 Oxford Street; London. 4 Napoleon 5 Kilimanjaro; Africa. 6 France; Switzerland OR Switzerland; France.

2 1 Himalayas 2 Denmark 3 Japanese 4 People's Republic of China 5 Trafalgar Square 6 Mediterranean 7 Ireland 8 United Kingdom 9 USA

page 161

3 1 the 2 the 3 the 4 – 5 the 6 the 7 – 8 –

4 1 – 2 – 3 the 4 the 5 – 6 the 7 – 8 the 9 the 10 – 11 – 12 the 13 – 14 – 15 the 16 – 17 – 18 the 19 the 20 the

page 162

1 1 lunch; Tuesday. 2 Easter. 3 next 4 winter. 5 Saturdays. 6 September 7 August 23rd. 8 1616. 9 Christmas. 10 last

2 1 bed 2 university 3 church 4 hospital 5 work; car 6 prison 7 foot 8 home 9 holiday. 10 school.

page 163

3 1 G a radio 2 C a garden 3 F a blanket 4 D a hundred 5 E a million 6 A an American passport 7 J a tourist guide 8 H a stupid idea 9 I a job

4 1 Patrick and I work in the same office.
2 We're going to the theatre tonight.
3 My room is at the top of the house.
4 Would you like to live in the country?
5 We usually go to the mountains at Christmas.
6 Joe always sits at the back of the class.
7 Suzie's office is on the right.
8 I would like to live near the sea.
9 Why are you driving in the middle of the road?
10 Please sign your name at the bottom of this paper.

page 164

1 1 a 2 the; the 3 an 4 the 5 – 6 – 7 The 8 – 9 – 10 a 11 – 12 the 13 –; – 14 – 15 the 16 the 17 – 18 – 19 – 20 –; –

2 1 ✗ 2 ✗ 3 ✗ 4 ✓ 5 ✗ 6 ✗ 7 ✓ 8 ✗ 9 ✓ 10 ✗

3 COUNTABLE: diamond; holiday; price; photo; shop
UNCOUNTABLE: coffee; hair; snow; information; music

page 165

4 1 – 2 – 3 – 4 a 5 a 6 the 7 the 8 the 9 a 10 – 11 a 12 a 13 the 14 the 15 the 16 a 17 The 18 the 19 the 20 the 21 a 22 the 23 the 24 The 25 the

page 166

1 1 an 2 a 3 an 4 a 5 a 6 an 7 a 8 an 9 a 10 an

2 1 – 2 a 3 –; – 4 – 5 –; – 6 a 7 – 8 a 9 a 10 –; –

3 1 – 2 – 3 – 4 the 5 – 6 the; the 7 – 8 an 9 the 10 the 11 – 12 – 13 the 14 a; the 15 – 16 – 17 a 18 –; – 19 –; – 20 a

4 1 to Professor Anderson 2 Correct. 3 the Czech Republic 4 Correct. 5 Correct. 6 Correct. 7 I'll see you next Tuesday. 8 a passport 9 a doctor 10 Correct.

page 168

1 1 these 2 This 3 These 4 These 5 this

2 1 those 2 those 3 that 4 Those 5 that

3 *(possible answers)*
This plate is blue. That plate is white. These glasses are green. Those glasses are red. These spoons are black. That spoon is silver. This saucer is blue. Those saucers are white. This bowl is green. That bowl is red.
(Other answers are possible.)

page 169

4 1 I'm enjoying 2 will be 3 Those 4 was 5 that 6 this 7 this 8 was 9 that 10 this

5 1 that 2 that 3 This 4 those 5 this 6 these 7 This 8 That 9 this 10 those 11 this 12 that 13 these 14 those 15 that 16 these 17 this 18 those 19 this 20 those

page 170

1 1 any 2 any 3 some 4 some 5 any 6 some 7 any 8 any 9 any

2 1 any more to drink. 2 any foreign languages. 3 any games 4 any sleep 5 any English newspapers

3 1 Could I have some coffee? 2 Would you like some bread? 3 Would you like some rice? 4 Could I have some tomatoes? 5 Would you like some more potatoes? 6 Could I have some more milk?

page 171

4 1 E 2 D 3 B 4 A 5 C 6 F

5 1 buy any. 2 some tomorrow. 3 some (in front of) you. 4 want any. 5 any good 6 put some

6 1 wasn't 2 didn't do 3 didn't have 4 didn't ask 5 didn't find

page 172

1 1 Nothing. 2 anywhere. 3 someone 4 anything 5 everywhere. 6 No one/Nobody 7 Nowhere 8 something. 9 Everyone/Everybody 10 anybody 11 Everything 12 somewhere

2 1 anybody/anyone 2 nowhere 3 anything. 4 Nobody/No one 5 nothing. 6 everything

3 1 knows 2 happens 3 is 4 Is 5 Has 6 agrees

4 1 ✗ 2 ✓ 3 ✓ 4 ✗ 5 ✗ 6 ✗ 7 ✓ 8 ✗ 9 ✗ 10 ✗

page 173

1 1 much 2 much 3 many 4 many 5 much 6 much 7 many 8 many 9 much 10 many 11 many 12 much 13 many 14 much 15 much

2
1 How many symphonies did Beethoven write?
2 How many cents are there in a dollar?
3 How many kilometres are there in a mile?
4 How many states are there in the USA?
5 How much blood is there in a person's body?
6 How much air do we breathe every minute?
7 How many points do you get for a try in rugby union?
8 How much food does an elephant eat every day?

page 174

1 1 have 2 are 3 has 4 a lot 5 work 6 A lot 7 need 8 is

2 1 plenty of food 2 plenty of time 3 plenty of patience 4 plenty of warm clothes 5 plenty of eggs 6 plenty of water 7 plenty of ideas

page 175

1 1 a little 2 a few 3 a few 4 a little 5 a few 6 a little 7 a few 8 a little 9 a little 10 a few

2 1 a little 2 little 3 few 4 a few 5 a few 6 few 7 few 8 A little

3
1 There was only a little room on the bus. OR There wasn't much room on the bus.
2 Only a few people learn foreign languages perfectly. OR Not many people learn foreign languages perfectly.
3 She only has a few friends. OR She doesn't have many friends.
4 We only get a little rain here in summer. OR We don't get much rain here in summer.
5 This car only uses a little petrol. OR This car doesn't use much petrol.
6 There are only a few flowers in the garden. OR There aren't many flowers in the garden.
7 Our town only gets a few tourists. OR Our town doesn't get many tourists.
8 We only have a little time to catch the train. OR We don't have much time to catch the train.

page 176

1 1 not enough food 2 not enough strings 3 not enough seats 4 not enough water

2 1 enough time 2 enough girls. 3 enough chairs. 4 enough work. 5 enough money 6 enough salt

3 1 not loud enough 2 not comfortable enough 3 not bright enough 4 not easy enough 5 not clear enough 6 not fresh enough 7 not deep enough

4 1 warm enough 2 early enough 3 enough beds 4 often enough 5 quiet enough 6 enough children 7 enough milk 8 enough help 9 sweet enough 10 young enough

page 177

1 1 too old 2 too much trouble 3 too many problems 4 too much money 5 too ill 6 too much work 7 too hot 8 too many students 9 too many cars 10 too difficult

2 1 too low 2 too short 3 too light 4 too soft 5 not wide enough 6 not cheap enough 7 not wet enough 8 not thin enough

3 *(possible answers)*
1 too many (pairs of) socks 2 enough (pairs of) boots 3 too many pocket torches 4 not enough (tubes of) suncream 5 too many waterproof jackets 6 too many pairs of sunglasses 7 too much bread 8 too much cheese 9 not enough water 10 not enough oranges 11 not enough chocolate 12 enough soap 13 too many toothbrushes *(Other answers are possible.)*

page 178

1 1 The films all start at 7 o'clock. 2 All our secretaries speak Arabic. 3 All the children went home. 4 These coats all cost the same. 5 Languages all have grammar. 6 All the people voted for the Radical Conservatives. 7 My friends all live in London. 8 All these houses need repairs. 9 Those shops all belong to the same family. 10 All children need love.

2 1 The offices all close at weekends. 2 The lessons will all start on Tuesday. 3 Those children can all swim. 4 Our windows are all dirty. 5 Sorry, the tickets have all gone. 6 We all went to New York for Christmas. 7 The shops will all be open tomorrow. 8 We all stopped for lunch at 12.30. 9 These watches are all too expensive. 10 The lights have all gone out.

page 179

1 1 Every animal breathes air. 2 She's read every book in the library. 3 I paid every bill. 4 Every computer is working today. 5 Every language has verbs. 6 Every London train stops at Reading. 7 I've written to every customer. 8 Every glass is dirty. 9 Every child can be difficult. 10 Every road was closed.

2 1 No. 2 Yes. … to every letter. 3 No. 4 No. 5 No. 6 Yes. Every house …

page 180

1 1 Both 2 both 3 either; both 4 Both; neither 5 either 6 both 7 Either 8 either; both 9 Either 10 Both; neither 11 both 12 either

2 1 both sides 2 Both (her) parents 3 both directions. 4 Both teams 5 both knees 6 both (my) earrings 7 both ends 8 both (of his) socks. 9 eyes 10 both sexes.

page 181

1 1 not much of the milk 2 any of my friends 3 enough of that meat 4 some of the big plates 5 a few of her ideas 6 most of these mistakes 7 too many of the students 8 more of those potatoes 9 not much of my money 10 not enough of his work

2 1 – 2 of 3 of 4 of 5 – 6 – 7 – 8 of 9 of 10 – 11 –; – 12 of

3 1 Most 2 most of the 3 Most of the 4 Most 5 Most 6 most of the 7 Most 8 most 9 most of the 10 most

page 182

1 1 this 2 that 3 those 4 This 5 these 6 anything 7 any 8 some 9 Nothing. 10 without

2 1 every 2 each/either 3 everything. 4 all 5 every 6 neither 7 either 8 both 9 everybody 10 all

3 1 a little 2 few 3 a few 4 a few 5 little 6 lots of 7 many 8 think 9 too 10 big enough

4 1 Most of 2 Most 3 A few of 4 any 5 some of 6 most of; all of 7 enough 8 too many 9 A lot. 10 many of

page 183

5 1 f 2 b 3 j 4 c 5 i 6 d 7 g 8 h 9 e 10 a

6 half of us; most of the rest; few; a lot; most of us; half; some of us; how many; a lot; all of us

page 184

1 1 He spoke fast, but I understood everything.
2 I'm hungry, but there isn't anything / there's nothing to eat.
3 She has a lot of / plenty of money.
4 A lot of us were at the party last night.
5 Most people think I'm right.
6 He was carrying a heavy bag in each hand.
7 Everything is very difficult.
8 I like every kind / all kinds of music.
9 I think you're driving too fast.
10 If everybody is ready, we can go.

2 1 this 2 That 3 those 4 that 5 This 6 somebody 7 I need 8 some 9 anything 10 anywhere

3 1 all 2 Is 3 Both 4 each 5 every 6 a little 7 little 8 a little 9 a few 10 A little. 11 lots of 12 many 13 too many 14 much 15 is 16 each 17 everything 18 every 19 neither 20 something

page 186

1 1 her 2 us 3 him 4 they 5 her 6 them 7 her; she

2 1 He 2 them 3 him 4 They 5 him 6 She

3 1 They 2 It 3 It 4 them 5 it 6 it 7 them. 8 they

page 187

5 1 He has moved to London. 2 They are on that chair. 3 I like them. 4 She is going to study medicine. 5 No, it is difficult. 6 I put it in the garage. 7 I/We play tennis. 8 It is beautiful.

6 1 It's warm. 2 It's windy. 3 It's snowing. 4 It's hot. 5 It's raining. 6 It's sunny. 7 It's cloudy. 8 It's cold.

page 188

1 1 her 2 his 3 Whose 4 its 5 my 6 their 7 his 8 her 9 your 10 his 11 its 12 her

page 189

2 1 James sold his bike to Carlos.
2 Carlos sold his dog to Sara.
3 Sara sold her house to Pat and Sam.
4 Pat and Sam sold their motorbike to Harry.
5 Harry sold his piano to Alice.
6 Alice sold her coat to Michael.
7 Michael sold his camera to Helen.
8 Helen sold her guitar to Marilyn.
9 Marilyn sold her hair dryer to Tom.
10 Tom sold his dictionary to Amy.

3 1 their son Joe 2 their daughter Emma 3 their camper van. 4 her brother Frank 5 her sister Lucy 6 his sister Louise 7 his brother Simon 8 their friend Pete

page 190

1 1 theirs. 2 looks better than yours. 3 Yours looks terrible. 4 That dog looks like ours. 5 That car's not hers. 6 This coat isn't mine. 7 My cooking is better than his. 8 Is this bike yours?

2 1 The towel is not theirs. 2 The razor is his. 3 The red toothbrush is his. 4 The green toothbrush is hers. 5 The toothpaste is theirs. 6 The make-up is hers. 7 The soap is hers. 8 The green washcloth is hers. 9 The hair dryer is hers. 10 The dressing-gown is his. 11 The shampoo is theirs.

In these answers, we usually give **either** contracted forms (for example *I'm, don't*) **or** full forms (for example *I am, do not*). Normally both are correct.

page 191

1 1 him 2 herself 3 themselves 4 yourselves 5 him

2 1 myself 2 'Himself.' 3 yourself. 4 ourselves 5 herself 6 yourselves 7 themselves.

3 1 yourself 2 themselves. 3 myself. 4 ourselves 5 herself.

4 1 each other 2 themselves. 3 each other 4 yourselves 5 each other

page 192

1 Column 2: us, NOT ~~our~~ Column 3: her, not ~~hers~~ Column 4: mine, NOT ~~mines~~ Column 5: themselves, NOT ~~theirselves~~

2 1 his wife 2 mine 3 ours 4 its 5 'I like it.' 6 It's five miles 7 It's Tuesday. 8 'It's over there.' 9 They were 10 it was wonderful 11 them 12 'It was me.' 13 That's her 14 It is cold 15 I have 16 her leg 17 It is 18 Is that my coat? 19 Whose 20 'It's me.'

3 1 her. 2 herself. 3 each other.

page 193

4 1 myself. 2 each other 3 himself 4 me; myself. 5 each other 6 themselves 7 you; yourself. 8 yourselves. 9 each other. 10 yourselves

5 1 myself 2 yourself 3 himself 4 myself 5 ourselves 6 yourself

6 1 his 2 each other 3 they 4 her 5 she 6 they 7 They 8 it's 9 Hers 10 their 11 his 12 she's 13 him 14 her 15 herself. 16 them 17 they're 18 each other 19 I 20 they

page 194

1

I	me	my	mine	myself
you	you	your	yours	yourself
he	him	his	his	himself
she	her	her	hers	herself
it	it	its	–	itself
we	us	our	ours	ourselves
you	you	your	yours	yourselves
they	them	their	theirs	themselves

2 1 I like it 2 It's 20 miles 3 It's Friday. 4 his sister 5 theirs 6 their children 7 Whose 8 each other 9 enjoyed myself 10 teaching myself 11 Where's my bike? 12 It is 13 his arm 14 I have 15 made myself comfortable

3 1 him; me. 2 her; herself. 3 each other 4 ourselves. 5 myself. 6 each other. 7 yourself; you 8 me; yourself. 9 me. 10 her 11 me; me; myself 12 her 13 his 14 myself; they 15 her

page 196

1 1 + *-s*: cats, chairs, gardens, hotels, planes, ships, tables, times, trees
+ *-es*: boxes, brushes, churches, classes, dresses, gases, glasses, watches, wishes

2 1 +*-s*: guys, holidays, keys, ways
+ *-es*: copies, countries. families, parties

3 1 children 2 students 3 want 4 cities 5 wives 6 do 7 teeth 8 watches 9 babies 10 matches 11 guys 12 work 13 people

page 197

1 1 class ✓ club ✓ Communist Party ✓ company ✓ crowd ✓ idea ✗ lunch ✗ question ✗ room ✗ school ✓ train ✗

2 1 D say 2 A want 3 B play 4 C haven't 5 G have 6 F are

3 1 dark glasses. 2 shorts. 3 scissors 4 black trousers 5 silk pyjamas. 6 tights

page 198

1 love, meat, music, oil, salt, snow, sugar, wool

2 some bread; a cheque; some baggage; a fridge; some furniture; a handbag; a holiday; some knowledge; some luck; a newspaper; a problem; a station; some travel; some work

3 1 baggage 2 travel. 3 spaghetti 4 news 5 advice 6 furniture 7 work 8 hair

4 1 a job 2 a journey 3 a piece of advice 4 a piece of information 5 a piece of news

page 199

5 1 a glass 2 glass 3 chocolate 4 a chocolate 5 paper 6 a paper 7 an iron 8 iron 9 a chicken 10 chicken

6 1 bottle 2 jug 3 box 4 cup 5 mug 6 jar 7 can 8 bag 9 glass 10 packet

page 200

1 1 this one. 2 a new one. 3 another one. 4 last one 5 small one. 6 blue ones.

page 201

1 1 Alice and John's house. 2 artists' ideas 3 my dog's ears 4 those dogs' ears 5 those men's faces 6 his girlfriend's piano 7 their grandchild's birthday 8 their grandchildren's school 9 ladies' hats 10 my aunt and uncle's shop 11 Patrick's books 12 a photographer's job 13 our postman's cat 14 postmen's uniforms 15 Joyce's pen 16 the thief's bag 17 the thieves' car 18 that woman's brother 19 most women's desks 20 your mum and dad's bedroom

2 1 That big building is a girls' school. 2 Is this your mother's office? 3 May I speak to the boss's secretary? 4 What's Jane and Peter's address? 5 This is a picture of my grandparents' wedding. 6 Do you know John's new girlfriend? 7 She writes for a women's magazine. 8 Is that Robert's car? 9 Let me have Ruth and Jack's phone number. 10 What's your wife's job?

3 1 My sister's secretary's office.
2 Jane's children's bicycles.
3 Rob's family's holiday flat.
4 Olivia's boyfriend's cat.
5 The Prime Minister's wife's problem.
6 Luke's uncle's farm.
7 Mr Patterson's doctor's car.
8 The President's niece's business.
9 Charlotte's boss's wife.
10 The Director's husband's friend's mother's cousin.

page 202

1 1 Astrid's house 2 the doctors' house 3 Oliver and Carla's book 4 the teacher's car 5 the girls' money 6 Susan's money

2 1 The builder's car is parked in front of Anna's house. 2 Do you know the tall woman's address? 3 The children's bedtime is eight o'clock. 4 Alice and Pat's brothers / Alice's and Pat's brothers are all in the army.

3 1 What's your brother's name? What's the name of that book? 2 Is there anything in the children's pockets? Is there anything in the pockets of that coat? 3 You can see the church from Emma's window. You can see the church from the window of the living room. 4 Why are John's arms so dirty? Why are the arms of your chair so dirty?

page 203

4 1 a year's course 2 a week's holiday 3 a day's journey 4 an hour's drive 5 a minute's wait

5 1 The handbag is probably Aunt Matilda's.
2 The gun is probably Texas Joe's.
3 The crown is probably Queen Lobelia's.
4 The big shoes are probably Oleg's.
5 The document case is probably Mr Brown's.

page 204

1 1 business address, email address, home address
2 aspirin bottle, milk bottle, perfume bottle
3 jazz singer, opera singer, pop singer
4 garden wall, prison wall (OR kitchen wall)
5 army uniform, police uniform, prison uniform
6 garden chair, kitchen chair

In these answers, we usually give **either** contracted forms (for example *I'm, don't*) **or** full forms (for example *I am, do not*). Normally both are correct.

2 1 F office building 2 D dog food 3 A computer engineer 4 B language school 5 E baby clothes 6 G knife drawer

3 1 a metal box 2 chocolate cakes 3 a plastic fork 4 vegetable soup 5 a leather jacket 6 cotton shirts 7 a paper plate 8 tomato salad 9 a stone wall

page 205

4 1 an office manager 2 a coffee maker 3 a coffee drinker 4 an animal lover 5 floor cleaner 6 a tennis player 7 a letter opener 8 a cigar smoker 9 a mountain climber

5 1 telephone book 2 teacher's book 3 Elizabeth's journey 4 train journey 5 aunt's home 6 holiday home 7 brother's interview 8 job interview

page 206

1 1 some 2 some 3 some 4 some 5 a 6 some 7 some 8 a 9 a 10 some

2 *(possible answers)* trousers, jeans, tights, shorts, pants, pyjamas, glasses, scissors

3 1 ✓ 2 ✓ 3 ✓ 4 ✗ 5 ✗ 6 ✓ 7 ✓ 8 ✓ 9 ✗ 10 ✓

4 1 That's Peter's house 2 children's 3 boys' 4 father's 5 boss's secretary OR secretary's boss 6 Jane and Peter's 7 parents' 8 teacher's 9 John's 10 men's

5 1 a shoe shop 2 orange juice 3 a leather jacket 4 a train driver 5 a coffee table 6 a window cleaner 7 news readers 8 a computer magazine 9 a street market 10 a gold watch

page 207

6 1 a bus driver 2 a mountain climber 3 a tennis player 4 a maths teacher 5 a dog trainer 6 a glass blower 7 a road cleaner 8 a butterfly collector 9 a computer programmer 10 a bird watcher

7 1 clothes shops 2 family business 3 Joe's wife 4 sons' 5 daughter's 6 plastic tables and chairs 7 have 8 Joe's 9 bus drivers 10 chocolate cake

page 208

1 foxes, journeys, matches, books, tables, feet, people, knives, mice, dogs, days, families, women, leaves, men, children, cars, wives, babies

2 1 ✗ 2 ✗ 3 ideas 4 ducks 5 ✗ 6 journeys 7 ✗ 8 governments 9 classes 10 ✗

3 1 tennis player 2 are 3 an hour's sleep 4 women's 5 countries 6 A large one 7 information 8 are 9 flower shop 10 phone book

4 1 milk chocolate 2 lives 3 book shops 4 were the people OR was the person 5 sister's son 6 the blue ones 7 I'd like one 8 a football player 9 journeys 10 street market 11 my brother's 12 an animal doctor 13 Anna's mother 14 silver earrings 15 orange juice 16 cities 17 door of the house 18 There's Peter's house. 19 Do you have Emma's address? 20 a big job

page 210

1 1 a beautiful little girl 2 in a red coat 3 was walking through a dark forest 4 with a big bag 5 of wonderful red apples 6 to see her old grandmother 7 Under a tall green tree 8 she saw a big bad wolf 9 with long white teeth

2 1 'Good morning, little girl,' said 2 the big bad wolf. 3 'Where are you going 4 with that heavy bag 5 on this fine day?' 6 'I'm going to see my old grandmother,' 7 said the little girl. 8 'She lives in a small house 9 near the new supermarket.'

3 1 friendly 2 little 3 stupid. 4 big

page 211

4 1 beautiful and intelligent 2 cold, hungry and tired

5 1 'That car looks expensive.' 2 'Jane seems happy.' 3 'I feel ill and tired.' 4 It gets dark very early here in winter. 5 My parents are getting old.

6 1 'The train is late.' 2 'He looks Australian.' 3 'Your hair looks beautiful.' 4 My memory is getting very bad.' 5 I want to become rich and famous.

page 212

1 1 slow 2 interestingly 3 beautifully 4 easy 5 perfect 6 badly 7 happy 8 angry 9 strong 10 quietly

2 1 finally 2 sincerely 3 loudly 4 thirstily 5 probably 6 usually 7 nicely 8 wonderfully 9 coldly 10 unhappily 11 comfortably

page 213

1 1 I read the letter carefully/slowly/yesterday.
2 I bought a computer yesterday.
3 Write your name carefully/clearly.
4 You must see the doctor tomorrow.
5 He speaks four languages correctly/perfectly.
6 You didn't write the address clearly/correctly.
7 I don't like skiing much/slowly.
8 Please speak clearly and slowly.

3 1 extremely/terribly 2 completely 3 beautifully/very well 4 extremely/terribly 5 beautifully/very well 6 nearly 7 badly/terribly 8 extremely/terribly

page 214

1 1 Jake always eats fish. He even eats fish for breakfast. 2 Ann often plays tennis, but she only plays in the evenings. 3 Edward usually puts tomato sauce on everything. He probably puts it on ice cream. 4 I sometimes forget names. I never forget faces. 5 Jane hardly ever gets angry, and she never shouts at people.
6 I always get to the station on time, and the train is always late. 7 I will definitely phone you tomorrow, and I will probably write next week.
8 I usually drink tea. I sometimes drink coffee.
9 Your sister is certainly a good singer. She is also a very interesting person. 10 My mother is still asleep. I think she is probably ill.

2 1 Do you often play cards? 2 Have you ever been to Tibet? 3 Are you always happy? 4 Does the boss ever take a holiday? 5 Do you usually eat in restaurants? 6 Is Barbara still ill?

page 215

3 *(possible answers)*
Eva never plays football. Tom plays football three times a week. Eva plays tennis once a week. Tom hardly ever plays tennis. Eva often goes skiing. Tom never goes skiing. Eva goes to the theatre every week. Tom goes to the theatre two or three times a year. Eva goes to the cinema three or four times a year. Tom goes to the cinema twice a month. Eva never goes to concerts. Tom goes to concerts every week.
(Other answers are possible.)

4 go climbing 1 go swimming 8 go sailing 4 go wind-surfing 12 go skiing 10 go skating 11 go fishing 3 go shopping 7 go to the opera 9 go to the theatre 2 go to concerts 5

page 216

1 1 boring 2 bored 3 interested 4 interesting

2 1 annoying 2 frightened; frightening 3 exciting; excited 4 surprising; surprised

page 217

1 1 well. 2 early 3 hard 4 weekly 5 hardly

2 1 Daily 2 lately 3 fast 4 hardly 5 early 6 well 7 late 8 weekly 9 hard 10 lately

3 1 ✗ 2 ✓ 3 ✗ 4 ✗ 5 ✓

page 218

1 1 She was driving a fast red car. 2 She speaks perfect Chinese. 3 She speaks Chinese perfectly. 4 I lost my keys yesterday.
5 I've got a very important meeting tomorrow.
6 Anna read Peter's letter slowly. 7 Tim plays the piano brilliantly. 8 Lucy is terribly unhappy.
9 They make very good ice cream here.
10 She's been happily unmarried for 15 years.

In these answers, we usually give **either** contracted forms (for example *I'm, don't*) **or** full forms (for example *I am, do not*). Normally both are correct.

2 1 terrible 2 slowly 3 hard 4 friendly 5 badly 6 unhappy 7 extremely; late 8 carefully 9 late 10 completely 11 beautiful 12 hard 13 unclearly 14 perfect 15 well

4 careful; extremely

page 219

5 1 interesting films 2 a good cheap restaurant 3 and good-looking 4 interested 5 I very much like OR I like ... very much. 6 'The poor girl/woman!' OR 'Poor Emma!' 7 terribly 8 my glasses yesterday. 9 happily 10 have often thought 11 difficult 12 in a friendly way/voice 13 Arabic very well. 14 beautiful 15 fast 16 carefully 17 perfect 18 is always 19 usually speak 20 hard

6 1 fast 2 daily 3 hard 4 late 5 hardly 6 friendly 7 silly 8 lonely.

7 1 a light/coffee 2 water 3 holidays 4 hair, skin 5 a light 6 a bed, water 7 hair, skin 8 milk 9 apples 10 children

page 220

1 1 really, completely, possibly, happily, nicely, easily, beautifully, probably, usually, incredibly, unhappily, rightly, sincerely, hungrily, carefully, perfectly, warmly, angrily, comprehensibly, slowly

2 1 I saw a good film yesterday. 2 Andy can definitely help you. 3 You speak Russian very well. 4 She never smiles. 5 Alice had some really interesting ideas. 6 They sell very good clothes here. 7 I have never been to Norway. 8 Karl plays the violin very badly. 9 I have already paid. 10 He was wearing a new blue suit. 11 We often see Annie and Seb. 12 Emma read the report slowly. 13 Judy and Simon are always late. 14 You are probably right. 15 I hardly ever go to the cinema.

3 1 ✗ 2 ✗ 3 ✓ 4 ✓ 5 ✗ 6 ✓ 7 ✗ 8 ✓ 9 ✗ 10 ✗ 11 ✓ 12 ✓ 13 ✗ 14 ✗ 15 ✗

4 1 and stupid-looking 2 are usually 3 bored 4 will never 5 always listen 6 'The poor girl/woman!' OR 'Poor Jenny!' 7 have often been 8 terribly 9 slowly 10 is already 11 You never tell me 12 beautiful 13 has probably 14 fast 15 slowly

page 222

1 1 greener, greenest 2 safer, safest 3 richer, richest 4 smaller, smallest 5 stranger, strangest 6 finer, finest 7 higher, highest 8 wider, widest 9 nearer, nearest 10 whiter, whitest

2 1 bigger, biggest 2 hotter, hottest 3 newer, newest 4 wetter, wettest 5 slimmer, slimmest

3 1 lazier, laziest 2 hungrier, hungriest 3 sleepier, sleepiest 4 angrier, angriest 5 dirtier, dirtiest

4 1 more careful, most careful 2 more beautiful, most beautiful 3 more intelligent, most intelligent 4 more dangerous, most dangerous 5 more important, most important 6 more boring, most boring 7 more interested, most interested

5 1 farther/further 2 better 3 worse.

page 223

1 1 the nicest 2 the best 3 more expensive 4 more dangerous 5 the most dangerous 6 bigger 7 the fastest 8 most

2 1 shorter 2 the most intelligent 3 quieter 4 the coldest 5 louder 6 the biggest 7 more intelligent 8 the most boring

page 224

1 1 Dogs are friendlier than cats. 2 Dogs are more intelligent than cats. 3 Train travel is cheaper than air travel. 4 Air travel is faster than train travel. 5 The Sahara is hotter than the Himalayas. 6 The Himalayas are colder than the Sahara. 7 English is easier than Chinese. 8 Chinese is more difficult than 9 English. 9 Canada is bigger than Ireland. 10 Ireland is smaller than Canada.

2 1 The Amazon is longer than all the other rivers in South America. 2 Blue whales are heavier than all the other whales. 3 Mont Blanc is higher than all the other mountains in the Alps. 4 Cheetahs are faster than all the other big cats. 5 The Atacama desert is drier than all the other deserts. 6 Redwoods are taller than all the other trees.

page 225

3 1 is more careful than him. / is more careful than he is. 2 hungrier than me. / hungrier than I am. 3 shorter than you. / shorter than you are. 4 are more excited than us. / are more excited than we are. 5 is more beautiful than her. / is more beautiful than she is.

4 1 Mark is a bit / a little taller than Simon. 2 Simon is a bit / a little older than Mark. 3 Mark is a bit / a little younger than Simon. 4 Mark is a lot / much richer than Simon. 5 Mark's car is a lot / much faster than Simon's car. 6 Simon's car is a lot / much slower than Mark's car. 7 Mark's car is a bit / a little more comfortable than Simon's car. 8 Simon's car is a lot / much quieter than Mark's car. 9 Mark's car is a lot / much noisier than Simon's car.

page 226

1 1 F n 2 E q 3 A r 4 C m 5 B p 6 J s 7 G u 8 I t 9 H v

2 1 In the 1970s, the Beatles were the richest musicians in the world. 2 Eric says that Eleanor is the best singer in the group. 3 When I was a child, my father was the tallest man in our town. 4 In this country, February is the coldest month of the year. 5 Who is the oldest of your three aunts? 6 Helen is very intelligent, but she is the quietest person in my class. 7 Which is the best of these three bikes? 8 Which is the biggest city in Argentina?

page 227

1 1 Lee talks to people more politely than Ben.
2 Liam works more carefully than John.
3 Simon goes swimming more often than Karen.
4 My car runs more quietly than my sister's car.
5 Annie talks more slowly than Rob.
6 Olivia thinks more clearly than most people.
7 Jack dresses more expensively than me.
8 I live more cheaply than my friends.

2 1 earlier. 2 later. 3 more. 4 nearer 5 less. 6 faster. 7 higher. 8 longer.

page 228

1 Picture A is Jenny. Picture B is Cassie.
1 Cassie is not as slim as Jenny. 2 Cassie is not as tall as Jenny. 3 Jenny's skirt is not as long as Cassie's. 4 Cassie's bag is not as big as Jenny's. 5 Jenny's coat is not as heavy as Cassie's. 6 Cassie's glass is not as big as Jenny's.

2 1 The other doctor isn't as nice as you. The other doctor isn't as nice as you are. 2 His boss isn't as interesting as him. His boss isn't as interesting as he is. 3 My mother isn't as slim as me. My mother isn't as slim as I am. 4 The Browns aren't as careful as us. The Browns aren't as careful as we are.

page 229

4 1 Eric has twice as many cousins as Tony. 2 Ben eats three times as many sandwiches as Jo. 3 Helen has nearly as many computer games as Adrian. 4 Chris drinks twice as much coffee as Liz. 5 Mike has just as many books as David. 6 Rebecca doesn't have nearly as much free time as Fred.

page 230

1 1 as; as 2 most; in 3 than 4 the; in 5 better; best 6 more 7 as; as 8 than 9 more; am. 10 than; less

2 1 in the world 2 than 3 most 4 more slowly 5 most 6 than me 7 as cold as ice 8 than his wife 9 higher 10 worst 11 most intelligent 12 happier 13 in 14 of 15 the best

In these answers, we usually give **either** contracted forms (for example *I'm, don't*) **or** full forms (for example *I am, do not*). Normally both are correct.

3 1 B is faster than C. 2 A is not as fast as B. 3 C is not as fast as B. 4 B is the fastest. 5 C is more expensive than A. 6 A is not as expensive as B. 7 B is the most expensive. 8 B is not as big as C. 9 C is bigger than A. 10 C is the biggest.

page 231

4 1 more than a year and less than a century
2 more than a week and less than a year
3 more than a day and less than a month
4 more than a minute and less than a day
5 more than an hour and less than a week
6 more than a month and less than a decade

5 1 John 2 Tom 3 Hannah

6 than

page 232

1 1 more interesting, most interesting 2 thinner, thinnest 3 cheaper, cheapest 4 easier, easiest 5 worse, worst 6 more beautiful, most beautiful 7 lazier, laziest 8 farther/further, farthest/furthest 9 better, best 10 older, oldest 11 fatter, fattest 12 happier, happiest 13 later, latest 14 hotter, hottest 15 slower, slowest 16 bigger, biggest 17 more expensive, most expensive 18 dirtier, dirtiest 19 more important, most important 20 stronger, strongest

2 1 as; as 2 than 3 that 4 than 5 than 6 as 7 that 8 than 9 as 10 than

3 1 than; more 2 am. 3 earlier; earliest 4 more 5 the; in 6 As; as 7 most; in 8 as; as 9 than 10 worse; worst.

4 1 in 2 worst 3 most 4 than 5 more quickly 6 as hard as stones 7 bigger 8 most beautiful 9 of 10 the worst

page 234

1 1 so 2 although 3 but 4 and 5 while 6 because 7 until 8 while 9 or 10 as soon as

2 1 We'll be glad when this job is finished. 2 I'll be very angry if you do that again. 3 I'd like to talk to you before you go home. 4 Sue watched TV until John came home. 5 We'll see you again after we come back from holiday. 6 I like her, although she's a difficult person. 7 Henry didn't like working in a bank, so he changed his job. 8 They think they can do what they like because they're rich. 9 I want to stop working before I'm 50. 10 You look beautiful when you're smiling.

page 235

1 1 I put on two sweaters because it was very cold. Because it was very cold, I put on two sweaters.
2 I'm going to work in Australia when I leave school. When I leave school, I'm going to work in Australia.
3 I go and see Felix if I want to talk to somebody. If I want to talk to somebody, I go and see Felix.
4 Ann made coffee while Bill fried some eggs. While Bill fried some eggs, Ann made coffee.
5 I was interested in the conversation, although I didn't understand everything. Although I didn't understand everything, I was interested in the conversation.
6 We went to a restaurant because there was no food in the house. Because there was no food in the house, we went to a restaurant.
7 We'll have a big party when John comes home. When John comes home, we'll have a big party.
8 I stayed with friends while my parents were travelling. While my parents were travelling, I stayed with friends.
9 I go for long walks at the weekend if the weather's fine. If the weather's fine, I go for long walks at the weekend.
10 Come and see us as soon as you arrive in Scotland. As soon as you arrive in Scotland, come and see us.

page 236

1 1 hear 2 make 3 leaves 4 write 5 get 6 am 7 stops. 8 go 9 arrive 10 finishes.

2 1 finds OR gets 2 travels 3 will help 4 starts 5 will tell 6 look after 7 will look 8 stops 9 come 10 will get

page 237

1 1 Because the rooms were dirty, I changed my hotel. I changed my hotel because the rooms were dirty. The rooms were dirty, so I changed my hotel.
2 Because the taxi was late, we missed the train. We missed the train because the taxi was late. The taxi was late, so we missed the train.
3 Because I didn't like the film, I walked out of the cinema. I walked out of the cinema because I didn't like the film. I didn't like the film, so I walked out of the cinema.

2 1 Although I felt ill, I went on working. I went on working, although I felt ill. I felt ill, but I went on working.
2 Although she was very kind, I didn't like her. I didn't like her, although she was very kind. She was very kind, but I didn't like her.
3 Although he's a big man, he doesn't eat much. He doesn't eat much, although he's a big man. He's a big man, but he doesn't eat much.

page 238

1 1 My company has offices in London, Tokyo, New York and Cairo. 2 I've invited Paul, Alexandra, Eric, Luke and Janet. 3 I'll be here on Tuesday, Thursday, Friday and Sunday. 4 She's got five cats, two dogs, a horse and a rabbit. 5 He plays golf, rugby, hockey and badminton. 6 She addressed, stamped and posted the letter.

2 1 She has painted the kitchen, (the) living room and (the) dining room. 2 Bob was wearing a pink shirt, blue jeans and white trainers. 3 Can you give me a knife, fork and spoon, please? 4 Many people speak English in India, Singapore and South Africa. 5 I've written and posted six letters this morning.

page 239

1 1 I think that she's either Scottish or Irish.
2 I'd like to work with either animals or children.
3 He did well in both mathematics and history.
4 This car is neither fast nor comfortable.
5 She neither looked at me nor said anything.
6 I've got problems both at home and in my job.
7 You can either stay here or go home.
8 I like both (the) theatre and (the) cinema.
9 She speaks neither English nor French.
10 I don't understand either politics or economics.

page 240

1 1 will have; go 2 will wait; arrives 3 come; will be 4 will be; goes 5 get; will cook 6 will send; receive 7 will be; are 8 go; will take 9 stops; will go 10 will have; gets up.

2 1 Because the teacher was ill, the children had a holiday. The children had a holiday because the teacher was ill.
2 When I was in China, I made a lot of friends. I made a lot of friends when I was in China.
3 Until they built the new road, it was difficult to get to our village. It was difficult to get to our village until they built the new road.
4 Although Jessica wrote three letters, Dylan never answered. Dylan never answered, although Jessica wrote three letters.
5 As soon as the work was finished, I phoned him. I phoned him as soon as the work was finished.

3 1 I both swim and play tennis.
2 He either lives or works in Birmingham.
3 My father speaks neither Greek nor French.
4 She likes neither pop music nor jazz.
5 She can have either orange juice or water.
6 I can neither sing nor dance.
7 He's either Scottish or Irish.
8 He's studying both physics and biology.
9 This sofa is neither nice-looking nor comfortable.
10 Anna neither looked at Henry nor spoke to him.

page 241

4 1 so 2 when 3 and 4 although 5 because 6 and 7 because 8 and 9 until 10 although 11 before

5 1 Karl plays neither the trombone nor the saxophone. 2 Melanie plays both the cello and the drums. 3 Neither Steve nor Karen play(s) the violin. 4 Both Joanna and Charles play the guitar. 5 Karen plays both the piano and the trumpet. 6 Sophie plays neither the guitar nor the trumpet. 7 Both Charles and Steve play the saxophone. 8 Neither Sophie nor Steve play(s) the trumpet.

page 242

1 1 I'm going to do some gardening until it gets dark. 2 I couldn't read because it was too dark. 3 The food wasn't very good, but he ate everything. 4 The lesson finished early, so we went for a walk. 5 After I got his letter, I went round to see him. 6 As soon as Jane gets up, she makes coffee. 7 You can't have any more coffee, because there isn't any. 8 I didn't go to work, because the buses weren't running. 9 The buses weren't running, so I didn't go to work. 10 The phone always rings while I'm having a bath. 11 I can't tell you the decision until I know myself. 12 He didn't work very hard, but he passed all his exams. 13 When the holiday was over, I had to start working very hard. 14 As soon as Andrew saw Zoe, he fell madly in love with her. 15 After I left school, I worked as a taxi driver.

2 1 He plays neither the piano nor the guitar. 2 Although the train was late, I got there in time. OR The train was late, but I got there in time. 3 small, cold and dirty 4 I/he/she/we/they went out 5 gets 6 Because it was cold, I put on a coat. OR It was cold, so I put on a coat. 7 or walk home 8 a knife and fork 9 Although I would like to help you, I don't have time. OR I would like to help you, but I don't have time. 10 both classical music and jazz. 11 I find 12 I'm old

page 244

1 1 If I can't sleep, I get up and read. I get up and read if I can't sleep. 2 If you take books from my room, please tell me. Please tell me if you take books from my room. 3 If you're hungry, why don't you cook some soup? Why don't you cook some soup if you're hungry? 4 If she's been travelling all day, she must be tired. She must be tired if she's been travelling all day. 5 If we catch the first train, we can be in London by 9.00. We can be in London by 9.00 if we catch the first train.

2 1 You can't park here unless you live in this street. 2 Unless you're over 15, you can't see this film. 3 I don't drive fast unless I'm really late. 4 Unless I'm going fishing, I get up late on Sundays. 5 We usually go for a walk after supper unless there's a good film on TV. 6 I see my mother at weekends unless I'm travelling. 7 Unless it's raining, I play tennis most evenings. 8 I can't help you unless you tell me the truth.

page 245

1 1 get 2 will bring 3 will give 4 phones 5 have 6 stop 7 will be 8 won't laugh 9 will cook 10 stops

2 1 will be; pass 2 leave; will catch 3 will work; needs 4 am not; will see 5 will study; has 6 will drive; can 7 marries; will not have 8 will (you) stop; tells 9 talk; will (he) lend

3
1 If I lose my job, I won't find another job.
2 If I don't find another job, I'll lose my flat.
3 If I lose my flat, I'll move back to my parents' house.
4 If I move back to my parents' house, I'll get very bored.
5 If I get very bored, I'll go swimming every day.
6 If I go swimming every day, I'll look very good.
7 If I look very good, I'll meet interesting people.
8 If I meet interesting people, I'll go to lots of parties.
9 If I go to lots of parties, I'll have a wonderful time.

page 246

1 1 could; would eat 2 were; would know 3 knew; would tell 4 asked; would (you) do 5 could; would (you) do 6 would buy; had 7 asked; would (you) say 8 would finish; did not talk 9 would study; had 10 were; would watch

2 1 If Jane and Peter were here, we would play cards. 2 If we had enough money, we would buy a new car. 3 If Fred answered letters, I would write to him. 4 If I could find my camera, I would take your photo. 5 If I could understand the words, I would enjoy opera. 6 If Carola didn't talk about herself all the time, I would like her. 7 If I had a dog, I would go for walks.

page 247

1 1 If I were you, I'd take a holiday. 2 If I were you, I'd join a club. 3 If I were you, I'd fly. 4 If I were you, I'd call the police at once. 5 If I were you, I wouldn't sell it.

2 1 If I were you, I'd start a business. 2 If I were you, I'd put the money in the bank. 3 If I were you, I'd buy a sports car. 4 If I were you, I'd have a big party. 5 If I were you, I'd travel round the world. 6 If I were you, I'd stop work.
7 If I were you, I'd give the money away.

page 248

1 1 lived 2 could 3 go 4 started 5 gave 6 need 7 gave 8 thought 9 was 10 go

2 1 have; 'll 2 had; 'd 3 get; will 4 got; would
5 did; would 6 do; will 7 go; won't
8 went; wouldn't 9 does; won't 10 did; would

page 249

1 1 had been 2 had worked 3 had taken
4 had not played 5 would have studied
6 Would (you) have crashed
7 would not have slept
8 had come; would have had
9 had not broken down; would have been
10 would (you) have studied; had liked
11 would not have got; had not wanted
12 would (you) have helped; had asked

2 1 If I had caught the 8.15 train, I would have sat by a beautiful foreign woman.
2 If I had sat by a beautiful foreign woman, I would have fallen in love and married her.
3 If I had fallen in love and married her, I would have gone to live in her country.
4 If I had gone to live in her country, I would have worked in her father's diamond business.
5 If I had worked in her father's diamond business, I would have become very rich.
6 If I had become very rich, I would have gone into politics.
7 If I had gone into politics, I would have died in a revolution.

page 250

1 *(possible answers)*
1 G 2 H 3 J 4 B 5 K 6 D 7 F 8 C 9 E 10 I
(Other answers are possible.)

2 1 bought; would 2 go; 'll 3 lived; would
4 went; wouldn't 5 start; won't 6 win; will
7 married; would 8 take; 'll 9 rains; won't
10 did; wouldn't

3 1 will 2 looks; it's 3 will; will; will take
4 will 5 won't 6 will

page 251

4 1 had not drunk; would have slept
2 had had; would have gone
3 would have gone; had not met
4 had not been; would have gone
5 would have caught; had run
6 had stopped; would have lived
7 would not have asked; had needed
8 would have been; had stayed
9 would have worn; had known
10 had had; would have gone

5 … the cat wouldn't have eaten her supper. If the cat hadn't eaten her supper, she wouldn't have gone to the shop to buy food. If she hadn't gone to the shop to buy food, she wouldn't have seen an advertisement for a secretary. If she hadn't seen an advertisement for a secretary, she wouldn't have got a new job and met my father.

6 1 If she goes to Egypt, she will have to learn Arabic. 2 If she goes to Brazil, she will have to learn Portuguese. 3 If she goes to Holland, she will have to learn Dutch. 4 If she goes to Kenya, she will have to learn Swahili. 5 If she goes to Greece, she will have to learn Greek. 6 If she goes to Austria, she will have to learn German.

page 252

1 1 cleaned 2 knows 3 will come
4 would understand 5 leave 6 would not sell
7 did not live 8 will translate 9 ask 10 gets

2 1 if I pass 2 Correct. 3 ate 4 will see
5 Correct. 6 Correct. 7 he works
8 Correct. 9 if we are 10 Correct.

3 1 had not asked; would not have known
2 had been; would have gone
3 would not have said; had known
4 would have been; had said
5 had not got; would not have met
6 would have died; had not taken
7 had not been; would have gone
8 had done; would have studied
9 would have gone; had had
10 had not helped; would have been

page 254

1 1 who 2 which 3 which 4 which 5 who 6 which 7 which 8 who 9 who 10 which 11 which 12 who

2 1 took 2 live 3 she is 4 lost 5 bought 6 is parked 7 it cuts 8 writes 9 make 10 I lent you

page 255

3 1 The man and woman who live in flat 1 play loud music all night. 2 The woman who lives in flat 2 broke her leg skiing. 3 The three men who live in flat 3 play golf all day. 4 The students who live in flat 4 haven't got much money. 5 The doctor who lives in flat 5 has three children. 6 The man who lives in flat 6 drives a Rolls-Royce. 7 The two women who live in flat 7 are hiding from the police.

4 1 The bus which goes to Oxford isn't running today. 2 Yesterday I met a man who works with your brother. 3 The child who didn't come to the party was ill. 4 Can you pick up the papers which are lying on the floor? 5 The eggs which I bought yesterday were bad. 6 Here's the book which you asked me to buy for you. 7 I don't like the man who is going out with my sister.

page 256

1 1 John's got a motorbike that can do 200km an hour. 2 Is that the computer that doesn't work? 3 Those are the trousers that I use for gardening. 4 A man that lives in New York wants to marry my sister. 5 The doctors that looked at my leg all said different things. 6 The flowers that you gave to Aunt Sarah are beautiful. 7 The children that play football with Paul have gone on holiday.

2 1 an insect that doesn't make honey and can bite you 2 a bird that can't fly 3 a bird that eats small animals and birds 4 an animal that flies at night and hears very well 5 a machine that can fly straight up 6 a plane that doesn't have an engine 7 a thing that can fly to the moon

page 257

1 1 O 2 S 3 O 4 O 5 O 6 S 7 O 8 S

2 1 the languages she spoke 2 the sweater I wore 3 a man I helped 4 the weather we have had 5 the car you bought

3 1 I'm working for a man I've known for twenty years. 2 They played a lot of music I didn't like. 3 The campsite we found was very dirty. 4 I'm going on holiday with some people I know. 5 That book you gave to me is very good. 6 The ring she lost belonged to her grandmother. 7 I'm driving a car I bought 15 years ago. 8 The papers you wanted are on the table.

page 258

1 1 the girl that I was talking about 2 the people that I work for 3 the house that I live in 4 the music that you are listening to 5 the bus that I go to work on

2 1 the girl I was talking about 2 the people I work for 3 the house I live in 4 the music you are listening to 5 the bus I go to work on

3 1 Eric is the man she works for. 2 Monica is the woman she plays tennis with. 3 Karen is the woman she reads to. 4 Emily and Jack are the people she babysits for. 5 Tom is the man she is in love with.

4 1 The man she works for gave her chocolates. 2 The woman she plays tennis with gave her a clock. 3 The woman she reads to gave her theatre tickets. 4 The people she babysits for gave her a picture. 5 The man she is in love with gave her flowers and earrings.

page 259

1 1 What he did made everybody angry. 2 Take what you want. 3 Soap – that's what I forgot to pack. 4 She gave me a watch. It was just what I wanted. 5 That child does what he likes. 6 What I read in the paper makes me unhappy. 7 Don't tell me what I know already. 8 What I like best in life is doing nothing.

3 1 that 2 What 3 what 4 that 5 what 6 What 7 that 8 that 9 what 10 that

page 260

1 1 I know a man who writes film music. 2 The bus which I took got to London twenty minutes late. 3 We have friends who live in Chicago. 4 The car which I bought last month isn't very good. 5 We stayed in a hotel which had a beautiful garden. 6 I didn't like the man who my sister married. 7 The people who were at the party weren't very interesting. 8 Tim uses long words which I can't understand. 9 The computer which I'm using crashes every five minutes. 10 The woman who works in the flower shop is terribly nice.

2 1 The tickets that I got were terribly expensive. 2 These are the scissors that I use for cutting paper. 3 The woman that gives me tennis lessons is from Brazil. 4 The man that lives next door is always very friendly. 5 I'm spending the day with some people that I know. 6 What did you do with the money that we collected? 7 People that study languages are called linguists. 8 We've got a cat that brings dead rats into the house. 9 The oranges that you bought are all bad. 10 Why did you throw away the soup that I cooked?

page 261

3 1 the clock I bought 2 the film I saw 3 No change. 4 No change. 5 a man I really disliked 6 No change. 7 that dog you had 8 No change. 9 No change. 10 those earrings I bought

4 The rooms they put us in; the beds they gave us; the extra blankets we asked for; The 'full English breakfast' they served; the 'French champagne' we ordered; that brochure you showed me; The 'view of the sea' they talked about; the gym they advertised; the bill we got

5 1 the book I was looking at 2 the people I work for 3 the hotel we stayed in 4 the place I drove to 5 those people we were talking to 6 the train we travelled on 7 some people I work with 8 the place I was telling you about 9 the pen I write with 10 the small village my mother lives in

6 1 Naomi got what Jessica wanted. 2 Sally got what Thalia wanted. 3 Jane got what Anna wanted. 4 Jessica got what Jane wanted. 5 Thalia got what Sally wanted.

page 262

1 1 A, B 2 A 3 A 4 B 5 A 6 A, B 7 A 8 A, B 9 A, B 10 A, B 11 A 12 A 13 A, B 14 B 15 A

2 2 which had 6 The woman who came 8 the man who 10 which I couldn't understand. 12 People who/that live 15 people that you can't relax with. *(The other sentences are all correct)*

3 1 that 2 that 3 What 4 that 5 what 6 that 7 what 8 what 9 What 10 that

page 264

1 1 he 2 she 3 her. 4 they; their 5 he 6 me. 7 they 8 he; his 9 she; her 10 their

2 1 told 2 said 3 said 4 say 5 told 6 tell 7 told 8 said

page 265

3
1 She said (that) her sister needed a car.
2 He said (that) he had to phone Andrew.
3 She said (that) nobody wanted to help her.
4 She said (that) the radio didn't work.
5 He said (that) he would be in Paris in July.
6 He said (that) he liked the red sweater.
7 He said (that) he couldn't swim.
8 She said (that) her parents were travelling.
9 She said (that) the lessons were very good.
10 They said (that) they hadn't heard from Joseph.

4 He thought (that) cats had nine lives. He thought (that) his father knew everything. He thought (that) spaghetti grew on trees. He thought (that) the teacher lived in the school. He thought (that) he would be rich one day. He thought (that) his mother had always been old.

page 266

1 1 She asked him where he lived. 2 She asked him where he worked. 3 She asked him where he was going. 4 She asked him where he had been. 5 She asked him what the number of his car was. 6 She asked him why he was driving on the right.

2 1 She asked him whether it was his car. 2 She asked him if/whether he had a driving licence. 3 She asked him if/whether he had it with him. 4 She asked him if/whether he always drove with the door open. 5 She asked him if/whether he was listening to her.

3 1 They asked him if/whether he was married. 2 They asked him if/whether he had children. 3 They asked him where he had worked before. 4 They asked him why he wanted to change his job. 5 They asked him if/whether he could speak any foreign languages. 6 They asked him what exams he had passed.

page 267

1 1 they live in Greece. 2 she went to Belfast yesterday. 3 he's been ill. 4 it's going to rain. 5 she'll ask her sister. 6 they're going to be rich. 7 if/whether lunch is ready. 8 where I put my keys. 9 I'm getting a cold. 10 this is the right answer.

2 1 Can you tell me where I can buy tickets? 2 Do you know how much it costs? 3 Can you tell me if/whether John has phoned? 4 Can you tell me if/whether I must pay now? 5 Can you tell me if/whether Maria likes steak? 6 Do you know where I parked the car?

page 268

1 1 now – then 2 this – that 3 tomorrow – the next day 4 yesterday – the day before 5 today – that day 6 tonight – that night 7 last week – the week before 8 next week – the next week

2 1 that place. 2 the week before. 3 the day before. 4 that day. 5 that night. 6 the next day.

3 1 He said he loved that place. 2 He said he'd seen a great film the day before. 3 He said he was going to another party that night. 4 He asked if I wanted to play tennis the next day. 5 He said his girlfriend would be there the next week.

page 269

1 1 Dave asked Sandra to give him her phone number. 2 The boss told James to work late. 3 Judy asked Kim not to tell Karen about Ryan. 4 Mr Sanders asked Fred not to smoke in his car. 5 The general told Colonel Walker to take 100 men and cross the river. 6 Ann told Polly not to study so hard.

2 1 His girlfriend told him to write to her every day. 2 His mother told him to keep his room clean. 3 His father told him to work hard. 4 His sister told him not to go to too many parties. 5 His brother told him to get a lot of exercise. 6 His mother told him to change his shirt every day. 7 His father told him not to go to bed late. 8 His brother told him to be careful with money. 9 His sister told him not to play cards for money. 10 His grandmother told him to eat properly.

page 270

1 1 He asked her if/whether he could have ice cream for breakfast. 2 He asked her why the stars only came out at night. 3 He asked her why Daddy / his father had to work. 4 He asked her where God was. 5 He asked her whether he would be taller than her one day. 6 He asked her if she believed in Father Christmas. 7 He asked her if/whether Scotland was in London. 8 He asked her when he would be rich. 9 He asked her why French people didn't speak English. 10 He asked her how big the universe was.

2 1 She told him to wash his hands before breakfast. 2 She told him not to eat with his mouth open. 3 She told him to eat everything on his plate. 4 She told him not to talk with his mouth full. 5 She told him to make his bed. 6 She told him to clean his room. 7 She told him to polish his shoes. 8 She told him to put on a clean shirt. 9 She told him not to shout at his sister. 10 She told him not to be late for school.

3 1 John doesn't know how to phone New York. 2 John doesn't know where to pay. 3 John doesn't know when to start work. 4 John doesn't know how to switch the computer on. 5 John doesn't know where to put his coat. 6 John doesn't know how much to pay. 7 John doesn't know what to study.

page 271

4 1 had been 2 told 3 was having 4 was doing 5 had had 6 the (week) before 7 would 8 said 9 had 10 had lost 11 to buy 12 if/whether 13 was 14 was 15 would 16 was living 17 had spent 18 to send 19 to give 20 told 21 hadn't heard 22 where 23 was living. 24 if/whether 25 wanted

page 272

1 1 said 2 told 3 told 4 said 5 said 6 told 7 told 8 told 9 said 10 told

2 1 ✗ 2 ✗ 3 ✓ 4 ✗ 5 ✓ 6 ✗ 7 ✓ 8 ✓ 9 ✗ 10 ✗

3 3 where the post office was. 4 when Jane is arriving? 7 tell me 8 was going 9 if/whether I was 10 what he wanted. 11 what this word means. 12 wanted. 15 why she said *(All the other sentences are correct.)*

page 274

1 1 on 2 at 3 on 4 on 5 at; on 6 on 7 on 8 at; on 9 at 10 on 11 at 12 on

2 1 at 2 in 3 in 4 at 5 at 6 in 7 at; in 8 in 9 in 10 at; in; on 11 in 12 in 13 at 14 in 15 in

page 275

3 1 I'll see you next Wednesday. 2 It rained non-stop last week. 3 Business was bad last month. 4 Shall we go out this evening? 5 We're going to America next month. 6 Ann had a car crash last Wednesday. 7 I'm going to change my job next year. 8 My holiday is in August every year. OR ... every August. 9 I've spent too much money already this month. 10 The new school will be open next March. OR ... in March next year.

4 1 In five days. 2 In a week. 3 In two weeks. 4 In a month. 5 In a year. 6 In a hundred years.

5 1 the twenty-first of March / March the twenty-first, nineteen ninety-nine 2 the fourteenth of February / February the fourteenth, nineteen sixty 3 the twenty-eighth of July / July the twenty-eighth, eighteen forty-six 4 the sixth of May / May the sixth, two thousand and three 5 the ninth of May / May the ninth, nineteen eighty-four 6 the seventeenth of December / December the seventeenth, two thousand and twelve

page 276

1 1 until lunchtime. 2 until Saturday. 3 until the age of 14. 4 until the end. 5 until July.

2 1 He washed the car from 8.00 to/till/until 9.00. 2 He talked to the woman next door from 9.00 to/till/until 9.15. 3 He played tennis from 10.00 to/till/until 11.00. 4 He talked to friends from 11.00 to/till/until 11.30. 5 He went for a walk from 11.30 to/till/until 12.45.

4 1 by 2 until 3 by 4 by 5 by 6 until

page 277

1 1 for 2 during 3 during 4 for; during 5 during 6 for 7 during 8 for

2 1 while they were playing 2 during the lesson 3 during the war 4 while she was teaching 5 while he was speaking 6 while they were talking 7 during her illness 8 while it was snowing

3 *(possible answers)*
1 for an hour or so 2 for ever 3 for a moment 4 for a couple of hours 5 for a minute or two 6 for a few minutes 7 for an hour or so 8 for life *(Other answers are possible.)*

page 278

1 1 in 2 on 3 in 4 on 5 in 6 on 7 on 8 in 9 on 10 on

2 1 in my diary. 2 in the office 3 on her first finger 4 in the cupboard. 5 on the roof of the car. 6 in your car 7 On his T-shirt 8 on the wall 9 in a little village 10 on a piece of paper; in my pocket

page 279

1 1 at the cinema 2 at the station. 3 at the party 4 at a Chinese restaurant 5 at a theatre 6 at work. 7 at breakfast 8 at Birmingham. 9 at the hotel bar 10 at the crossroads.

2 1 at the bottom 2 at the end 3 at the top 4 at the top 5 at the beginning

page 281

1 1 above 2 by 3 above 4 by 5 behind 6 under 7 against

2 1 under 2 between; opposite 3 against 4 behind 5 near 6 in front of 7 near

3 1 opposite 2 between 3 behind 4 near 5 in front of 6 under 7 against 8 between 9 by

page 282

1 1 up the steps 2 through the gate 3 over the fence 4 past the café 5 round the corner 6 out of the shop 7 across the river 8 along the yellow line 9 under the bridge 10 into the water 11 off the bike 12 down the mountain

page 283

2 1 along the road 2 up the mountain 3 down the stairs 4 over the wall 5 into the bank 6 round the corner 7 through the door 8 off the table 9 out of the church 10 under the bridge 11 past the bank 12 across the river

3 1 out of; along 2 down; over 3 along; through; into 4 up; into; off 5 past; under; round 6 off; into 7 out of; across; out of 8 up; down

4 1 to 2 in 3 to 4 from; to 5 in 6 to 7 at 8 at 9 in 10 to

page 284

1 1 on 2 on 3 at 4 for 5 on 6 at 7 at 8 in 9 in 10 on 11 by 12 until 13 during 14 while 15 at

2 1 last Saturday 2 next year 3 in September every year OR every September 4 this month 5 last week 6 tomorrow evening 7 next Saturday 8 last month 9 next month 10 next August OR in August next year

3 1 along the road 2 down the mountain 3 into the church 4 off the table 5 out of the church 6 up the mountain 7 over the wall 8 past the church 9 round the corner 10 through the door

4 1 between 2 above 3 in front of 4 opposite 5 against 6 through 7 along; by 8 out of; across 9 off; into 10 past; under; round

page 285

5 1 out of the church 2 on the bus 3 up the stairs 4 under the bridge 5 into the river 6 behind the door 7 at the bottom of the stairs 8 down the mountain 9 in front of the police station 10 at the end

6 1 the twenty-third of April or April the twenty-third 2 the first of September or September the first 3 the fifth of August, two thousand and ten or August the fifth … 4 the second of March, nineteen eighty or March the second … 5 the tenth of January, two thousand and two OR January the tenth … 6 the third of April, two thousand and eight OR April the third … 7 the fourth of October OR October the fourth 8 the twenty-first of March, nineteen thirty-six OR March the twenty-first … 9 the twenty-second of October, two thousand and six OR October the twenty-second ... 10 the first of January, two thousand and one OR January the first …

7 *(possible answers)* 1 for a moment. 2 for life. 3 for a long time. 4 for a few minutes. 5 for a long time. 6 for a couple of hours 7 for years and years. 8 for a moment 9 for a few minutes. 10 for an hour or so. (Other answers are possible.)

8 1 on 2 on 3 opposite 4 off 5 by 6 along 7 at 8 under 9 up 10 round 11 down 12 across 13 through 14 out of 15 in front of 16 in 17 by

page 286

1 1 on 2 over 3 on 4 at 5 off 6 by 7 in 8 for 9 through 10 while

2 1 on 2 from; until 3 for 4 during 5 in 6 at/in front of/opposite 7 on 8 on 9 on 10 at 11 by/before 12 between 13 at 14 in 15 along/by/near

3 1 for three hours 2 by Saturday 3 out of the room 4 opposite our house 5 across this river 6 on the ceiling 7 across the town 8 next Monday 9 at Christmas 10 off the bus

page 288

1 1 , won't you? 2 , has he? 3 –? 4 , isn't it? 5 , can he? 6 , isn't it? 7 , was it? 8 –? 9 , aren't I?

2 1 isn't it? 2 aren't we? 3 isn't she? 4 won't you 5 can't he? 6 doesn't she? 7 doesn't it?

3 1 is he? 2 can you? 3 do they? 4 does she? 5 do they? 6 has he/she?

page 289

4 1 wasn't there? 2 aren't there? 3 isn't there? 4 has there? 5 were there?

5 1 do you? 2 isn't she? 3 isn't it? 4 can you? 5 wouldn't you? 6 do they? 7 hasn't she? 8 aren't I? 9 isn't there? 10 don't you?

6 1 They've lived in France, haven't they? 2 They all went home early, didn't they? 3 It rained all last week, didn't it? 4 Her brother writes for the newspapers, doesn't he? 5 I need a visa, don't I? 6 You'd like a holiday, wouldn't you? 7 The train was late, wasn't it? 8 Sarah forgot your birthday, didn't she? 9 There was a letter for me, wasn't there? 10 I'm in time for lunch, aren't I?

page 290

1 1 'No, it isn't.' OR 'No, it's not.' 2 'No, he hasn't.' 3 'Yes, they do.' 4 'No, it isn't.' OR 'No, it's not.' 5 No, he doesn't.' 6 'Yes, I/we do.' 7 'No, thanks, she wouldn't.' 8 'No, it wasn't.' 9 'No, I'm afraid I'm not.'

3 1 'No, I'm not.' 2 'Yes, it is.' 3 'Yes, she does,' 4 'No, it doesn't.' 5 'Yes, he did.' 6 'Yes, he did.'

page 291

1 1 Have you? 2 Did he? 3 Is there? 4 Can't you? 5 Doesn't it? 6 Is she? 7 Do they? 8 Don't they?

2 1 C Don't you? 2 B Are they? 3 F Is it? 4 D Has he? 5 E Can't you?

3 *(possible answers)*
1 'Congratulations!' 2 'Say 'hello' to her for me.' 3 'Good luck!' 4 'That's interesting.' 5 'What a pity!' 6 'What a nuisance!' 7 'I am sorry.' 8 'That's a surprise.' 9 'That's terrible.' *(Other answers are possible.)*

page 292

1 1 Are you? 2 Joe didn't phone yesterday. 3 I'm feeling ill. 4 John needs help. 5 You don't remember David, 6 Have you? 7 can't they?

2 1 don't you? 2 Yes, I do. 3 didn't he? 4 he didn't. 5 Is he? 6 does he? 7 Yes, it is. 8 Aren't you? 9 don't you? 10 Yes, I do 11 haven't you? 12 Yes, I have. 13 Are you? 14 Yes, I would. 15 can I? 16 Yes, you can. 17 Are you?

page 293

1 1 … but I do. 2 … I have. 3 … I don't think she will. 4 … I hope he has. 5 … Of course I will. 6 … I can tomorrow.

2 1 'They hope to.' 2 she didn't want to. 3 I'd like to. 4 I used to. 5 'Sorry, I forgot to.' 6 'It's starting to.'

In these answers, we usually give **either** contracted forms (for example *I'm, don't*) **or** full forms (for example *I am, do not*). Normally both are correct.

3 1 I couldn't understand what he wanted from me. 2 She doesn't know what she's doing. 3 The bus is late again. 4 Do you speak French? 5 I haven't seen them. 6 I don't think so.

page 294

1 1 'So is Alice.' 2 'So does my father.' 3 'So can I.' 4 'So does Carla.' 5 'So has Edward.'

2 1 neither/nor was the meat. 2 'Neither/Nor has Gemma.' 3 'Neither/Nor does this one.' 4 'Neither/Nor can I.' 5 neither/nor will his friends.

3 1 'My car does.' 2 her sister hasn't. 3 our dog can't. 4 'The train doesn't.' 5 the back door was. 6 'Her second one did.'

page 295

4 1 Eric plays tennis, and so does Dan. 2 Julie isn't tall, but Denise is. 3 Denise doesn't laugh a lot, and neither/nor does Paul. 4 Dan can ski, but Rachel can't. 5 Julie has been to America, and so has Denise. 6 Eric isn't tall, and neither/nor is Paul. 7 Julie doesn't play tennis, but Dan does. 8 Paul doesn't like dancing, but Rachel does.

page 296

1 1 she wasn't. 2 he does. 3 she wouldn't. 4 it doesn't. 5 I can. 6 I haven't. 7 he doesn't. 8 she did. 9 they won't. 10 I do.

2 *(possible answers)*
1 'Say 'hello' to him for me.' 2 'Congratulations!' 3 'I don't believe it!' 4 'Good luck!' 5 'That's interesting.' 6 'That's terrible.' 7 'What a nuisance!' 8 'I am sorry.' 9 'That's a surprise.' 10 'What a pity.'

3 1 nor/neither do cats. 2 nor/neither has the 3.15. 3 'Nor/Neither was I.' 4 nor/neither did Sally. 5 so does his brother. 6 so are the potatoes. 7 nor/neither does her brother. 8 so were we. 9 'Nor/Neither do her parents.' 10 'So will I.'

page 297

4 1 … but I do. 2 … 'I have.' 3 … but I don't think he will. 4 … 'I'm trying to.' 5 … 'Of course I won't.' 6 … but I can't. 7 … but I don't want to. 8 … but I haven't. 9 … 'No, I didn't.' 10 … but I hope to soon.

5 1 I don't know why. 2 Have you seen my mother today? 3 I don't think so. 4 Sorry, you can't come in here. 5 Do you want some help? 6 Do you know what I think? 7 I can't understand a word. 8 The house is cold. 9 It's raining again. 10 I've lost my keys.

6 1 They're paper clips, aren't they? 2 It's a diary, isn't it? 3 It's a hole-punch, isn't it? 4 It's an address book, isn't it? 5 They're rulers, aren't they? 6 They're calculators, aren't they?

page 298

1 1 ✓ 2 ✗ 3 ✗ 4 ✗ 5 ✓ 6 ✗ 7 ✓ 8 ✓ 9 ✗ 10 ✗

2 1 can't you? 2 won't she? 3 have you? 4 doesn't he? 5 was there? 6 didn't she? 7 does he? 8 isn't it? 9 is it? 10 will you? 11 haven't they? 12 have they? 13 aren't I? 14 don't they? 15 did it?

3
1 They haven't gone home, have they?
2 We need tickets, don't we?
3 You'd like some more coffee, wouldn't you?
4 Mike was away yesterday, wasn't he?
5 Angela didn't tell you her news, did she?
6 Sophie can't play the piano, can she?
7 There will be room for everybody, won't there?
8 Your father doesn't eat meat, does he?
9 These books don't belong to the library, do they?
10 You're tired, aren't you?

4 1 it wasn't. 2 he wouldn't. 3 it doesn't. 4 it did. 5 it won't.

5 1 Have they? 2 Won't you? 3 Do you? 4 Has it? 5 Didn't I?

index